Effective Robotics Programming with ROS

Third Edition

Find out everything you need to know to build powerful robots with the most up-to-date ROS

Anil Mahtani

Luis Sánchez

Enrique Fernández

Aaron Martinez

BIRMINGHAM - MUMBAI

Effective Robotics Programming with ROS
Third Edition

First published: September 2013

Second edition: August 2015

Third edition: December 2016

Production reference: 1231216

Published by Packt Publishing Ltd.
Livery Place
35 Livery Street
Birmingham B3 2PB, UK.

ISBN 978-1-78646-365-4

www.packtpub.com

Credits

Authors
Anil Mahtani
Luis Sánchez
Enrique Fernández
Aaron Martinez

Reviewer
Lentin Joseph

Commissioning Editor
Kartikey Pandey

Acquisition Editor
Narsimha Pai

Content Development Editor
Abhishek Jadhav

Technical Editor
Gaurav Suri

Copy Editors
Safis Editing
Dipti Mankame

Project Coordinator
Judie Jose

Proofreader
Safis Editing

Indexer
Pratik Shirodkar

Graphics
Kirk D'Penha

Production Coordinator
Shantanu N. Zagade

Cover Work
Shantanu N. Zagade

About the Authors

Anil Mahtani is a computer scientist who has dedicated an important part of his career to underwater robotics. He first started working in the field with his master thesis, where he developed a software architecture for a low-cost ROV. During the development of his thesis, he also became the team leader and lead developer of AVORA, a team of university students that designed and developed an autonomous underwater vehicle for the Students Autonomous Underwater Challenge – Europe (SAUC-E) in 2012. That same year, Anil Mahtani completed his thesis and his MSc in Computer Science at the University of Las Palmas de Gran Canaria and then became a Software Engineer at SeeByte Ltd, a world leader in smart software solutions for underwater systems. In 2015, he joined Dell Secureworks as a Software Engineer, where he applies his knowledge and skills toward developing intrusion detection and prevention systems.

During his time at SeeByte Ltd, Anil Mahtani played a key role in the development of several semi-autonomous and autonomous underwater systems for the military and oil and gas industries. In those projects, he was heavily involved in the development of autonomy systems, the design of distributed software architectures, and low-level software development and also contributed in providing Computer Vision solutions for front-looking sonar imagery. At SeeByte Ltd, he also achieved the position of project manager, managing a team of engineers developing and maintaining the internal core C++ libraries.

His professional interests lie mainly in software engineering, algorithms, data structures, distributed systems, networks, and operating systems. Anil's main role in robotics is to provide efficient and robust software solutions, addressing not only the current problems at hand but also foreseeing future problems or possible enhancements. Given his experience, he is also an asset when dealing with Computer Vision, machine learning, or control problems. Anil has also interests in DIY and electronics, and he has developed several Arduino libraries, which he has contributed back to the community.

First of all, I would like to thank my family and friends for their support and for always being there when I needed them. I would also like to thank my girlfriend Alex for her support and patience, and for being a constant source of inspiration. Finally, I would like to thank my colleagues Ihor Bilyy and Dan Good, who have taught me a lot, both personally and professionally, during these new steps in my career as a software engineer.

Luis Sánchez has completed his dual master's degree in electronics and telecommunication engineering at the University of Las Palmas de Gran Canaria.

He has collaborated with different research groups as the Institute for Technological Development and Innovation (IDETIC), the Oceanic Platform of Canary Islands (PLOCAN), and the Institute of Applied Microelectronics (IUMA) where he actually researches on imaging super-resolution algorithms.

His professional interests lie in Computer Vision, signal processing, and electronic design applied on robotics systems. For this reason, he joined the AVORA team, a group of young engineers and students working on the development of Underwater Autonomous Vehicles (AUV) from scratch. Inside this project, Luis has started developing acoustic and Computer Vision systems, extracting information from different sensors such as hydrophones, sonar, or camera.

With a strong background gained in marine technology, Luis cofounded Subsea Mechatronics, a young start-up, where he works on developing remotely operated and autonomous vehicles for underwater environments.

Here's what Dario Sosa Cabrera, a marine technologies engineer and entrepreneur (and the cofounder and maker of LPA Fabrika: Gran Canaria Maker Space) has to say about Luis:

"He is very enthusiastic and an engineer in multiple disciplines. He is responsible for his work. He can manage himself and can take up responsibilities as a team leader, as demonstrated at the euRathlon competition. His background in electronics and telecommunications allows him to cover a wide range of expertise from signal processing and software, to electronic design and fabrication."

Luis has participated as a technical reviewer of the previous version of *Learning ROS for Robotics Programming* and as a cowriter of the second edition.

First, I have to acknowledge Aaron, Anil, and Enrique for inviting me to participate in this book. It has been a pleasure to return to work with them. Also, I want to thank the Subsea Mechatronics team for the great experience working with heavy underwater robots, we grew together during these years. I have to mention LPA Fabrika – Gran Canaria Maker Space for the enthusiasm preparing and teaching educational robotics and technological projects; sharing a workspace with kids can be really motivating.

Finally, I will have to thank my family and my girlfriend for the big support and encouragement in every project where I'm involved. I want to dedicate my contribution in this book to them.

Enrique Fernández has a PhD in computer engineering and an extensive background in robotics. His PhD thesis addressed the problem of Path Planning for Autonomous Underwater Gliders, but he also worked on other robotics projects, including SLAM, perception, vision, and control. During his doctorate, he joined the Center of Underwater Robotics Research in the University of Girona, where he developed Visual SLAM and INS modules in ROS for Autonomous Underwater Vehicles (AUVs), and participated in the Student Autonomous Underwater Challenge, Europe (SAUC-E) in 2012, and collaborated in the 2013 edition; in 2012, he was awarded a prize.

During his PhD, Enrique published several conference papers and publications to top robotics conferences, such as the International Conference of Robotics and Automation (ICRA). He has also authored some book chapters and ROS books.

Later, Enrique joined PAL Robotics as a SLAM engineer in June 2013. There he worked with the REEM and REEM-C humanoid robots using ROS software and also contributed to the open source community, mainly to ROS Control repository, being one of the maintainers nowadays. In 2015, he joined Clearpath Robotics to work on the Autonomy team, developing perception algorithms. He has worked on the software that runs on the industrial mobile robots OTTO 1500 and OTTO 100, which has been deployed into the facilities of multiple large industry companies, such as General Electric and John Deere.

I would like to thank the coauthors of the book for their dedication. I also want to say thanks to the members of my research group in Las Palmas de Gran Canaria and the Center of Underwater Robotics Research in Girona. I learned a lot about robotics then, and I started to work with ROS. Thanks also to the ex-colleagues from PAL Robotics, who received me with open hands, and have given me the opportunity to learn even more from ROS and (humanoid) robots. Last by not least, to my current colleagues at Clearpath Robotics, where I have mastered ROS and contributed to the software that runs 24/7 in the self-driving robots we have sold for the Industry 4.0. Finally, thanks to my family and friends for their help and support, especially Eva.

Aaron Martinez is a computer engineer, entrepreneur, and expert in digital fabrication. He did his master's thesis in 2010 at the IUCTC (Instituto Universitario de Ciencias y Tecnologias Ciberneticas) in the University of Las Palmas de Gran Canaria. He prepared his master's thesis in the field of telepresence using immersive devices and robotic platforms. After completing his academic career, he attended an internship program at The Institute for Robotics in the Johannes Kepler University in Linz, Austria. During his internship program, he worked as part of a development team of a mobile platform using ROS and the navigation stack. After that, he was involved in some projects related to robotics; one of them is the AVORA project in the University of Las Palmas de Gran Canaria. In this project, he worked on the creation of an AUV to participate in the Student Autonomous Underwater Challenge-Europe (SAUC-E) in Italy. In 2012, he was responsible for manufacturing this project; in 2013, he helped to adapt the navigation stack and other algorithms from ROS to the robotic platform.

Recently, Aaron created his own company named SubSeaMechatronics, SL. This company works with projects related with underwater robotics and telecontrol systems. They are also designing and manufacturing subsea sensors. The company manufactures devices for other companies and research and development institutes.

Aaron has experience in many fields, such as programming, robotics, mechatronics, and digital fabrication as well as many devices, such as Arduino, BeagleBone, Servers, and LIDAR, and nowadays he is designing in SubSeaMechatronics SL some robotics platforms for underwater and aerial environments.

I would like to thank my girlfriend who has supported me while writing this book and gave me motivation to continue growing professionally. I also want to thank Donato Monopoli, Head of Biomedical Engineering Department at ITC (Canary-Islands Institute of Technology), and all the staff there. Thanks for teaching me all I know about digital fabrication, machinery, and engineering tissue. I spent the best years of my life in your workshop.

Thanks to my colleagues in the university, especially Alexis Quesada, who gave me the opportunity to create my first robot in my master's thesis. I have learned a lot about robotics working with them.

Finally, thanks to my family and friends for their help and support.

About the Reviewer

Lentin Joseph is an author, entrepreneur, electronics engineer, robotics enthusiast, machine vision expert, embedded programmer, and the founder and CEO of Qbotics Labs (`http://www.qboticslabs.com`) in India.

He completed his bachelor's degree in electronics and communication engineering at the Federal Institute of Science and Technology (FISAT), Kerala. For his final year engineering project, he made a social robot that can interact with people (`http://www.technolabsz.com/2012/07/social-robot-my-final-year.html`). The project was a huge success and was mentioned in many forms of visual and print media. The main features of this robot were that it can communicate with people and reply intelligently and has some image processing capabilities, such as face, motion, and color detection. The entire project was implemented using the Python programming language. His interest in robotics, image processing, and Python started with that project.

After his graduation, for 3 years he worked at a start-up company focusing on robotics and image processing. In the meantime, he learned famous robotic software platforms, such as Robot Operating System (ROS), V-REP, Actin (a robotic simulation tool), and image processing libraries, such as OpenCV, OpenNI, and PCL. He also knows about robot 3D designing and embedded programming on Arduino and Tiva Launchpad.

After 3 years of work experience, he started a new company named Qbotics Labs, which mainly focuses on research to build up some great products in domains, such as robotics and machine vision. He maintains a personal website (`http://www.lentinjoseph.com`) and a technology blog named technolabsz (`http://www.technolabsz.com`). He publishes his works on his tech blog. He was also a speaker at PyCon2013, India, on the topic *Learning Robotics using Python*.

Lentin is the author of the books *Learning Robotics using Python* (refer to `http://learn-robotics.com` to find out more) and *Mastering ROS for Robotics Programming* (refer to `http://mastering-ros.com` to find out more) by Packt Publishing. The first book was about building an autonomous mobile robot using ROS and OpenCV. This book was launched in ICRA 2015 and was featured in the ROS blog, Robohub, OpenCV, the Python website, and various other such forums. The second book is for mastering robot operating system; this was also launched ICRA 2016, and it is one of the best seller book in ROS.

Lentin and his team was a winner of HRATC 2016 challenge conducted as a part of ICRA 2016, and he was Also a finalist in the ICRA 2015 challenge, HRATC (`http://www.icra2016.org/conference/challenges/`).

www.PacktPub.com

eBooks, discount offers, and more

Did you know that Packt offers eBook versions of every book published, with PDF and ePub files available? You can upgrade to the eBook version at www.PacktPub.com and as a print book customer, you are entitled to a discount on the eBook copy. Get in touch with us at customercare@packtpub.com for more details.

At www.PacktPub.com, you can also read a collection of free technical articles, sign up for a range of free newsletters and receive exclusive discounts and offers on Packt books and eBooks.

https://www.packtpub.com/mapt

Get the most in-demand software skills with Mapt. Mapt gives you full access to all Packt books and video courses, as well as industry-leading tools to help you plan your personal development and advance your career.

Why subscribe?

- Fully searchable across every book published by Packt
- Copy and paste, print, and bookmark content
- On demand and accessible via a web browser

Customer Feedback

Thank you for purchasing this Packt book. We take our commitment to improving our content and products to meet your needs seriously—that's why your feedback is so valuable. Whatever your feelings about your purchase, please consider leaving a review on this book's Amazon page. Not only will this help us, more importantly it will also help others in the community to make an informed decision about the resources that they invest in to learn.

You can also review for us on a regular basis by joining our reviewers' club. **If you're interested in joining, or would like to learn more about the benefits we offer, please contact us**: customerreviews@packtpub.com.

Table of Contents

Preface

Effective Robotics Programming with ROS, Third Edition gives you a comprehensive review of ROS, the Robot Operating System framework, which is used nowadays by hundreds of research groups and companies in the robotics industry. More importantly, ROS is also the painless entry point to robotics for nonprofessionals and students. This book will guide you through the installation process of ROS, and soon enough, you will be playing with the basic tools and understanding the different elements of the framework.

The content of the book can be followed without any special devices, and each chapter comes with a series of source code examples and tutorials that you can run on your own computer. This is the only thing you need to follow the book.

However, we also show you how to work with hardware so that you can connect your algorithms with the real world. Special care has been taken in choosing devices that are affordable for amateur users, but at the same time, the most typical sensors or actuators in robotics research are covered.

Finally, the potential of ROS is illustrated with the ability to work with whole robots in a real or simulated environment. You will learn how to create your own robot and integrate it with a simulation by using the Gazebo simulator. From here, you will have the chance to explore the different aspects of creating a robot, such as perceiving the world using computer vision or point cloud analysis, navigating through the environment using the powerful navigation stack, and even being able to control robotic arms to interact with your surroundings using the MoveIt! package. By the end of the book, it is our hope that you will have a thorough understanding of the endless possibilities that ROS gives you when developing robotic systems.

What this book covers

Chapter 1, Getting Started with ROS, shows the easiest way you must follow in order to have a working installation of ROS. You will see how to install ROS on different platforms, and you will use ROS Kinetic throughout the rest of the book. This chapter describes how to make an installation from Debian packages, compile the sources, and make installations in virtual machines, Docker, and ARM CPU.

Chapter 2, ROS Architecture and Concepts, is concerned with the concepts and tools provided by the ROS framework. We will introduce you to nodes, topics, and services, and you will also learn how to use them. Through a series of examples, we will illustrate how to debug a node and visualize the messages published through a topic.

Chapter 3, Visualization and Debugging Tools, goes a step further in order to show you powerful tools to debug your nodes and visualize the information that goes through the node's graph along with the topics. ROS provides a logging API that allows you to diagnose node problems easily. In fact, we will see some powerful graphical tools, such as rqt_console and rqt_graph, as well as visualization interfaces, such as rqt_plot and rviz. Finally, this chapter explains how to record and play back messages using rosbag and rqt_bag.

Chapter 4, 3D Modeling and Simulation, constitutes one of the first steps in order to implement your own robot in ROS. It shows you how to model a robot from scratch and run it in simulation using the Gazebo simulator. You will simulate sensors, such as cameras and laser range sensors. This will later allow you to use the whole navigation stack provided by ROS and other tools.

Chapter 5, The Navigation Stack – Robot Setups, is the first of two chapters concerned with the ROS navigation stack. This chapter describes how to configure your robot so that it can be used with the navigation stack. In the same way, the stack is explained, along with several examples.

Chapter 6, The Navigation Stack – Beyond Setups, continues the discussion of the previous chapter by showing how we can effectively make our robot navigate autonomously. It will use the navigation stack intensively for that. This chapter shows the great potential of ROS using the Gazebo simulator and RViz to create a virtual environment in which we can build a map, localize our robot, and do path planning with obstacle avoidance.

Chapter 7, Manipulation with MoveIt!, is a set of tools for mobile manipulation in ROS. This chapter contains the documentation that you need to install this package. The chapter also contains example demonstrations with robotic arms that use MoveIt! for manipulation tasks, such as grasping, picking and placing, or simple motion planning with inverse kinematics.

Chapter 8, Using Sensors and Actuators with ROS, literally connects ROS with the real world. This chapter goes through a number of common sensors and actuators that are supported in ROS, such as range lasers, servo motors, cameras, RGB-D sensors, and GPS. Moreover, we explain how to use embedded systems with microcontrollers, similar to the widely known Arduino boards.

Chapter 9, Computer Vision, shows the support for cameras and computer vision tasks in ROS. This chapter starts with drivers available for FireWire and USB cameras so that you can connect them to your computer and capture images. You will then be able to calibrate your camera using the ROS calibration tools. Later, you will be able to use the image pipeline, which is explained in detail. Then, you will see how to use several APIs for vision and integrate OpenCV. Finally, the installation and usage of a visual odometry software is described.

Chapter 10, Point Clouds, shows how to use Point Cloud Library in your ROS nodes. This chapter starts with the basics utilities, such as read or write a PCL snippet and the conversions needed to publish or subscribe to these messages. Then, you will create a pipeline with different nodes to process 3D data, and you will downsample, filter, and search for features using PCL.

What you need for this book

This book was written with the intention that almost everybody can follow it and run the source code examples provided with it. Basically, you need a computer with a Linux distribution. Although any Linux distribution should be fine, it is recommended that you use a version of Ubuntu 16.04 LTS. Then, you will use ROS Kinetic, which is installed according to the instructions given in *Chapter 1, Getting Started with ROS.*

As regards the hardware requirements of your computer, in general, any computer or laptop is enough. However, it is advisable to use a dedicated graphics card in order to run the Gazebo simulator. Also, it will be good to have a good number of peripherals so that you can connect several sensors and actuators, including cameras and Arduino boards.

You will also need Git (the git-core Debian package) in order to clone the repository with the source code provided with this book. Similarly, you are expected to have a basic knowledge of the Bash command line, GNU/Linux tools, and some C/C++ programming skills.

Who this book is for

This book is targeted at all robotics developers, from amateurs to professionals. It covers all the aspects involved in a whole robotic system and shows how ROS helps with the task of making a robot really autonomous. Anyone who is learning robotics and has heard about ROS but has never tried it will benefit from this book. Also, ROS beginners will learn advanced concepts and tools of this framework. Indeed, even regular users may learn something new from some particular chapters. Certainly, only the first three chapters are intended for new users; so those who already use ROS can skip these ones and go directly to the rest.

Conventions

In this book, you will find a number of text styles that distinguish between different kinds of information. Here are some examples of these styles and an explanation of their meaning.

Code words in text, database table names, folder names, filenames, file extensions, pathnames, dummy URLs, user input, and Twitter handles are shown as follows: "The rosdep command-line tool must be installed and initialized before you can use ROS."

A block of code is set as follows:

```
#include <ros/ros.h>
#include <dynamic_reconfigure/server.h>
#include <chapter2_tutorials/chapter2Config.h>
```

When we wish to draw your attention to a particular part of a code block, the relevant lines or items are set in bold:

```
dynamic_reconfigure::Server<chapter2_tutorials::chapter2Config>::Call
backType f;

    f = boost::bind(&callback, _1, _2);
```

Any command-line input or output is written as follows:

```
$ sudo apt-get install python-rosdep
$ sudo rosdep init
$ rosdep update
```

New terms and **important words** are shown in bold. Words that you see on the screen, for example, in menus or dialog boxes, appear in the text like this: "When it finishes, you can start your virtual machine by clicking on the **Start** button."

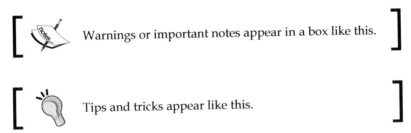

Warnings or important notes appear in a box like this.

Tips and tricks appear like this.

Reader feedback

Feedback from our readers is always welcome. Let us know what you think about this book—what you liked or disliked. Reader feedback is important for us as it helps us develop titles that you will really get the most out of.

To send us general feedback, simply e-mail feedback@packtpub.com, and mention the book's title in the subject of your message.

If there is a topic that you have expertise in and you are interested in either writing or contributing to a book, see our author guide at www.packtpub.com/authors.

Customer support

Now that you are the proud owner of a Packt book, we have a number of things to help you to get the most from your purchase.

Downloading the example code

You can download the example code files from your account at http://www.packtpub.com for all the Packt Publishing books you have purchased. If you purchased this book elsewhere, you can visit http://www.packtpub.com/support and register to have the files e-mailed directly to you. You can also download these code files from https://github.com/rosbook/effective_robotics_programming_with_ros. The same code files are also available at https://github.com/PacktPublishing/Effective-Robotics-Programming-with-ROS.

Downloading the color images of this book

We also provide you with a PDF file that has color images of the screenshots/diagrams used in this book. The color images will help you better understand the changes in the output. You can download this file from `https://www.packtpub.com/sites/default/files/downloads/EffectiveRoboticsProgrammingwithROSThirdEdition_ColorImages.pdf`.

Errata

Although we have taken every care to ensure the accuracy of our content, mistakes do happen. If you find a mistake in one of our books—maybe a mistake in the text or the code—we would be grateful if you could report this to us. By doing so, you can save other readers from frustration and help us improve subsequent versions of this book. If you find any errata, please report them by visiting `http://www.packtpub.com/submit-errata`, selecting your book, clicking on the **Errata Submission Form** link, and entering the details of your errata. Once your errata are verified, your submission will be accepted and the errata will be uploaded to our website or added to any list of existing errata under the Errata section of that title.

To view the previously submitted errata, go to `https://www.packtpub.com/books/content/support` and enter the name of the book in the search field. The required information will appear under the **Errata** section.

Piracy

Piracy of copyrighted material on the Internet is an ongoing problem across all media. At Packt, we take the protection of our copyright and licenses very seriously. If you come across any illegal copies of our works in any form on the Internet, please provide us with the location address or website name immediately so that we can pursue a remedy.

Please contact us at `copyright@packtpub.com` with a link to the suspected pirated material.

We appreciate your help in protecting our authors and our ability to bring you valuable content.

Questions

If you have a problem with any aspect of this book, you can contact us at `questions@packtpub.com`, and we will do our best to address the problem.

Getting Started with ROS

Welcome to the first chapter of this book, where you will learn how to install ROS, the new standard software framework in robotics. This book is an update on *Learning ROS for Robotics Programming - Second Edition*, based in ROS Hydro/ Indigo. With ROS, you will learn how to program and control your robots the easy way, using tons of examples and source code that will show you how to use sensors and devices, or how to add new functionalities, such as autonomous navigation, visual perception, and others, to your robot. Thanks to the open source ethos and a community that is developing state-of-the-art algorithms and providing new functionalities, ROS is growing every day.

This book will cover the following topics:

- Installing ROS Kinetic framework on a compatible version of Ubuntu
- The basic operation of ROS
- Debugging and visualizing data
- Programming your robot using this framework
- Connecting sensors, actuators, and devices to create your robot
- Creating a 3D model to use in the simulator
- Using the navigation stack to make your robot autonomous

In this chapter, we are going to install a full version of ROS Kinetic in Ubuntu. ROS is fully supported and recommended for Ubuntu, and it is experimental for other operative systems. The version used in this book is the 15.10 (Wily Werewolf), and you can download it for free from `http://releases.ubuntu.com/15.10`. Note that you can also use Ubuntu 16.04 (Xenial), following the same steps shown here; indeed, for the BeagleBone Black installation we will use Ubuntu Xenial.

Before starting with the installation, we are going to learn about the origin of ROS and its history.

The **Robot Operating System (ROS)** is a framework that, nowadays, is widely accepted and used in the robotics community. Its main goal is to make the multiple components of a robotics system easy to develop and share so they can work on other robots with minimal changes. This basically allows for code reuse, and improves the quality of the code by having it tested by a large number of users and platforms. ROS was originally developed in 2007 by the **Stanford Artificial Intelligence Laboratory (SAIL)** in support of the Stanford AI Robot project. Since 2008, Willow Garage continued the development, and recently **Open Source Robotics Foundation (OSRF)** began to oversee the maintenance of ROS and partner projects, like Gazebo, including the development of new features.

A lot of research institutions have started to develop in ROS, adding hardware and sharing their code. Also, companies have started to adapt their products to be used in ROS. In the following set of images, you can see some of the platforms that are fully supported. Normally, these platforms are published with a lot of code, examples, and simulators to permit the developers to start work easily. The first three humanoid robots are examples of robots with published code. The last one is an AUV developed by the *University of Las Palmas de Gran Canaria*, and the code has not been published yet. You can find many other examples at `http://wiki.ros.org/Robots`.

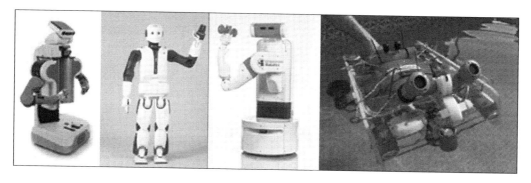

Most of the sensors and actuators used in robotics are supported by ROS as drivers. Furthermore, some companies benefit from ROS and open hardware to create cheaper and easier to use sensors, as existing software can be used for them at zero cost. The Arduino board is a good example because you can add many different kinds of sensors to this cheap electronic board, such as encoders, light and temperature sensors, and many others, and then expose their measurements to ROS to develop robotic applications.

ROS provides a hardware abstraction, low-level device control with ROS control, implementations of commonly used functionalities and libraries, message passing between processes, and package management with `catkin` and `cmake`.

It uses graph architecture with a centralized topology, where processing takes place in nodes that may receive and send messages to communicate with other nodes on the graph net. A node is any process that can read data from a sensor, control an actuator, or run high level, complex robotic or vision algorithms for mapping or navigating autonomously in the environment.

The `*-ros-pkg` is a community repository for developing high-level libraries easily. Many of the capabilities frequently associated with ROS, such as the navigation library and the rviz visualizer, are developed in this repository. These libraries provide a powerful set of tools for working with ROS easily; visualization, simulators, and debugging tools are among the most important features that they have to offer. In the following image you can see two of these tools, the **rviz** and **rqt_plot**. The screenshot in the center is rqt_plot, where you can see the plotted data from some sensors. The other two screenshots are rviz; in the screenshot you can see a 3D representation of a real robot.

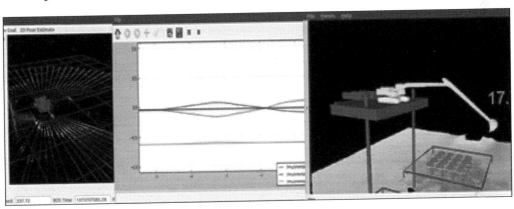

ROS is released under the terms of the **Berkeley Software Distribution (BSD)** license and is an open source software. It is free for commercial and research use. The `ros-pkg` contributed packages are licensed under a variety of open source licenses.

With ROS, you can take a code from the repositories, improve it, and share it again. This philosophy is the underlying principle of open source software.

ROS has numerous versions, the last one being Indigo. In this book, we are going to use Kinetic because it is the latest version. Now we are going to show you how to install ROS Kinetic. As we mentioned before, the operating system used in the book is Ubuntu, and we are going to use it throughout this book and with all the tutorials. If you use another operating system and you want to follow the book, the best option is to install a virtual machine with a copy of Ubuntu. At the end of this chapter, we will explain how to install a virtual machine to use the ROS inside it, or download a virtual machine with ROS installed.

If you want to try installing it on an operating system other than Ubuntu, you can find instructions on how to do so with many other operating systems at `http://wiki.ros.org/kinetic/Installation`.

PC installation

We assume that you have a PC with a copy of Ubuntu 15.10. It will also be necessary to have a basic knowledge of Linux and command tools such as the terminal, Vim, folder creation, and so on. If you need to learn these tools, you can find a lot of relevant resources on the Internet, or you can find books on these topics instead.

Installing ROS Kinetic using repositories

Last year, the ROS web page was updated with a new design and a new organization of contents. The following is a screenshot of the web page:

In the menu, you can find information about ROS and whether ROS is a good choice for your system. You can also find blogs, news, and other features.

Instructions for ROS installation can be found under the **Install** tab in the **Getting Started** section.

ROS recommends that you install the system using the repository instead of the source code, unless you are an advanced user and you want to make a customized installation; in that case, you may prefer installing ROS using the source code.

To install ROS using the repositories, we will start by configuring the Ubuntu repository in our system.

Configuring your Ubuntu repositories

In this section, you will learn the steps for installing ROS Kinetic in your computer. This process has been based on the official installation page, which can be found at `http://wiki.ros.org/kinetic/Installation/Ubuntu`.

We assume that you know what an Ubuntu repository is and how to manage it. If you have any doubts about it, refer to `https://help.ubuntu.com/community/Repositories/Ubuntu`.

Before we start the installation, we need to configure our repositories. To do that, the repositories need to allow **restricted**, **universe**, and **multiverse**. To check if your Ubuntu accepts these repositories, click on **Ubuntu Software Center** in the menu on the left-hand side of your desktop, as shown in the following screenshot:

Click on **Edit | Software Sources** and you will see the following window. Make sure that all the listed options are checked as shown in the following screenshot (choose the appropriate country for the server from which you download the sources):

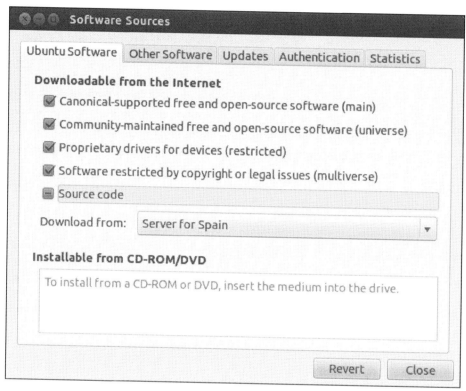

Normally these options are marked, so you should not have any problem with this step.

Setting up your source.list file

In this step, you have to select your Ubuntu version. It is possible to install ROS Kinetic in various versions of the operating system. You can use any of them, but we recommend version 15.10 to follow the chapters of this book. Keep in mind that Kinetic works in the Wily Werewolf (15.10) and Xenial Xerus (16.04) versions of Ubuntu. Type the following command to add the repositories:

```
sudo sh -c 'echo "deb http://packages.ros.org/ros/ubuntu $(lsb_release
-cs) main" > /etc/apt/sources.list.d/ros-latest.list'
```

Downloading the example code

Detailed steps to download the code bundle are mentioned in the Preface of this book. Please have a look.

The code bundle for the book is also hosted on GitHub at `https://github.com/rosbook/effective_robotics_programming_with_ros`. We also have other code bundles from our rich catalog of books and videos available at `https://github.com/PacktPublishing/`. Check them out!

Once you've added the correct repository, your operating system will know where to download programs to install them into your system.

Setting up your keys

This step is to confirm that the origin of the code is correct and that no one has modified the code or programs without the knowledge of the owner. Normally, when you add a new repository, you have to add the keys of that repository, so it's added to your system's trusted list.

```
$ wget http://packages.ros.org/ros.key -O - | sudo apt-key add -
```

Now we can be sure that the code came from an authorized site and has not been modified.

Installing ROS

We are ready to start the installation now, but before we do that, we'd better make an update to avoid problems with the libraries and versions of software that are not ideal for ROS. This is done with the following command:

```
$ sudo apt-get update
```

ROS is huge; sometimes you will install libraries and programs that you will never use. Normally it has four different installations, but this depends on the final use. For example, if you are an advanced user, you might only need the basic installation for a robot without much space on the hard disk. For this book, we recommend you use the full installation because it will install everything necessary to practice the examples and tutorials.

It doesn't matter if you don't know what are you installing right now — rviz, simulators, navigation, and so on. You will learn everything in the upcoming chapters:

- The easiest (and recommended if you have enough hard disk space) installation is known as `desktop-full`. It comes with ROS, the rqt tools, the rviz visualizer (for 3D), many generic robot libraries, the simulator in 2D (like a stage plan) and 3D (usually Gazebo), the navigation stack (to move, localize, do mapping, and control arms), and also perception libraries using vision, lasers, or RGBD cameras:

  ```
  $ sudo apt-get install ros-kinetic-desktop-full
  ```

- If you do not have enough disk space, or if you prefer to install only a few packages, install only the desktop install initially, which only comes with ROS, the rqt tools, rviz, and generic robot libraries. You can install the rest of the packages as and when you need them, for example, by using `aptitude` and looking for `ros-kinetic-*` packages with the following command:

  ```
  $ sudo apt-get install ros-kinetic-desktop
  ```

- If you only want the bare bones, install ROS-base, which is usually recommended for the robot itself, or for computers without a screen or just a **TTY**. It will install the ROS package with the build and communication libraries and no GUI tools at all. With **BeagleBone Black (BBB)**, we will install the system with the following option:

  ```
  $ sudo apt-get install ros-kinetic-ros-base
  ```

- Finally, whichever of the previous options you choose, you can also install individual/specific ROS packages (for a given package name):

  ```
  $ sudo apt-get install ros-kinetic-PACKAGE
  ```

Initializing rosdep

Before using ROS we need to initialize `rosdep`. The `rosdep` command-line tool helps with the installation of system dependencies for the source code that we are going to compile or install. For this reason, it is required by some of the core components in ROS, so it is installed by default with it. To initialize `rosdep`, you have to run the following commands:

```
$ sudo rosdep init
$ rosdep update
```

Setting up the environment

Congratulations! If you are at this step, you have an installed version of ROS on your system! To start using it, the system needs to know the location of the executable or binary files, as well as the other commands. To do this, normally you need to execute the next script; if you also install another ROS distro, you can work with both just by calling the script of the one you need each time, since this script simply sets your environment. Here, we use the one for ROS Kinetic, but just replace `kinetic` with `indigo` or `jade`, for example, if you want to try other distros:

```
$ source /opt/ros/kinetic/setup.bash
```

If you type `roscore` in the shell, you will see something starting up. This is the best test for finding out if you have ROS, and if it is installed correctly.

Note that if you open another terminal you also have to source the `setup.bash` file to set the environment variables to detect the ROS packages installed on your system. Otherwise, `roscore` or other ROS commands will not work. This is because the script must be sourced again to configure the environment variables, which include the path where ROS is installed, as well as other packages and additional paths for compiling new code properly.

It is very easy to solve this; you just need to add the script at the end of your `.bashrc` script file so that when you start a new shell, the script will execute and you will have the environment configured.

The `.bashrc` file is within the user home (`/home/USERNAME/.bashrc`). It has the configuration of the shell or terminal, and each time the user opens the terminal, this file is loaded. That way, you can add commands or configuration to make the user's life easy. For this reason, we will add the script at the end of the `.bashrc` file to avoid keying it in each time we open a terminal. We do this with the following command:

```
$ echo "source /opt/ros/kinetic/setup.bash" >> ~/.bashrc
```

To see the results, you have to execute the file using the following command, or close the current terminal and open another:

```
$ source ~/.bashrc
```

Some users need more than a single ROS distribution installed in their system, so you'll have several distros living in the same system and may need to switch between them. Your `~/.bashrc` file must only source the `setup.bash` file of the version you are currently using, since the last call will override the environment set by the others.

For example, you might have the following lines in your `.bashrc` file:

```
...
source /opt/ros/indigo/setup.bash
source /opt/ros/jade/setup.bash
source /opt/ros/kinetic/setup.bash
...
```

The ROS Kinetic version will be executed in this case. Make sure that the version you are running is the last one in the file. It's also recommended to source a single setup.bash.

If you want to check the version used in a terminal, you can do so easily running the `echo $ROS_DISTRO` command.

Getting rosinstall

Now the next step is to install a command tool that will help us install other packages with a single command. This tool is based in Python, but don't worry, you don't need to know Python to use it. You will learn how to use this tool in the upcoming chapters:

To install this tool on Ubuntu, run the following command:

```
$ sudo apt-get install python-rosinstall
```

And that's it! You have a complete ROS system installed in your system. When I finish a new installation of ROS, I personally like to test two things: that `roscore` and `turtlesim` both work.

If you want to do the same, type the following commands in different shells:

```
$ roscore
```

```
$ rosrun turtlesim turtlesim_node
```

If everything is okay, you will see the following screenshot:

How to install VirtualBox and Ubuntu

VirtualBox is a general-purpose, full virtualizer for x86 hardware, targeted at server, desktop, and embedded use. VirtualBox is free and supports all the major operating systems and pretty much every Linux flavor out there.

If you don't want to change the operating system of your computer to Ubuntu, tools such as VirtualBox help us virtualize a new operating system in our computers without making any changes.

In the following section, we are going to show you how to install VirtualBox and a new installation of Ubuntu. After this virtual installation, you should have a clean installation for restarting your development machine if you have any problems, or to save all the setups necessary for your robot in the machine.

Downloading VirtualBox

The first step is to download the VirtualBox installation file. The latest version at the time of writing this book is 4.3.12; you can download the Linux version of it from `http://download.virtualbox.org/virtualbox/4.3.12/`. If you're using Windows, you can download it from `http://download.virtualbox.org/virtualbox/4.3.12/VirtualBox-4.3.12-93733-Win.exe`.

Once installed, you need to download the image of Ubuntu; for this tutorial we will use a copy of Ubuntu 15.10 from *OSBOXES* found at `http://www.osboxes.org/ubuntu/`; then we will simply install ROS Kinetic following the same instructions described in the previous section. In particular, the Ubuntu 15.10 image can be downloaded from `http://sourceforge.net/projects/osboxes/files/vms/vbox/Ubuntu/15.10/Ubuntu_15.10-64bit.7z/download`.

This would download a .7z file. In Linux, it can be uncompressed with the following:

```
$ 7z x Ubuntu_15.10-64bit.7z
```

If the .7z command is not installed, it can be installed with the following:

```
$ sudo apt-get install p7zip-full
```

The virtual machine file will go into the 64-bit folder with the name: Ubuntu 15.10 Wily (64bit).vdi

Creating the virtual machine

Creating a new virtual machine with the downloaded file is very easy; just proceed with the following steps. Open VirtualBox and click on **New**. We are going to create a new virtual machine that will use the Ubuntu 15.10 Wily (64bit).vdi file downloaded before, which is a hard disk image with Ubuntu 15.10 already installed. Set the name, type, and version of the virtual machine as shown in the following screenshot:

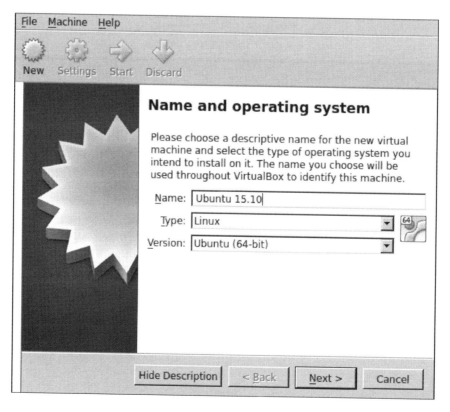

You can configure the parameters of the new virtual machine in the windows that follow. Keep the default configuration and change only the name for the virtual system. This name is how you distinguish this virtual machine from others. For the RAM, we advise that you use as much as possible, but 8 GB should be enough.

For the hard drive, use the existing virtual hard drive file `Ubuntu 15.10 Wily (64bit).vdi` downloaded before, as shown in the following screenshot:

After this, you can start your virtual machine by clicking on the **Start** button. Remember to select the right machine before you start it. In our case, we only have one, but you could have more:

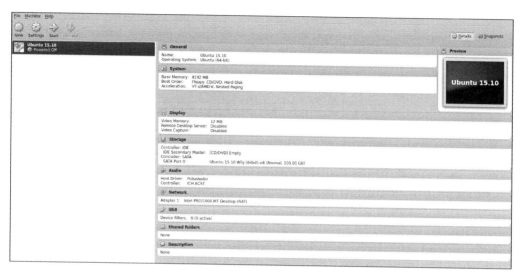

Once the virtual machine starts, you should see another window, as seen in the following screenshot. It is the Ubuntu 15.10 OS with ROS installed (use `osboxes.org` as the password to log in):

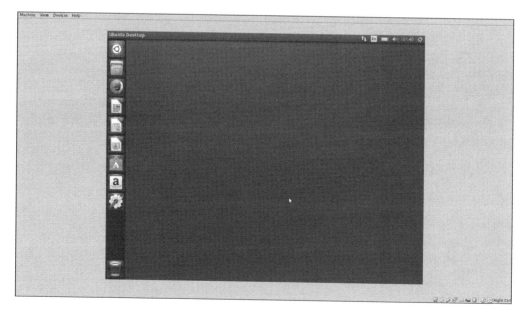

When you finish these steps, install ROS Kinetic as you would on a regular computer following the steps of the previous sections, and you will have a full copy of ROS Kinetic that can be used with this book. You can run all the examples and stacks that we are going to work with. Unfortunately, VirtualBox has problems when working with real hardware, and it's possible that you may not be able to use this copy of ROS Kinetic with the examples given in *Chapter 4, 3D Modeling and Simulation*.

Using ROS from a Docker image

Docker is an open platform that helps to distribute applications and complete systems. In some ways, it is similar to a virtual machine, but it is much faster and more flexible; see `https://www.docker.com` or `https://dockerproject.org` for more information.

Installing Docker

In order to install it in Ubuntu, you only have to run the following:

```
$ sudo apt-get install docker.io
```

Getting and using ROS Docker images and containers

Docker images are like virtual machines or systems already set up. There are servers that provide images like this, so the users only have to download them. The main server is Docker hub, found at `https://hub.docker.com`. There, it is possible to search for Docker images for different systems and configurations. In our case, we are going to use ROS Kinetic images already available. All ROS Docker images are listed in the official ROS repo images on the web at `https://hub.docker.com/_/ros/`. The ROS container image is pulled down with the following command:

```
$ docker pull ros
```

There's a possibility that you may see this error:

```
~$ docker pull ros
FATA[0000] Post http:///var/run/docker.sock/v1.18/images/create?fromImage=ros%3
Alatest: dial unix /var/run/docker.sock: permission denied. Are you trying to c
onnect to a TLS-enabled daemon without TLS?
```

You should either update your system or try adding your user to the `docker` group to resolve this:

```
$ sudo usermod -a -G docker $(whoami)
```

You should see multiple Docker images getting downloaded simultaneously. Each image has a different hash name. This will take some time, especially on slow networks. You will see something like the following once it is done:

```
~$ docker pull ros
latest: Pulling from ros
808ef855e5b6: Pull complete
267903aa9bd1: Pull complete
d28d8a6a946d: Pull complete
ab035c88d533: Pull complete
0b409bfffca0: Pull complete
aa8ec2450c6b: Pull complete
fea18d173ca4: Pull complete
5c9bb5cbe512: Pull complete
ae87b758dd0d: Pull complete
9cadeb3affd3: Pull complete
9c28b2d84bd7: Pull complete
0c7cd879039b: Pull complete
e8530b0325b8: Pull complete
8ab2cb273ccb: Pull complete
c7411052df49: Pull complete
ec05b0e2ef74: Pull complete
c366f9bb95b3: Pull complete
e795c4487953: Pull complete
Digest: sha256:078fbd221da8a3126eff2e283655f5a58e0342de272e38ef94631a1017568b86
Status: Downloaded newer image for ros:latest
```

The ROS Kinetic distribution can be pulled down using the corresponding tag, using the following command:

```
$ docker pull ros:kinetic-robot
```

Although you do not need to know it, the images and containers are stored by Docker in `/var/lib/docker` by default.

Once the container is downloaded, we can run it interactively with the following command:

```
$ docker run -it ros
```

This will be like entering a session inside the Docker container. This command will create a new container from the main image. Inside it we have a full Ubuntu system with ROS Kinetic already installed. We can install additional packages and run ROS nodes, as in a regular system. With `docker ps -a`, you can check all the containers available and the image they come from.

We have to set up the ROS environment inside the container in order to start using ROS. That is, we have to run the following command:

```
$ source /opt/ros/kinetic/setup.bash
```

Docker containers can be stopped from other terminals using `docker stop`, and they can also be removed with `docker rm`. Docker also allows you to configure the container to expose the network, as well as mounting a host folder as volumes into it. In addition to this, it also supports a Python API, and has many other features. All this can be found in the official documentation at `https://docs.docker.com`. However, in principle, `docker run` should be enough, and we can even *SSH* into a running Docker container, as a regular machine, using its name. We can also open another terminal for a running container with the following command (where NAME is the name of the Docker container, that you can fine using `docker ps -a`):

```
$ docker exec -it NAME bash
```

You can also create your own Docker images using `docker build` and specify what should be installed in them in `Dockerfile`. You can even publish them online with `docker push`, contributing them to the community or simply sharing your working setup. This book comes with a working Docker image and `Dockerfile` to build it, and you can find this by running `docker build` from the same folder where `Dockerfile` is. This Docker image is basically an extension of the ROS Kinetic one with the code of the book. The instructions to download and install it would be on the GitHub repository with the rest of the code.

Installing ROS in BeagleBone Black

BeagleBone Black is a low-cost development platform based on an ARM Cortex A8 processor. This board is fabricated with a Linux distribution called **Ångström**. Ångström was developed by a small group who wanted to unify Linux distribution for embedded systems. They wanted an operating system that was stable and user-friendly.

Texas Instruments designed BeagleBone Black thinking that the community of developers needed an on-board computer with some **general purpose input/ output (GPIO)** pins. The BeagleBone Black platform is an evolution of the original BeagleBone. The main features of the board are an ARM Cortex A8 processor at 1 GHz with 512 MB RAM, and with Ethernet, USB, and HDMI connections and two headers of 46 GPIO pins.

This GPIO can be set up as digital I/O, ADC, PWM, or for communication protocol like I2C, SPI, or UART. The GPIO is an easy way to communicate with sensors and actuators directly from the BeagleBone without intermediaries. The following is a labeled image of BeagleBone:

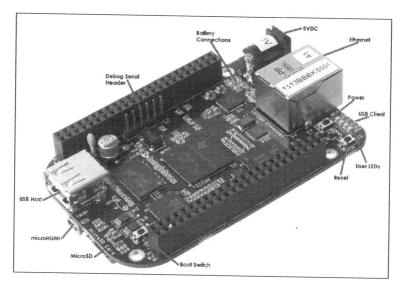

When the BeagleBone board came out, it was not possible to install ROS on the Ångström distribution. For this reason, it was common to install an operating system based on Ubuntu on the BeagleBone. There are different versions of Ubuntu ARM compatible with the BeagleBone Black and ROS; we recommend that you use an image of Ubuntu ARM 16.04 Xenial armhf on the platform to work with ROS.

Now, an ROS version for Ångström distribution is ready to be installed; you can do so following the installation steps given at `http://wiki.ros.org/kinetic/Installation/Angstrom`. Despite this possibility, we have chosen to install ROS on Ubuntu ARM because these distributions are more common and can be used on other ARM-based boards such as UDOO, ODROIDU3, ODROIDX2, or Gumstick.

ARM technology is booming with the use of mobile devices such as smartphones and tablets. Apart from the increasing computer power of the ARM cortex, the great level of integration and low consumption has made this technology suitable for autonomous robotic systems. In the last few years, multiple ARM platforms for developers have been launched in the market. Some of them have features similar to the BeagleBone Black, such as the Raspberry PI or the Gumstick Overo. Additionally, more powerful boards like GumstickDuoVero with a Dual Core ARM Cortex A9 or some quad core boards like OdroidU3, OdroidX2 or UDOO are now available.

Prerequisites

Before installing ROS on BeagleBone Black, we have to achieve some prerequisites. As this book is focused on ROS, we will list them without going into detail. There is a lot of information about BeagleBone Black and Ubuntu ARM available on websites, forums, and books that you can check out.

First, we have to install an Ubuntu ARM distribution compatible with ROS, so an image of Ubuntu ARM is needed. You can obtain an Ubuntu 16.04 Xenial armhf using `wget` with the following command:

```
$ wget https://rcn-ee.com/rootfs/2016-10-06/elinux/ubuntu-16.04.1-
console-armhf-2016-10-06.tar.xz
```

From the URL `https://rcn-ee.com/rootfs` you can look for newer versions too. This version is the one mentioned in the official documentation at `http://elinux.org/BeagleBoardUbuntu`.

Once the image is downloaded, the next step is installing it on a microSD card. First, unpack the image with the following commands:

```
$ tar xf ubuntu-16.04.1-console-armhf-2016-10-06.tar.xz
```

```
$ cd ubuntu-16.04.1-console-armhf-2016-10-06
```

Insert a microSD of 2 GB or more on the card reader of your computer and install the Ubuntu image on it with the following setup script:

```
$ sudo ./setup_sdcard.sh --mmc DEVICE --dtb BOARD
```

In the preceding script, `DEVICE` is the device where the microSD appears on the system, for example `/dev/sdb`, and `BOARD` is the board name. For the BeagleBone Black it would be `beaglebone`. So, assuming the microSD is in `/dev/mmcblk0`, and you are using a BeagleBone Black, the command would be as follows:

```
$ sudo ./setup_sdcard.sh --mmc /dev/mmcblk0 --dtb beaglebone
```

If you do not know the device assigned to the microSD, you can use the following command:

```
$ sudo ./setup_sdcard.sh --probe-mmc
```

Once we have Ubuntu ARM on our platform, the BeagleBone Black network interfaces must be configured to provide access to the network, so you will have to configure the network settings, such as the IP, DNS, and gateway.

Remember that the easiest way could be mounting the SD card in another computer and editing `/etc/network/interfaces`.

Another easy way consists on using an Ethernet cable and running the DHCP client to obtain an IP address.

```
$ sudo dhclient eth0
```

For this, you need to boot up the BeagleBone Black with the microSD. For that, you need to keep the **S2** button press before you power on the board, either with the DC or USB connector. After some minutes the system will show the login prompt. Log in with the user `ubuntu` and password `temppwd` (default ones) and then run the DHCP client command shown above with the Ethernet cable connected. Then, you can check the IP address assigned using (look at the `inet addr: value`):

```
$ ifconfig eth0
```

In our setup, we have connected to the BeagleBone Black the following devices (as shown in the image below):

- HDMI (with microHDMI adapter) cable to see terminal prompt on the screen during the network setup; after that we can SSH into the board
- Keyboard connected through USB
- Power supplied through the microUSB connector
- Ethernet cable to access the Internet, as explained so far

After setting up the network, we should install the packages, programs, and libraries that ROS will need. Now that the network is up, we can also SSH into the board with (assuming the IP address assigned to it is `192.168.1.6`):

```
$ ssh ubuntu@192.168.1.6
```

We are going to follow the instructions in `http://wiki.ros.org/indigo/Installation/UbuntuARM`, but with the changes required so they work for ROS kinetic (note they are still for indigo on the web). The first step consists on setting up the repository sources so we can install ROS.

```
$ sudo vi /etc/apt/sources.list
```

And add restricted to the sources, so you have something like this:

```
deb http://ports.ubuntu.com/ubuntu-ports/ xenial main restricted universe
multiverse

#deb-src http://ports.ubuntu.com/ubuntu-ports/ xenial main restricted
universe multiverse

deb http://ports.ubuntu.com/ubuntu-ports/ xenial-updates main restricted
universe multiverse

#deb-src http://ports.ubuntu.com/ubuntu-ports/ xenial-updates main
restricted universe multiverse

#Kernel source (repos.rcn-ee.com) : https://github.com/RobertCNelson/
linux-stable-rcn-ee

#

#git clone https://github.com/RobertCNelson/linux-stable-rcn-ee

#cd ./linux-stable-rcn-ee

#git checkout `uname -r` -b tmp

#

deb [arch=armhf] http://repos.rcn-ee.com/ubuntu/ xenial main

#deb-src [arch=armhf] http://repos.rcn-ee.com/ubuntu/ xenial main
```

Then, update the sources running:

```
$ sudo apt-get update
```

The operating system for BeagleBone Black is set up for micro SD cards with 1-4 GB. This memory space is very limited if we want to use a large part of the ROS Kinetic packages. In order to solve this problem, we can use SD cards with more space and expand the file system to occupy all the space available with re-partitioning.

So if we want to work with a bigger memory space, it is recommended to expand the BeagleBone Black memory file system. This process is further explained at `http://elinux.org/Beagleboard:Expanding_File_System_Partition_On_A_microSD`.

Although the following steps are not needed in general, they are here in case you need them in your particular case. You can Proceed by following these commands:

1. We need to become a super user, so we will type the following command and our password:

   ```
   $ sudo su
   ```

2. We will look at the partitions of our SD card:

   ```
   $ fdisk /dev/mmcblk0
   ```

3. On typing p, the two partitions of the SD card will be shown:

   ```
   $ p
   ```

4. After this, we will delete one partition by typing d and then we will type 2 to indicate that we want to delete /dev/mmcblk0p2:

   ```
   $ d
   $ 2
   ```

5. On typing n, a new partition will be created; if we type p it will be a primary partition. We will indicate that we want to number it as the second partition by typing 2:

   ```
   $ n
   $ p
   $ 2
   ```

6. You can write these changes by typing w if everything is right, or eliminate the changes with *Ctrl + Z*:

   ```
   $ w
   ```

7. We should reboot the board after finishing:

   ```
   $ reboot
   ```

8. Once again, become a super user once the reboot is complete:

   ```
   $ sudosu
   ```

9. Finally, run the following command to execute the expansion of the memory file system of the operating system:

   ```
   $ resize2fs /dev/mmcblk0p2
   ```

Now we should be ready to install ROS. At this point, the process of installation is pretty similar to the PC installation previously explained in this chapter, so we should be familiar with it. We will see that the main difference when installing ROS on BeagleBone Black is that we can't install the ROS full-desktop; we must install it package by package.

Setting up the local machine and source.list file

Now you will start setting up your local machine:

```
$ sudo update-locale LANG=C LANGUAGE=C LC_ALL=C LC_MESSAGES=POSIX
```

After this, we will configure the source lists depending on the Ubuntu version that we have installed in BeagleBone Black. The number of Ubuntu versions compatible with BeagleBone Black is limited, and only active builds can be found for Ubuntu 16.40 Xenial armhf, the most popular version of Ubuntu ARM. Run the following to install the Ubuntu armhf repositories:

```
$ sudo sh -c 'echo "deb http://packages.ros.org/ros/ubuntu $(lsb_release
-cs) main" > /etc/apt/sources.list.d/ros-latest.list'
```

Setting up your keys

As explained previously, this step is needed to confirm that the origin of the code is correct and that no one has modified the code or programs without the knowledge of the owner:

```
$ sudo apt-key adv --keyserver hkp://ha.pool.sks-keyservers.net --recv-
key 0xB01FA116
```

Installing the ROS packages

Before the installation of ROS packages, we must update the system to see all the packages on the ROS repository just added:

```
$ sudo apt-get update
```

This part of the installation is slightly different for the BeagleBone Black. There are a lot of libraries and packages in ROS, and not all of them compile fully on an ARM, so it is not possible to make a full desktop installation. It is recommended that you install them package by package to ensure that they will work on an ARM platform.

You can try to install ROS-base, known as ROS Bare Bones. ROS-base installs the ROS package along with the build and communications libraries but does not include the GUI tools (press *ENTER* (*Y*) when prompted):

```
$ sudo apt-get install ros-kinetic-ros-base
```

We can install specific ROS packages with the following command:

```
$ sudo apt-get install ros-kinetic-PACKAGE
```

If you need to find the ROS packages available for BeagleBone Black, you can run the following command:

```
$ apt-cache search ros-kinetic
```

For example, the following packages are the basics (already installed as ros-base dependencies) that work with ROS and can be installed individually using `apt-get install`:

```
$ sudo apt-get install ros-kinetic-ros
$ sudo apt-get install ros-kinetic-roslaunch
$ sudo apt-get install ros-kinetic-rosparam
$ sudo apt-get install ros-kinetic-rosservice
```

Although, theoretically, not all the packages of ROS are supported by BeagleBone Black, in practice, we have been able to migrate entire projects developed on PC to BeagleBone Black. We tried a lot of packages, and the only one that we could not install was rviz, which is indeed not recommended to run on it.

Initializing rosdep for ROS

The `rosdep` command-line tool must be installed and initialized before you can use ROS. This allows you to easily install libraries and solve system dependencies for the source you want to compile, and is required to run some core components in ROS. You can use the following commands to install and initialize `rosdep`:

```
$ sudo apt-get install python-rosdep
$ sudo rosdep init
$ rosdep update
```

Setting up the environment in the BeagleBone Black

If you have arrived at this step, congratulations, because you have installed ROS in your BeagleBone Black. The ROS environment variables can be added to your bash, so they will be added every time a shell is launched:

```
$ echo "source /opt/ros/kinetic/setup.bash" >> ~/.bashrc
$ source ~/.bashrc
```

We have to be careful if we have more than one version of ROS in our system. The bashrc setup must use the variables of the version being used only.

If we want to set up the environment in the current shell, we will run the following command:

```
$ source /opt/ros/kinetic/setup.bash
```

Getting rosinstall for BeagleBone Black

Rosinstall is a common command-line tool in ROS that helps us to install packages easily. It can be installed on Ubuntu with the following command:

```
$ sudo apt-get install python-rosinstall
```

Basic ROS example on the BeagleBone Black

As a basic example, you can run a ROS core on one terminal on the BeagleBone Black:

```
$ roscore
```

And from another terminal publish a pose message (note you can press *Tab Tab* after geometry_msgs/Pose and it'd autocomplete the message fields, that then you need to change since it'd have the default values):

```
$ rostopic pub /dummy geometry_msgs/Pose
Position:
x: 1.0
y: 2.0
z: 3.0
Orientation:
x: 0.0
y: 0.0
z: 0.0
w: 1.0 -r 10
```

Now, from your laptop (in the same network), you can set ROS_MASTER_URI to point to the BeagleBone Black (IP 192.168.1.6 in our case):

```
$ export ROS_MASTER_URI=http://192.168.1.6:11311
```

And now you should be able to see the pose published from the BeagleBone Black on your laptop doing:

```
$ rostopic echo -n1 /dummy
Position:
x: 1.0
y: 2.0
z: 3.0
Orientation:
x: 0.0
y: 0.0
z: 0.0
w: 1.0
---
```

If you use a PoseStamped, you can even visualize it on rviz.

From this point, you can check multiple projects at http://wiki.ros.org/BeagleBone, as well as another installation option, which uses the Angstrom OS instead of Ubuntu, but it does not support ROS Kinetic at the moment.

Summary

In this chapter, we have installed ROS Kinetic on different physical and virtual devices (PC, VirtualBox, and BeagleBone Black) in Ubuntu. With these steps, you should have everything needed to start working with ROS installed on your system, and you can also practice the examples in this book. You also have the option of installing ROS using the source code. This option is for advanced users and we recommend you use only the installation from the apt repositories as it is more common and normally does not give any errors or problems.

It is a good idea to play around with ROS and its installation on a virtual machine. That way, if you have problems with the installation or with something else, you can reinstall a new copy of your operating system and start again.

Normally, with virtual machines, you will not have access to real hardware, such as sensors or actuators. In any case, you can use it for testing the algorithms.

2
ROS Architecture and Concepts

Once you have installed ROS, you're probably be thinking, *OK, I have installed it, so now what?* In this chapter, you will learn the structure of ROS and the parts it is made up of. Furthermore, you will start to create nodes and packages and use ROS with examples using **Turtlesim**.

The ROS architecture has been designed and divided into three sections or levels of concepts:

- The Filesystem level
- The Computation Graph level
- The Community level

The first level is the **Filesystem level**. In this level, a group of concepts are used to explain how ROS is internally formed, the folder structure, and the minimum number of files that it needs to work.

The second level is the **Computation Graph level**, where communication between processes and systems happens. In this section, we will see all the concepts and mechanisms that ROS has to set up systems, handle all the processes, and communicate with more than a single computer, and so on.

The third level is the **Community level**, which comprises a set of tools and concepts to share knowledge, algorithms, and code between developers. This level is of great importance; as with most open source software projects, having a strong community not only improves the ability of newcomers to understand the intricacies of the software, as well as solve the most common issues, it is also the main force driving its growth.

Understanding the ROS Filesystem level

The ROS Filesystem is one of the strangest concepts to grasp when starting to develop projects in ROS, but with time and patience, the reader will easily become familiar with it and realize its value for managing projects and its dependencies. The main goal of the ROS Filesystem is to centralize the build process of a project, while at the same time provide enough flexibility and tooling to decentralize its dependencies.

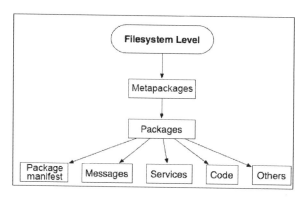

Similar to an operating system, an ROS program is divided into folders, and these folders have files that describe their functionalities:

- **Packages**: Packages form the atomic level of ROS. A package has the minimum structure and content to create a program within ROS. It may have ROS runtime processes (nodes), configuration files, and so on.

- **Package manifests**: Package manifests provide information about a package, licenses, dependencies, compilation flags, and so on. A package manifest is managed with a file called `package.xml`.

- **Metapackages**: When you want to aggregate several packages in a group, you will use metapackages. In **ROS Fuerte**, this form for ordering packages was called *Stacks*. To maintain the simplicity of ROS, the stacks were removed, and now, metapackages make up this function. In ROS, there exists a lot of these metapackages; for example, the navigation stack.

- **Metapackage manifests**: Metapackage manifests (`package.xml`) are similar to a normal package, but with an export tag in XML. It also has certain restrictions in its structure.

- **Message (msg) types**: A message is the information that a process sends to other processes. ROS has a lot of standard types of messages. Message descriptions are stored in `my_package/msg/MyMessageType.msg`.

- **Service (srv) types**: Service descriptions, stored in `my_package/srv/MyServiceType.srv`, define the request and response data structures for services provided by each process in ROS.

In the following screenshot, you can see the content of the `turtlesim` package. What you see is a series of files and folders with code, images, launch files, services, and messages. Keep in mind that the screenshot was edited to show a short list of files; the real package has more:

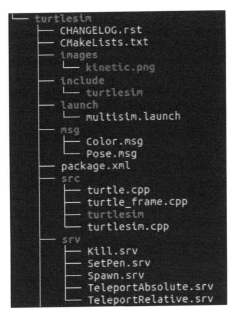

The workspace

In general terms, the workspace is a folder which contains packages, those packages contain our source files and the environment or workspace provides us with a way to compile those packages. It is useful when you want to compile various packages at the same time and it is a good way of centralizing all of our developments.

A typical workspace is shown in the following screenshot. Each folder is a different space with a different role:

```
└── catkin_ws
    ├── build
    │   ├── catkin
    │   ├── catkin_generated
    │   ├── Makefile
    │   └── ...
    ├── devel
    │   ├── setup.zsh
    │   └── ...
    └── src
        ├── CMakeLists.txt -> /opt/ros/kinetic/share/catkin/cmake/toplevel.cmake
        └── ...
```

- **The source space**: In the source space (the `src` folder), you put your packages, projects, clone packages, and so on. One of the most important files in this space is `CMakeLists.txt`. The `src` folder has this file because it is invoked by `cmake` when you configure the packages in the workspace. This file is created with the `catkin_init_workspace` command.

- **The build space**: In the `build` folder, `cmake` and `catkin` keep the cache information, configuration, and other intermediate files for our packages and projects.

- **Development (devel) space**: The `devel` folder is used to keep the compiled programs. This is used to test the programs without the installation step. Once the programs are tested, you can install or export the package to share with other developers.

You have two options with regard to building packages with `catkin`. The first one is to use the standard CMake workflow. With this, you can compile one package at a time, as shown in the following commands:

```
$ cmake packageToBuild/
$ make
```

If you want to compile all your packages, you can use the `catkin_make` command line, as shown in the following commands:

```
$ cd workspace
$ catkin_make
```

Both commands build the executable in the build space directory configured in ROS.

Another interesting feature of ROS is its overlays. When you are working with a package of ROS, for example, Turtlesim, you can do it with the installed version, or you can download the source file and compile it to use your modified version.

ROS permits you to use your version of this package instead of the installed version. This is very useful information if you are working on an upgrade of an installed package. You might not understand the utility of this at the moment, but in the following chapters we will use this feature to create our own plugins.

Packages

Usually when we talk about packages, we refer to a typical structure of files and folders. This structure looks as follows:

- `include/package_name/`: This directory includes the headers of the libraries that you would need.
- `msg/`: If you develop nonstandard messages, put them here.
- `scripts/`: These are executable scripts that can be in Bash, Python, or any other scripting language.
- `src/`: This is where the source files of your programs are present. You can create a folder for nodes and nodelets or organize it as you want.
- `srv/`: This represents the service (`srv`) types.
- `CMakeLists.txt`: This is the `CMake` build file.
- `package.xml`: This is the package manifest.

To create, modify, or work with packages, ROS gives us tools for assistance, some of which are as follows:

- `rospack`: This command is used to get information or find packages in the system.
- `catkin_create_pkg`: This command is used when you want to create a new package.
- `catkin_make`: This command is used to compile a workspace.
- `rosdep`: This command installs the system dependencies of a package.

- `rqt_dep`: This command is used to see the package dependencies as a graph. If you want to see the package dependencies as a graph, you will find a plugin called package graph in `rqt`. Select a package and see the dependencies.

To move between packages and their folders and files, ROS gives us a very useful package called `rosbash`, which provides commands that are very similar to Linux commands. The following are a few examples:

- `roscd`: This command helps us change the directory. This is similar to the `cd` command in Linux.

- `rosed`: This command is used to edit a file.

- `roscp`: This command is used to copy a file from a package.

- `rosd`: This command lists the directories of a package.

- `rosls`: This command lists the files from a package. This is similar to the `ls` command in Linux.

Every package must contain a `package.xml` file, as it is used to specify information about the package. If you find this file inside a folder, it is very likely that this folder is a package or a metapackage.

If you open the `package.xml` file, you will see information about the name of the package, dependencies, and so on. All of this is to make the installation and the distribution of these packages easier .

Two typical tags that are used in the `package.xml` file are `<build_depend>` and `<run _depend>`.

The `<build_depend>` tag shows which packages must be installed before installing the current package. This is because the new package might use functionality contained in another package.

The `<run_depend>` tag shows the packages that are necessary for running the code of the package. The following screenshot is an example of the `package.xml` file:

```
<?xml version="1.0"?>
<package>
  <name>example</name>
  <version>0.0.1</version>
  <description>
    this is a example.
  </description>
  <maintainer email="test@test.com">test</maintainer>
  <license>BSD</license>

  <url type="website">http://www.test.com</url>
  <author>test</author>

  <buildtool_depend>catkin</buildtool_depend>
  <build_depend>geometry_msgs</build_depend>

  <run_depend>geometry_msgs</run_depend>
</package>
```

Metapackages

As we have shown earlier, metapackages are special packages with only one file inside; this file is package.xml. This package does not have other files, such as code, includes, and so on.

Metapackages are used to refer to others packages that are normally grouped following a feature-like functionality, for example, navigation stack, ros_tutorials, and so on.

You can convert your stacks and packages from ROS Fuerte to Kinetic and catkin using certain rules for migration. These rules can be found at http://wiki.ros.org/catkin/migrating_from_rosbuild.

In the following screenshot, you can see the content from the `package.xml` file in the `ros_tutorials` metapackage. You can see the `<export>` tag and the `<run_depend>` tag. These are necessary in the package manifest, which is also shown in the following screenshot:

```xml
<?xml version="1.0"?>
<package>
  ...
  <buildtool_depend>catkin</buildtool_depend>
  ...
  <run_depend>roscpp_tutorials</run_depend>
  <run_depend>rospy_tutorials</run_depend>
  <run_depend>turtlesim</run_depend>
  ...
  <export>
    <metapackage/>
  </export>
  ...
</package>
```

If you want to locate the `ros_tutorials` metapackage, you can use the following command:

```
$ rosstack find ros_tutorials
```

The output will be a path, such as `/opt/ros/kinetic/share/ros_tutorials`.

To see the code inside, you can use the following command line:

```
$ vim /opt/ros/kinetic/ros_tutorials/package.xml
```

Remember that Kinetic uses metapackages, not stacks, but the `rosstack find` command-line tool is also capable of finding metapackages.

Messages

ROS uses a simplified message description language to describe the data values that ROS nodes publish. With this description, ROS can generate the right source code for these types of messages in several programming languages.

ROS has a lot of messages predefined, but if you develop a new message, it will be in the `msg/` folder of your package. Inside that folder, certain files with the `.msg` extension define the messages.

A message must have two main parts: *fields* and *constants*. Fields define the type of data to be transmitted in the message, for example, `int32`, `float32`, and `string`, or new types that you created earlier, such as `type1` and `type2`. Constants define the name of the fields.

An example of an `msg` file is as follows:

```
int32 id
float32 vel
string name
```

In ROS, you can find a lot of standard types to use in messages, as shown in the following table list:

Primitive type	Serialization	C++	Python
bool (1)	unsigned 8-bit int	uint8_t(2)	bool
int8	signed 8-bit int	int8_t	int
uint8	unsigned 8-bit int	uint8_t	int(3)
int16	signed 16-bit int	int16_t	int
uint16	unsigned 16-bit int	uint16_t	int
int32	signed 32-bit int	int32_t	int
uint32	unsigned 32-bit int	uint32_t	int
int64	signed 64-bit int	int64_t	long
uint64	unsigned 64-bit int	uint64_t	long
float32	32-bit IEEE float	float	float
float64	64-bit IEEE float	double	float
string	ascii string (4)	std::string	string
time	secs/nsecs signed 32-bit ints	ros::Time	rospy.Time
duration	secs/nsecs signed 32-bit ints	ros::Duration	rospy.Duration

A special type in ROS is the header type. This is used to add the time, frame, and sequence number. This permits you to have the messages numbered, to see who is sending the message, and to have more functions that are transparent for the user and that ROS is handling.

The header type contains the following fields:

```
uint32 seq
time stamp
string frame_id
```

You can see the structure using the following command:

```
$ rosmsg show std_msgs/Header
```

Thanks to the header type, it is possible to record the timestamp and frame of what is happening with the robot, as we will see in upcoming chapters.

ROS provides certain tools to work with messages. The rosmsg tool prints out the message definition information and can find the source files that use a message type.

In upcoming sections, we will see how to create messages with the right tools.

Services

ROS uses a simplified service description language to describe ROS service types. This builds directly upon the ROS msg format to enable request/response communication between nodes. Service descriptions are stored in .srv files in the srv/ subdirectory of a package.

To call a service, you need to use the package name, along with the service name; for example, you will refer to the sample_package1/srv/sample1.srv file as sample_package1/sample1.

Several tools exist to perform operations on services. The rossrv tool prints out the service descriptions and packages that contain the .srv files and finds source files that use a service type.

If you want to create a service, ROS can help you with the service generator. These tools generate code from an initial specification of the service. You only need to add the gensrv() line to your CMakeLists.txt file.

In upcoming sections, you will learn how to create your own services.

Understanding the ROS Computation Graph level

ROS creates a network where all the processes are connected. Any node in the system can access this network, interact with other nodes, see the information that they are sending, and transmit data to the network:

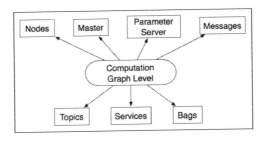

The basic concepts in this level are nodes, the master, Parameter Server, messages, services, topics, and bags, all of which provide data to the graph in different ways and are explained in the following list:

- **Nodes**: Nodes are processes where computation is done. If you want to have a process that can interact with other nodes, you need to create a node with this process to connect it to the ROS network. Usually, a system will have many nodes to control different functions. You will see that it is better to have many nodes that provide only a single functionality, rather than have a large node that makes everything in the system. Nodes are written with an ROS client library, for example, `roscpp` or `rospy`.

- **The master**: The master provides the registration of names and the lookup service to the rest of the nodes. It also sets up connections between the nodes. If you don't have it in your system, you can't communicate with nodes, services, messages, and others. In a distributed system, you will have the master in one computer, and you can execute nodes in this or other computers.

- **Parameter Server**: Parameter Server gives us the possibility of using keys to store data in a central location. With this parameter, it is possible to configure nodes while it's running or to change the working parameters of a node.

- **Messages**: Nodes communicate with each other through messages. A message contains data that provides information to other nodes. ROS has many types of messages, and you can also develop your own type of message using standard message types.

- **Topics**: Each message must have a name to be routed by the ROS network. When a node is sending data, we say that the node is publishing a topic. Nodes can receive topics from other nodes by simply subscribing to the topic. A node can subscribe to a topic even if there aren't any other nodes publishing to this specific topic. This allows us to decouple the production from the consumption. It's important that topic names are unique to avoid problems and confusion between topics with the same name.

- **Services**: When you publish topics, you are sending data in a many-to-many fashion, but when you need a request or an answer from a node, you can't do it with topics. Services give us the possibility of interacting with nodes. Also, services must have a unique name. When a node has a service, all the nodes can communicate with it, thanks to ROS client libraries.

- **Bags**: Bags are a format to save and play back the ROS message data. Bags are an important mechanism to store data, such as sensor data, that can be difficult to collect but is necessary to develop and test algorithms. You will use bags a lot while working with complex robots.

In the following diagram, you can see the graphic representation of this level. It represents a real robot working in real conditions. In the graph, you can see the nodes, the topics, which node is subscribed to a topic, and so on. This graph does not represent messages, bags, Parameter Server, and services. It is necessary for other tools to see a graphic representation of them. The tool used to create the graph is `rqt_graph`; you will learn more about it in *Chapter 3, Visualization and Debugging Tools*.

These concepts are implemented in the `ros_comm` repository.

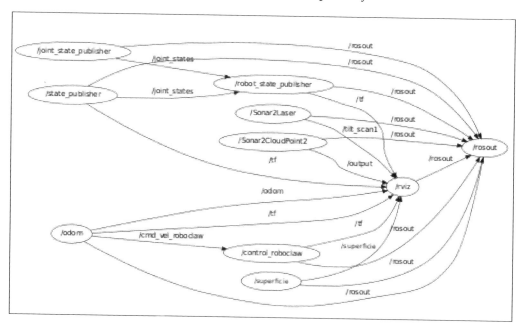

Nodes and nodelets

Nodes are executable that can communicate with other processes using topics, services, or the Parameter Server. Using nodes in ROS provides us with fault tolerance and separates the code and functionalities, making the system simpler.

ROS has another type of node called **nodelets**. These special nodes are designed to run multiple nodes in a single process, with each nodelet being a thread (light process). This way, we avoid using the ROS network among them, but permit communication with other nodes. With that, nodes can communicate more efficiently, without overloading the network. Nodelets are especially useful for camera systems and 3D sensors, where the volume of data transferred is very high.

A node must have a unique name in the system. This name is used to permit the node to communicate with another node using its name without ambiguity. A node can be written using different libraries, such as `roscpp` and `rospy`; `roscpp` is for C++ and `rospy` is for Python. Throughout this book, we will use `roscpp`.

ROS has tools to handle nodes and give us information about it, such as `rosnode`. The `rosnode` tool is a command-line tool used to display information about nodes, such as listing the currently running nodes. The supported commands are as follows:

- `rosnode info NODE`: This prints information about a node
- `rosnode kill NODE`: This kills a running node or sends a given signal
- `rosnode list`: This lists the active nodes
- `rosnode machine hostname`: This lists the nodes running on a particular machine or lists machines
- `rosnode ping NODE`: This tests the connectivity to the node
- `rosnode cleanup`: This purges the registration information from unreachable nodes

In upcoming sections, you will learn how to use these commands with examples.

A powerful feature of ROS nodes is the possibility of changing parameters while you start the node. This feature gives us the power to change the node name, topic names, and parameter names. We use this to reconfigure the node without recompiling the code so that we can use the node in different scenes.

An example of changing a topic name is as follows:

```
$ rosrun book_tutorials tutorialX topic1:=/level1/topic1
```

This command will change the topic name `topic1` to `/level1/topic1`. It's likely that you will not understand this at this stage, but you will find the utility of it in upcoming chapters.

To change parameters in the node, you can do something similar to changing the topic name. For this, you only need to add an underscore (_) to the parameter name; for example:

```
$ rosrun book_tutorials tutorialX _param:=9.0
```

The preceding command will set `param` to the float number `9.0`.

Bear in mind that you cannot use names that are reserved by the system. They are as follows:

- `__name`: This is a special, reserved keyword for the name of the node
- `__log`: This is a reserved keyword that designates the location where the node's log file should be written
- `__ip` and `__hostname`: These are substitutes for `ROS_IP` and `ROS_HOSTNAME`
- `__master`: This is a substitute for `ROS_MASTER_URI`
- `__ns`: This is a substitute for `ROS_NAMESPACE`

Topics

Topics are buses used by nodes to transmit data. Topics can be transmitted without a direct connection between nodes, which means that the production and consumption of data is decoupled. A topic can have various subscribers and can also have various publishers, but you should be careful when publishing the same topic with different nodes as it can create conflicts.

Each topic is strongly typed by the ROS message type used to publish it, and nodes can only receive messages from a matching type. A node can subscribe to a topic only if it has the same message type.

The topics in ROS can be transmitted using TCP/IP and UDP. The TCP/IP-based transport is known as **TCPROS** and uses the persistent TCP/IP connection. This is the default transport used in ROS.

The UDP-based transport is known as **UDPROS** and is a low-latency, lossy transport, so it is best suited to tasks such as teleoperation.

ROS has a tool to work with topics called `rostopic`. It is a command-line tool that gives us information about the topic or publishes data directly on the network. This tool has the following parameters:

- `rostopic bw /topic`: This displays the bandwidth used by the topic.
- `rostopic echo /topic`: This prints messages to the screen.
- `rostopic find message_type`: This finds topics by their type.
- `rostopic hz /topic`: This displays the publishing rate of the topic.
- `rostopic info /topic`: This prints information about the topic, such as its message type, publishers, and subscribers.
- `rostopic list`: This prints information about active topics.
- `rostopic pub /topic type args`: This publishes data to the topic. It allows us to create and publish data in whatever topic we want, directly from the command line.
- `rostopic type /topic`: This prints the topic type, that is, the type of message it publishes.

We will learn how to use this command-line tool in upcoming sections.

Services

When you need to communicate with nodes and receive a reply in an RPC fashion, you cannot do it with topics; you need to do it with services.

Services are developed by the user and standard services don't exist for nodes. The files with the source code of the services are stored in the `srv` folder.

Similar to topics, services have an associated service type that is the package resource name of the `.srv` file. As with other ROS filesystem-based types, the service type is the package name and the name of the `.srv` file. For example, the `chapter2_tutorials/srv/chapter2_srv1.srv` file has the `chapter2_tutorials/chapter2_srv1` service type.

ROS has two command-line tools to work with services: `rossrv` and `rosservice`. With `rossrv`, we can see information about the services' data structure, and it has exactly the same usage as `rosmsg`.

With `rosservice`, we can list and query services. The supported commands are as follows:

- `rosservice call /service args`: This calls the service with the arguments provided
- `rosservice find msg-type`: This finds services by service type
- `rosservice info /service`: This prints information about the service
- `rosservice list`: This lists the active services
- `rosservice type /service`: This prints the service type
- `rosservice uri /service`: This prints the ROSRPC URI service

Messages

A node publishes information using messages which are linked to topics. The message has a simple structure that uses standard types or types developed by the user.

Message types use the following standard ROS naming convention; the name of the package, then / and then the name of the `.msg` file. For example, `std_msgs/ msg/ String.msg` has the `std_msgs/String` message type.

ROS has the `rosmsg` command-line tool to get information about messages. The accepted parameters are as follows:

- `rosmsg show`: This displays the fields of a message
- `rosmsg list`: This lists all messages
- `rosmsg package`: This lists all of the messages in a package
- `rosmsg packages`: This lists all of the packages that have the message
- `rosmsg users`: This searches for code files that use the message type
- `rosmsg md5`: This displays the MD5 sum of a message

Bags

A **bag** is a file created by ROS with the `.bag` format to save all of the information of the messages, topics, services, and others. You can use this data later to visualize what has happened; you can play, stop, rewind, and perform other operations with it.

The bag file can be reproduced in ROS just as a real session can, sending the topics at the same time with the same data. Normally, we use this functionality to debug our algorithms.

To use bag files, we have the following tools in ROS:

- `rosbag`: This is used to record, play, and perform other operations
- `rqt_bag`: This is used to visualize data in a graphic environment
- `rostopic`: This helps us see the topics sent to the nodes

The ROS master

The **ROS master** provides naming and registration services to the rest of the nodes in the ROS system. It tracks publishers and subscribers to topics as well as services. The role of the master is to enable individual ROS nodes to locate one another. Once these nodes have located each other, they communicate with each other in a peer-to-peer fashion. You can see in a graphic example the steps performed in ROS to advertise a topic, subscribe to a topic, and publish a message, in the following diagram:

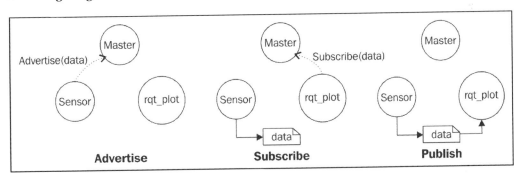

The master also provides Parameter Server. The master is most commonly run using the `roscore` command, which loads the ROS master, along with other essential components.

Parameter Server

Parameter Server is a shared, multivariable dictionary that is accessible via a network. Nodes use this server to store and retrieve parameters at runtime.

Parameter Server is implemented using XMLRPC and runs inside the ROS master, which means that its API is accessible via normal XMLRPC libraries. XMLRPC is a **Remote Procedure Call (RPC)** protocol that uses XML to encode its calls and HTTP as a transport mechanism.

Parameter Server uses XMLRPC data types for parameter values, which include the following:

- 32-bit integers
- Booleans
- Strings
- Doubles
- ISO8601 dates
- Lists
- Base64-encoded binary data

ROS has the `rosparam` tool to work with Parameter Server. The supported parameters are as follows:

- `rosparam list`: This lists all the parameters in the server
- `rosparam get parameter`: This gets the value of a parameter
- `rosparam set parameter value`: This sets the value of a parameter
- `rosparam delete parameter`: This deletes a parameter
- `rosparam dump file`: This saves Parameter Server to a file
- `rosparam load file`: This loads a file (with parameters) on Parameter Server

Understanding the ROS Community level

The ROS Community level concepts are the ROS resources that enable separate communities to exchange software and knowledge. These resources include the following:

- **Distributions**: ROS distributions are collections of versioned metapackages that you can install. ROS distributions play a similar role to Linux distributions. They make it easier to install a collection of software, and they also maintain consistent versions across a set of software.

- **Repositories**: ROS relies on a federated network of code repositories, where different institutions can develop and release their own robot software components.

- **The ROS Wiki**: The ROS Wiki is the main forum for documenting information about ROS. Anyone can sign up for an account, contribute their own documentation, provide corrections or updates, write tutorials, and more.

- **Bug ticket system**: If you find a problem or want to propose a new feature, ROS has this resource to do it.

- **Mailing lists**: The ROS user-mailing list is the primary communication channel about new updates to ROS, as well as a forum to ask questions about the ROS software.

- **ROS answers**: Users can ask questions on forums using this resource.

- **Blog**: You can find regular updates, photos, and news at `http://www.ros.org/news`.

Tutorials to practise with ROS

It is time for you to practise what you have learned until now. In upcoming sections, you will see examples for you to practise along with the creation of packages, using nodes, using Parameter Server, and moving a simulated robot with Turtlesim.

Navigating through the ROS filesystem

As explained before, ROS provides a number of command-line tools for navigating through the filesystem. In this subsection, we will explain the most used ones, with examples.

To get information about the packages and stacks in our environment, such as their paths, dependencies, and so on, we can use `rospack` and `rosstack`. On the other hand, to move through packages and stacks, as well as listing their contents, we will use `roscd` and `rosls`.

For example, if you want to find the path of the `turtlesim` package, you can use the following command:

```
$ rospack find turtlesim
```

Which will then result in the following output:

```
/opt/ros/kinetic/share/turtlesim
```

The same thing happens with the metapackages that you have installed in the system. An example of this is as follows:

```
$ rosstack find ros_comm
```

You will obtain the path for the `ros_comm` metapackage as follows:

```
/opt/ros/kinetic/share/ros_comm
```

To list the files inside the pack or stack, you will use the following command:

```
$ rosls turtlesim
```

The following is the output of the preceding command:

```
cmake      images      srv      package.xml   msg
```

Changing the current working directory, essentially moving to a new folder, can be done with `roscd` as follows:

```
$ roscd turtlesim
$ pwd
```

The new path will be as follows:

```
/opt/ros/kinetic/share/turtlesim
```

Creating our own workspace

Before proceeding to further examples, we are going to create our own workspace. In this workspace, we will centralize all the code used throughout this book.

To see the workspace that ROS is using, use the following command:

```
$ echo $ROS_PACKAGE_PATH
```

You will see output similar to the following:

```
/opt/ros/kinetic/share:/opt/ros/kinetic/stacks
```

The folder that we are going to create is in `~/dev/catkin_ws/src/`. To add this folder, we use the following commands:

```
$ mkdir -p ~/dev/catkin_ws/src
$ cd ~/dev/catkin_ws/src
$ catkin_init_workspace
```

Once we've created the workspace folder, there are no packages inside — only a `CMakeList.txt` file. The next step is building the workspace. To do this, we use the following commands:

```
$ cd ~/dev/catkin_ws
$ catkin_make
```

Now, if you type the `ls` command in the directory, you can see new folders created with the previous command. These are the `build` and `devel` folders.

To finish the configuration, use the following command:

```
$ source devel/setup.bash
```

This step is only for reloading the `setup.bash` file. You will obtain the same result if you close and open a new shell. You should have this command at the end in your `~/.bashrc` file because we used it in *Chapter 1, Getting Started with ROS*; otherwise, you can add it using the following command:

```
$ echo "source /opt/ros/kinetic/setup.bash" >> ~/.bashrc
```

Creating an ROS package and metapackage

As explained before, creating packages can be done manually, but to avoid the tedious work involved, we will use the `catkin_create_pkg` command-line tool.

We will create the new package in our recently initialized workspace using the following commands:

```
$ cd ~/dev/catkin_ws/src
$ catkin_create_pkg chapter2_tutorials std_msgs roscpp
```

The format of this command includes the name of the package and the dependencies that will have the package, in our case, `std_msgs` and `roscpp`. This is shown in the following command:

```
catkin_create_pkg [package_name] [dependency1] ... [dependencyN]
```

The following dependencies are included:

- `std_msgs`: This contains common message types representing primitive data types and other basic message constructs, such as multiarray.

- `roscpp`: This is a C++ implementation of ROS. It provides a client library that enables C++ programmers to quickly interface with ROS topics, services, and parameters.

If all the parameters are correct, the output will look as follows:

```
Created file chapter2_tutorials/package.xml
Created file chapter2_tutorials/CMakeLists.txt
Created folder chapter2_tutorials/include/chapter2_tutorials
Created folder chapter2_tutorials/src
Successfully created files in /home/aaronmr/dev/catkin_ws/src/chapter2_tutorials. Please adjust the values in package.xml.
```

As we saw earlier, you can use the `rospack`, `roscd`, and `rosls` commands to retrieve information about the new package. The following are some of the operations which can be performed:

- `rospack profile`: This command informs you about the newly-added packages to the ROS system. It is useful after installing any new package.

- `rospack find chapter2_tutorials`: This command helps us find the path.

- `rospack depends chapter2_tutorials`: This command helps us see the dependencies.

- `rosls chapter2_tutorials`: This command helps us see the content.

- `roscd chapter2_tutorials`: This command changes the actual path.

Building an ROS package

Once you have your package created and you have some code, it is necessary to build the package. When the package is built, the code contained in it is compiled; this includes not only the code added by the user, but also the code generated from the messages and services.

To build a package, we will use the `catkin_make` tool, as follows:

```
$ cd ~/dev/catkin_ws/
```

```
$ catkin_make
```

In a few seconds, you will see something similar to the following screenshot:

```
. . .
Base path: /home/aaronmr/dev/catkin_ws
Source space: /home/aaronmr/dev/catkin_ws/src
Build space: /home/aaronmr/dev/catkin_ws/build
Devel space: /home/aaronmr/dev/catkin_ws/devel
Install space: /home/aaronmr/dev/catkin_ws/install
. . .
-- BUILD_SHARED_LIBS is on
-- ~~~~~~~~~~~~~~~~~~~~~~~~~~~~~~~~~~~~~~~~~~~~~~~~~~~~~~~~~~~~~
-- ~~  traversing 29 packages in topological order:
-- ~~   - chapter2_tutorials
. . .
-- ~~~~~~~~~~~~~~~~~~~~~~~~~~~~~~~~~~~~~~~~~~~~~~~~~~~~~~~~~~~~~
-- +++ processing catkin package: 'chapter2_tutorials'
-- ==> add_subdirectory(chapter2_tutorials)
. . .
[100%] Built target . . . . . . . . . .
```

If you don't encounter any failures, the package is compiled.

Remember that you should run the `catkin_make` command in the `workspace` folder.
If you try to do it in any other folder, the command will fail. An example of this is
provided in the following command lines:

```
$ roscd chapter2_tutorials/
$ catkin_make
```

When you are in the `chapter2_tutorials` folder and try to build the package using
`catkin_make`, you will get the following error:

```
The specified base path "/home/your_user/dev/catkin_ws/src/chapter2_
tutorials" contains a CMakeLists.txt but "catkin_make" must be invoked in
the root of workspace
```

If you execute `catkin_make` in the `catkin_ws` folder, you will obtain a good
compilation. Finally, compiling a single package using `catkin_make` can be done
using the following command:

```
$ catkin_make --pkg <package name>
```

Playing with ROS nodes

As we explained in the *Nodes and nodelets* section, nodes are executable programs
and, once built, these executables can be found in the `devel` space. To practise and
learn about nodes, we are going to use a typical package called `turtlesim`.

If you have installed the desktop installation, you will have the `turtlesim` package preinstalled; if not, install it with the following command:

```
$ sudo apt-get install ros-kinetic-ros-tutorials
```

Before starting this tutorial, it is important that you open a terminal and start `roscore` using the following command:

```
$ roscore
```

To get information on nodes, we have the `rosnode` tool. To see what parameters are provided, type the following command:

```
$ rosnode
```

You will obtain a list of accepted parameters, as shown in the following screenshot:

```
rosnode is a command-line tool for printing information about ROS Nodes.

Commands:
        rosnode ping     test connectivity to node
        rosnode list     list active nodes
        rosnode info     print information about node
        rosnode machine list nodes running on a particular machine or list machines
        rosnode kill     kill a running node
        rosnode cleanup purge registration information of unreachable nodes

Type rosnode <command> -h for more detailed usage, e.g. 'rosnode ping -h'
```

If you want a more detailed explanation of the use of these parameters, use the following command:

```
$ rosnode <param> -h
```

Now that `roscore` is running, we are going to get information about the nodes that are running, using the following command:

```
$ rosnode list
```

You will see that the only node running is `/rosout`. This is normal, as this node is usually launched with `roscore`.

We can get all the information about this node using the parameters provided by the rosnode tool. Try to use the following commands for more information:

```
$ rosnode info
$ rosnode ping
$ rosnode machine
$ rosnode kill
$ rosnode cleanup
```

Now we are going to start a new node with rosrun using the following command:

```
$ rosrun turtlesim turtlesim_node
```

We will then see a new window appear with a little turtle in the middle, as shown in the following screenshot:

If we see the node list now, we will see a new node with the name /turtlesim. You can see information about the node using rosnode info nameNode.

You can see a lot of information that can be used to debug your programs, using the following command:

```
$ rosnode info /turtlesim
```

The preceding command line prints the following information:

```
Node [/turtlesim]
Publications:
 * /turtle1/color_sensor [turtlesim/Color]
 * /rosout [rosgraph_msgs/Log]
 * /turtle1/pose [turtlesim/Pose]

Subscriptions:
 * /turtle1/cmd_vel [geometry_msgs/Twist]

Services:
 * /turtle1/teleport_absolute
 * /turtlesim/get_loggers
 * /turtlesim/set_logger_level
 * /reset
 * /spawn
 * /clear
 * /turtle1/set_pen
 * /turtle1/teleport_relative
 * /kill


contacting node http://daneel:38674/ ...
Pid: 3881
Connections:
 * topic: /rosout
    * to: /rosout
    * direction: outbound
    * transport: TCPROS
 * topic: /turtle1/cmd_vel
    * to: /teleop_turtle (http://daneel:44645/)
    * direction: inbound
    * transport: TCPROS
```

In the information, we can see the Publications (*topics*), Subscriptions (*topics*), and Services (*srv*) that the node has and the unique name of each.

Now, let's see how you interact with the node using topics and services.

Learning how to interact with topics

To interact and get information about topics, we have the rostopic tool. This tool accepts the following parameters:

* rostopic bw TOPIC: This displays the bandwidth used by topics

- `rostopic echo TOPIC`: This prints messages to the screen
- `rostopic find TOPIC`: This finds topics by their type
- `rostopic hz TOPIC`: This displays the publishing rate of topics
- `rostopic info TOPIC`: This prints information about active topics
- `rostopic list`: This lists the active topics
- `rostopic pubs TOPIC`: This publishes data to the topic
- `rostopic type TOPIC`: This prints the topic type

If you want to see more information on these parameters, use `-h`, as follows:

```
$ rostopic bw -h
```

With the `pub` parameter, we can publish topics that can be subscribed to by any node. We only need to publish the topic with the correct name. We will do this test later; we are now going to use a node that will do this work for us:

```
$ rosrun turtlesim turtle_teleop_key
```

With this node, we can move the turtle using the arrow keys, as illustrated in the following screenshot:

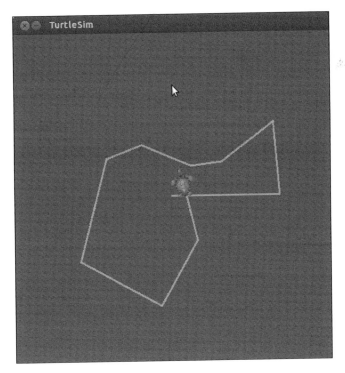

Why does the turtle move when `turtle_teleop_key` is executed?

Checking the information provided by `rosnode` about the `/teleop_turtle` and `/turtlesim` nodes, we can see that there exists a topic called `/turtle1/cmd_vel [geometry_msgs/Twist]` in the `Publications` section of the node `/teleop_turtle`, and in the `Subscriptions` section of the `/turtlesim` node, there is `/turtle1/cmd_vel [geometry_msgs/Twist]`:

```
$ rosnode info /teleop_turtle
```

```
Node [/teleop_turtle]
Publications:
 * /turtle1/cmd_vel [geometry_msgs/Twist]
 * /rosout [rosgraph_msgs/Log]

Subscriptions: None

Services:
 * /teleop_turtle/get_loggers
 * /teleop_turtle/set_logger_level


contacting node http://daneel:44645/ ...
Pid: 4156
Connections:
 * topic: /rosout
    * to: /rosout
    * direction: outbound
    * transport: TCPROS
 * topic: /turtle1/cmd_vel
    * to: /turtlesim
    * direction: outbound
    * transport: TCPROS
```

This means that the first node is publishing a topic that the second node can subscribe to. You can see the topic list using the following command line:

```
$ rostopic list
```

The output will be as follows:

```
/rosout
  /rosout_agg
/turtle1/colour_sensor
```

```
/turtle1/cmd_vel
```

```
/turtle1/pose
```

With the echo parameter, you can see the information sent by the node. Run the following command line and use the arrow keys to see the data that is being sent:

```
$ rostopic echo /turtle1/cmd_vel
```

You will see something similar to the following output:

```
---
linear:
x: 0.0
y: 0.0
z: 0.0
angular:
x: 0.0
y: 0.0
z: 2.0
---
```

You can see the type of message sent by the topic using the following command line:

```
$  rostopic type /turtle1/cmd_vel
```

You will see something similar to the following output:

```
Geometry_msgs/Twist
```

If you want to see the message fields, you can do it with the following command:

```
$ rosmsg show geometry_msgs/Twist
```

You will see something similar to the following output:

```
geometry_msgs/Vector3 linear
   float64 x
   float64 y
   float64 z
geometry_msgs/Vector3 angular
   float64 x
   float64 y
   float64 z
```

These tools are useful because, with this information, we can publish topics using the `rostopic pub [topic] [msg_type] [args]` command:

```
$ rostopic pub /turtle1/cmd_vel  geometry_msgs/Twist -r 1 -- "linear:
x: 1.0
y: 0.0
z: 0.0
angular:
x: 0.0
y: 0.0
z: 1.0"
```

You will see the turtle doing a curve, as shown in the following screenshot:

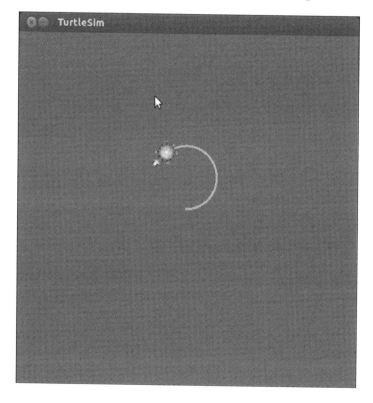

Learning how to use services

Services are another way through which nodes can communicate with each other. Services allow nodes to send a request and receive a response.

The tool that we are going to use to interact with services is called `rosservice`. The accepted parameters for this command are as follows:

- `rosservice args /service`: This prints the service arguments
- `rosservice call /service`: This calls the service with the arguments provided
- `rosservice find msg-type`: This finds services by their service type
- `rosservice info /service`: This prints information about the service
- `rosservice list`: This lists the active services
- `rosservice type /service`: This prints the service type
- `rosservice uri /service`: This prints the ROSRPC URI service

We are going to list the services available for the `turtlesim` node using the following command, so if it is not working, run `roscore` and run the `turtlesim` node:

```
$ rosservice list
```

You will obtain the following output:

```
/clear
/kill
/reset
/rosout/get_loggers
/rosout/set_logger_level
/spawn
/teleop_turtle/get_loggers
/teleop_turtle/set_logger_level
/turtle1/set_pen
/turtle1/teleport_absolute
/turtle1/teleport_relative
/turtlesim/get_loggers
/turtlesim/set_logger_level
```

If you want to see the type of any service, for example, the `/clear` service, use the following command:

```
$ rosservice type /clear
```

You will see something similar to the following output:

```
std_srvs/Empty
```

To invoke a service, you will use `rosservice call [service] [args]`. If you want to invoke the /clear service, use the following command:

```
$ rosservice call /clear
```

In the `turtlesim` window, you will now see that the lines created by the movements of the turtle will be deleted.

Now we are going to try another service, for example, the /spawn service. This service will create another turtle in another location with a different orientation. To start with, we are going to see the following type of message:

```
$ rosservice type /spawn | rossrv show
```

You will see something similar to the following output:

```
float32 x
float32 y
float32 theta
string name
---
string name
```

The preceding command is the same as the following commands. If you want to know why these lines are the same, search in Google about *piping Linux*:

```
$ rosservice type /spawn
```

You will see something similar to the following output:

```
turtlesim/Spawn
```

Type in the following command:

```
$ rossrv show turtlesim/Spawn
```

You will see something similar to the following output:

```
float32 x
float32 y
float32 theta
string name
---
string name
```

With these fields, we know how to invoke the service. We need the position of x and y, the orientation (theta), and the name of the new turtle:

```
$ rosservice call /spawn 3 3 0.2 "new_turtle"
```

We then obtain the following result:

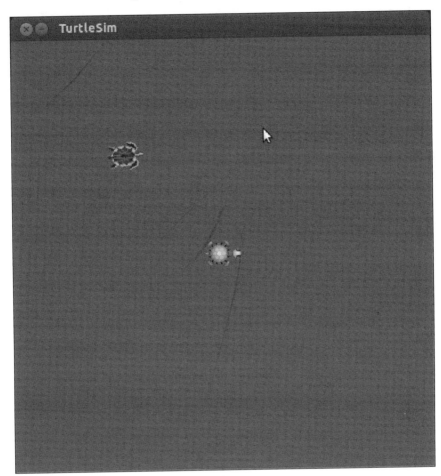

Using Parameter Server

Parameter Server is used to store data that is accessible to all nodes. ROS has a tool called rosparam to manage Parameter Server. The accepted parameters are as follows:

- rosparam set parameter value: This sets the parameter
- rosparam get parameter: This gets the parameter

- `rosparam load file`: This loads parameters from the file
- `rosparam dump file`: This dumps parameters to the file
- `rosparam delete parameter`: This deletes the parameter
- `rosparam list`: This lists the parameter names

For example, we can see the parameters in the server that are used by all nodes:

```
$ rosparam list
```

We obtain the following output:

```
/background_b
/background_g
/background_r
/rosdistro
/roslaunch/uris/host_aaronmr_laptop__60878
/rosversion
/run_id
```

The background parameters are of the `turtlesim` node. These parameters change the color of the windows that are initially blue. If you want to read a value, you will use the `get` parameter:

```
$ rosparam get /background_b
```

To set a new value, you will use the `set` parameter:

```
$ rosparam set /background_b 100
```

Another important feature of `rosparam` is the `dump` parameter. With this parameter, you can save or load the contents of Parameter Server.

To save Parameter Server, use `rosparam dump [file_name]` as follows:

```
$ rosparam dump save.yaml
```

To load a file with new data for Parameter Server, use `rosparam load [file_name] [namespace]` as follows:

```
$ rosparam load load.yaml namespace
```

Creating nodes

In this section, we are going to learn how to create two nodes: one to publish data and the other to receive this data. This is the basic way of communicating between two nodes, that is, to handle data and do something with this data.

Navigate to the `chapter2_tutorials/src/` folder using the following command:

```
$ roscd chapter2_tutorials/src/
```

Create two files with the names `example1_a.cpp` and `example1_b.cpp`. The `example1_a.cpp` file will send the data with the node name, and the `example1_b.cpp` file will show the data in the shell. Copy the following code inside the `example1_a.cpp` file or download it from the repository:

```cpp
#include "ros/ros.h"
#include "std_msgs/String.h"
#include <sstream>

int main(int argc, char **argv)
{
  ros::init(argc, argv, "example1_a");
  ros::NodeHandle n;
  ros::Publisher chatter_pub =
    n.advertise<std_msgs::String>("message", 1000);
  ros::Rate loop_rate(10);
  while (ros::ok())
  {
    std_msgs::String msg;
    std::stringstream ss;
    ss<< " I am the example1_a node ";
    msg.data = ss.str();
    //ROS_INFO("%s", msg.data.c_str());
    chatter_pub.publish(msg);
    ros::spinOnce();
    loop_rate.sleep();
  }
  return 0;
}
```

Here is a further explanation of the preceding code. The headers to be included are `ros/ros.h`, `std_msgs/String.h`, and `sstream`. Here, `ros/ros.h` includes all the files necessary for using the node with ROS, and `std_msgs/String.h` includes the header that denotes the type of message that we are going to use:

```cpp
#include "ros/ros.h"
#include "std_msgs/String.h"
#include <sstream>
```

At this point, we initialize the node and set the name; remember that the name must be unique:

```
ros::init(argc, argv, "example1_a");
```

This is the handler of our process; it allows us to interact with the environment:

```
ros::NodeHandle n;
```

We instantiate a publisher and tell the master the name of the topic and the type. The name is message, and the second parameter is the buffer size. If the topic is publishing data quickly, the buffer will keep at least 1000 messages:

```
ros::Publisher chatter_pub =
n.advertise<std_msgs::String>("message", 1000);
```

The next step is to set the data sending frequency, which in this case is 10 Hz:

```
ros::Rate loop_rate(10);
```

The ros::ok() line stops the node if *Ctrl* + *C* is pressed or if ROS stops all the nodes:

```
while (ros::ok())
{
```

In this part, we create a variable for the message with the correct type to send the data:

```
std_msgs::String msg;
std::stringstream ss;
ss<< " I am the example1_a node ";
msg.data = ss.str();
```

We continue by sending the message, in this case, the semantic is to publish a message, using the previously defined publisher:

```
chatter_pub.publish(msg);
```

The spinOnce function takes care of handling all of ROS's internal events and actions, such as reading from subscribed topics; spinOnce performs one iteration in the main loop of ROS in order to allow the user to perform actions between iterations, in contrast with the spin function, which runs the main loop without interruption:

```
ros::spinOnce();
```

Finally, we sleep for the required time to get a 10 Hz frequency:

```
loop_rate.sleep();
```

Now we will create the other node. Copy the following code inside the `example1_b.cpp` file or download it from the repository:

```
#include "ros/ros.h"
#include "std_msgs/String.h"

void chatterCallback(const std_msgs::String::ConstPtr& msg)
{
  ROS_INFO("I heard: [%s]", msg->data.c_str());
}

int main(int argc, char **argv)
{
  ros::init(argc, argv, "example1_b");
  ros::NodeHandle n;
  ros::Subscriber sub = n.subscribe("message", 1000,
    chatterCallback);
  ros::spin();
  return 0;
}
```

Let's explain the code. Include the headers and the type of message to use for the topic:

```
#include "ros/ros.h"
#include "std_msgs/String.h"
```

The following type of function is a `callback` and happens in response to an action, which in this case is the reception of a `String` message. This function allows us to do something with the data; in this case, we display it in the terminal:

```
void messageCallback(const std_msgs::String::ConstPtr& msg)
{
  ROS_INFO("I heard: [%s]", msg->data.c_str());
}
```

We create a subscriber and start to listen to the topic with the name `message`. The buffer will be of `1000`, and the function to handle the message will be `messageCallback`:

```
ros::Subscriber sub = n.subscribe("message", 1000,
  messageCallback);
```

The `ros::spin()` line is the main loop where the node starts to read the topic and when a message arrives, `messageCallback` is called. When the user presses *Ctrl + C*, the node exits the loop and ends:

```
ros::spin();
```

Building the node

As we are using the `chapter2_tutorials` package, we are going to edit the `CMakeLists.txt` file. You can use your favorite editor or the `rosed` tool. This will open the file with the Vim editor:

```
$ rosed chapter2_tutorials CMakeLists.txt
```

At the end of the file, we will copy the following lines:

```
include_directories(
include
  ${catkin_INCLUDE_DIRS}
)

add_executable(example1_a src/example1_a.cpp)
add_executable(example1_b src/example1_b.cpp)

add_dependencies(example1_a
chapter2_tutorials_generate_messages_cpp)
add_dependencies(example1_b
chapter2_tutorials_generate_messages_cpp)

target_link_libraries(example1_a ${catkin_LIBRARIES})
target_link_libraries(example1_b ${catkin_LIBRARIES})
```

Now, to build the package and compile all the nodes, use the `catkin_make` tool as follows:

```
$ cd ~/dev/catkin_ws/
$ catkin_make --pkg chapter2_tutorials
```

If ROS is not running on your computer, you will have to use the following command:

```
$ roscore
```

You can check whether ROS is running using the `rosnode` list command as follows:

```
$ rosnode list
```

Now run both nodes in different shells:

```
$ rosrun chapter2_tutorials example1_a
```

```
$ rosrun chapter2_tutorials example1_b
```

If you check the shell where the `example1_b` node is running, you will see something similar to the following screenshot:

```
...
[ INFO] [1403252419.452448698]: I heard: [ I am the example1_a node ]
[ INFO] [1403252419.552163326]: I heard: [ I am the example1_a node ]
[ INFO] [1403252419.653701929]: I heard: [ I am the example1_a node ]
[ INFO] [1403252419.752261663]: I heard: [ I am the example1_a node ]
[ INFO] [1403252419.854459847]: I heard: [ I am the example1_a node ]
...
```

Everything that is happening can be viewed in the following diagram. You can see that the `example1_a` node is publishing the `message` topic, and the `example2_b` node is subscribing to the topic:

You can use `rosnode` and `rostopic` to debug and see what the nodes are doing. Try the following commands:

```
$ rosnode list
$ rosnode info /example1_a
$ rosnode info /example1_b
$ rostopic list
$ rostopic info /message
$ rostopic type /message
$ rostopic bw /message
```

Creating msg and srv files

In this section, we are going to learn how to create msg and srv files for use in our nodes. They are files where we put a specification about the type of data to be transmitted and the values of this data. ROS will use these files to create the necessary code for us to implement the msg and srv files to be used in our nodes.

Let's start with the msg file first.

In the example used in the *Building the node* section, we created two nodes with a standard type message. Now we are going to learn how to create custom messages with the tools that ROS has.

First, create a new msg folder in our chapter2_tutorials package; create a new chapter2_msg1.msg file and add the following lines:

```
int32 A
int32 B
int32 C
```

Now, edit package.xml and remove <!--   --> from the <build_depend>message_ generation</build_depend> and <run_depend>message_runtime</run_depend> lines.

Edit CMakeList.txt and add the message_generation line as follows:

```
find_package(catkin REQUIRED COMPONENTS
roscpp
  std_msgs
  message_generation
)
```

Find the next lines, uncomment and add the name of the new message as follows:

```
## Generate messages in the 'msg' folder
add_message_files(
       FILES
       chapter2_msg1.msg
)


## Generate added messages and services with any dependencies
listed here
 generate_messages(
   DEPENDENCIES
   std_msgs
 )
```

And now you can compile using the following lines:

```
$ cd ~/dev/catkin_ws/
$ catkin_make
```

To check whether all is OK, you can use the `rosmsg` command:

```
$ rosmsg show chapter2_tutorials/chapter2_msg1
```

If you see the same content as that of the `chapter2_msg1.msg` file, all is OK.

Now we are going to create a `srv` file. Create a new folder in the `chapter2_tutorials` folder with the name `srv`, create a new `chapter2_srv1.srv` file and add the following lines:

```
int32 A
int32 B
int32 C
---
int32 sum
```

To compile the new `msg` and `srv` files, you have to uncomment the following lines in the `package.xml` and `CMakeLists.txt` files. These lines permit the configuration of the messages and services and tell ROS how and what to build.

First of all, open the `package.xml` folder from your `chapter2_tutorials` package as follows:

```
$ rosed chapter2_tutorials package.xml
```

Search for the following lines and uncomment them:

```
<build_depend>message_generation</build_depend>
<run_depend>message_runtime</run_depend>
```

Open `CMakeLists.txt` using the following command:

```
$ rosed chapter2_tutorials CMakeLists.txt
```

Find the following lines, uncomment them and complete them with the correct data:

```
catkin_package(
  CATKIN_DEPENDS message_runtime
)
```

To generate messages, you need to add the `message_generation` line in the `find_package` section:

```
find_package(catkin REQUIRED COMPONENTS
```

```
roscpp
  std_msgs
message_generation
)
```

Add the names of the message and service files in the add_message_files section, as follows:

```
## Generate messages in the 'msg' folder
add_message_files(
    FILES
    chapter2_msg1.msg
)

## Generate services in the 'srv' folder
add_service_files(
    FILES
    chapter2_srv1.srv
)
```

Uncomment the generate_messages section to make sure that the generation of messages and services can be done:

```
## Generate added messages and services with any dependencies
listed here
 generate_messages(
   DEPENDENCIES
   std_msgs
 )
```

You can test whether all is OK using the rossrv tool as follows:

```
$ rossrv show chapter2_tutorials/chapter2_srv1
```

If you see the same content as that of the chapter2_srv1.srv file, all is OK.

Using the new srv and msg files

First, we are going to learn how to create a service and how to use it in ROS. Our service will calculate the sum of three numbers. We need two nodes: a server and a client.

In the chapter2_tutorials package, create two new nodes with the following names: example2_a.cpp and example2_b.cpp. Remember to put the files in the src folder.

In the first file, example2_a.cpp, add the following code:

```
#include "ros/ros.h"
#include "chapter2_tutorials/chapter2_srv1.h"

bool add(chapter2_tutorials::chapter2_srv1::Request  &req,
         chapter2_tutorials::chapter2_srv1::Response &res)
{
  res.sum = req.A + req.B + req.C;
  ROS_INFO("request: A=%ld, B=%ld C=%ld", (int)req.A, (int)req.B,
    (int)req.C);
  ROS_INFO("sending back response: [%ld]", (int)res.sum);
  return true;
}

int main(int argc, char **argv)
{
  ros::init(argc, argv, "add_3_ints_server");
  ros::NodeHandle n;
  ros::ServiceServer service = n.advertiseService("add_3_ints",
    add);
  ROS_INFO("Ready to add 3 ints.");
  ros::spin();

  return 0;
}
```

Let's explain the code. These lines include the necessary headers and the srv file that we created:

```
#include "ros/ros.h"
#include "chapter2_tutorials/chapter2_srv1.h"
```

This function will add three variables and send the result to the other node:

```
bool add(chapter2_tutorials::chapter2_srv1::Request  &req,
         chapter2_tutorials::chapter2_srv1::Response &res)
```

Here, the service is created and advertised over ROS:

```
ros::ServiceServer service = n.advertiseService("add_3_ints",
    add);
```

In the second file, example2_b.cpp, add this code:

```
#include "ros/ros.h"
```

```
#include "chapter2_tutorials/chapter2_srv1.h"
#include <cstdlib>

int main(int argc, char **argv)
{
  ros::init(argc, argv, "add_3_ints_client");
  if (argc != 4)
  {
    ROS_INFO("usage: add_3_ints_client A B C ");
    return 1;
  }

  ros::NodeHandle n;
  ros::ServiceClient client =
    n.serviceClient<chapter2_tutorials::chapter2_srv1>("add_3_ints");
  chapter2_tutorials::chapter2_srv1 srv;
  srv.request.A = atoll(argv[1]);
  srv.request.B = atoll(argv[2]);
  srv.request.C = atoll(argv[3]);
  if (client.call(srv))
  {
    ROS_INFO("Sum: %ld", (long int)srv.response.sum);
  }
  else
  {
    ROS_ERROR("Failed to call service add_3_ints");
    return 1;
  }
  return 0;
}
```

As usual, let's explain the code. Create a client for the service with the name
add_3_ints:

```
ros::ServiceClient client =
n.serviceClient<chapter2_tutorials::chapter2_srv1>("add_3_ints");
```

Here, we create an instance of our srv request type and fill all the values to be sent.
If you remember, the message has three fields:

```
chapter2_tutorials::chapter2_srv1 srv;
srv.request.A = atoll(argv[1]);
srv.request.B = atoll(argv[2]);
srv.request.C = atoll(argv[3]);
```

With this line, the service is called and the data is sent. If the call succeeds, `call()` will return `true`, and if not, `call()` will return `false`:

```
if (client.call(srv))
```

To build the new nodes, edit `CMakeList.txt` and add the following lines:

```
add_executable(example2_a src/example2_a.cpp)
add_executable(example2_b src/example2_b.cpp)

add_dependencies(example2_a
chapter2_tutorials_generate_messages_cpp)
add_dependencies(example2_b
chapter2_tutorials_generate_messages_cpp)
target_link_libraries(example2_a ${catkin_LIBRARIES})
target_link_libraries(example2_b ${catkin_LIBRARIES})
```

Now execute the following command:

```
$ cd ~/dev/catkin_ws
$ catkin_make
```

To start the nodes, execute the following command lines:

```
$ rosrun chapter2_tutorials example2_a
$ rosrun chapter2_tutorials example2_b 1 2 3
```

You should see something similar to this output:

```
Node example2_a
[ INFO] [1355256113.014539262]: Ready to add 3 ints.
[ INFO] [1355256115.792442091]: request: A=1, B=2 C=3
[ INFO] [1355256115.792607196]: sending back response: [6]
Node example2_b
[ INFO] [1355256115.794134975]: Sum: 6
```

Now we are going to create nodes with our custom `msg` file. The example is the same, that is, `example1_a.cpp` and `example1_b.cpp`, but with the new message, `chapter2_msg1.msg`.

The following code snippet is present in the `example3_a.cpp` file:

```
#include "ros/ros.h"
#include "chapter2_tutorials/chapter2_msg1.h"
#include <sstream>
```

```
int main(int argc, char **argv)
{
  ros::init(argc, argv, "example3_a");
  ros::NodeHandle n;
  ros::Publisher pub =
    n.advertise<chapter2_tutorials::chapter2_msg1>("message", 1000);
  ros::Rate loop_rate(10);
  while (ros::ok())
  {
    chapter2_tutorials::chapter2_msg1 msg;
    msg.A = 1;
    msg.B = 2;
    msg.C = 3;
    pub.publish(msg);
    ros::spinOnce();
    loop_rate.sleep();
  }
  return 0;
}
```

The following code snippet is present in the example3_b.cpp file:

```
#include "ros/ros.h"
#include "chapter2_tutorials/chapter2_msg1.h"

void messageCallback(const
chapter2_tutorials::chapter2_msg1::ConstPtr& msg)
{
  ROS_INFO("I heard: [%d] [%d] [%d]", msg->A, msg->B, msg->C);
}

int main(int argc, char **argv)
{
  ros::init(argc, argv, "example3_b");
  ros::NodeHandle n;
  ros::Subscriber sub = n.subscribe("message", 1000,
    messageCallback);
  ros::spin();
  return 0;
}
```

If we run both nodes now, we will see something similar to the following output:

```
...
[ INFO] [1355270835.920368620]: I heard: [1] [2] [3]
```

```
[ INFO] [1355270836.020326372]: I heard: [1] [2] [3]
[ INFO] [1355270836.120367449]: I heard: [1] [2] [3]
[ INFO] [1355270836.220266466]: I heard: [1] [2] [3]
...
```

The launch file

The `launch` file is a useful feature in ROS for launching more than one node. In these sections, we have created nodes and we have been executing them in different shells. Imagine working with 20 nodes and the nightmare of executing each one in a shell!

With the `launch` file, we can do it in the same shell by launching a configuration file with the extension `.launch`.

To practise using this utility, we are going to create a new folder in our package as follows:

```
$ roscd chapter2_tutorials/
$ mkdir launch
$ cd launch
$ vim chapter2.launch
```

Now put the following code inside the `chapter2.launch` file:

```xml
<?xml version="1.0"?>
<launch>
  <node name ="example1_a" pkg="chapter2_tutorials"
    type="example1_a"/>
  <node name ="example1_b" pkg="chapter2_tutorials"
    type="example1_b"/>
</launch>
```

This file is simple, although you can write a very complex file if you want, for example, to control a complete robot, such as PR2 or Robonaut. Both are real robots and they are simulated in ROS.

The file has a `launch` tag; inside this tag, you can see the `node` tag. The `node` tag is used to launch a node from a package, for example, the `example1_a` node from the `chapter2_tutorials` package.

This launch file will execute two nodes—the first two examples of this chapter. If you remember, the `example1_a` node sends a message to the `example1_b` node. To launch the file, you can use the following command:

```
$ roslaunch chapter2_tutorials chapter2.launch
```

You will see something similar to the following screenshot on your screen:

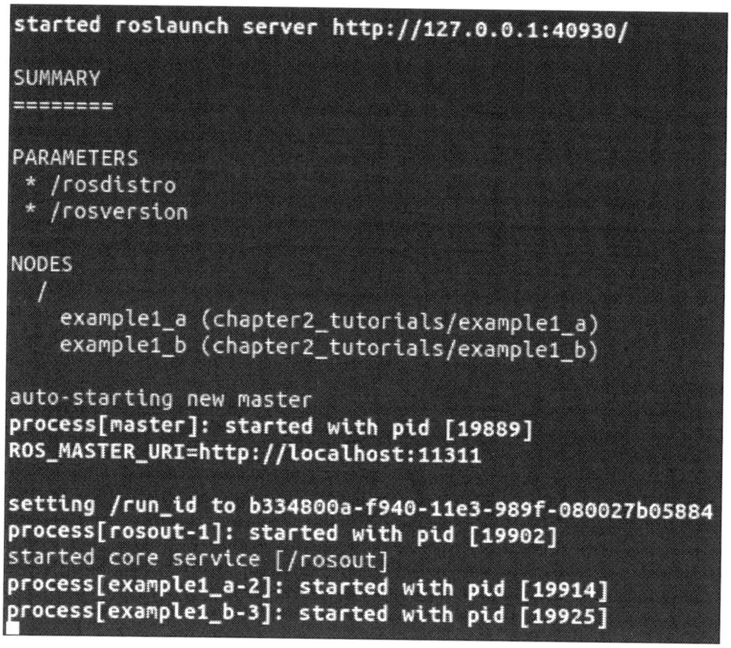

```
started roslaunch server http://127.0.0.1:40930/

SUMMARY
========

PARAMETERS
 * /rosdistro
 * /rosversion

NODES
  /
      example1_a (chapter2_tutorials/example1_a)
      example1_b (chapter2_tutorials/example1_b)

auto-starting new master
process[master]: started with pid [19889]
ROS_MASTER_URI=http://localhost:11311

setting /run_id to b334800a-f940-11e3-989f-080027b05884
process[rosout-1]: started with pid [19902]
started core service [/rosout]
process[example1_a-2]: started with pid [19914]
process[example1_b-3]: started with pid [19925]
```

The running nodes are listed in the screenshot. You can also see the running nodes using the following command:

```
$ rosnode list
```

You will see the three nodes listed as follows:

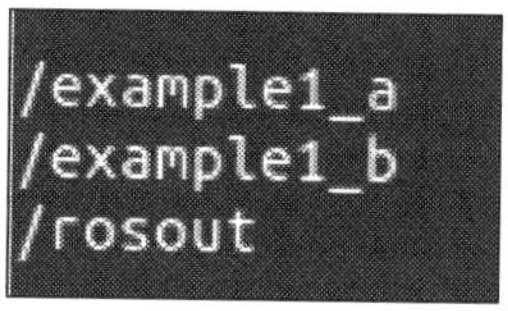

```
/example1_a
/example1_b
/rosout
```

When you launch a launch file, it is not necessary to execute it before the `roscore` command; `roslaunch` does it for us.

Remember that the `example1_b` node prints on the screen the message received from the other node. If you take a look, you won't see anything. This is because `example1_b` prints the message using `ROS_INFO`, and when you run only a node in a shell, you can see it, but when you run a launch file, you can't.

Now, to see the message printed on the screen, you can use the `rqt_console` utility. You will learn more about this utility in the following chapters. Now run the following command:

```
$ rqt_console
```

You will see the message sent by `example1_b`, as shown in the following screenshot:

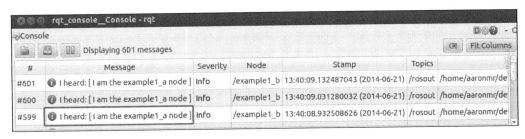

On the line, you can see the message, the node that has sent it, and the path of the source file.

Dynamic parameters

Another utility in ROS is the **Dynamic Reconfigure** utility. Normally, when you are programming a new node, you initialize the variables with data that can only be changed within the node. If you want to change these values dynamically from outside the node, you can use Parameter Server, services, or topics. If you are working in a PID node to control a motor, for example, you should use the Dynamic Reconfigure utility.

In this section, you will learn how to configure a basic node with this feature. Add the necessary lines in the `CMakeLists.txt` and `package.xml` files.

To use Dynamic Reconfigure, you should write a configuration file and save it in the `cfg` folder in your package. Create the folder and a new file as follows:

```
$ roscd chapter2_tutorials
$ mkdir cfg
$ vim chapter2.cfg
```

Write the following code in the `chapter2.cfg` file:

```python
#!/usr/bin/env python
PACKAGE = "chapter2_tutorials"

from dynamic_reconfigure.parameter_generator_catkin import *

gen = ParameterGenerator()

gen.add("double_param", double_t, 0, "A double parameter", .1, 0,
1)
gen.add("str_param", str_t, 0, "A string parameter",
"Chapter2_dynamic_reconfigure")
gen.add("int_param", int_t, 0, "An Integer parameter", 1,  0, 100)
gen.add("bool_param",   bool_t, 0, "A Boolean parameter",  True)

size_enum = gen.enum([ gen.const("Low", int_t, 0, "Low is 0"),
gen.const("Medium", int_t, 1, "Medium is 1"),
gen.const("High", int_t, 2, "High is 2")],
                "Select from the list")

gen.add("size", int_t, 0, "Select from the list", 1, 0, 3,
edit_method=size_enum)

exit(gen.generate(PACKAGE, "chapter2_tutorials", "chapter2_"))
```

Let's explain the code. These lines initialize ROS and import the parameter generator:

```python
#!/usr/bin/env python
PACKAGE = "chapter2_tutorials"

from dynamic_reconfigure.parameter_generator_catkin import *
```

The following line initializes the parameter generator, and thanks to that, we can start to add parameters in the following lines:

```python
gen = ParameterGenerator()

gen.add("double_param", double_t, 0, "A double parameter", .1, 0,
1)
gen.add("str_param", str_t, 0, "A string parameter",
"Chapter2_dynamic_reconfigure")
gen.add("int_param", int_t, 0, "An Integer parameter", 1,  0, 100)
gen.add("bool_param",   bool_t, 0, "A Boolean parameter",  True)
```

These lines add different parameter types and set the default values, description, range, and so on. The parameter has the following arguments:

```
gen.add(name, type, level, description, default, min, max)
```

- `name`: This is the name of the parameter
- `type`: This is the type of the value stored
- `level`: This is a bitmask that is passed to the callback
- `description`: This is a short description of the parameter
- `default`: This is the default value when the node starts
- `min`: This is the minimum value for the parameter
- `max`: This is the maximum value for the parameter

The names of the parameters must be unique, and the values have to be in the range and have `min` and `max` values:

```
exit(gen.generate(PACKAGE, "chapter2_tutorials", "chapter2_"))
```

The last line generates the necessary files and exits the program. Notice that the `.cfg` file was written in Python. This book is for C++ snippets, but we will sometimes use Python snippets.

It is necessary to change the permissions for the file because the file will be executed by ROS. To make the file executable and runnable by any user, we will use the `chmod` command with the `a+x` parameter as follows:

```
$ chmod a+x cfg/chapter2.cfg
```

Open `CMakeList.txt` and add the following lines:

```
find_package(catkin REQUIRED COMPONENTS
roscpp
  std_msgs
  message_generation
  dynamic_reconfigure
)

generate_dynamic_reconfigure_options(
  cfg/chapter2.cfg
)

add_dependencies(example4 chapter2_tutorials_gencfg)
```

Now we are going to write our new node with Dynamic Reconfigure support. Create a new file in your src folder as follows:

```
$ roscd chapter2_tutorials
$ vim src/example4.cpp
```

Write the following code snippet in the file:

```
#include <ros/ros.h>
#include <dynamic_reconfigure/server.h>
#include <chapter2_tutorials/chapter2Config.h>

void callback(chapter2_tutorials::chapter2Config &config, uint32_t
level) {
  ROS_INFO("Reconfigure Request: %d %f %s %s %d",
        config.int_param,
        config.double_param,
        config.str_param.c_str(),
        config.bool_param?"True":"False",
        config.size);
}

int main(int argc, char **argv) {
  ros::init(argc, argv, "example4_dynamic_reconfigure");

  dynamic_reconfigure::Server<chapter2_tutorials::chapter2Config>
  server;
  dynamic_reconfigure::Server<chapter2_tutorials::chapter2Config>::
  CallbackType f;

  f = boost::bind(&callback, _1, _2);
  server.setCallback(f);

  ros::spin();
  return 0;
}
```

Let's explain the code and note the important lines. As usual, these lines include the headers for ROS, Parameter Server, and our config file created earlier:

```
#include <ros/ros.h>
#include <dynamic_reconfigure/server.h>
#include <chapter2_tutorials/chapter2Config.h>
```

The `callback` function will print the new values for the parameters. The way to access the parameters is, for example, `config.int_param`. The name of the parameter must be the same as the one that you configured in the `example2.cfg` file:

```
void callback(chapter2_tutorials::chapter2Config &config, uint32_t
level) {
  ROS_INFO("Reconfigure Request: %d %f %s %s %d",
          config.int_param,
          config.double_param,
          config.str_param.c_str(),
          config.bool_param?"True":"False",
          config.size);
}
```

To continue, the server is initialized in the line where we pass the `chapter2_Config` configuration file:

```
dynamic_reconfigure::Server<chapter2_tutorials::chapter2Config>
server;

dynamic_reconfigure::Server<chapter2_tutorials::chapter2Config>::
CallbackType f;

  f = boost::bind(&callback, _1, _2);
server.setCallback(f);
```

Now we send the `callback` function to the server. When the server gets a reconfiguration request, it will call the `callback` function.

Once we are done with the explanation, we need to add lines to the `CMakeLists.txt` file as follows:

```
add_executable(example4 src/example4.cpp)

add_dependencies(example4 chapter2_tutorials_gencfg)

target_link_libraries(example4 ${catkin_LIBRARIES})
```

Now you have to compile and run the node and the Dynamic Reconfigure GUI as follows:

```
$ roscore
$ rosrun chapter2_tutorials example4
$ rosrun rqt_reconfigure rqt_reconfigure
```

When you execute the last command, you will see a new window where you can dynamically modify the parameters of the node, as shown in the following screenshot:

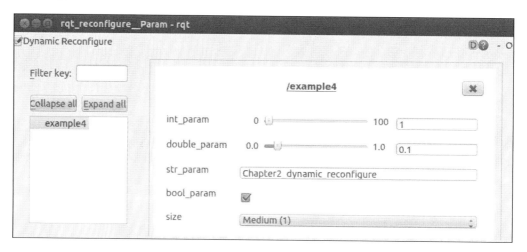

Each time you modify a parameter with the slider, the checkbox, and so on, you will see the changes made in the shell where the node is running. You can see an example in the following screenshot:

```
[ INFO] [1403367196.752115948]: Reconfigure Request: 20 0.800000 qwert True 1
[ INFO] [1403367196.942722848]: Reconfigure Request: 20 0.800000 qwerty True 1
[ INFO] [1403367196.973132691]: Reconfigure Request: 20 0.800000 qwerty True 1
[ INFO] [1403367197.183714401]: Reconfigure Request: 20 0.800000 qwertyu True 1
[ INFO] [1403367197.217819018]: Reconfigure Request: 20 0.800000 qwertyu True 1
[ INFO] [1403367203.160337570]: Reconfigure Request: 1 0.800000 qwertyu True 1
[ INFO] [1403367203.188864110]: Reconfigure Request: 1 0.800000 qwertyu True 1
```

Thanks to Dynamic Reconfigure, you can program and test your nodes more efficiently and faster. Using the program with hardware is a good choice and you will learn more about it in the following chapters.

Summary

This chapter provided you with general information about the ROS architecture and how it works. You saw certain concepts, tools, and samples of how to interact with nodes, topics, and services. In the beginning, all of these concepts might look complicated and without use, but in upcoming chapters, you will start to understand their applications.

It is useful to practise using these terms and tutorials before continuing because in upcoming chapters we will assume that you know all of the concepts and uses.

Remember that if you have queries about something and you cannot find the solution in this book, you can use the official resources of ROS from `http://www.ros.org`. Additionally, you can ask the ROS Community questions at `http://answers.ros.org`.

In the next chapter, you will learn how to debug and visualize data using ROS tools. This will help you to find problems, know whether what ROS is doing is correct, and better define what your expectations from it are.

3
Visualization and Debugging Tools

ROS has a good number of tools which allow the user and the developer to visualize and debug their code in order to detect and solve issues with both hardware and software. This comprises a message logging system similar to `log4cxx`, diagnostic messages, and also visualization and inspection tools, which provide a comprehensive list of the running nodes as well as how are they interconnected.

In this chapter, we will also show you how to debug an ROS node with the GDB debugger. The message logging API will be explained, and advice will be given on how to choose the logging level. Then, we will explain the set of ROS tools that allows us to inspect which processes are running and what information is communicated between them. For instance, the following figure shows a tool that visualizes the graph of the system, where the nodes are the processes running and the edges represent the data workflow through communication topics. This tool is `rqt_graph`, and in this case, it shows the nodes and topics which compose the **REEM robot** software system running on a Gazebo simulation.

You can see multiple controllers for the arms, torso, head, **MoveIt!** `move_group` node, pick and place action servers, and the `play_motion` node for pre-recorded movements. Other nodes publish `joint_states`, spawn the robot controllers, and control the joystick to move the mobile base.

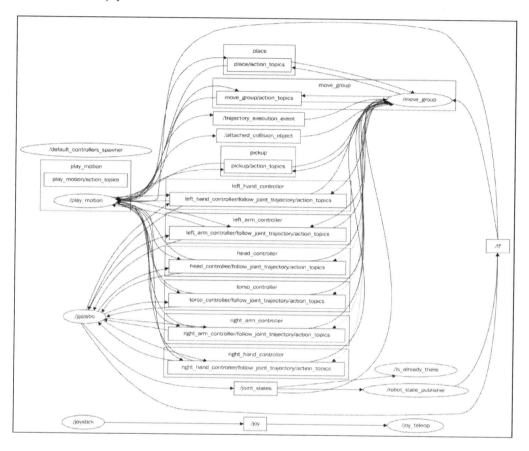

Similarly, this chapter will show you how to plot scalar data in a time series, visualize images from a video stream, and represent different types of data in a 3D representation using (the widely known) `rviz` (or `rqt_rviz`), as shown in the following screenshot:

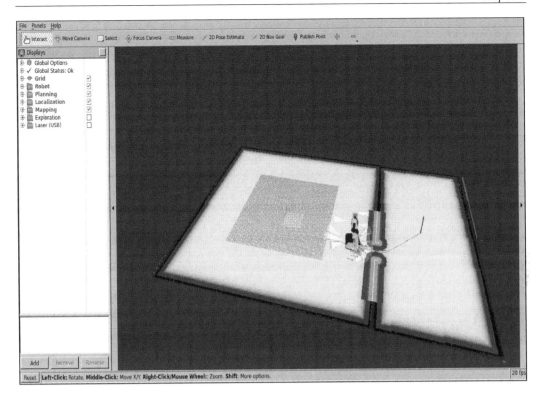

The preceding screenshot shows the REEM robot, which can be run in simulation with the following command:

```
$ roslaunch reem_2dnav_gazebo reem_navigation.launch
```

Note that before you install it, you need to follow the instructions provided at `http://wiki.ros.org/Robots/REEM`. The following sections in this chapter will cover the following topics on visualization and debugging: debugging our code in ROS; using logging messages in our code, with different severity levels, names, conditions, and throttling options. Here, we will explain the `rqt_logger_level` and `rqt_console` interfaces, which allow you to set the severity level of a node and visualize the message, respectively. We will also inspect the state of the ROS system by listing the nodes running, the topics, services, and actions they use to transfer messages among them, and the parameters declared in the ROS master server. We will explain `rqt_graph`, which shows nodes and topics in a directed graph representation, and `rqt_reconfigure`, which allows you to change dynamic parameters. We will also take a look at visualizing diagnostics information using the `runtime_monitor` and `robot_monitor` interfaces, as well as plotting scalar data from messages using `rqt_plot`.

For non-scalar data, we will explain other `rqt` tools available in ROS, such as `rqt_image_view` to visualize images and `rqt_rviz` to show multiple data in a 3D representation. We will also show you how to visualize markers and interactive markers, and what frames are and how they are integrated into ROS messages and visualization tools. We will also explain how to use `rqt_tf_tree` to visualize the **Transform Frame (tf)** tree, along with how to save messages and replay them for simulation or evaluation purposes. We will also cover the `rqt_bag` interface.

Finally, other `rqt_gui` interfaces will be explained, as well as how to arrange them in a single GUI.

Most of the `rqt` tools can be run by simply inputting their name in the terminal, such as `rqt_console`, but in some cases this does not work and we must use `rosrun rqt_reconfigure rqt_reconfigure`, which always works; note that the name seems to be repeated, but it is actually the package and node names, one after the other.

Debugging ROS nodes

ROS nodes can be debugged as regular programs. They run as a process in the operating system and have a PID. Therefore, you can debug them as with any program using standard tools, such as `gdb`. Similarly, you can check for memory leaks with `memcheck` or profile the performance of your algorithm with `callgrind`. However, remember that in order to run a node, you must run the following command:

```
$ rosrun chapter3_tutorials example1
```

Unfortunately, you cannot simply run the command through `gdb` in the following way:

```
$ gdb rosrun chapter3_tutorials example1
```

In the following sections, we will explain how to call these tools for an ROS node to overcome this issue. Later, we will see how to add logging messages to our code in order to make it simple to diagnose problems; in practice, using logging messages helps to diagnose basic (and not so basic) problems without the need to debug the binaries. Similarly, we will discuss ROS introspection tools, which allow you to easily detect broken connections between nodes. Finally, even though we will provide a bottom-up overview, in practice we usually follow a top-down approach to diagnosing issues.

Using the GDB debugger with ROS nodes

In order to debug a C/C++ node with the gdb debugger, all we need to know is the location of the node executable. With the ROS Kinetic and catkin packages, the node executable is placed inside the devel/lib/<package> folder within the workspace. For example, in order to run the example1 node from the chapter3_tutorials package in gdb, we have to proceed as follows, starting from the workspace folder (/home/<user>/book_ws):

```
$ cd devel/lib/chapter3_tutorials
```

If you have run catkin_make install, you can also navigate to the install/lib/chapter3_tutorials directory using the following command:

```
$ cd install/lib/chapter3_tutorials
```

Now we can run the node executable inside gdb with the following command:

```
$ gdb example1
```

 Remember that you must have roscore running before you start your node because it will need the master/server running.

Once roscore is running, you can start your node in gdb by pressing the *R* key (and *Enter*), and you can also list the associated source code with the *L* key as well as set breakpoints or any of the functionalities that gdb comes with. If everything is correct, you should see the following output in the gdb terminal after running the node:

```
(gdb) r
Starting program: /home/luis/devel/catkin_ws/devel/lib/chapter3_tutorials/exampl
e1
[Thread debugging using libthread_db enabled]
Using host libthread_db library "/lib/x86_64-linux-gnu/libthread_db.so.1".
[New Thread 0x7ffff170d700 (LWP 6618)]
[New Thread 0x7ffff0f0c700 (LWP 6619)]
[New Thread 0x7fffebfff700 (LWP 6620)]
[New Thread 0x7fffeb7fe700 (LWP 6625)]
[DEBUG] [1476313631.940149636]: This is a simple DEBUG message!
[DEBUG] [1476313631.940214159]: This is a DEBUG message with an argument: 3.1400
00
[DEBUG] [1476313631.940246937]: This is DEBUG stream message with an argument: 3
.14
[Thread 0x7fffeb7fe700 (LWP 6625) exited]
[Thread 0x7ffff170d700 (LWP 6618) exited]
[Thread 0x7ffff0f0c700 (LWP 6619) exited]
[Thread 0x7fffebfff700 (LWP 6620) exited]
[Inferior 1 (process 6613) exited normally]
(gdb)
```

Attaching a node to GDB while launching ROS

In many cases, we might get a `launch` file that takes care of starting the node, as you can see in the following example:

```
<launch>
  <node pkg="chapter3_tutorials" type="example1" name="example1"/>
</launch>
```

In order to attach it to `gdb`, we must add `launch-prefix="xterm -e gdb --args"` as follows:

```
<launch>
  <node pkg="chapter3_tutorials" type="example1" name="example1"
  launch-prefix="xterm -e gdb --args"/>
</launch>
```

Similarly, you can also add `output="screen"` to make the node output appear on the terminal. With this launch prefix, a new `xterm` terminal will be created with the node attached to `gdb`. Set breakpoints if needed, and then press the *C* or *R* key to run the node and debug it. One of the common uses you will find of this simple workflow is to obtain a **backtrace (bt)** if the node crashes.

Profiling a node with valgrind while launching ROS

Additionally, we can use the same attribute to attach the node to diagnosis tools. For example, we can run our program through `valgrind` (see `http://valgrind.org` for further information) to detect memory leaks using `memcheck` and perform profiling analysis using `callgrind`. Contrary to attaching to `gdb`, we do not need to start `xterm`:

```
<launch>
  <node pkg="chapter3_tutorials" type="example1"
  name="example1" output="screen"
  launch-prefix="valgrind"/>
</launch>
```

Enabling core dumps for ROS nodes

Although ROS nodes are actually regular executables, there is a tricky point to enabling core dumps, which can later be used in a gdb session. First of all, we have to set an unlimited core size; the current value can be checked with ulimit -c. Note that this is also required for any executable and not just ROS nodes:

```
$ ulimit -c unlimited
```

Then, to allow core dumps to be created, we must set the core filename to use the pid process by default. Otherwise, they will not be created because at $ROS_HOME, there is already a core directory to prevent core dumps. Therefore, in order to create core dumps with the name and path $ROS_HOME/core.PID, we must run the following command:

```
$ echo 1 | sudo tee /proc/sys/kernel/core_uses_pid
```

Logging messages

It is good practice to include messages that indicate what the program is doing; we must do it without compromising the efficiency of our software and the clarity of its output. In ROS, we have an API which covers both features, built on top of log4cxx (a port of the well-known log4j logger library). In brief, we have several levels of messages, which might have a name (named messages) and depend on a condition or even throttle. All of them have a negligible footprint on performance if they are masked by the current verbosity level (even at compile time). They also have full integration with other ROS tools to visualize and filter the messages from all the nodes running.

Outputting logging messages

ROS comes with a great number of functions/macros to output logging messages. It supports different levels, conditions, STL streams, throttling, and other features that we will see in this section. To start with something simple, an information message is printed with this code in C++:

```
$ ROS_INFO("My INFO message.");
```

In order to have access to these logging functions/macros, the following header is required:

```
#include <ros/ros.h>
```

This includes the following header (where the logging API is defined):

```
#include <ros/console.h>
```

As a result of running a program with the preceding message, we will get the following output:

```
[ INFO] [1356440230.837067170]: My INFO message.
```

All messages are printed with their level and the current timestamp (your output might differ for this reason) before the actual message, with both between square brackets. The timestamp is the epoch time, that is, the number of seconds and nanoseconds since January 1, 1970. Then, we have our message—always with a new line.

This function allows parameters in the same way as the C printf function does. For example, we can print the value of a floating point number in the variable val with this code:

```
floatval = 1.23;
ROS_INFO("My INFO message with argument: %f", val);
```

C++ STL streams are also supported with *_STREAM functions. Therefore, the previous instruction is equivalent to the following using streams:

```
ROS_INFO_STREAM("My INFO message with argument: " <<val);
```

Note that we did not specify any stream since the API takes care of that by redirecting to cout/cerr, a file, or both.

Setting the debug message level

ROS supports the following logging levels (in increasing order of relevance):

- DEBUG
- INFO
- WARN
- ERROR
- FATAL

These levels are part of the function used to output messages, so it's something you can easily experiment with, simply by using the syntax below:

```
ROS_<LEVEL>[_<OTHER>]
```

Each message is printed with a particular color. The colors are as follows:

```
DEBUG in green
INFO in white
WARN in yellow
ERROR in red
FATAL in purple
```

Each message level is meant to be used for a different purpose. Here, we suggest the uses for each of the levels:

- DEBUG: Use them only when debugging; this information should not be displayed in a deployed application, as it's only for testing purposes

- INFO: These should be standard messages to indicate significant steps or what the node is doing

- WARN: As the name suggests, use them to provide a warning that something might be wrong, missed, or abnormal, but that the application can still run regardless

- ERROR: These can be used to indicate errors, although the node can still recover from them; however, they set a certain expectation regarding the node's behavior

- FATAL: These messages usually expose errors that prevent the node from continuing its operation

Configuring the debugging level of a particular node

By default, only messages of INFO or higher levels are shown. ROS uses these levels to filter the messages printed by a particular node. There are many ways to do so. Some of them are set at the time of compilation and some messages aren't even compiled below a given verbosity level; others can be changed before execution using a configuration file, and it is also possible to change the logging level dynamically using the rqt_console and rqt_logger_level tools.

It is possible to set the logging level at compile time in our source code, but this is very uncommon and not recommended as it it requires us to modify the source code to change the logging level.

Nevertheless, in some cases we need to remove the overhead of all the logging functions below a given level. In those cases, we won't be able to see those messages later because they get removed from the code and are not simply disabled. To do so, we must set ROSCONSOLE_MIN_SEVERITY to the minimum severity level desired, or even none, in order to avoid any message (even FATAL). The macros are as follows:

```
ROSCONSOLE_SEVERITY_DEBUG
ROSCONSOLE_SEVERITY_INFO
ROSCONSOLE_SEVERITY_WARN
ROSCONSOLE_SEVERITY_ERROR
ROSCONSOLE_SEVERITY_FATAL
ROSCONSOLE_SEVERITY_NONE
```

The ROSCONSOLE_MIN_SEVERITY macro is defined in <ros/console.h> to the DEBUG level if not given. Therefore, we can pass it as a build argument (with -D) or put it before all the headers. For example, to show only ERROR (or higher) messages, we will put this in our source code:

```
#define ROSCONSOLE_MIN_SEVERITY ROSCONSOLE_SEVERITY_ERROR
```

Alternatively, we can set this to all the nodes in a package, setting this macro in CMakeLists.txt by adding this line:

```
add_definitions(-DROSCONSOLE_MIN_SEVERITY
=ROSCONSOLE_SEVERITY_ERROR)
```

On the other hand, we have the more flexible solution of setting the minimum logging level in a configuration file. We create a config folder with a file, such as chapter3_tutorials.config, and this content (edit the file provided since it is set to DEBUG):

```
log4j.logger.ros.chapter3_tutorials=ERROR
```

Then, we must set the ROSCONSOLE_CONFIG_FILE environment variable to point to our file. We can do this on a launch file that also runs the node. Therefore, we will extend the launch file shown earlier to do so with the env (environment variable) element, as shown here:

```
<launch>
  <!-- Logger config -->
  <env name="ROSCONSOLE_CONFIG_FILE"
  value="$(find
  chapter3_tutorials)/config/chapter3_tutorials.config"/>

  <!-- Example 1 -->
  <node pkg="chapter3_tutorials" type="example1" name="example1"
  output="screen"/>
</launch>
```

The environment variable takes the configuration file shown previously, which contains the logging level specification for each named logger; in this case, it is for the package name.

Giving names to messages

By default, ROS assigns several names to the node loggers. The messages discussed until now will be named after the node's name. In complex nodes, we can give a name to those messages of a given module or functionality. This is done with `ROS_<LEVEL>[_STREAM]_NAMED` functions (see the `example2` node):

```
ROS_INFO_STREAM_NAMED(
  "named_msg",
  "My named INFO stream message; val = " <<val
);
```

With named messages, we can set different initial logging levels for each named message using the configuration file and modify them individually later. We must use the name of the messages as children of the package in the specification; for example, for `named_msg` messages, we will use the following code:

```
log4j.logger.ros.chapter3_tutorials.named_msg=ERROR
```

Conditional and filtered messages

Conditional messages are printed only when a given condition is satisfied. To use them, we have the `ROS_<LEVEL>[_STREAM]_COND[_NAMED]` functions; note that they can be named messages as well (see the `example2` node for more examples and combinations):

```
ROS_INFO_STREAM_COND(
  val< 0.,
    "My conditional INFO stream message; val (" <<val<< ") < 0"
);
```

Filtered messages are similar to conditional messages in essence, but they allow us to specify a user-defined filter that extends `ros::console::FilterBase`; we must pass a pointer to such a filter in the first argument of a macro with the format `ROS_<LEVEL>[_STREAM]_FILTER[_NAMED]`. The following example is taken from the `example2` node:

```
structMyLowerFilter : public ros::console::FilterBase {
  MyLowerFilter(const double&val ) : value( val ) {}
  inline virtual boolisEnabled() { return value < 0.; }
  double value;
```

```
};

MyLowerFilterfilter_lower(val );

ROS_INFO_STREAM_FILTER(&filter_lower,
  "My filter INFO stream message; val (" <<val<< ") < 0"
);
```

Showing messages once, throttling, and other combinations

It is also possible to control how many times a given message is shown. We can print it only once with ROS_<LEVEL>[_STREAM]_ONCE[_NAMED]:

```
for(int i = 0; i< 10; ++i ) {
  ROS_INFO_STREAM_ONCE("My once INFO stream message; i = " <<i);
}
```

This code from the `example2` node will show the message only once.

However, it is usually better to show the message with a certain frequency. For that, we have throttle messages. They have the same format as the once message, but here ONCE is replaced with THROTTLE. They also include a first argument, which is `period` in seconds, that is, it is printed only every `period` seconds:

```
for(int i = 0; i< 10; ++i ) {
  ROS_INFO_STREAM_THROTTLE(2,
    "My throttle INFO stream message; i = " <<i);
  ros::Duration( 1 ).sleep();
}
```

Finally, note that named, conditional, and once/throttle messages can be used together with all the available levels.

Nodelets also have some support in terms of logging messages. Since they have their own namespace, they have a specific name to differentiate the message of one nodelet from another. Simply put, all the macros shown until now are valid, but instead of ROS_*, we have NODELET_*. These macros will only compile inside nodelets. In addition, they operate by setting up a named logger with the name of the nodelet running so that you can differentiate between the outputs of two nodelets of the same type running in the same nodelet manager. They also have an advantage in that you can turn one specific nodelet into the debug level instead of all the nodelets of a specific type.

Using rqt_console and rqt_logger_level to modify the logging level on the fly

ROS provides a series of tools to manage logging messages. In ROS Kinetic, we have two separate GUIs: `rqt_logger_level` to set the logging level of the nodes or named loggers and `rqt_console` to visualize, filter, and analyze the logging messages.

In order to test this, we are going to use `example3`. Run `roscore` and `rqt_console` to see the logging messages:

```
$ rosrun rqt_console rqt_console
```

The following window will open:

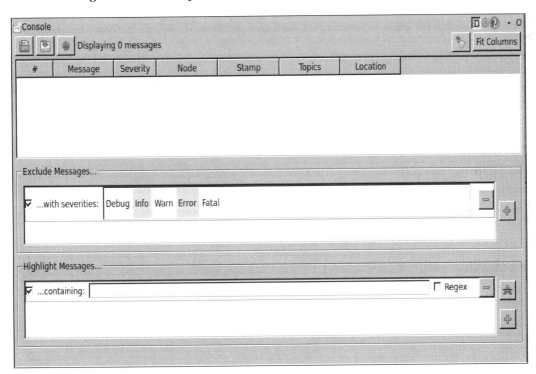

Now, run the node:

```
$ rosrun chapter3_tutorials example3
```

You will start seeing the logging messages, as the following screenshot shows. Note that `roscore` must be running and that you must press the recording button on `rqt_console`.

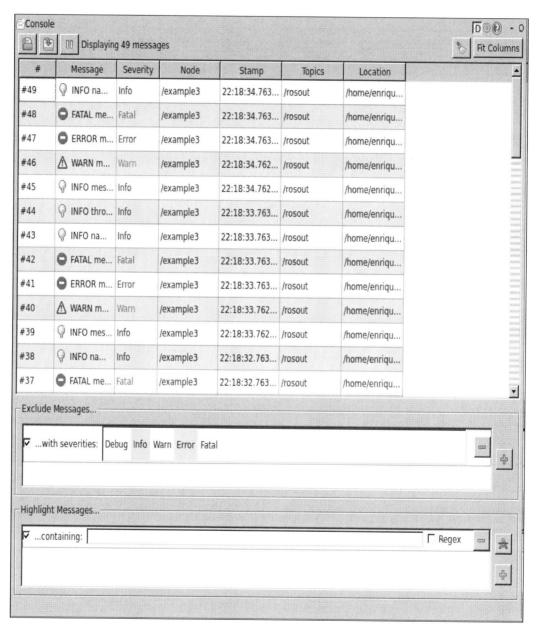

In `rqt_console`, the messages are collected and shown in a table where different columns separate the timestamp, the message itself, the severity level, and the node that produced the message, alongside other information. You can fit the columns automatically by pressing the **Resize columns** button. If you double-click on a message, you can see all the information, including the line of code that generated it, as shown in the following screenshot:

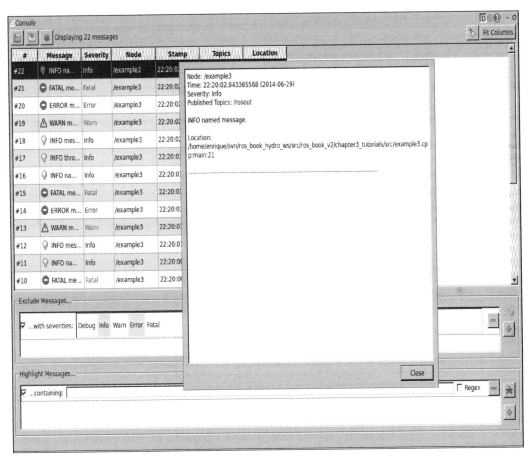

This interface allows you to pause, save, and load previous/saved logging messages. We can clear the list of messages and filter them. In ROS Kinetic, excluding those that are filtered, messages have specific interfaces depending on the filter criteria. For instance, nodes can be filtered with a single rule, where we select the nodes we want to exclude. Additionally, in the same way, we can set highlighting filters. This is shown in the following screenshot:

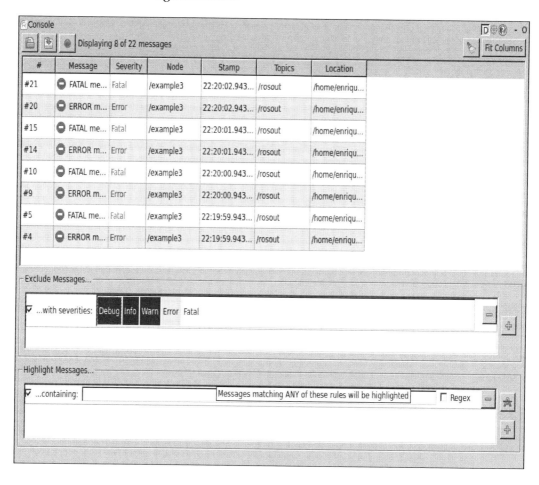

As an example, the messages from the previous image are filtered by excluding those with a severity different to **Error** and **Fatal**.

In order to set the severity of the loggers, we must run the following command:

```
$ rosrun rqt_logger_level rqt_logger_level
```

Here, we can select the node, then the named logger, and finally its severity. Once we modify it, the new messages received with a severity below the desired level will not appear in `rqt_console`:

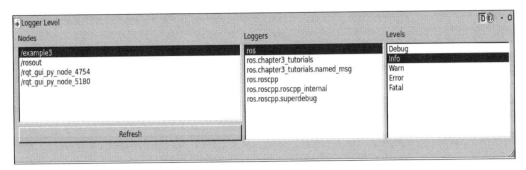

Shown in the following screenshot is an example where we have set the severity level to the minimum (**Debug**) for the named logger, `ros.chapter3_tutorials.named_msg`, of the `example3` node; remember that the named loggers are created by the `*_NAMED` logging functions:

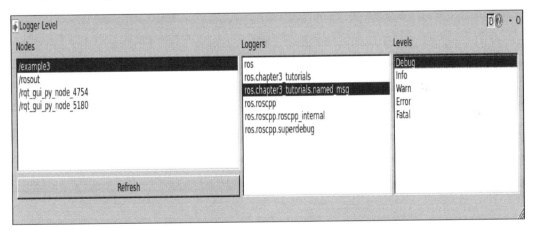

As you can see, every node has several internal loggers by default, which are related to the ROS communication API, among others; in general, you should not reduce their severity.

Inspecting the system

When our system is running, we might have several nodes and many more topics publishing messages amongst each other. We might also have nodes providing actions or services. For large systems, it is important to have tools that let us see what is running at a given time. ROS provides basic but very powerful tools with this goal in mind, from the CLI to GUI applications.

Listing nodes, topics, services, and parameters from our perspective, we should start with the most basic level of introspection. We are going to see how to obtain the list of nodes running and topics and services available at a given time:

Obtain the list of all	Command
Nodes running	rosnode list
Topics of all nodes running	rostopic list
Services of all nodes running	rosservice list
Parameters on the server	rosparam list

We recommend that you go back to *Chapter 2*, *ROS Architecture and Concepts*, to see how these commands also allow us to obtain the message type sent by a particular topic, as well as its fields, using rosmsg show.

Any of these commands can be combined with regular bash commands, such as grep, to look for the desired nodes, topics, services, or parameters. For example, action goal topics can be found using the following command:

```
$ rostopic list | grep goal
```

The grep command looks for text or patterns in a list of files or the standard output.

Additionally, ROS provides several GUIs for you to play with topics and services. First, `rqt_top` shows the nodes running in an interface, similar to a **table of processes** (**ToP**), which allows us to rapidly see all the nodes and resources they are using. For the following screenshot, we have used the REEM simulation with the navigation stack running as an example:

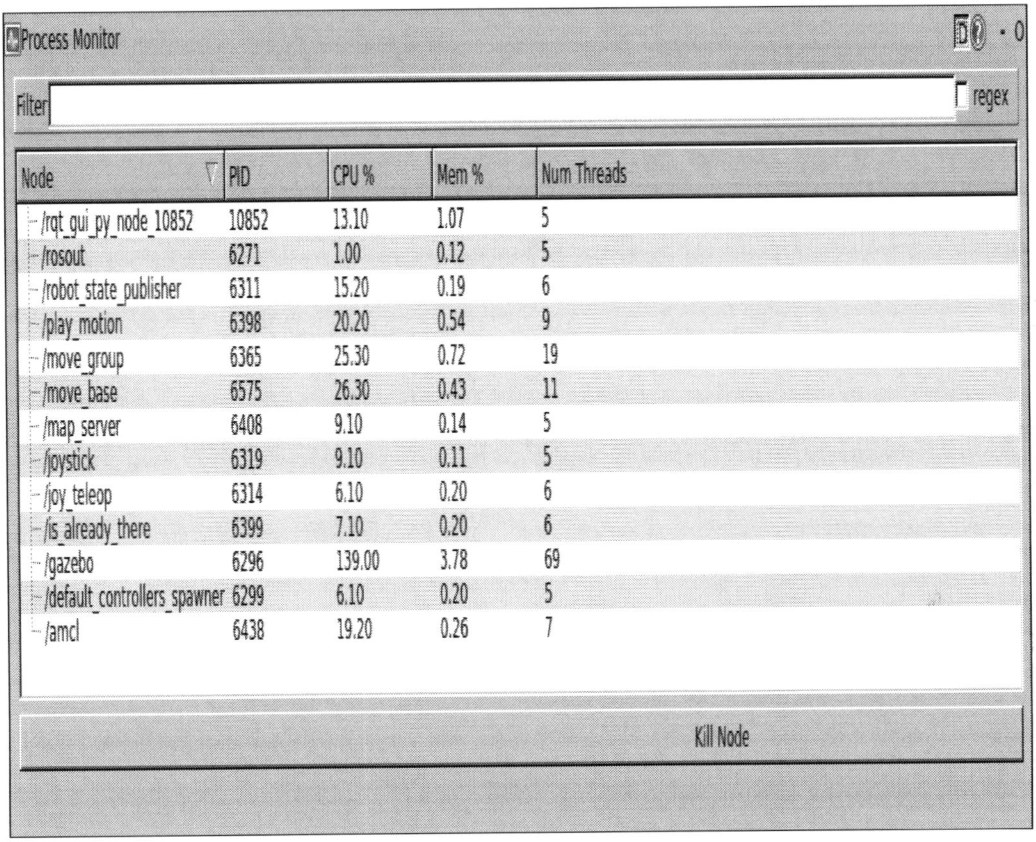
Process Monitor
Filter
regex
Node PID CPU % Mem % Num Threads
/rqt_gui_py_node_10852 10852 13.10 1.07 5
/rosout 6271 1.00 0.12 5
/robot_state_publisher 6311 15.20 0.19 6
/play_motion 6398 20.20 0.54 9
/move_group 6365 25.30 0.72 19
/move_base 6575 26.30 0.43 11
/map_server 6408 9.10 0.14 5
/joystick 6319 9.10 0.11 5
/joy_teleop 6314 6.10 0.20 6
/is_already_there 6399 7.10 0.20 6
/gazebo 6296 139.00 3.78 69
/default_controllers_spawner 6299 6.10 0.20 5
/amcl 6438 19.20 0.26 7
Kill Node

On the other hand, `rqt_topic` provides us with information about topics, including publishers, subscribers, the publishing rate, and messages published. You can view the message fields and select the topics you want to subscribe to in order to analyze their bandwidth and rate (Hz) and see the latest message published; note that latched topics do not usually publish continuously, so you will not see any information about them. The following screenshot shows this:

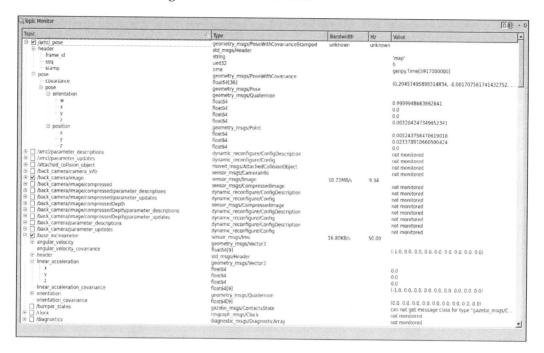

Similarly, `rqt_publisher` allows us to manage multiple instances of `rostopic pub` commands in a single interface. It also supports Python expressions for the published messages and fixed values. In the following screenshot, we will see two example topics being published (we will see the messages using `rostopic echo <topic>` in two different terminals):

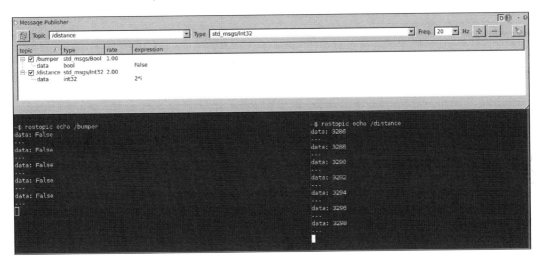

Note that `rqt_service_caller` does the same thing for multiple instances of `rosservice call` commands. In the following screenshot, we will call the `/move_base/NavfnROS/make_plan` service, which is where we have to set up the request; for empty services, this is not needed, due to the `/global_localization` service from the `/amcl` node. After clicking on the **Call** button, we will obtain the response message. For this example, we have used the REEM simulation with the navigation stack running:

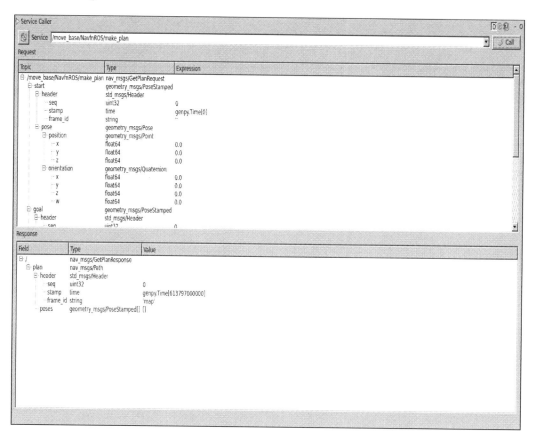

Inspecting the node's graph online with rqt_graph

The current state of an ROS session can be shown as a directed graph where the nodes running are the graph nodes and the edges are the publisher-subscriber connections amongst these nodes through the topics. This graph is drawn dynamically by `rqt_graph`:

```
$ rosrun rqt_graph rqt_graph
```

In order to illustrate how to inspect the nodes, topics, and services with `rqt_graph`, we are going to run the `example4` and `example5` nodes simultaneously with the following `launch` file:

```
$ roslaunch chapter3_tutorials example4_5.launch
```

The `example4` node publishes in two different topics and calls a service. Meanwhile, `example5` subscribes to those topics and also has the service server to attend the request queries and provide the response. Once the nodes are running, we have the node's topology, as shown in the following screenshot:

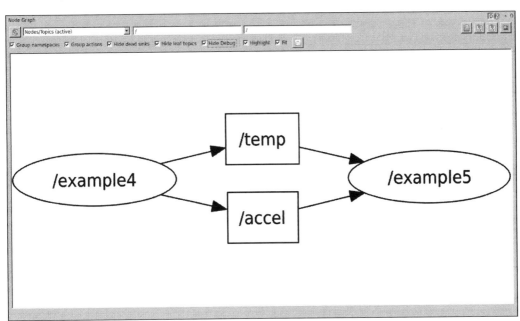

In this screenshot, we have the nodes `example4` and `example5` connected by the topics `temp` and `accel`. Since **Hide Debug** is selected, we do not see the ROS server node `rosout` as well as the `rosout` topic that publishes the logging messages for the diagnostic aggregator in the server as we did previously. We can deselect this option to show the debug nodes/topics so that the ROS server is shown, as well as the `rqt_graph` node itself (see the following screenshot). It is useful to hide these nodes for larger systems because it simplifies the graph. Additionally, with ROS Kinetic, the nodes in the same namespace are grouped - for example, the image pipeline nodes:

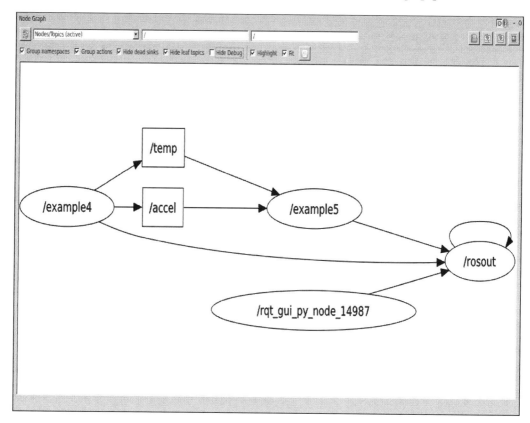

When there is a problem in the system, the nodes appear in red all the time (not just when we move the mouse over them). In those cases, it is useful to select **All Topics** to also show unconnected topics. This usually shows misspelled topic names that break connections among nodes.

When running nodes on different machines, `rqt_graph` shows its great high-level debugging capabilities, as it shows whether the nodes see each other from one machine to the other, enumerating the connections.

Finally, we can enable statistics to see the message rate and bandwidth represented in the topic edge, with the rate written and the line width. We must set this parameter before running `rqt_graph` in order to have this information available:

```
$ rosparam set enable_statistics true
```

But this is not the only thing we need to do to enable statistics. To be able to get the desired information, the `rqt_topic` utility needs to be launched and the appropriate topics need to be ticked. It should also be noted that the parameter might need to be enabled before the relevant nodes are launched.

Setting dynamic parameters

If a node implements a dynamic reconfigure parameter server, we can use `rqt_reconfigure` to modify it on the fly. Run the following example, which implements a dynamic reconfigure server with several parameters (see the `cfg` file in the `cfg` folder of the package):

```
$ roslaunch chapter3_tutorials example6.launch
```

With the dynamic reconfigure server running, open the GUI with the following command:

```
$ rosrun rqt_reconfigure rqt_reconfigure
```

Select the `example6` server in the left-hand side panel, and you will see its parameters, which you can modify directly. The parameter changes take effect immediately, running the code inside a callback method in the example source code, which checks for the validity of the values. In this example, the parameters are printed every time they are changed, that is, when the callback method is executed. The following screenshot is an example of the expected behavior:

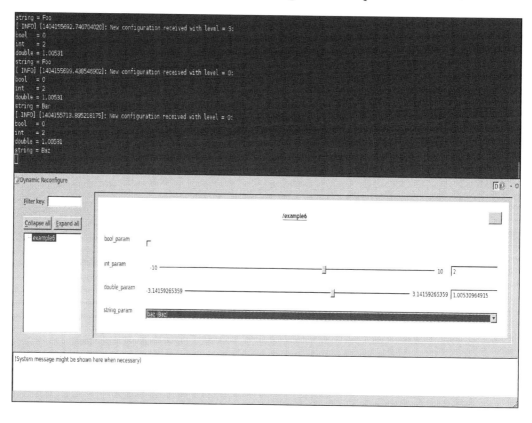

Dynamic parameters were originally meant for drivers, in order to make it easier to modify them on the fly. For this reason, several drivers already implement them; nevertheless, they can be used for any other node. Examples of drivers that implement them are the `hokuyo_node` driver for the Hokuyo laser rangefinders or the Firewire `camera1394` driver. Indeed, in the case of Firewire cameras, it is common for drivers to support changing configuration parameters of the sensor, such as the frame rate, shutter speed, and brightness, among others. The ROS driver for FireWire (IEEE 1394, a and b) cameras can be run with the following command:

```
$ rosrun camera1394 camera1394_node
```

Once the camera is running, we can configure its parameters with `rqt_reconfigure`, and we should see something similar to what's shown in the following screenshot:

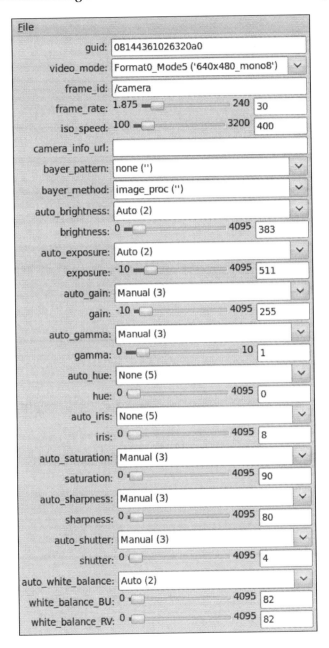

Note that we will cover how to work with cameras in *Chapter 9, Computer Vision*, where we will also explain these parameters from a developer's point of view.

Dealing with the unexpected

ROS has several tools for detecting potential problems in all the elements of a given package. Just move with roscd to the package you want to analyze. Then, run roswtf. For chapter3_tutorials, we have the following output. Note that if you have something running, the ROS graph will be analyzed too. We have run the roslaunch chapter3_tutorials example6.launch command, which yields an output similar to the following screenshot:

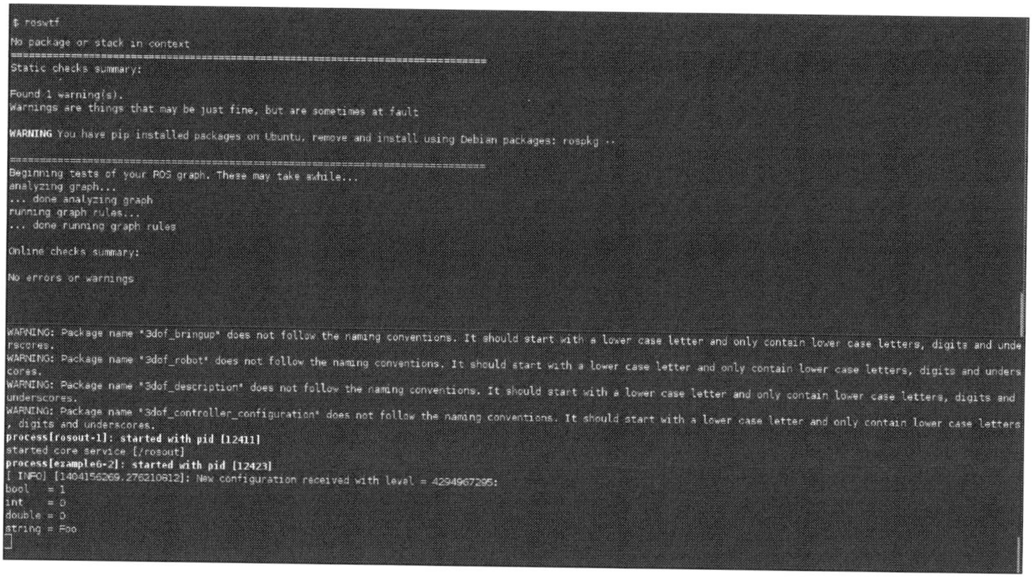

In general, we should expect no error or warning, but even then some of them are innocuous. In the previous screenshot, we can see that roswtf does not detect any error; it only issues a warning about pip, which may sometimes generate problems with the Python code installed in the system. Note that the purpose of roswtf is to signal potential problems; we are responsible for checking whether they are real or meaningless ones, as in the previous case.

Another useful tool is catkin_lint, which helps to diagnose errors with catkin, usually in the CMakeLists.txt and package.xml files. For chapter3_tutorials, we have the following output:

```
$ catkin_lint -W2 --pkg chapter3_tutorials
```

With `-W2`, we see warnings that can be usually ignored, such as the ones shown in the following screenshot:

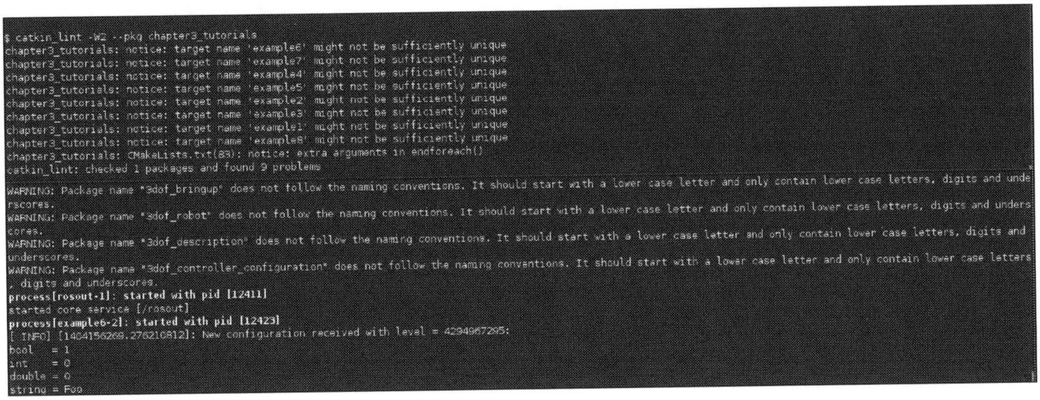

Please be aware that you might need to install `catkinlint` separately; it is usually contained in the package `python-catkin-lint`.

Visualizing nodes diagnostics

ROS nodes can provide diagnostic information using the `diagnostics` topic. For that, there is an API that helps to publish diagnostic information in a standard way. The information follows the `diagnostic_msgs/DiagnosticStatus` message type, which allows us to specify a level (`OK`, `WARN`, `ERROR`), name, message, and hardware ID as well as a list of `diagnostic_msgs/KeyValue`, which are pairs of `key` and `value` strings.

The interesting part comes with the tools that collect and visualize this diagnostic information. At the basic level, `rqt_runtime_monitor` allows us to visualize the information directly published through the `diagnostics` topic. Run the `example7` node, which publishes information through the diagnostics topic, and this visualization tool, to see the diagnostic information:

```
$ roslaunch chapter3_tutorials example7.launch
$ rosrun rqt_runtime_monitor rqt_runtime_monitor
```

The previous commands display the following output:

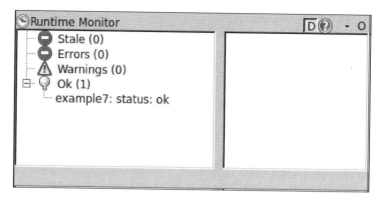

When the system is large, we can aggregate diagnostic information using the `diagnostic_aggregator`. It processes and categorizes the `diagnostics` topic messages and republishes them on `diagnostics_agg`. These aggregated diagnostic messages can be visualized with `rqt_robot_monitor`. The diagnostic aggregator is configured with a configuration file, such as the following one (see `config/diagnostic_aggregator.yaml` in `chapter3_tutorials`), where we define different `analyzers`, in this case using an `AnalyzerGroup`:

```
type: AnalyzerGroup
path: Sensors
analyzers:
status:
type: GenericAnalyzer
path: Status
startswith: example7
num_items: 1
```

The `launch` file used in the previous code already runs the diagnostic `aggregator_node` with the previous configuration, so you can run the following command:

```
$ rosrun rqt_robot_monitor rqt_robot_monitor
```

Now, we can compare the visualization of `rqt_runtime_monitor` with the one of `rqt_robot_monitor`, as shown in the following screenshot:

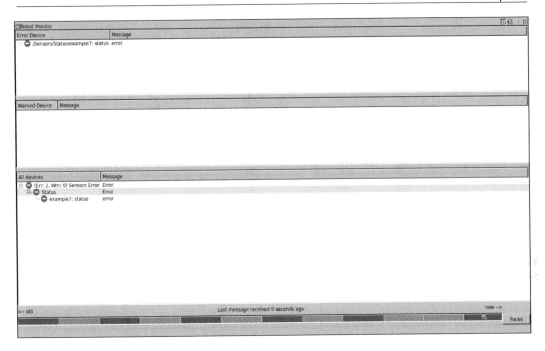

Plotting scalar data

Scalar data can be easily plotted with generic tools already available in ROS. Even non-scalar data can be plotted, but with each scalar field plotted separately. That is why we talk about scalar data, because most non-scalar structures are better represented with ad-hoc visualizers, some of which we will see later; for instance, images, poses, orientation/attitude, and so on.

Creating a time series plot with rqt_plot

Scalar data can be plotted as a time series over the time provided by the timestamps of the messages. Then, in the y axis, we can plot our scalar data. The tool for doing so is `rqt_plot`. It has a powerful argument syntax, which allows you to specify several fields of a structured message in a concise manner; we can also add or remove topics or fields manually from the GUI.

To show `rqt_plot` in action, we are going to use the `example4` node, as it publishes a scalar and a vector (non-scalar) in two different topics, which are `temp` and `accel`, respectively. The values put in these messages are synthetically generated, so they have no actual meaning, but they are useful for our plotting demonstration purposes. Start by running the node using the following command:

```
$ rosrun chapter3_tutorials example4
```

To plot a message, we must know its format; use `rosmg show <msg type>` if you do not know it. In the case of scalar data, we always have a `data` field that has the actual value. Hence, for the `temp` topic, which is of the `Int32` type, we will run the following command:

```
$ rosrun rqt_plot rqt_plot /temp/data
```

With the node running, we will see a plot that changes over time with the incoming messages, as shown in the following screenshot:

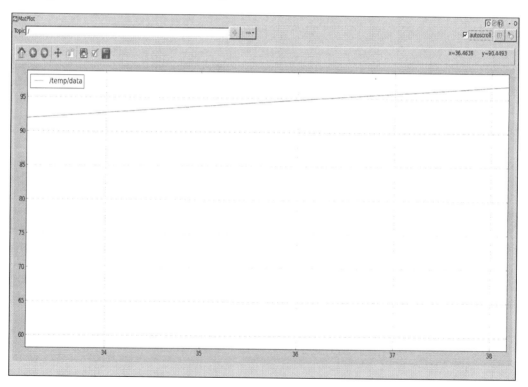

For `accel`, we have a `Vector3` message (as you can check with `rostopic type /accel`), which contains three fields that we can visualize in a single plot. The `Vector3` message has the x, y, and z fields. We can specify the fields separated by colons (`:`) or in the more concise manner, as shown in the following command:

```
$ rosrun rqt_plot rqt_plot /accel/x:y:z
```

The plot should look similar to the one in the following screenshot:

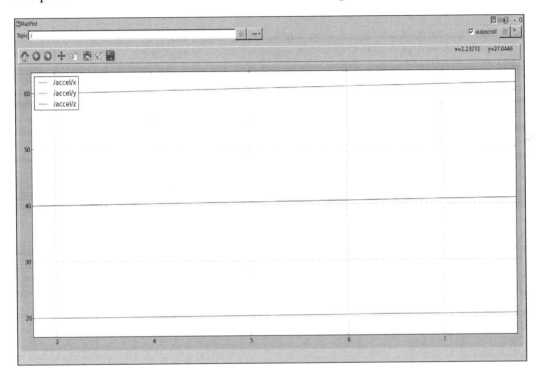

We can also plot each field in a separate axis. However, `rqt_plot` does not support this directly. Instead, we must use `rqt_gui` and arrange three plots manually, as shown in the following command and the screenshot after that:

```
$ rosrun rqt_gui rqt_gui
```

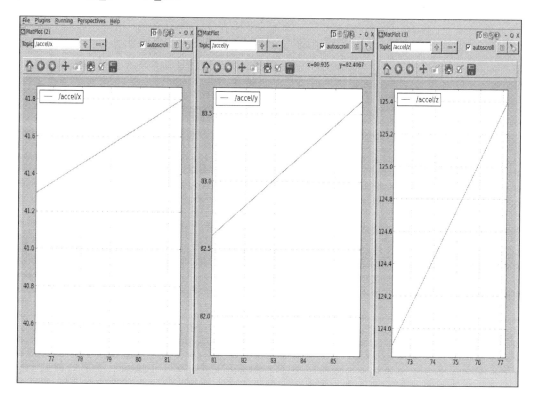

The `rqt_plot` GUI supports three plotting frontends. We can use QT frontends, which are faster and support more time series simultaneously. You can access and select them from the configuration button:

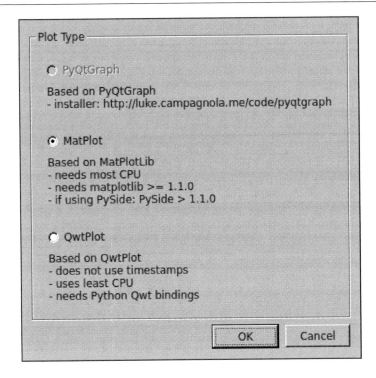

Image visualization

In ROS, we have a node that enables you to display images coming from a camera on-the-fly. This is an example of a topic with complex data, which is better visualized or analyzed with special tools. You only need a camera to do this, such as your laptop webcam. The `example8` node implements a basic camera capture program using OpenCV and ROS bindings to convert `cv::Mat` images into ROS `Image` messages that can be published in a topic. This node publishes the camera frames in the `/camera` topic.

We are only going to run the node with a `launch` file created to do so. The code inside the node is still new for the reader, but in the followings chapters we will cover how to work with cameras and images in ROS, so we will be able to come back to this node and understand it:

```
$ roslaunch chapter3_tutorials example8.launch
```

Once the node is running, we can list the topics (`rostopic list`) and see that the /camera topic is there. A straightforward way to verify that we are actually capturing images is to see which frequency we are receiving images at in the topic with `rostopic hz/camera`. It should be something in the region of 30 Hz. This is shown in the following screenshot:

```
~$ rostopic hz /camera
subscribed to [/camera]
average rate: 10.728
        min: 0.084s max: 0.099s std dev: 0.00474s window: 10
average rate: 10.746
        min: 0.084s max: 0.099s std dev: 0.00441s window: 21
average rate: 10.725
        min: 0.084s max: 0.099s std dev: 0.00426s window: 31
average rate: 10.710
        min: 0.084s max: 0.100s std dev: 0.00409s window: 42
average rate: 10.702
        min: 0.084s max: 0.100s std dev: 0.00398s window: 53
```

Visualizing a single image

We cannot use `rostopic echo /camera` because, as it's an image, the amount of information in plain text would be huge and not human-readable. Hence, we are going to use the following command:

```
$ rosrun image_view image_view image:=/camera
```

This is the `image_view` node, which shows the images in the given topic (the `image` argument) in a window. This way, we can visualize every image or frame published in a topic in a very simple and flexible manner—even over a network. If you press the right button of your mouse in the window, you can save the current frame in the disk, usually in your home directory, or `~/.ros`.

ROS Kinetic also has `rqt_image_view`, which supports viewing multiple images in a single window but does not allow the saving of images by right-clicking. We can select the `image` topic manually on the GUI or as we do with `image_view`:

```
$ rosrun rqt_image_view rqt_image_view
```

The previous command yields an output shown in the following screenshot:

ROS provides a camera calibration interface built on top of the OpenCV calibration API. We will cover this in *Chapter 9, Computer Vision*, when we will see how to work with cameras. There, we will see monocular and stereo cameras as well as the ROS image pipeline (`image_proc` and `stereo_image_proc`), which allows the rectification of the camera image distortion and computes the depth image disparity for stereo pairs so that we obtain a point cloud.

3D visualization

There are certain devices (such as stereo cameras, 3D lasers, the Kinect sensor, and so on) that provide 3D data—usually in the form of point clouds (organized/ordered or not). For this reason, it is extremely useful to have tools that visualize this type of data. In ROS, we have `rviz` or `rqt_rviz`, which integrates an OpenGL interface with a 3D world that represents sensor data in a world representation, using the frame of the sensor that reads the measurements in order to draw such readings in the correct position in respect to each other.

Visualizing data in a 3D world using rqt_rviz

With `roscore` running, start `rqt_rviz` (note that `rviz` is still valid in ROS Kinetic) with:

```
$ rosrun rqt_rviz rqt_rviz
```

We will see the graphical interface of the following screenshot, which has a simple layout:

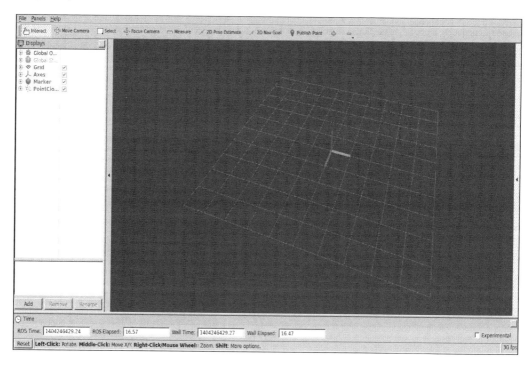

On the left-hand side, we have the **Displays** panel, in which we have a tree list of the different elements in the world, which appears in the middle. In this case, we have certain elements already loaded. This layout is saved in the config/example9.rviz file, which can be loaded in the **File | Open Config** menu.

Below the **Displays** area is the **Add** button, which allows you to add more elements by topic or type. Also note that there are global options, which are basically tools to set the fixed frame in the world in respect to others. Then, we have **Axes** and a **Grid** as a reference for the rest of the elements. In this case, for the example9 node, we are going to see **Marker** and **PointCloud2**.

Finally, on the status bar, we have information regarding the time, and on the right-hand side, there are menus. The **Tools** properties allows us to configure certain plugin parameters, such as the **2D Nav Goal** and **2D Pose Estimate** topic names. The **Views** menu gives different view types, where **Orbit** and **TopDownOrtho** are generally enough; one for a 3D view and the other for a 2D top-view. Another menu shows elements selected in the environment. At the top, we also have a menu bar with the current operation mode (**Interact**, **Move Camera**, **Measure**, and so on) and certain plugins.

Now we are going to run the example9 node using the following command:

```
$ roslaunch chapter3_tutorials example9.launch
```

In `rqt_rviz`, we are going to set `frame_id` of the marker, which is `frame_marker`, in the fixed frame. We will see a red cubic marker moving, as shown in the following screenshot:

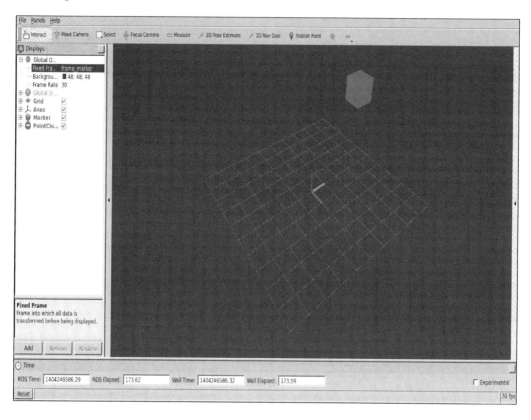

Similarly, if we set **Fixed Frame** to `frame_pc`, we will see a point cloud that represents a plane of 200 x 100 points, as shown in the following screenshot:

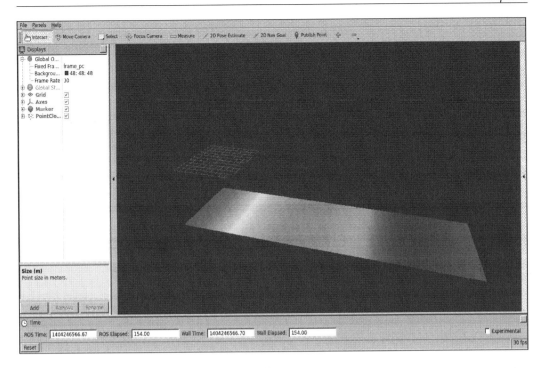

The list of supported built-in types in `rqt_viz` includes **Camera** and **Image**, which are shown in a window—similar to `image_view`. In the case of **Camera**, its calibration is used, and in the case of stereo images, they allow us to overlay the point cloud. We can also see the **LaserScan** data from range lasers, **Range** cone values from IR/sonar sensors, or **PointCloud2** from 3D sensors, such as the Kinect sensor.

For the navigation stack, which we will cover the in following chapters, we have several data types, such as `Odometry` (which plots the robot odometry poses), `Path` (which draws the path plan followed by the robot), `Pose` objects, `PoseArray` for particle clouds with the robot pose estimate, the **Occupancy Grid Map** (**OGM**) as a `Map`, and `costmaps` (which are of the `Map` type in ROS Kinetic and were `GridCell` before ROS Kinetic).

Among other types, it is also worth mentioning the `RobotModel`, which shows the CAD model of all the robot parts, taking the transformation among the frames of each element into account. Indeed, `tf` elements can also be drawn, which is very useful for debugging the frames in the system; we will see an example of this in the following section. In `RobotModel`, we also have the links that belong to the robot **Unified Robot Description Format (URDF)** description with the option to draw a trail showing how they move over time.

Basic elements can also be represented, such as a **Polygon** for the robot footprint; several kind of **Markers**, which support basic geometric elements, such as cubes, spheres, lines, and so on; and even **Interactive Marker** objects, which allow the user to set a pose (position and orientation) in the 3D world. Run the `example8` node to see an example of a simple interactive marker:

```
$ roslaunch chapter3_tutorials example10.launch
```

You will see a marker that you can move in the interactive mode of `rqt_rviz`. Its pose can be used to modify the pose of another element in the system, such as the joint of a robot:

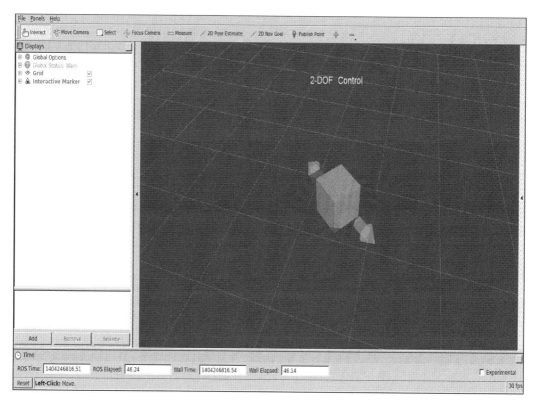

The relationship between topics and frames

All topics must have a frame if they are publishing data from a particular sensor that has a physical location in the real world. For example, a laser is located in a position with respect to the base link of the robot (usually in the middle of the traction wheels in wheeled robots). If we use the laser scans to detect obstacles in the environment or to build a map, we must use the transformation between the laser and the base link. In ROS, stamped messages have `frame_id`, apart from the timestamp (which is also extremely important when synchronizing different messages). A `frame_id` gives a name to the frame it belongs to.

However, the frames themselves are meaningless; we need the transformation among them. We already have the `tf` frame, which usually has the `base_link` frame as its root (or map if the navigation stack is running). Then, in `rqt_rviz`, we can see how this and other frames move in respect to each other.

Visualizing frame transformations

To illustrate how to visualize frame transformations, we are going to use the `turtlesim` example. Run the following command to start the demonstration:

```
$ roslaunch turtle_tf turtle_tf_demo.launch
```

This is a very basic example with the purpose of illustrating the `tf` visualization in `rqt_rviz`; note that, for the full extent of the capabilities offered by the `tf` API, you should wait until you have reached later chapters of this book. For now, it is enough to know that it allows us to make computations in one frame and then transform them to another, including time delays. It is also important to know that `tf` is published at a certain frequency in the system, so it is like a subsystem, where we can traverse the `tf` tree to obtain the transformation between any frames; we can do this in any node of our system just by consulting `tf`.

If you receive an error, it is probably because the listener died on the launch startup due to another required node that was not ready. If so, run the following command on another terminal to start it again:

```
$ rosrun turtle_tf turtle_tf_listener
```

Now you should see a window with two turtles, one following the other. You can control one of the turtles with the arrow keys as long as your focus is the terminal where you run the `launch` file. The following screenshot shows how one turtle has been following the other for some time:

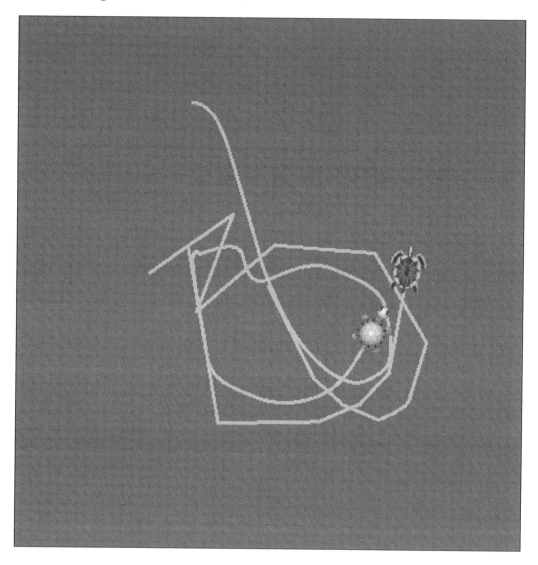

Each turtle has its own frame, so we can see it in `rqt_rviz`:

```
$ rosrun rqt_rviz rqt_rviz
```

Now, instead of viewing the `turtlesim` window, we are going to see how the turtles' frames move in `rqt_rviz` as we move our turtle with the arrow keys. We have to set the fixed frame to `/world` and then add the `tf` tree to the left-hand side area. We will see that we have the `/turtle1` and `/turtle2` frames both as children of the root `/world` frame. In the world representation, the frames are shown as axes and the parent-child links are shown with a yellow arrow that has a pink end. Set the view type to **TopDownOrtho** so it is easier to see how the frames move, as they only move on the 2D ground plane. You might also find it useful to translate the world center, which is done with the mouse with the *Shift* key pressed.

In the following screenshot, you can see how the two turtle frames are shown in respect to the `/world` frame. You can change the fixed frame to experiment with this example and `tf`. Note that `config/example_tf.rviz` is provided to give the basic layout for this example:

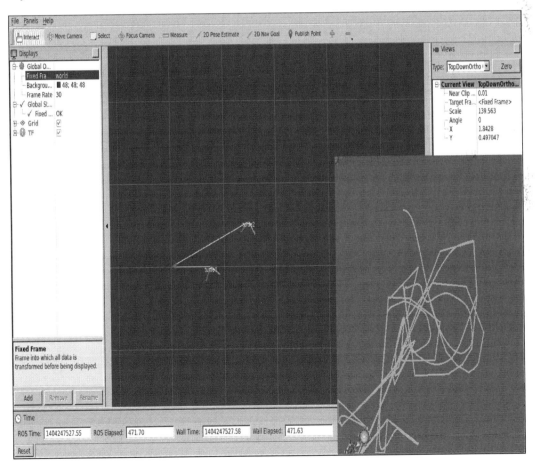

Saving and playing back data

Usually, when we work with robotic systems, we have to deal with our resources either being shared or not always available, or with the fact that experiments cannot be done regularly because of the cost or time required for preparing and performing them. For this reason, it is good practice to record the data of the experiment session for later analysis and to work, develop, and test our algorithms. However, the process of saving good data so that we can reproduce the experiment offline is not trivial. Fortunately, in ROS we have powerful tools that have already solved this problem.

ROS can save all the messages published on any topic. It has the ability to create a bag file containing the messages as they are, with all their fields and timestamps. This allows for the reproduction of the experiment offline, with its real conditions on the robot as the latency of message transmissions. What's more, ROS tools do all this efficiently, with a high bandwidth, and in an adequate manner, to organize the saved data.

In the following section, we will explain the tools provided by ROS to save and play back data stored in `bag` files, which use a binary format designed for and by ROS developers. We will also see how to manage these files, that is, inspect the contents (number of messages, topics, and so on), compress them, and split or merge several of them.

What is a bag file?

A `bag` file is a container of messages sent by topics that were recorded during a session using a robot or nodes. In brief, they are the log files for the messages transferred during the execution of our system, and they allow us to play back everything, even with time delays, since all messages are recorded with a timestamp—not only the timestamp in the header, but also for the packets contained within the `bag` file. The difference between the timestamp used to record and the one in the header is that the first one is set once the message is recorded, while the other is set by the producer/publisher of the message.

The data stored in a `bag` file is in the binary format. The particular structure of this container allows for extremely fast recording throughput, which is the most important concern when saving data. Additionally, the size of the `bag` file is relevant, but usually at the expense of speed. Nonetheless, we have the option to compress the file on the fly with the `bz2` algorithm; just use the `-j` parameter when you record with `rosbag record`.

Every message is recorded along with the topic that published it. Therefore, we can specify which topics to record or we can record them all (with -a). Later, when we play the bag file back, we can also select a particular subset of the topics contained in the bag file by indicating the name of the topics we want to publish.

Recording data in a bag file with rosbag

The first thing we have to do is simply record some data. We are going to use a very simple system as an example—our example4 node. Hence, we will first run the node:

```
$ rosrun chapter3_tutorials example4
```

Now, we have two options. First, we can record all the topics with the following command:

```
$ rosbag record -a
```

Otherwise, we can record only specific topics. In this case, it makes sense to record only the example4 topics, so we will run the following command:

```
$ rosbag record /temp /accel
```

By default, when we run the previous command, the rosbag program subscribes to the node and starts recording the message in a bag file in the current directory with the date as the name. Once the experiment has been completed, you only need to hit *Ctrl + C* in the running terminal. The following is an example of a recording session and the resulting bag file:

```
[ INFO] [1404248014.668263731]: Subscribing to /temp
[ INFO] [1404248014.671339658]: Subscribing to /accel
[ INFO] [1404248014.674950564]: Recording to 2014-07-01-22-54-34.bag.
```

You can find more options with rosbag help record, which include the bag file size, the duration of the recording, options to split the files into several smaller files of a given size, and so on. As we mentioned before, the file can be compressed on the fly (the -j option). This is only useful for small data rate recording, as it also consumes CPU time and might end up dropping messages. If messages are dropped, we can increase the buffer (-b) size for the recorder in MB, which defaults to 256 MB, although it can be increased to a couple of GB if the data rate is very high (especially with images).

It is also possible to include the call to `rosbag record` into a `launch` file, which is useful when we want to set up a recorder for certain topics. To do so, we must add the following node:

```
<node pkg="rosbag" type="record" name="bag_record"
args="/temp /accel"/>
```

Note that topics and other arguments are passed to the command using the `args` argument. It is also important to note that when `rosbag` is run from the `launch` file, the `bag` file is created by default in `~/.ros`, unless we give the name of the file with `-o` (prefix) or `-O` (full name).

Playing back a bag file

Now that we have a `bag` file recorded, we can use it to play back all the messages for the topics contained in it; note that we need `roscore` running and nothing else. We will move to the folder in which the `bag` file is located (there are two examples in the `bag` folder of this chapter's tutorials) and run this command:

```
$ rosbag play 2014-07-01-22-54-34.bag
```

Hopefully, `rosbag` will produce the following output:

```
[ INFO] [1404248314.594700096]: Opening 2014-07-01-22-54-34.bag


Waiting 0.2 seconds after advertising topics... done.


Hit space to toggle paused, or 's' to step.
 [RUNNING]  Bag Time: 1404248078.757944   Duration: 2.801764 / 39.999515
```

In the terminal in which the `bag` file is being played, we can pause (hit spacebar) or move step by step (hit *S*). As usual, press *Ctrl* + *C* to finish the execution. Once we have reached the end of the file, it will close; however, there is an option to loop (`-l`), which may sometimes be useful.

We will see the topics with `rostopic list` automatically, as follows:

```
/accel
/clock
/rosout
/rosout_agg
/temp
```

The /clock topic appears because we can simulate the system clock to produce a faster playback. This can be configured using the -r option. The /clock topic publishes the time for the simulation at a configurable frequency with the --hz argument (it defaults to 100 Hz).

We can also specify a subset of the topics in the file to be published. This is done with the --topics option.

Inspecting all the topics and messages in a bag file

There are two main ways to inspect the contents of a bag file. The first one is very simple: we just type rosbag info <bag_file>, and the result is something similar to the one shown in the following screenshot:

```
~$ rosbag info 2014-07-01-22-54-34.bag
path:         2014-07-01-22-54-34.bag
version:      2.0
duration:     40.0s
start:        Jul 01 2014 22:54:35.96 (1404248075.96)
end:          Jul 01 2014 22:55:15.96 (1404248115.96)
size:         10.9 KB
messages:     82
compression:  none [1/1 chunks]
types:        geometry_msgs/Vector3 [4a842b65f413084dc2b10fb484ea7f17]
              std_msgs/Int32        [da5909fbe378aeaf85e547e830cc1bb7]
topics:       /accel    41 msgs    : geometry_msgs/Vector3
              /temp     41 msgs    : std_msgs/Int32
```

We have information about the bag file itself, such as the creation date, duration, size, the number of messages, and the compression (if any). Then, we have the list of data types inside the file, and finally the list of topics with their corresponding name, number of messages, and type.

The second way to inspect a `bag` file is extremely powerful. It is a GUI called `rqt_bag` which also allows you to play back the files, view the images (if any), plot scalar data, and also view the **Raw** structure of the messages; it is `rxbag` behavior's replacement. We only have to pass the name of the `bag` file to see something similar to the following screenshot (for the previous `bag` file):

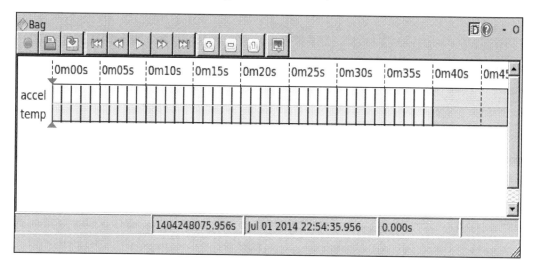

We have a timeline for all the topics where each message appears with a mark. If the bag file we're inspecting contains images, we can enable thumbnails to see them in the timeline.

In the following screenshot, we can see how to access the **Raw**, **Plot**, and **Image** (if the topic is of the **Image** type) views for the topics in the file. This pop-up menu appears with a right-click over the timeline:

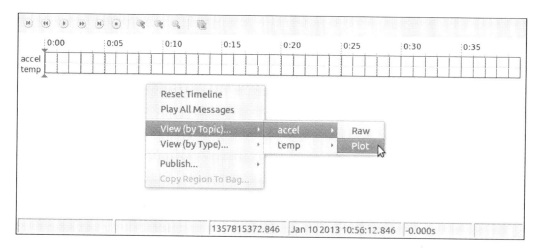

As an alternative, we can use `rqt_gui` and put the `rqt_bag` and `rqt_plot` plugins in the same window; the layout of the following screenshot can be imported from the perspective given in the `config/bag_plot.perspective` folder. However, we have to use **Publish All** and play to actually see the plot, which differs from the `rxbag` behavior. For `/accel`, we can plot all the fields in a single axis. To do so, once we have the plot view, we add each field by pressing the + button/icon. Note that we can remove them later or create different axes. As mentioned previously, the plot is not generated for all the values in the file, rather it simply shows the data that is played back and published:

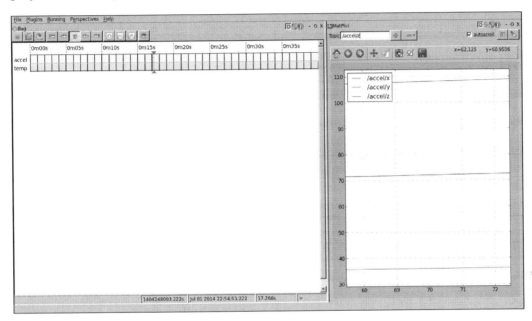

Remember that with the `rxbag` behavior, we must press the play button at least once to be able to plot the data. Then we can play, pause, stop, and move to the beginning or the end of the file. The images are straightforward, and a simple window appears with the current frame with options to save them as image files.

Using the rqt_gui and rqt plugins

Since **ROS Fuerte**, the `rx` applications or tools have been deprecated, so we should use the `rqt` nodes instead. They are basically the same, and only a few of them incorporate small updates, bug fixes, and new features. The following table shows the equivalences for the tools shown in this chapter (the ROS Kinetic `rqt` tool and the one it replaces from previous ROS distributions):

ROS Kinetic rqt tool	Replaces (ROS Fuerte or before)
`rqt_console` and `rqt_logger_level`	`rxconsole`
`rqt_graph`	`rxgraph`
`rqt_reconfigurerqt_reconfigure`	`dynamic_reconfigurereconfigure_gui`
`rqt_plot`	`rxplot`
`rqt_image_view`	`image_view`
`rqt_bag`	`rxbag`

In ROS Kinetic, there are even more standalone plugins, such as a shell (`rqt_shell`), a topic publisher (`rqt_publisher`), a message type viewer (`rqt_msg`), and many more (the most important ones have been covered in this chapter). Even `rqt_viz` is a plugin, which replaces `rviz`, which can also be integrated into the new `rqt_gui` interface. We can run this GUI and add and arrange several plugins manually on the window, as it has been seen in several examples in this chapter:

```
$ rosrun rqt_gui rqt_gui
```

Summary

After reading and running the code of this chapter, you will have learned how to use many tools that will help you to develop robotic systems faster, debug errors, and visualize your results, so as to evaluate their quality or validate them. Some of the specific concepts and tools you will require in your life as a robotics developer have been summarized here.

Now you know how to include logging messages in your code with different levels of verbosity, which will help you to debug errors in your nodes. For this purpose, you can also use the powerful tools included in ROS, such as the `rqt_console` interface. Additionally, you can inspect or list the nodes running, topics published, and services provided in the whole system. This includes the inspection of the node graph using `rqt_graph`.

Regarding the visualization tools, you should now be able to plot scalar data using `rqt_plot` for a more intuitive analysis of certain variables published by your nodes. Similarly, you can view more complex types (non-scalar ones). This includes images and 3D data using `rqt_image_view` and `rqt_rviz`, respectively. Similarly, you can use tools to calibrate and rectify camera images.

Finally, you are now able to record and play back messages in a session thanks to `rosbag`. You have also learned how to view the contents of a `bag` file with `rqt_bag`. This allows you to record the data from your experiments and process them later with your AI or robotics algorithms.

In the following chapter, you will use many of the tools covered here to visualize data of very different types. Several sensors are presented, along with instructions on to use them in ROS and visualize their output data.

3D Modeling and Simulation

Programming directly on a real robot gives us good feedback and is more impressive than simulations, but not everybody has access to real robots. For this reason, we have programs that simulate the physical world.

In this chapter, we are going to learn how to do the following:

- Create a 3D model of our robot
- Provide movements, physical limits, inertia, and other physical aspects to our robot model
- Add simulated sensors to our 3D model
- Use the model on the simulator

A 3D model of our robot in ROS

The way ROS uses the 3D model of a robot or its parts, whether to simulate them or to simply help the developers in their daily work, is by means of the URDF files.

Unified Robot Description Format (URDF) is an XML format that describes a robot, its parts, its joints, dimensions, and so on. Every time you see a 3D robot on ROS, for example, the **PR2 (Willow Garage)** or the **Robonaut (NASA)**, a URDF file is associated with it. In the next few sections, we will learn how to create this file, as well as the format for defining different values.

Creating our first URDF file

The robot that we are going to build in the following sections is a mobile robot with four wheels and an arm with a gripper.

To start with, we create the base of the robot with four wheels. Create a new file in the `chapter4_tutorials/robot1_description/urdf` folder with the name `robot1.urdf`, and enter the following code:

```
<?xml version="1.0"?>
<robot name="Robot1">
  <link name="base_link">
    <visual>
      <geometry>
        <box size="0.2 .3 .1" />
      </geometry>
      <origin rpy="0 0 0" xyz="0 0 0.05" />
      <material name="white">
        <color rgba="1 1 1 1" />
      </material>
    </visual>
  </link>
  <link name="wheel_1">
    <visual>
      <geometry>
        <cylinder length="0.05" radius="0.05" />
      </geometry>
      <origin rpy="0 1.5 0" xyz="0.1 0.1 0" />
      <material name="black">
        <color rgba="0 0 0 1" />
      </material>
    </visual>
  </link>
  <link name="wheel_2">
    <visual>
      <geometry>
        <cylinder length="0.05" radius="0.05" />
      </geometry>
      <origin rpy="0 1.5 0" xyz="-0.1 0.1 0" />
      <material name="black" />
    </visual>
  </link>
  <link name="wheel_3">
```

```
      <visual>
        <geometry>
          <cylinder length="0.05" radius="0.05" />
        </geometry>
        <origin rpy="0 1.5 0" xyz="0.1 -0.1 0" />
        <material name="black" />
      </visual>
  </link>
  <link name="wheel_4">
      <visual>
        <geometry>
          <cylinder length="0.05" radius="0.05" />
        </geometry>
        <origin rpy="0 1.5 0" xyz="-0.1 -0.1 0" />
        <material name="black" />
      </visual>
  </link>
  <joint name="base_to_wheel1" type="fixed">
      <parent link="base_link" />
      <child link="wheel_1" />
      <origin xyz="0 0 0" />
  </joint>
  <joint name="base_to_wheel2" type="fixed">
      <parent link="base_link" />
      <child link="wheel_2" />
      <origin xyz="0 0 0" />
  </joint>
  <joint name="base_to_wheel3" type="fixed">
      <parent link="base_link" />
      <child link="wheel_3" />
      <origin xyz="0 0 0" />
  </joint>
  <joint name="base_to_wheel4" type="fixed">
      <parent link="base_link" />
      <child link="wheel_4" />
      <origin xyz="0 0 0" />
  </joint>
</robot>
```

This URDF code is based on XML, and the indentation is not mandatory but advisable. Use an editor that supports it or an adequate plugin or configuration (for example, an appropriate `.vimrc` file in Vim).

Explaining the file format

As you can see in the code, there are two principal fields that describe the geometry of a robot: `links` and `joints`.

The first link has the name `base_link`; this name must be unique to the file:

```
<link name="base_link">
  <visual>
    <geometry>
      <box size="0.2 .3 .1" />
    </geometry>
    <origin rpy="0 0 0" xyz="0 0 0.05" />
    <material name="white">
      <color rgba="1 1 1 1" />
    </material>
  </visual>
</link>
```

In order to define what we will see on the simulator, we use the visual field in the preceding code. Inside the code, you can define the geometry (cylinder, box, sphere, or mesh), the material (color or texture), and the origin. We then have the code for the joint, shown as follows:

```
<joint name="base_to_wheel1" type="fixed">
  <parent link="base_link"/>
  <child link="wheel_1"/>
  <origin xyz="0 0 0"/>
</joint>
```

In the `joint` field, we define the name, which must be unique as well. Also, we define the type of joint (`fixed`, `revolute`, `continuous`, `floating`, or `planar`), the parent, and the child. In our case, `wheel_1` is a child of `base_link`. It is fixed, but, as it is a wheel, we can set it to `revolute`.

To check whether the syntax is fine or whether we have errors, we can use the `check_urdf` command tool:

```
$ check_urdf robot1.urdf
```

The output of the command will be as follows:

```
robot name is: Robot1
---------- Successfully Parsed XML ----------------

root Link: base_link has 4 child(ren)
child(1): wheel_1
child(2): wheel_2
child(3): wheel_3
child(4): wheel_4
```

If you want to see it graphically, you can use the `urdf_to_graphiz` command tool:

```
$ urdf_to_graphiz robot1.urdf
```

This command generates two files: `origins.pdf` and `origins.gv`. You can open the file using `evince`:

```
$ evince origins.pdf
```

The following image is what you will receive as an output:

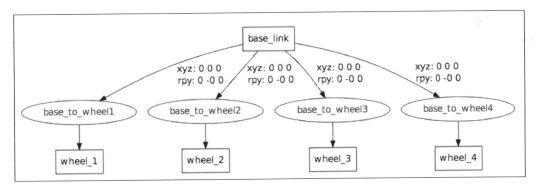

Watching the 3D model on rviz

Now that we have the model of our robot, we can use it on `rviz` to watch it in 3D and see the movements of the joints.

We will create the `display.launch` file in the `robot1_description/launch` folder and put the following code in it:

```xml
<?xml version="1.0"?>

<launch>
  <arg name="model" />
  <arg name="gui" default="False" />
  <param name="robot_description" textfile="$(arg model)" />
  <param name="use_gui" value="$(arggui)" />
  <node name="joint_state_publisher" pkg="joint_state_publisher"
    type="joint_state_publisher" />
  <node name="robot_state_publisher" pkg="robot_state_publisher"
    type="state_publisher" />
</launch>
```

We will then launch it with the following command:

```
$ roslaunch robot1_description display.launch model:="'rospack find
robot1_description'/urdf/robot1.urdf"
```

If everything is fine, you will see the following window with the 3D model on it:

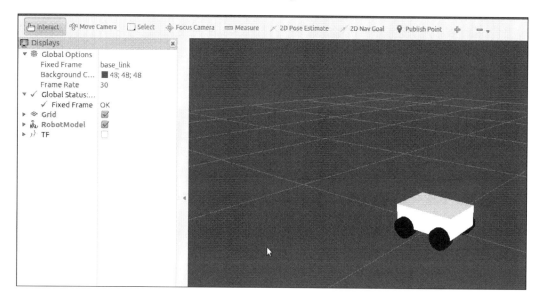

Let's finish the design by adding some parts: A base arm, an articulatered arm, and a gripper. Try to finish the design yourself. You can find the final model in the `chapter4_tutorials/robot1_description/urdf/robot1.urdf` file. You can see the final design in the following screenshot as well:

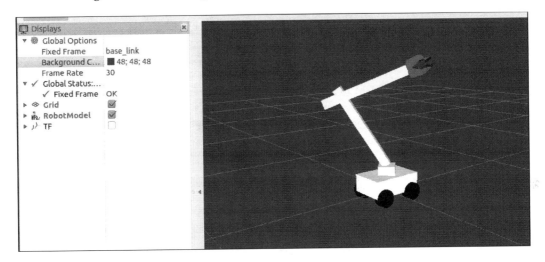

Loading meshes to our models

Sometimes, we want to give our model more realistic elements, or make a more elaborate design, rather than using basic geometric objects/blocks. It is possible to load meshes generated by us or to use meshes of other models. URDF models support `.stl` and `.dae` meshes. For our model, we used the PR2's gripper. In the following code, you can see an example of how to use it:

```
<link name="left_gripper">
  <visual>
    <origin rpy="0 0 0" xyz="0 0 0" />
    <geometry>
      <mesh filename="package://pr2_description/meshes/gripper_v0/
      l_finger.dae" />
    </geometry>
  </visual>
</link>
```

This looks like the sample link that we used before, but in the geometry section we added the mesh that we are going to use. You can see the result in the following screenshot:

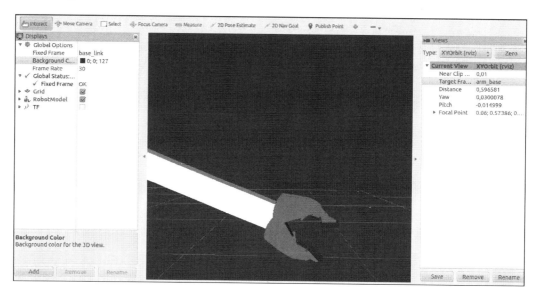

Making our robot model movable

To convert the model into a robot that can actually move, the only thing you have to do is pay attention to the type of joints it uses. If you check the URDF model file, you will see the different types of joints used in this model.

The most used type of joint is the revolute joint. You can see it being used on `arm_1_to_arm_base` in the following code:

```
<joint name="arm_1_to_arm_base" type="revolute">
  <parent link="arm_base" />
  <child link="arm_1" />
  <axis xyz="1 0 0" />
  <origin xyz="0 0 0.15" />
  <limit effort="1000.0" lower="-1.0" upper="1.0" velocity="0.5" />
</joint>
```

This means that they rotate in the same way that the continuous joints do, but they have strict limits. The limits are fixed using the `<limit effort ="1000.0" lower="-1.0" upper="1.0" velocity="0.5"/>` line, and you can select the axis to move with `axis xyz="1 0 0"`. The `<limit>` tag is used to set the following attributes: `effort` (maximum force supported by the joint), `lower` to assign the lower limit of a joint (radian per revolute joints, meters for prismatic joints), `upper` for the upper limit, and `velocity` for enforcing the maximum joint velocity.

A good way of testing whether or not the axis and limits of the joints are fine is by running `rviz` with the `Join_State_Publisher` GUI:

```
$ roslaunch robot1_description display.launch model:="'rospack find
robot1_description'/urdf/robot1.urdf" gui:=true
```

You will see the `rviz` interface in another window with some sliders, each one controlling a joint:

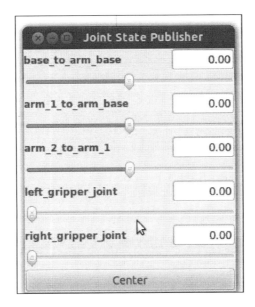

Physical and collision properties

If you want to simulate the robot on Gazebo or any other simulation software, you have to add physical and collision properties. This means that we need to set the dimensions of the geometry to calculate the possible collisions; for example, we need to define the weight of an object in order to figure out its inertia.

It is vital that all links on the model file have these parameters; if not, the robot will not be simulated.

For the mesh models, it is easier to calculate collisions by using simplified geometry rather than the actual mesh. Calculating the collision between two meshes is more computationally complex than it is to calculate a simple geometry.

In the following code, you will see the new parameters added to the link with the name `wheel_1`:

```
<link name="wheel_1">
  ...
  <collision>
    <geometry>
      <cylinder length="0.05" radius="0.05" />
    </geometry>
  </collision>
  <inertial>
    <mass value="10" />
    <inertia ixx="1.0" ixy="0.0" ixz="0.0" iyy="1.0" iyz="0.0"
      izz="1.0" />
  </inertial>
</link>
```

It is the same for the other links. Remember to put `collision` and `inertial` elements in all the links, because if you do not, Gazebo will not take the model.

You can find a complete file with all the parameters at `robot1_description/urdf/robot1_physics.urdf`.

Xacro – a better way to write our robot models

Notice the size of the `robot1_physics.urdf` file. It has 314 lines of code to define our robot. Imagine adding cameras, legs, and other geometries—the file will start increasing, and the maintenance of the code will become more complicated.

Xacro (short for **XML Macros**) helps in reducing the overall size of the URDF file and makes it easier to read and maintain. It also allows us to create modules and reutilize them to create repeated structures, such as several arms or legs.

To start using xacro, we need to specify a namespace so that the file is parsed properly. For example, these are the first two lines of a valid .xacro file:

```
<?xml version="1.0"?>
<robot xmlns:xacro="http://www.ros.org/wiki/xacro"
name="robot1_xacro">
```

In the preceding lines, we define the name of the model, which in this case is robot1_xacro. Remember that the file extension will be .xacro instead of .urdf.

Using constants

We can use xacro to declare constant values. As a result, we can avoid putting the same value in a lot of lines. Without the use of xacro, it would be almost impossible to maintain the changes if we had to change some values.

For example, the four wheels have the same values for length and radius. If we want to change the value, we will need to change it in each line, but if we use the next lines, we can change all the values easily:

```
<xacro:property name="length_wheel" value="0.05" />
<xacro:property name="radius_wheel" value="0.05" />
```

To use these variables, you only have to replace the old value with the following new value:

```
${name_of_variable}:
<cylinder length="${length_wheel}" radius="${radius_wheel}"/>
```

Using math

You can build up arbitrarily complex expressions in the ${} construct using the four basic operations (+, -, *, /), the unary minus, and the parenthesis. Exponentiation and modulus are, however, not supported:

```
<cylinder radius="${wheeldiam/2}" length=".1"/>
<origin xyz="${reflect*(width+.02)} 0 .25" />
```

By using mathematics, we can resize the model by only changing a value. To do this, we need a parameterized design.

Using macros

Macros are the most useful component of the xacro package. To reduce the file size even more, we are going to use the following macro for inertial:

```
<xacro:macro name="default_inertial" params="mass">
  <inertial>
    <mass value="${mass}" />
  <inertia ixx="1.0" ixy="0.0" ixz="0.0"
    iyy="1.0" iyz="0.0"
    izz="1.0" />
  </inertial>
</xacro:macro>
<xacro:default_inertial mass="100"/>
```

If we compare the robot1.urdf file with robot1.xacro, we will have eliminated 30 duplicate lines without effort. It is possible to reduce it further using more macros and variables.

To use the .xacro file with rviz and Gazebo, you need to convert it to .urdf. To do this, we execute the following command inside the robot1_description/urdf folder:

```
$ rosrun xacro xacro.pyrobot1.xacro > robot1_processed.urdf
```

You can also execute the following command everywhere and it should give the same result as the other command:

```
$ rosrun xacro xacro.py "'rospack find robot1_description'/urdf/robot1.
xacro" > "'rospack find robot1_description'/urdf/robot1_processed.urdf"
```

So, in order to make the commands easier to write, we recommend that you continue working in the same folder.

Moving the robot with code

Okay, we have the 3D model of our robot and we can see it on rviz, but how do we move the robot using a node?

We are going to create a simple node to move the robot. If you want to learn more, ROS offers great tools to control robots, such as the ros_control package. Create a new file in the robot1_description/src folder with the name state_publisher. cpp and copy the following code:

```
#include <string>
#include <ros/ros.h>
#include <sensor_msgs/JointState.h>
```

```
#include <tf/transform_broadcaster.h>

int main(int argc, char** argv) {
  ros::init(argc, argv, "state_publisher");
  ros::NodeHandle n;
  ros::Publisher joint_pub =
  n.advertise<sensor_msgs::JointState>("joint_states", 1);
  tf::TransformBroadcaster broadcaster;
  ros::Rate loop_rate(30);

  const double degree = M_PI/180;

  // robot state
  doubleinc= 0.005, base_arm_inc= 0.005, arm1_armbase_inc= 0.005,
  arm2_arm1_inc= 0.005, gripper_inc= 0.005, tip_inc= 0.005;
  double angle= 0 ,base_arm = 0, arm1_armbase = 0, arm2_arm1 = 0,
  gripper = 0, tip = 0;
  // message declarations
  geometry_msgs::TransformStampedodom_trans;
  sensor_msgs::JointStatejoint_state;
  odom_trans.header.frame_id = "odom";
  odom_trans.child_frame_id = "base_link";

  while (ros::ok()) {
    //update joint_state
    joint_state.header.stamp = ros::Time::now();
    joint_state.name.resize(7);
    joint_state.position.resize(7);
    joint_state.name[0] ="base_to_arm_base";
    joint_state.position[0] = base_arm;
    joint_state.name[1] ="arm_1_to_arm_base";
    joint_state.position[1] = arm1_armbase;
    joint_state.name[2] ="arm_2_to_arm_1";
    joint_state.position[2] = arm2_arm1;
    joint_state.name[3] ="left_gripper_joint";
    joint_state.position[3] = gripper;
    joint_state.name[4] ="left_tip_joint";
    joint_state.position[4] = tip;
    joint_state.name[5] ="right_gripper_joint";
    joint_state.position[5] = gripper;
    joint_state.name[6] ="right_tip_joint";
    joint_state.position[6] = tip;

    // update transform
```

```
// (moving in a circle with radius 1)
// (moving in a circle with radius 1)
odom_trans.header.stamp = ros::Time::now();
odom_trans.transform.translation.x = cos(angle);
odom_trans.transform.translation.y = sin(angle);
odom_trans.transform.translation.z = 0.0;
odom_trans.transform.rotation =
tf::createQuaternionMsgFromYaw(angle);

//send the joint state and transform
joint_pub.publish(joint_state);
broadcaster.sendTransform(odom_trans);

// Create new robot state
arm2_arm1 += arm2_arm1_inc;
if (arm2_arm1<-1.5 || arm2_arm1>1.5) arm2_arm1_inc *= -1;
arm1_armbase += arm1_armbase_inc;
if (arm1_armbase>1.2 || arm1_armbase<-1.0) arm1_armbase_inc *= -1;
base_arm += base_arm_inc;
if (base_arm>1. || base_arm<-1.0) base_arm_inc *= -1;
gripper += gripper_inc;
if (gripper<0 || gripper>1) gripper_inc *= -1;
angle += degree/4;

// This will adjust as needed per iteration
loop_rate.sleep();
  }
  return 0;
}
```

Let's see what we can do to the code to get these movements.

For moving the model, first we have to know some `tf` frames that are generally used in ROS, such as `map`, `odom`, and `base_link`. The `tf` frame map is a world-fixed frame that is useful as a long-term global reference. The `odom` frame is useful as an accurate, short-term local reference. The coordinate frame called `base_link` is rigidly attached to the mobile robot base. Normally, these frames are attached and their relationship can be illustrated as `map | odom | base_link`.

First, we create a new frame called `odom`, and all the transformations will be referred to this new frame. As you might remember, all the links are children of `base_link` and all the frames will be linked to the `odom` frame:

```
...
geometry_msgs::TransformStampedodom_trans;
odom_trans.header.frame_id = "odom";
odom_trans.child_frame_id = "base_link";
...
```

Now, we are going to create a new topic to control all the joints of the model. `Joint_state` is a message that holds data to describe the state of a set of torque-controlled joints. As our model has seven joints, we'll create a message with seven elements:

```
sensor_msgs::JointStatejoint_state;

joint_state.header.stamp = ros::Time::now();
joint_state.name.resize(7);
joint_state.position.resize(7);
joint_state.name[0] ="base_to_arm_base";
joint_state.position[0] = base_arm;
...
```

In our example, the robot will move in circles. We calculate the coordinates and the movement in the next portion of our code:

```
odom_trans.header.stamp = ros::Time::now();
odom_trans.transform.translation.x = cos(angle)*1;
odom_trans.transform.translation.y = sin(angle)*1;
odom_trans.transform.translation.z = 0.0;
odom_trans.transform.rotation =
tf::createQuaternionMsgFromYaw(angle);
```

Finally, we publish the new state of our robot:

```
joint_pub.publish(joint_state);
broadcaster.sendTransform(odom_trans);
```

We are also going to create a launch file to launch the node, the model, and all the necessary elements. Create a new file with the name `display_xacro.launch` (content given as follows), and put it in the `robot1_description/launch` folder:

```xml
<?xml version="1.0"?>

<launch>
  <arg name="model" />
  <arg name="gui" default="False" />
  <param name="robot_description" command="$(find xacro)/xacro.py
  $(arg model)" />
  <param name="use_gui" value="$(arggui)"/>
  <node name="state_publisher_tutorials" pkg="robot1_description"
  type="state_publisher_tutorials" />
  <node name="robot_state_publisher" pkg="robot_state_publisher"
  type="state_publisher" />
  <node name="rviz" pkg="rviz" type="rviz" args="-d $(find
  robot1_description)/urdf.rviz" />
</launch>
```

Before starting our node, we have to install the following packages:

```
$ sudo apt-get install ros-kinetic-map-server
$ sudo apt-get install ros-kinetic-fake-localization
$ cd ~/catkin_ws && catkin_make
```

Using the following command, we will start our new node with the complete model. We will see the 3D model on `rviz`, moving all the articulations:

```
$ roslaunch robot1_description state_xacro.launch model:="'rospack find robot1_description'/urdf/robot1.xacro"
```

In the following screenshot, you can see a mix of four screens captured to show you the movements that we obtained with the node. If you see it clearly, you will see the the arms moving through their trajectory in a circle:

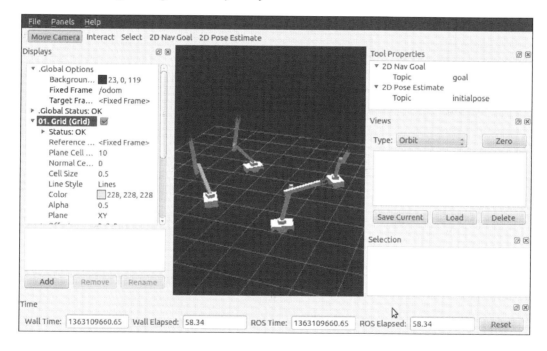

3D modeling with SketchUp

It is possible to generate the model using 3D programs such as **SketchUp**. In this section, we will show you how to make a simple model, export it, generate `urdf`, and watch the model on `rviz`. Notice that SketchUp works on Windows and Mac, and that this model was developed using Mac and not Linux.

First, you need to have SketchUp installed on your computer. When you have it, make a model similar to the following:

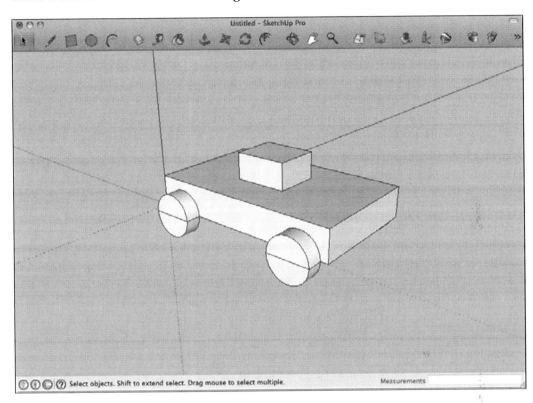

The model was exported only to one file, so the wheels and chassis are the same object. If you want to make a robot model with mobile parts, you must export each part in a separate file.

To export the model, navigate to **Export | 3D Model | Save As COLLADA File** (*.dae).

We named the file bot.dae and saved it in the robot1_description/meshes folder.

Now, to use the 3D model, we are going to create a new file in the robot1_ description/urdf folder with the name dae.urdf and type in the following code:

```
<?xml version="1.0"?>
<robot name="robot1">
  <link name="base_link">
    <visual>
      <geometry>
```

```
        <mesh scale="0.025 0.025 0.025" filename="package://robot1_
        description/meshes/bot.dae" />
      </geometry>
      <origin xyz="0 0 0.226" />
    </visual>
  </link>
</robot>
```

As you can see, when we load the mesh, we can choose the scale of the model with the command line `<mesh scale="0.025 0.025 0.025" filename="package:// robot1_description/meshes/bot.dae"/>`. Test the model with the following command:

```
$ roslaunch robot1_description display.launch model:="'rospack find
robot1_description'/urdf/dae.urdf"
```

You will see the following output:

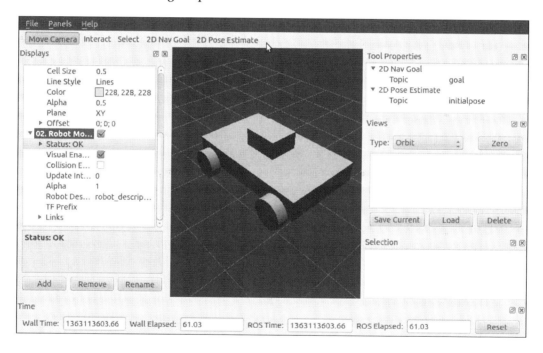

Simulation in ROS

In order to make simulations with our robots in ROS, we are going to use Gazebo.

Gazebo (`http://Gazebosim.org/`) is a multi-robot simulator for complex indoor and outdoor environments. It is capable of simulating a population of robots, sensors, and objects in a three-dimensional world. It generates both realistic sensor feedback and physically plausible interactions between objects.

Gazebo is now independent from ROS and is installed as a standalone package in Ubuntu. In this section, we will learn how to interface Gazebo and ROS. You will learn how to use the model created before, how to include a laser sensor and a camera, and how to move it as a real robot.

Using our URDF 3D model in Gazebo

We are going to use the model that we designed in the last section, but to make it simple, we won't include the arm.

Make sure that you have Gazebo installed by typing the following command in a terminal:

```
$ gazebo
```

Before starting to work with Gazebo, we will install ROS packages to interface Gazebo:

```
$ sudo apt-get install ros-kinetic-gazebo-ros-pkgsros-kinetic-Gazebo-ros-control
```

The Gazebo GUI will open after this command. Assuming that all is working well, we will now prepare our robot model to be used on Gazebo. You can test the integration of Gazebo with ROS using the following commands and checking that the GUI is open:

```
$ roscore & rosrun gazebo_ros Gazebo
```

To introduce the robot model in Gazebo, we must complete the URDF model. In order to use it in Gazebo, we need to declare more elements. We will also use the `.xacro` file; although this may be more complex, it is more powerful for the development of the code. You will find a file with all the modifications at `chapter4_tutorials/robot1_description/urdf/robot1_base_01.xacro`.

```
<link name="base_link">
  <visual>
  <geometry>
    <box size="0.2 .3 .1"/>
  </geometry>
```

```
        <origin rpy="0 0 1.54" xyz="0 0 0.05"/>
        <material name="white">
        <color rgba="1 1 1 1"/>
      </material>
      </visual>
      <collision>
      <geometry>
        <box size="0.2 .3 0.1"/>
        </geometry>
      </collision>
      <xacro:default_inertial mass="10"/>
    </link>
```

This is the new code for the chassis of the robot base_link. Notice that the collision and inertial sections are necessary to run the model on Gazebo in order to calculate the physics of the robot.

To launch everything, we are going to create a new .launch file. Create a new file with the name gazebo.launch in the chapter4_tutorials/robot1_gazebo/ gazebo.launch folder and put in the following code:

```
<?xml version="1.0"?>

<launch>
  <!-- these are the arguments you can pass this launch file, for
  example paused:=true -->
  <arg name="paused" default="true" />
  <arg name="use_sim_time" default="false" />
  <arg name="gui" default="true" />
  <arg name="headless" default="false" />
  <arg name="debug" default="true" />
  <!-- We resume the logic in empty_world.launch, changing only the
  name of the world to be launched -->
  <include file="$(find gazebo_ros)/launch/empty_world.launch">
    <arg name="world_name" value="$(find
    robot1_gazebo)/worlds/robot.world" />
    <arg name="debug" value="$(arg debug)" />
    <arg name="gui" value="$(arggui)" />
    <arg name="paused" value="$(arg paused)" />
    <arg name="use_sim_time" value="$(arg use_sim_time)" />
    <arg name="headless" value="$(arg headless)" />
  </include>
  <!-- Load the URDF into the ROS Parameter Server -->
  <arg name="model" />
```

```
<param name="robot_description" command="$(find xacro)/xacro.py
$(arg model)" />
<!-- Run a python script to the send a service call to gazebo_ros
to spawn a URDF robot -->
<node name="urdf_spawner" pkg="gazebo_ros" type="spawn_model"
respawn="false" output="screen" args="-urdf -model robot1 -
paramrobot_description -z 0.05" />
</launch>
```

To launch the file, use the following command:

```
$ roslaunch robot1_gazebo gazebo.launch model:="'rospack find robot1_
description'/urdf/robot1_base_01.xacro"
```

You will now see the robot in Gazebo. The simulation is initially paused; you can click on play to start it. Congratulations! This is your first step in the virtual world:

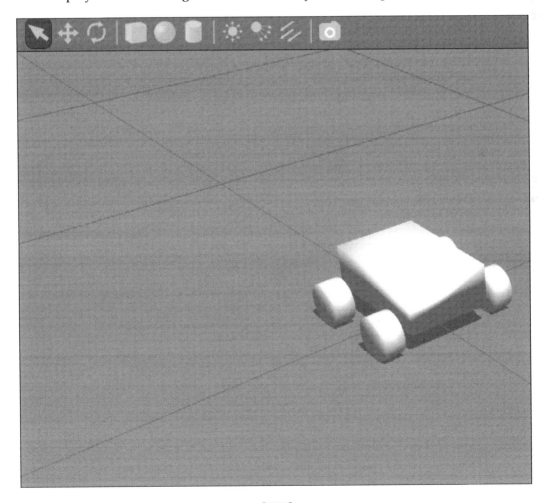

As you can see, the model has no texture. In `rviz`, you saw the textures that were declared in the URDF file, but in Gazebo you cannot see them.

To add visible textures in Gazebo, use the following code on your model `.gazebo` file. In `robot1_description/urdf`, create a file `robot.gazebo`:

```
<gazebo reference="base_link">
<material>gazebo/Orange</material>
</gazebo>

<gazebo reference="wheel_1">
<material>gazebo/Black</material>
</gazebo>

<gazebo reference="wheel_2">
<material>gazebo/Black</material>
</gazebo>

<gazebo reference="wheel_3">
<material>gazebo/Black</material>
</gazebo>

<gazebo reference="wheel_4">
<material>gazebo/Black</material>
</gazebo>
```

Copy the `robot1_description/urdf/robot1_base_01.xacro` file, save it with the name `robot1_base_02.xacro`, and add the following code inside:

```
<xacro:include filename="$(find
robot1_description)/urdf/robot.gazebo" />
```

Launch the new file and you will see the same robot, but with the added textures:

```
$ roslaunch robot1_gazebo gazebo.launch model:="'rospack find robot1_
description'/urdf/robot1_base_02.xacro"
```

You will see the following output:

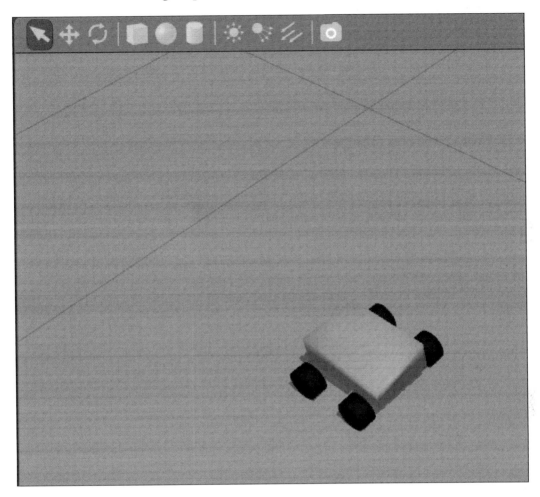

Adding sensors to Gazebo

In Gazebo, you can simulate the physics of the robot and its movement, and you can also simulate sensors.

Normally, when you want to add a new sensor, you need to implement the behavior. Fortunately, some sensors are already developed for Gazebo and ROS.

In this section, we are going to add a camera and a laser sensor to our model. These sensors will be a new part on the robot. Therefore, you need to select where to put them. In Gazebo, you will see a new 3D object that looks like a Hokuyo laser and a red cube that will be the camera. We talked about these sensors in the previous chapters.

We are going to take the laser from the `gazebo_ros_demos` package. This is the magic of ROS — you can use code from other packages for your development.

We must add the following lines to our `.xacro` file to add the 3D model of a Hokuyo laser to our robot:

```
<?xml version="1.0" encoding="UTF-8"?>
  <link name="hokuyo_link">
  <collision>
    <origin xyz="0 0 0" rpy="0 0 0" />
    <geometry>
      <box size="0.1 0.1 0.1" />
    </geometry>
  </collision>
  <visual>
    <origin xyz="0 0 0" rpy="0 0 0" />
    <geometry>
      <mesh filename="package://robot1_description/meshes/hokuyo.dae"
      />
    </geometry>
  </visual>
  <inertial>
    <massvalue="1e-5" />
    <originxyz="0 0 0" rpy="0 0 0" />
    <inertiaixx="1e-6" ixy="0" ixz="0" iyy="1e-6" iyz="0" izz="1e-6"
  />
  </inertial>
</link>
```

In our `.gazebo` file, we are going to add the plugin `libgazebo_ros_laser.so` that will simulate the behavior of a Hokuyo range laser:

```
<gazebo reference="hokuyo_link">
  <sensor type="ray" name="head_hokuyo_sensor">
    <pose>0 0 0 0 0 0</pose>
    <visualize>false</visualize>
    <update_rate>40</update_rate>
    <ray>
      <scan>
        <horizontal>
```

```
            <samples>720</samples>
            <resolution>1</resolution>
            <min_angle>-1.570796</min_angle>
            <max_angle>1.570796</max_angle>
          </horizontal>
        </scan>
        <range>
          <min>0.10</min>
          <max>30.0</max>
          <resolution>0.01</resolution>
        </range>
        <noise>
          <type>gaussian</type>
          <!-- Noise parameters based on published spec for Hokuyo
          laser achieving "+-30mm" accuracy at range <10m. A mean of
          0.0m and stddev of 0.01m will put 99.7% of samples within
          0.03m of the true reading. -->
          <mean>0.0</mean>
          <stddev>0.01</stddev>
        </noise>
      </ray>
      <plugin name="gazebo_ros_head_hokuyo_controller"
        filename="libgazebo_ros_laser.so">
        <topicName>/robot/laser/scan</topicName>
        <frameName>hokuyo_link</frameName>
      </plugin>
    </sensor>
  </gazebo>
```

Launch the new model with the following command:

```
$ roslaunch robot1_gazebo gazebo.launch model:="'rospack find robot1_
description'/urdf/robot1_base_03.xacro"
```

You will see the robot with the laser module attached to it.

In a similar way, we have added lines to `robot.gazebo` and `robot1_base_03.xacro` to add another sensor: a camera. Check these files!

In the following screenshot, you can see the robot model with the Hokuyo laser and a red cube that simulates the camera model:

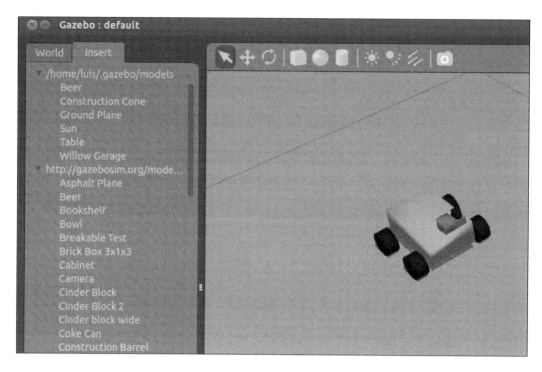

Notice that this laser is generating real data as a real laser. You can see the data generated using the `rostopic echo` command:

```
$ rostopic echo /robot/laser/scan
```

We can say the same about the camera. If you want to see the Gazebo simulation of the images taken, you can write the following command in a terminal:

```
$ rosrun image_view image_view image:=/robot/camera1/image_raw
```

Gazebo allows us to add objects to the world using the right menu. We have added some elements like a traffic cone, a table, and a can to check how the sensors react to them. You can see three screenshots showing this. The first image is that of Gazebo and our simulated world, then we have a top-down view of rviz with the laser data, and finally, an image visualization of the camera.

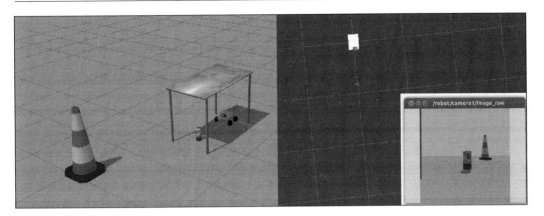

Loading and using a map in Gazebo

In Gazebo, you can use virtual worlds such as offices, mountains, and so on.

In this section, we are going to use a map of the office of Willow Garage that is installed by default with ROS.

This 3D model is in the `gazebo_worlds` package. If you do not have the package, install it before you continue.

To check the model, all you have to do is start the `.launch` file using the following command:

```
$ roslaunch gazebo_ros willowgarage_world.launch
```

You will see the 3D office in Gazebo. The office only has walls. You can add tables, chairs, and much more, if you want. By inserting and placing objects, you can create your own worlds in Gazebo to simulate your robots. You have the option of saving your world by selecting **Menu | Save As**.

Please note that Gazebo requires a good machine, with a relatively recent GPU. You can check whether your graphics are supported at the Gazebo home page. Also, note that sometimes this software crashes, but great effort is being taken by the community to make it more stable. Usually, it is enough to run it again (probably several times) if it crashes. If the problem persists, our advice is to try it with a newer version, which will be installed by default with more recent distributions of ROS.

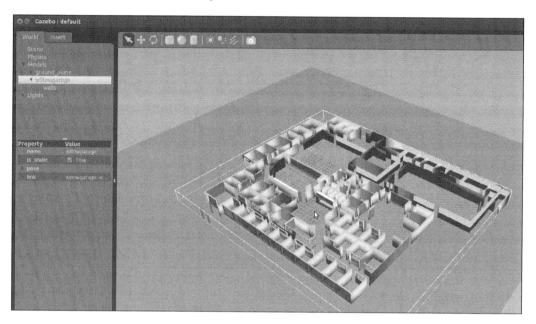

What we are going to do now is create a new `.launch` file to load the map and the robot together. To do that, create a new file in the `robot1_gazebo/launch` folder with the name `gazebo_wg.launch` and add the following code:

```xml
<?xml version="1.0"?>
<launch>
  <include file="$(find
    gazebo_ros)/launch/willowgarage_world.launch" />
  </include>
  <!-- Load the URDF into the ROS Parameter Server -->
  <param name="robot_description"
  command="$(find xacro)/xacro.py '$(find
  robot1_description)/urdf/robot1_base_03.xacro'" />
  <!-- Run a python script to the send a service call to Gazebo_ros
  to spawn a URDF robot -->
```

```
<node name="urdf_spawner" pkg="gazebo_ros" type="spawn_model"
respawn="false" output="screen"
args="-urdf -model robot1 -paramrobot_description -z 0.05"/>

</launch>
```

Now, launch the file of the model with the laser:

```
$ roslaunch robot1_gazebo gazebo_wg.launch
```

You will see the robot and the map on the Gazebo GUI. The next step is to command the robot to move and receive the simulated readings of its sensors as it moves around the virtual world loaded in the simulator.

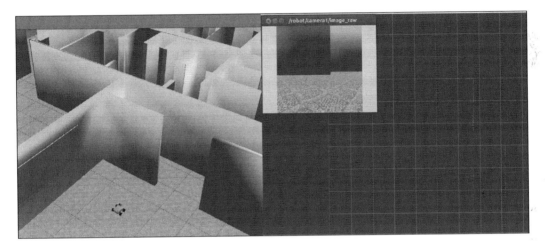

Moving the robot in Gazebo

A skid-steer robot is a mobile robot whose movement is based on separately driven wheels placed on either side of the robot body. It can thus change its direction by varying the relative rate of rotation of its wheels, and it does not require an additional steering motion.

As we said before, in Gazebo you need to program the behaviors of the robot, joints, sensors, and so on. As for the laser, Gazebo already has a skid drive implemented, and we can use it to move our robot.

To use this controller, you only have to add the following code to the model file:

```
<gazebo>
  <plugin name="skid_steer_drive_controller"
    filename="libgazebo_ros_skid_steer_drive.so">
    <updateRate>100.0</updateRate>
    <robotNamespace>/</robotNamespace>
    <leftFrontJoint>base_to_wheel1</leftFrontJoint>
    <rightFrontJoint>base_to_wheel3</rightFrontJoint>
    <leftRearJoint>base_to_wheel2</leftRearJoint>
    <rightRearJoint>base_to_wheel4</rightRearJoint>
    <wheelSeparation>4</wheelSeparation>
    <wheelDiameter>0.1</wheelDiameter>
    <robotBaseFrame>base_link</robotBaseFrame>
    <torque>1</torque>
    <topicName>cmd_vel</topicName>
    <broadcastTF>0</broadcastTF>
  </plugin>
</gazebo>
```

The parameters that you can see in the code are simply the configuration set up to make the controller work with our four-wheeled robot. For example, we selected the `base_to_wheel1`, `base_to_wheel2`, `base_to_wheel3`, and `base_to_wheel4` joints as wheels to move the robot.

Another interesting parameter is `topicName`. We need to publish commands with this name in order to control the robot. In this case, when you publish a `sensor_msgs/Twist` topic call `/cmd_vel`, the robot will move. It is important to have a well-configured orientation of the wheel joints. With the current orientation on the `.xacro` file, the robot will move upside-down, so we need to change the origin `rpy` for the four wheels, as shown in the following lines for the joint of the base link and the `wheel1` joint:

```
<joint name="base_to_wheel1" type="continuous">
  <parent link="base_link"/>
  <child link="wheel_1"/>
  <origin rpy="-1.5707 0 0" xyz="0.1 0.15 0"/>
  <axis xyz="0 0 1" />
</joint>
```

All these changes are in the `chapter4_tutorials/robot1_description/urfd/robot1_base_04.xacro` file. In `gazebo_wg.launch`, we have to update the robot model in order to use the new file `robot1_base_04.xacro`.

Now, to launch the model with the controller and the map, we use the following command:

```
$ roslaunch robot1_gazebo gazebo_wg.launch
```

You will see the map with the robot on the Gazebo screen. We are going to move the robot using the keyboard. This node is in the teleop_twist_keyboard package that publishes the /cmd_vel topic.

Run the following commands in a terminal to install the package:

```
$ sudo apt-get install ros-kinetic-teleop-twist-keyboard
$ rosstack profile
$ rospack profile
```

Then, you can run the node as follows:

```
$ rosrun teleop_twist_keyboard teleop_twist_keyboard.py
```

You will see a new shell with some instructions and the keys to move the robot (u, i, o, j, k, l, m, ",", ".") and adjust maximum speeds.

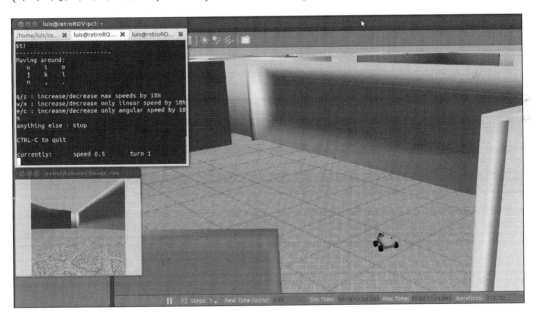

If everything has gone well, you can drive the robot across the Willow Garage office. You can see the laser data or visualized images from the camera.

Summary

For people learning robotics, the ability to have access to real robots is fun and useful, but not everyone has access to a real robot. Simulators are a great tool when we have limited access to a real robot. They were created for testing the behavior of algorithms before trying them on a real robot. This is why simulators exist.

In this chapter, you learned how to create a 3D model of your own robot. This included a detailed explanation of how to add textures and creating joints, s as well as how to use a node to move the robot.

Then, we introduced Gazebo, a simulator where you can load the 3D model of your robot and simulate it moving and sensing a virtual world. This simulator is widely used by the ROS community, and it already supports many real robots in simulation.

We saw how we can reuse parts of other robots to design ours. In particular, we included a gripper and added sensors, such as a laser range finder and a camera.

As you can see, you don't have to create a robot from scratch to start using the simulator. The community has developed a lot of robots, and you can download the code, execute them in ROS and Gazebo, and modify them if it turns out to be necessary.

You can find a list of the robots supported on ROS at `http://www.ros.org/wiki/Robots`. Also, you can find tutorials about Gazebo at `http://gazebosim.org/tutorials`.

5
The Navigation Stack – Robot Setups

In the previous chapters, we have seen how to create our robot, mount some sensors and actuators, and move it through the virtual world using a joystick or the keyboard. In this chapter, you will learn what is probably one of the most powerful features in ROS, something that will let you move your robot autonomously.

Thanks to the community and the shared code, ROS has many algorithms that can be used for navigation.

First of all, in this chapter, you will learn all the necessary ways to configure the navigation stack with your robot. In the next chapter, you will learn how to configure and launch the navigation stack on the simulated robot, giving goals and configuring some parameters to get the best results. In particular, we will cover the following topics in this chapter:

- Introduction to the navigation stacks and their powerful capabilities—clearly one of the greatest pieces of software that comes with ROS.

- The `tf` library—showing the transformation of one physical element to the other from the frame; for example, the data received using a sensor or the command for the desired position of an actuator. `tf` is a library for keeping track of the coordinate frames.

- Creating a laser driver or simulating it.

- Computing and publishing the odometry and how this is provided by Gazebo.

- Base controllers and creating one for your robot.

- Executing **Simultaneous Localization and Mapping (SLAM)** with ROS—building a map from the environment with your robot as it moves through it. Localizing your robot in the map using the **Adaptive Monte Carlo Localization (AMCL)** algorithm of the navigation stack. AMCL is a probabilistic localization system for a robot moving in 2D. It implements the AMCL approach, which uses a particle filter to track the pose of a robot against a known map.

The navigation stack in ROS

In order to understand the navigation stack, you should think of it as a set of algorithms that use the sensors of the robot and the odometry so that you can control the robot using a standard message. It can move your robot without any problems, such as crashing, getting stuck in a location, or getting lost to another position.

You would assume that this stack can be easily used with any robot. This is almost true, but it is necessary to tune some configuration files and write some nodes to use the stack.

The robot must satisfy some requirements before it uses the navigation stack:

- The navigation stack can only handle a differential drive and holonomic-wheeled robots. The shape requisites of the robot must either be a square or a rectangle. However, it can also do certain things with biped robots, such as robot localization, as long as the robot does not move sideways.

- It requires that the robot publishes information about the relationships between the positions of all the joints and sensors.

- The robot must send messages with linear and angular velocities.

- A planar laser must be on the robot to create the map and localization. Alternatively, you can generate something equivalent to several lasers or a sonar, or you can project the values to the ground if they are mounted at another place on the robot.

The following diagram shows you how the navigation stacks are organized. You can see three groups of boxes with colors (gray and white) and dotted lines. The plain white boxes indicate the stacks that are provided by ROS, and they have all the nodes to make your robot really autonomous:

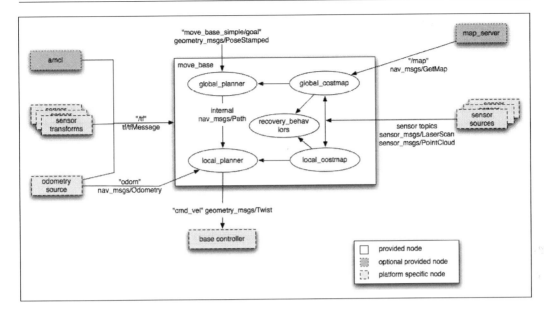

In the following sections, we will see how to create the parts marked in gray in the diagram. These parts depend on the platform used; this means that it is necessary to write code to adapt the platform to be used in ROS and to be used by the navigation stack.

Creating transforms

The navigation stack needs to know the position of the sensors, wheels, and joints.

To do that, we use the **Transform Frames (tf)** software library. It manages a transform tree. You could do this with mathematics, but if you have a lot of frames to calculate, it will be a bit complicated and messy.

Thanks to `tf`, we can add more sensors and parts to the robot, and `tf` will handle all the relations for us.

If we put the laser 10 cm backwards and 20 cm above with reference to the origin of the `base_link coordinates`, we would need to add a new frame to the transformation tree with these offsets.

Once inserted and created, we could easily know the position of the laser with reference to the `base_link` value or the wheels. The only thing we need to do is call the `tf` library and get the transformation.

Creating a broadcaster

Let's test this with a simple code. Create a new file in `chapter5_tutorials/src` with the name `tf_broadcaster.cpp`, and put the following code inside it:

```
#include <ros/ros.h>
#include <tf/transform_broadcaster.h>

int main(int argc, char** argv){
  ros::init(argc, argv, "robot_tf_publisher");
  ros::NodeHandle n;

  ros::Rate r(100);

  tf::TransformBroadcaster broadcaster;

  while(n.ok()){
    broadcaster.sendTransform(
      tf::StampedTransform(
        tf::Transform(tf::Quaternion(0, 0, 0, 1), tf::Vector3(0.1,
        0.0, 0.2)),
        ros::Time::now(),"base_link", "base_laser"));
    r.sleep();
  }
}
```

Remember to add the following line in your `CMakelist.txt` file to create the new executable:

```
add_executable(tf_broadcaster src/tf_broadcaster.cpp)
target_link_libraries(tf_broadcaster ${catkin_LIBRARIES})
```

We also create another node that will use the transform, and which will give us the position of a point on the sensor with reference to the center of `base_link` (our robot).

Creating a listener

Create a new file in `chapter5_tutorials/src` with the name `tf_listener.cpp` and input the following code:

```
#include <ros/ros.h>
#include <geometry_msgs/PointStamped.h>
#include <tf/transform_listener.h>
```

```cpp
void transformPoint(const tf::TransformListener& listener){
  //we'll create a point in the base_laser frame that we'd like to
  transform to the base_link frame
  geometry_msgs::PointStamped laser_point;
  laser_point.header.frame_id = "base_laser";

  //we'll just use the most recent transform available for our
  simple example
  laser_point.header.stamp = ros::Time();

  //just an arbitrary point in space
  laser_point.point.x = 1.0;
  laser_point.point.y = 2.0;
  laser_point.point.z = 0.0;

  geometry_msgs::PointStamped base_point;
  listener.transformPoint("base_link", laser_point, base_point);

  ROS_INFO("base_laser: (%.2f, %.2f. %.2f) -----> base_link: (%.2f,
  %.2f, %.2f) at time %.2f",
  laser_point.point.x, laser_point.point.y, laser_point.point.z,
  base_point.point.x, base_point.point.y, base_point.point.z,
  base_point.header.stamp.toSec());
  ROS_ERROR("Received an exception trying to transform a point from
  \"base_laser\" to \"base_link\": %s", ex.what());

}


int main(int argc, char** argv){
  ros::init(argc, argv, "robot_tf_listener");
  ros::NodeHandle n;

  tf::TransformListener listener(ros::Duration(10));

  //we'll transform a point once every second
  ros::Timer timer = n.createTimer(ros::Duration(1.0),
  boost::bind(&transformPoint, boost::ref(listener)));

  ros::spin();
}
```

Remember to add the line in the `CMakeList.txt` file to create the executable. Compile the package and run both the nodes using the following commands in each terminal:

```
$ catkin_make
$ rosrun chapter5_tutorials tf_broadcaster
$ rosrun chapter5_tutorials tf_listener
```

Remember, always run `roscore` before starting with the examples. You will see the following message:

```
[ INFO] [1368521854.336910465]: base_laser: (1.00, 2.00. 0.00) ----->
base_link: (1.10, 2.00, 0.20) at time 1368521854.33
[ INFO] [1368521855.336347545]: base_laser: (1.00, 2.00. 0.00) ----->
base_link: (1.10, 2.00, 0.20) at time 1368521855.33
```

This means that the point that you published on the node, with the position (`1.00, 2.00, 0.00`) relative to `base_laser`, has the position (`1.10, 2.00, 0.20`) relative to `base_link`.

As you can see, the `tf` library performs all the mathematics for you to get the coordinates of a point or the position of a joint relative to another point.

A transform tree defines offsets in terms of both translation and rotation between different coordinate frames. Let us see an example to help you understand this.

In our robot model used in *Chapter 4*, *3D Modeling and Simulation*, we are going to add another laser, say, on the back of the robot (`base_link`):

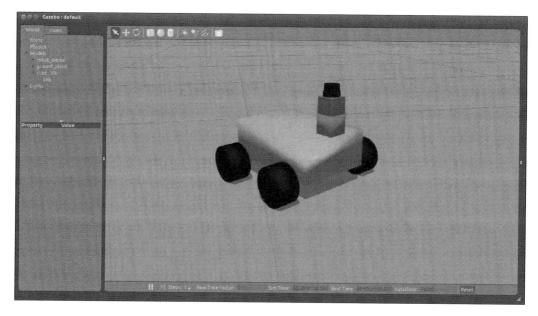

The system in our robot had to know the position of the new laser to detect collisions, such as the one between the wheels and walls. With the `tf` tree, this is very simple to do and maintain, apart from being scalable. Thanks to `tf`, we can add more sensors and parts, and the `tf` library will handle all the relations for us. All the sensors and joints must be correctly configured on `tf` to permit the navigation stack to move the robot without problems, and to know exactly where each one of their components is.

Before starting to write the code to configure each component, keep in mind that you have the geometry of the robot specified in the URDF file. So, for this reason, it is not necessary to configure the robot again. Perhaps you do not know it, but you have been using the `robot_state_publisher` package to publish the transform tree of your robot. In *Chapter 4, 3D Modeling and Simulation*, we used it for the first time; therefore, you do have the robot configured to be used with the navigation stack.

Watching the transformation tree

If you want to see the transformation tree of your robot, use the following command:

```
$ roslaunch chapter5_tutorials gazebo_map_robot.launch model:="'rospack
find chapter5_tutorials'/urdf/robot1_base_01.xacro"

$ rosrun tf view_frames
```

The resultant frame is depicted as follows:

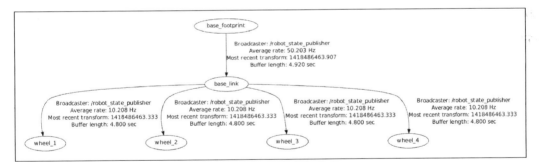

And now, if you run `tf_broadcaster` and run the `rosrun tf view_frames` command again, you will see the frame that you have created using code:

```
$ rosrun chapter5_tutorials tf_broadcaster

$ rosrun tf view_frames
```

The resultant frame is depicted as follows:

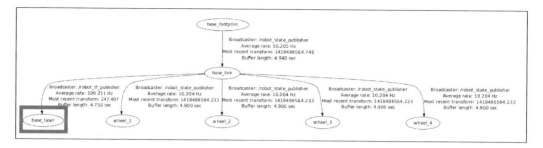

Publishing sensor information

Your robot can have a lot of sensors to see the world; you can program a lot of nodes to take this data and do something, but the navigation stack is prepared only to use the planar laser's sensor. So, your sensor must publish the data with one of these types: `sensor_msgs/LaserScan` or `sensor_msgs/PointCloud2`.

We are going to use the laser located in front of the robot to navigate in Gazebo. Remember that this laser is simulated on Gazebo, and it publishes data on the `hokuyo_link` frame with the topic name `/robot/laser/scan`.

In our case, we do not need to configure anything in our laser to use it on the navigation stack. This is because we have `tf` configured in the `.urdf` file, and the laser is publishing data with the correct type.

If you use a real laser, ROS might have a driver for it. Indeed, in *Chapter 8, Using Sensors and Actuators with ROS*, we will show you how to connect the Hokuyo laser to ROS. Anyway, if you are using a laser that has no driver on ROS and want to write a node to publish the data with the `sensor_msgs/LaserScan` sensor, you have an example template to do it, which is shown in the following section.

But first, remember the structure of the message `sensor_msgs/LaserScan`. Use the following command:

```
$ rosmsg show sensor_msgs/LaserScan
```

The preceding command will generate the following output:

```
std_msgs/Header header
  uint32 seq
  time stamp
  string frame_id
float32 angle_min
float32 angle_max
```

```
float32 angle_increment
float32 time_increment
float32 scan_time
float32 range_min
float32 range_max
float32[] ranges
float32[] intensities
```

Creating the laser node

Now we will create a new file in `chapter5_tutorials/src` with the name `laser.cpp` and put the following code in it:

```cpp
#include <ros/ros.h>
#include <sensor_msgs/LaserScan.h>

int main(int argc, char** argv){
  ros::init(argc, argv, "laser_scan_publisher");

  ros::NodeHandle n;
  ros::Publisher scan_pub = n.advertise<sensor_
  msgs::LaserScan>("scan", 50);

  unsigned int num_readings = 100;
  double laser_frequency = 40;
  double ranges[num_readings];
  double intensities[num_readings];

  int count = 0;
  ros::Rate r(1.0);
  while(n.ok()){
    //generate some fake data for our laser scan
    for(unsigned int i = 0; i < num_readings; ++i){
      ranges[i] = count;
      intensities[i] = 100 + count;
    }
    ros::Time scan_time = ros::Time::now();
    //populate the LaserScan message
    sensor_msgs::LaserScan scan;
    scan.header.stamp = scan_time;
    scan.header.frame_id = "base_link";
    scan.angle_min = -1.57;
    scan.angle_max = 1.57;
    scan.angle_increment = 3.14 / num_readings;
```

```
scan.time_increment = (1 / laser_frequency) / (num_readings);
scan.range_min = 0.0;
scan.range_max = 100.0;

scan.ranges.resize(num_readings);
scan.intensities.resize(num_readings);
for(unsigned int i = 0; i < num_readings; ++i){
  scan.ranges[i] = ranges[i];
  scan.intensities[i] = intensities[i];
}

scan_pub.publish(scan);
++count;
r.sleep();
  }
}
```

As you can see, we are going to create a new topic with the name `scan` and the message type `sensor_msgs/LaserScan`. You will become familiar with this message type when you reach *Chapter 8, Using Sensors and Actuators with ROS*. The name of the topic must be unique. When you configure the navigation stack, you will select this topic to be used for navigation. The following command line shows how to create the topic with the correct name:

```
ros::Publisher scan_pub =
n.advertise<sensor_msgs::LaserScan>("scan", 50);
```

It is important to publish data with `header`, `stamp`, `frame_id`, and many more elements because, if not, the navigation stack could fail with such data:

```
scan.header.stamp = scan_time;
scan.header.frame_id = "base_link";
```

Other important data on `header` is `frame_id`. It must be one of the frames created in the `.urdf` file and must have a frame published on the `tf` frame transforms. The navigation stack will use this information to know the real position of the sensor and make transforms, such as the one between the data sensor and obstacles.

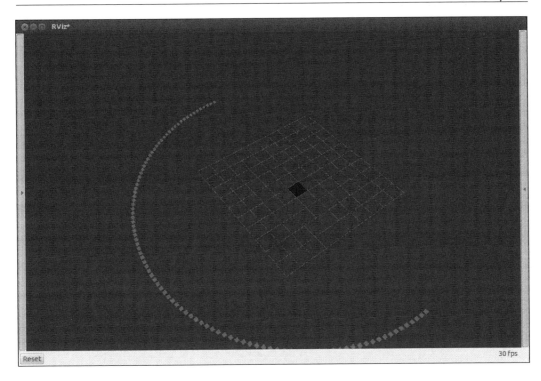

With this template, you can use any laser, even if it has no driver for ROS. You only have to change the fake data with the right data from your laser.

This template can also be used to create something that looks like a laser but is not. For example, you could simulate a laser using stereoscopy or using a sensor such as a sonar.

Publishing odometry information

The navigation stack also needs to receive data from the robot odometry. The odometry is the distance of something relative to a point. In our case, it is the distance between base_link and a fixed point in the frame odom.

The type of message used by the navigation stack is `nav_msgs/Odometry`. We can see its structure using the following command:

```
$ rosmsg show nav_msgs/Odometry
```

```
std_msgs/Header header
  uint32 seq
  time stamp
  string frame_id
string child_frame_id
geometry_msgs/PoseWithCovariance pose
  geometry_msgs/Pose pose
    geometry_msgs/Point position
      float64 x
      float64 y
      float64 z
    geometry_msgs/Quaternion orientation
      float64 x
      float64 y
      float64 z
      float64 w
  float64[36] covariance
geometry_msgs/TwistWithCovariance twist
  geometry_msgs/Twist twist
    geometry_msgs/Vector3 linear
      float64 x
      float64 y
      float64 z
    geometry_msgs/Vector3 angular
      float64 x
      float64 y
      float64 z
  float64[36] covariance
```

As you can see in the message structure, `nav_msgs/Odometry` gives the position of the robot between `frame_id` and `child_frame_id`. It also gives us the pose of the robot using the `geometry_msgs/Pose` message, and the velocity with the `geometry_msgs/Twist` message.

The pose has two structures that show the position in Euler coordinates and the orientation of the robot using a quaternion. The orientation is the angular displacement of the robot.

The velocity has two structures that show the linear velocity and the angular velocity. For our robot, we will use only the linear x velocity and the angular z velocity. We will use the linear x velocity to know whether the robot is moving forward or backward. The angular z velocity is used to check whether the robot is rotating towards the left or right.

As the odometry is the displacement between two frames, it is necessary to publish its transform. We did it in the last section, but later on in this section, we will show you an example for publishing the odometry and the transform of our robot.

Now, let us show you how Gazebo works with the odometry.

How Gazebo creates the odometry

As you have seen in other examples with Gazebo, our robot moves in the simulated world just like a robot in the real world. We use a driver for our robot, `diffdrive_plugin`. We configured this plugin in *Chapter 4, 3D Modeling and Simulation*, when you created the robot to use it in Gazebo.

This driver publishes the odometry generated in the simulated world, so we do not need to write anything for Gazebo.

Execute the robot sample in Gazebo to see the odometry working. Type the following commands in the shell:

```
$ roslaunch chapter5_tutorials gazebo_xacro.launch model:="'rospack find robot1_description'/urdf/robot1_base_04.xacro"
$ rosrun teleop_twist_keyboard teleop_twist_keyboard.py
```

Then, with the `teleop` node, move the robot for a few seconds to generate new data on the odometry topic.

On the screen of the Gazebo simulator, if you click on `robot_model1`, you will see some properties of the object. One of these properties is the pose of the robot. Click on the pose, and you will see some fields with data. What you are watching is the position of the robot in the virtual world. If you move the robot, the data changes:

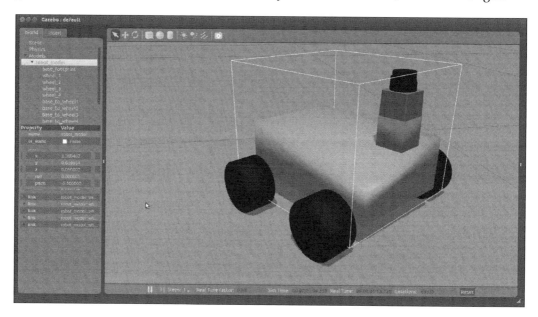

Gazebo continuously publishes the odometry data. Check the topic and see what data it is sending. Type the following command in a shell:

```
$ rostopic echo /odom/pose/pose
```

The following is the output that you will receive:

```
pose:
  pose:
    position:
      x: 0.11499976476
      y: 0.0
      z: 0.0
    orientation:
      x: 0.0
      y: 0.0
      z: 0.0
      w: 1.0
    covariance: [0.001, 0.0, 0.0, 0.0, 0.0, 0.0, 0.0, 0.001, 0.0, 0.0, 0.0, 0.0, 0.0, 0.0, 0.0, 1e-06, 0.0, 0.0, 0.0, 0.0, 0.0, 0.0, 1e-06, 0.0, 0.0,
0.0, 0.0, 0.0, 0.0, 1e-06, 0.0, 0.0, 0.0, 0.0, 0.0, 0.0, 0.001]
twist:
  twist:
    linear:
      x: 0.01
      y: 0.0
      z: 0.0
    angular:
      x: 0.0
      y: 0.0
      z: 0.0
    covariance: [0.001, 0.0, 0.0, 0.0, 0.0, 0.0, 0.0, 0.001, 0.0, 0.0, 0.0, 0.0, 0.0, 0.0, 0.0, 0.001, 0.0, 0.0, 0.0, 0.0, 0.0, 0.0, 0.001, 0.0, 0.0,
0.0, 0.0, 0.0, 0.0, 0.0, 0.0, 0.0, 0.0, 0.0, 0.0, 0.0, 0.001]
---
```

As you can observe, Gazebo is creating the odometry as the robot moves. We are going to see how Gazebo creates it by looking inside the plugin's source code.

The plugin file is located in the `gazebo_plugins` package, and the file is `gazebo_ros_skid_steer_drive.cpp`. You can find the code at `https://github.com/ros-simulation/gazebo_ros_pkgs/blob/kinetic-devel/gazebo_plugins/src/gazebo_ros_skid_steer_drive.cpp`.

The file has a lot of code, but the important part for us now is the following function, `publishOdometry()`:

```
void GazeboRosSkidSteerDrive::publishOdometry(double step_time)
{
  ros::Time current_time = ros::Time::now();
  std::string odom_frame =
  tf::resolve(tf_prefix_, odometry_frame_);
  std::string base_footprint_frame =
  tf::resolve(tf_prefix_, robot_base_frame_);
  // TODO create some non-perfect odometry!
  // getting data for base_footprint to odom transform
  math::Pose pose = this->parent->GetWorldPose();
  tf::Quaternion qt(pose.rot.x, pose.rot.y, pose.rot.z, pose.rot.w);
  tf::Vector3 vt(pose.pos.x, pose.pos.y, pose.pos.z);
  tf::Transform base_footprint_to_odom(qt, vt);
  if (this->broadcast_tf_)
  {
    transform_broadcaster_->sendTransform(
    tf::StampedTransform(base_footprint_to_odom, current_time,
    odom_frame, base_footprint_frame));
  }
  // publish odom topic
  odom_.pose.pose.position.x = pose.pos.x;
  odom_.pose.pose.position.y = pose.pos.y;
  odom_.pose.pose.orientation.x = pose.rot.x;
  odom_.pose.pose.orientation.y = pose.rot.y;
  odom_.pose.pose.orientation.z = pose.rot.z;
  odom_.pose.pose.orientation.w = pose.rot.w;
  odom_.pose.covariance[0] = 0.00001;
  odom_.pose.covariance[7] = 0.00001;
  odom_.pose.covariance[14] = 1000000000000.0;
  odom_.pose.covariance[21] = 1000000000000.0;
  odom_.pose.covariance[28] = 1000000000000.0;
  odom_.pose.covariance[35] = 0.01;
  // get velocity in /odom frame
  math::Vector3 linear;
```

```
linear = this->parent->GetWorldLinearVel();
odom_.twist.twist.angular.z = this->parent->
GetWorldAngularVel().z;
// convert velocity to child_frame_id (aka base_footprint)
float yaw = pose.rot.GetYaw();
odom_.twist.twist.linear.x = cosf(yaw) * linear.x + sinf(yaw) *
linear.y;
odom_.twist.twist.linear.y = cosf(yaw) * linear.y - sinf(yaw) *
linear.x;
odom_.header.stamp = current_time;
odom_.header.frame_id = odom_frame;
odom_.child_frame_id = base_footprint_frame;
odometry_publisher_.publish(odom_);
}
```

The `publishOdometry()` function is where the odometry is published. You can see how the fields of the structure are filled and the name of the topic for the odometry is set (in this case, it is `odom`). The pose is generated in the other part of the code that we will see in the following section.

Once you have learned how and where Gazebo creates the odometry, you will be ready to learn how to publish the odometry and the transform for a real robot. The following code will show a robot doing circles continuously. The final outcome does not really matter; the important thing to know here is how to publish the correct data for our robot.

Using Gazebo to create the odometry

To obtain some insight of how Gazebo does that, we are going to take a sneak peek inside the `diffdrive_plugin.cpp` file. You can find it at `https://github.com/ros-simulation/gazebo_ros_pkgs/blob/kinetic-devel/gazebo_plugins/src/gazebo_ros_skid_steer_drive.cpp`.

The `Load` function performs the function of registering the subscriber of the topic, and when a `cmd_vel` topic is received, the `cmdVelCallback()` function is executed to handle the message:

```
void GazeboRosSkidSteerDrive::Load(physics::ModelPtr _parent,
sdf::ElementPtr _sdf)
{
  …
  …
  // ROS: Subscribe to the velocity command topic (usually
  "cmd_vel")
```

```
ros::SubscribeOptions so =
ros::SubscribeOptions::create<geometry_msgs::Twist>(command_topic_
, 1,
boost::bind(&GazeboRosSkidSteerDrive::cmdVelCallback, this, _1),
ros::VoidPtr(), &queue_);
...
...
}
```

When a message arrives, the linear and angular velocities are stored in the internal variables to run operations later:

```
void GazeboRosSkidSteerDrive::cmdVelCallback(
const geometry_msgs::Twist::ConstPtr& cmd_msg)
{
  boost::mutex::scoped_lock scoped_lock(lock);
  x_ = cmd_msg->linear.x;
  rot_ = cmd_msg->angular.z;
}
```

The plugin estimates the velocity for each motor, using the formulas from the kinematic model of the robot, in the following manner:

```
void GazeboRosSkidSteerDrive::getWheelVelocities() {
  boost::mutex::scoped_lock scoped_lock(lock);
  double vr = x_;
  double va = rot_;
  wheel_speed_[RIGHT_FRONT] = vr + va * wheel_separation_ / 2.0;
  wheel_speed_[RIGHT_REAR] = vr + va * wheel_separation_ / 2.0;
  wheel_speed_[LEFT_FRONT] = vr - va * wheel_separation_ / 2.0;
  wheel_speed_[LEFT_REAR] = vr - va * wheel_separation_ / 2.0;
}
```

And finally, it estimates the distance traversed by the robot using more formulas from the kinematic motion model of the robot. As you can see in the code, you must know the wheel diameter and the wheel separation of your robot:

```
// Update the controller
void GazeboRosSkidSteerDrive::UpdateChild()
{
  common::Time current_time = this->world->GetSimTime();
  double seconds_since_last_update =
  (current_time - last_update_time_).Double();
  if (seconds_since_last_update > update_period_)
  {
```

```
        publishOdometry(seconds_since_last_update);
        // Update robot in case new velocities have been requested
        getWheelVelocities();
        joints[LEFT_FRONT]->SetVelocity(0, wheel_speed_[LEFT_FRONT] /
        wheel_diameter_);
        joints[RIGHT_FRONT]->SetVelocity(0, wheel_speed_[RIGHT_FRONT] /
        wheel_diameter_);
        joints[LEFT_REAR]->SetVelocity(0, wheel_speed_[LEFT_REAR] /
        wheel_diameter_);
        joints[RIGHT_REAR]->SetVelocity(0, wheel_speed_[RIGHT_REAR] /
        wheel_diameter_);
        last_update_time_ += common::Time(update_period_);
    }
}
```

This is the way `gazebo_ros_skid_steer_drive` controls our simulated robot in Gazebo.

Creating our own odometry

Create a new file in `chapter5_tutorials/src` with the name `odometry.cpp`, and write a code to publish odometry, you can use the following code snippets or check the code repository to have the entire code:

```
#include <string>
#include <ros/ros.h>
#include <sensor_msgs/JointState.h>
#include <tf/transform_broadcaster.h>
#include <nav_msgs/Odometry.h>

int main(int argc, char** argv) {

  ros::init(argc, argv, "state_publisher");
  ros::NodeHandle n;
  ros::Publisher odom_pub = n.advertise<nav_msgs::Odometry>("odom",
  10);
  ...

  while (ros::ok()) {
    current_time = ros::Time::now();

    double dt = (current_time - last_time).toSec();
    double delta_x = (vx * cos(th) - vy * sin(th)) * dt;
    double delta_y = (vx * sin(th) + vy * cos(th)) * dt;
    double delta_th = vth * dt;

    x += delta_x;
    y += delta_y;
```

```
      th += delta_th;

      geometry_msgs::Quaternion odom_quat;
      odom_quat = tf::createQuaternionMsgFromRollPitchYaw(0,0,th);

      // update transform
      odom_trans.header.stamp = current_time;
      odom_trans.transform.translation.x = x;
      odom_trans.transform.translation.y = y;
      odom_trans.transform.translation.z = 0.0;
      odom_trans.transform.rotation =
      tf::createQuaternionMsgFromYaw(th);

      // filling the odometry
      nav_msgs::Odometry odom;
      odom.header.stamp = current_time;
      odom.header.frame_id = "odom";
      odom.child_frame_id = "base_footprint";
      // position
      odom.pose.pose.position.x = x;
      odom.pose.pose.position.y = y;
      odom.pose.pose.position.z = 0.0;
      odom.pose.pose.orientation = odom_quat;

      // velocity
      odom.twist.twist.linear.x = vx;
      odom.twist.twist.linear.y = vy;


      ...
      odom.twist.twist.angular.z = vth;

      last_time = current_time;

      // publishing the odometry and the new tf
      broadcaster.sendTransform(odom_trans);
      odom_pub.publish(odom);

      loop_rate.sleep();
    }
    return 0;
}
```

First, create the transformation variable and fill it with `frame_id` and the `child_frame_id` values in order to know when the frames have to move. In our case, the `base_footprint` will move relatively towards the frame `odom`:

```
geometry_msgs::TransformStamped odom_trans;
odom_trans.header.frame_id = "odom";
odom_trans.child_frame_id = "base_footprint";
```

In this part, we generate the pose of the robot. With the linear velocity and the angular velocity, we can calculate the theoretical position of the robot after a while:

```
double dt = (current_time - last_time).toSec();
double delta_x = (vx * cos(th) - vy * sin(th)) * dt;
double delta_y = (vx * sin(th) + vy * cos(th)) * dt;
double delta_th = vth * dt;

x += delta_x;
y += delta_y;
th += delta_th;

geometry_msgs::Quaternion odom_quat;
odom_quat = tf::createQuaternionMsgFromRollPitchYaw(0,0,th);
```

In the transformation, we will only fill in the x and `rotation` fields, as our robot can only move forward and backward and can turn:

```
odom_trans.header.stamp = current_time;
odom_trans.transform.translation.x = x;
odom_trans.transform.translation.y = 0.0;
odom_trans.transform.translation.z = 0.0;
odom_trans.transform.rotation = tf::createQuaternionMsgFromYaw(th);
```

With the odometry, we will do the same. Fill the `frame_id` and `child_frame_id` fields with `odom` and `base_footprint`.

As the odometry has two structures, we will fill in the x, y, and `orientation` of the pose. In the twist structure, we will fill in the linear velocity x and the angular velocity z:

```
// position
odom.pose.pose.position.x = x;
odom.pose.pose.position.y = y;
odom.pose.pose.orientation = odom_quat;

// velocity
odom.twist.twist.linear.x = vx;
odom.twist.twist.angular.z = vth;
```

Once all the necessary fields are filled in, publish the data:

```
// publishing the odometry and the new tf
broadcaster.sendTransform(odom_trans);
odom_pub.publish(odom);
```

Remember to create the following line in the `CMakeLists.txt` file before compiling it:

```
add_executable(odometry src/odometry.cpp)
target_link_libraries(odometry ${catkin_LIBRARIES})
```

Compile the package and launch the robot without using Gazebo, using only `rviz` to visualize the model and the movement of the robot. Use the following command to do this:

```
$ roslaunch chapter5_tutorials display_xacro.launch model:="'rospack find chapter5_tutorials'/urdf/robot1_base_04.xacro"
```

Now, run the `odometry` node with the following command:

```
$ rosrun chapter5_tutorials odometry
```

The following output is what you will get:

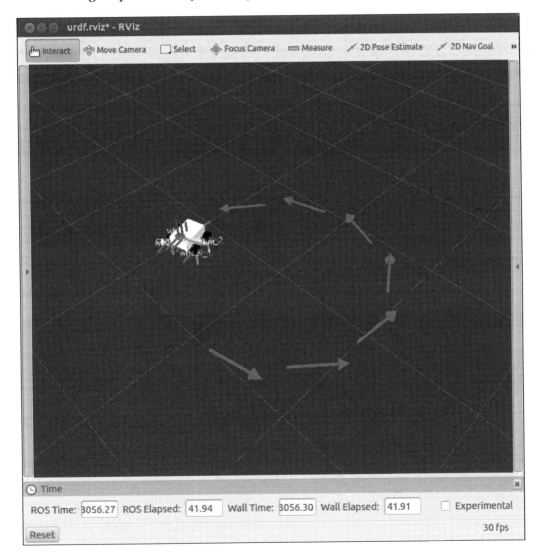

On the `rviz` screen, you can see the robot moving over some red arrows (grid). The robot moves over the grid because you published a new `tf` frame transform for the robot. The red arrows are the graphical representation for the `Odometry` message. You will see the robot moving in circles continuously as we programmed in the code.

Creating a base controller

A base controller is an important element in the navigation stack because it is the only way to effectively control your robot. It communicates directly with the electronics of your robot.

ROS does not provide a standard base controller, so you must write a base controller for your mobile platform.

Your robot has to be controlled with the message type `geometry_msgs/Twist`. This message was used on the `Odometry` message that we saw before.

So, your base controller must subscribe to a topic with the name `cmd_vel`, and must generate the correct commands to move the platform with the correct linear and angular velocities.

We are now going to recall the structure of this message. Type the following command in a shell to see the structure:

```
$ rosmsg show geometry_msgs/Twist
```

The output of this command is as follows:

```
geometry_msgs/Vector3 linear
    float64 x
    float64 y
    float64 z
geometry_msgs/Vector3 angular
    float64 x
    float64 y
    float64 z
```

The vector with the name `linear` indicates the linear velocity for the axes x, y, and z. The vector with the name `angular` is for the angular velocity on the axes.

For our robot, we will only use the linear velocity x and the angular velocity z. This is because our robot is on a differential-wheeled platform; it has two motors to move the robot forward and backward and to turn.

We are working with a simulated robot on Gazebo, and the base controller is implemented on the driver used to move/simulate the platform. This means that we will not have to create the base controller for this robot.

Anyway, in this chapter, you will see an example to implement the base controller on your physical robot. Before that, let's execute our robot on Gazebo to see how the base controller works. Run the following commands on different shells:

```
$ roslaunch chapter5_tutorials gazebo_xacro.launch model:="'rospack find
robot1_description'/urdf/robot1_base_04.xacro"
$ rosrun teleop_twist_keyboard teleop_twist_keyboard.py
```

When all the nodes are launched and working, open rxgraph to see the relation between all the nodes:

```
$ rqt_graph
```

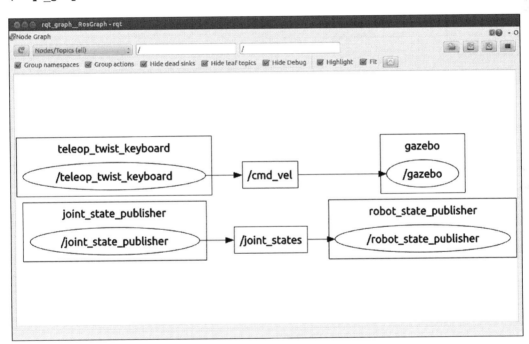

You can see that Gazebo subscribes automatically to the cmd_vel topic that is generated by the teleop node.

Inside the Gazebo simulator, the plugin of our robot is running and is getting the data from the cmd_vel topic. Also, this plugin moves the robot in the virtual world and generates the odometry.

Creating our base controller

Now, we are going to do something similar, that is, prepare a code to be used with a real robot with two wheels and encoders.

Create a new file in `chapter5_tutorials/src` with the name `base_controller.cpp` and put in the following code:

```cpp
#include <ros/ros.h>
#include <sensor_msgs/JointState.h>
#include <tf/transform_broadcaster.h>
#include <nav_msgs/Odometry.h>
#include <iostream>

using namespace std;

double width_robot = 0.1;
double vl = 0.0;
double vr = 0.0;
ros::Time last_time;
double right_enc = 0.0;
double left_enc = 0.0;
double right_enc_old = 0.0;
double left_enc_old = 0.0;
double distance_left = 0.0;
double distance_right = 0.0;
double ticks_per_meter = 100;
double x = 0.0;
double y = 0.0;
double th = 0.0;
geometry_msgs::Quaternion odom_quat;
```

In this part of the code, we have declared global variables and including the libraries to calculate the odometry and making the spatial transformation for positioning our robot. Now, you should create a call back function to receive velocity commands. Applying some kinematics equations, you could relate velocity commands with the speed of each wheels of your robot.

```cpp
void cmd_velCallback(const geometry_msgs::Twist &twist_aux)
{
  geometry_msgs::Twist twist = twist_aux;
  double vel_x = twist_aux.linear.x;
  double vel_th = twist_aux.angular.z;
  double right_vel = 0.0;
```

```
        double left_vel = 0.0;

    if(vel_x == 0){
        // turning
        right_vel = vel_th * width_robot / 2.0;
        left_vel = (-1) * right_vel;
    }else if(vel_th == 0){
        // forward / backward
        left_vel = right_vel = vel_x;
    }else{
        // moving doing arcs
        left_vel = vel_x - vel_th * width_robot / 2.0;
        right_vel = vel_x + vel_th * width_robot / 2.0;
    }
    vl = left_vel;
    vr = right_vel;
}
```

In the `main` function, you are going to code a loop that will update the real velocity of your robot using data from encoders and calculate the odometry.

```
int main(int argc, char** argv){
    ros::init(argc, argv, "base_controller");
    ros::NodeHandle n;
    ros::Subscriber cmd_vel_sub = n.subscribe("cmd_vel", 10,
    cmd_velCallback);
    ros::Rate loop_rate(10);

    while(ros::ok())
    {

        double dxy = 0.0;
        double dth = 0.0;
        ros::Time current_time = ros::Time::now();
        double dt;
        double velxy = dxy / dt;
        double velth = dth / dt;

        ros::spinOnce();
        dt = (current_time - last_time).toSec();;
        last_time = current_time;

        // calculate odomety
        if(right_enc == 0.0){
```

```
    distance_left = 0.0;
    distance_right = 0.0;
  }else{
    distance_left = (left_enc - left_enc_old) / ticks_per_meter;
    distance_right = (right_enc - right_enc_old) / ticks_per_meter;
  }
```

Once, the distance traversed by each wheel is known, you will be able to update the robot position calculating the increment of distance dxy and the angle increment dth.

```
    left_enc_old = left_enc;
    right_enc_old = right_enc;

    dxy = (distance_left + distance_right) / 2.0;
    dth = (distance_right - distance_left) / width_robot;

    if(dxy != 0){
        x += dxy * cosf(dth);
        y += dxy * sinf(dth);
    }

    if(dth != 0){
        th += dth;
    }
```

Position of the robot is calculated in x and y, for a base controller of a 2D robot platform you will suppose z is 0 and constant. For the robot orientation, you can assume that pitch and roll are also equal to zero and only the yaw angle should be update.

```
    odom_quat = tf::createQuaternionMsgFromRollPitchYaw(0,0,th);
    loop_rate.sleep();
  }
}
```

Do not forget to insert the following in your CMakeLists.txt file to create the executable of this file:

```
add_executable(base_controller src/base_controller.cpp)
target_link_libraries(base_controller ${catkin_LIBRARIES})
```

This code is only a common example and must be extended with more code to make it work with a specific robot. It depends on the controller used, the encoders, and so on. We assume that you have the right background to add the necessary code in order to make the example work fine. In *Chapter 8, Using Sensors and Actuators with ROS* a fully functional example will be provided with a real robot platform with wheels and encoders.

Creating a map with ROS

Getting a map can sometimes be a complicated task if you do not have the correct tools. ROS has a tool that will help you build a map using the odometry and a laser sensor. This tool is the map_server (http://wiki.ros.org/map_server). In this example, you will learn how to use the robot that we created in Gazebo, as we did in the previous chapters, to create a map, save it, and load it again.

We are going to use a .launch file to make it easy. Create a new file in chapter5_tutorials/launch with the name gazebo_mapping_robot.launch and put in the following code:

```
<?xml version="1.0"?>
<launch>
  <param name="/use_sim_time" value="true" />
  <include file="$(find
  gazebo_ros)/launch/willowgarage_world.launch"/>
  <arg name="model" />
  <param name="robot_description" command="$(find xacro)/xacro.py
  $(arg model)" />
  <node name="joint_state_publisher" pkg="joint_state_publisher"
  type="joint_state_publisher" ></node>
  <!-- start robot state publisher -->
  <node pkg="robot_state_publisher" type="robot_state_publisher"
  name="robot_state_publisher" output="screen" >
  <param name="publish_frequency" type="double" value="50.0" />
  </node>
  <node name="spawn_robot" pkg="gazebo_ros" type="spawn_model"
  args="-urdf -param robot_description -z 0.1 -model robot_model"
  respawn="false" output="screen" />
  <node name="rviz" pkg="rviz" type="rviz" args="-d $(find
  chapter5_tutorials)/launch/mapping.rviz"/>
  <node name="slam_gmapping" pkg="gmapping" type="slam_gmapping">
    <remap from="scan" to="/robot/laser/scan"/>
    <param name="base_link" value="base_footprint"/>
  </node>
</launch>
```

With this `.launch` file, you can launch the Gazebo simulator with the 3D model, the `rviz` program with the correct configuration file, and `slam_mapping` to build a map in real time. Launch the file in a shell, and in the other shell, run the `teleop` node to move the robot:

```
$ roslaunch chapter5_tutorials gazebo_mapping_robot.launch
model:="'rospack find robot1_description'/urdf/robot1_base_04.xacro"
$ rosrun teleop_twist_keyboard teleop_twist_keyboard.py
```

When you start to move the robot with the keyboard, you will see the free and unknown space on the `rviz` screen, as well as the map with the occupied space; this is known as an **Occupancy Grid Map** (**OGM**). The `slam_mapping` node updates the map state when the robot moves, or more specifically, when (after some motion) it has a good estimate of the robot's location and how the map is. It takes the laser scans and the odometry to build the OGM for you.

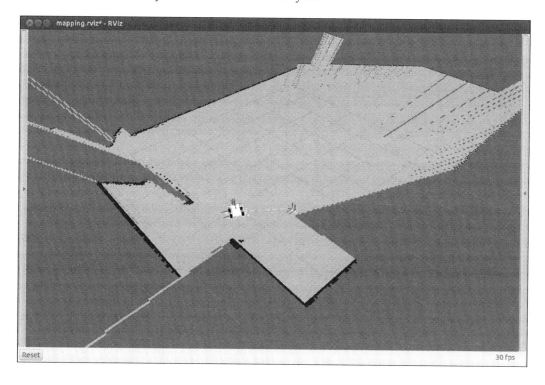

Saving the map using map_server

Once you have a complete map or something acceptable, you can save it to use it later in the navigation stack. To save it, use the following command:

```
$ rosrun map_server map_saver -f map
```

This command would give the following result:

```
[ INFO] [1418594807.613374681]: Waiting for the map
[ INFO] [1418594807.958979924, 126.530000000]: Received a 4000 X 4000 map @ 0.050 m/pix
[ INFO] [1418594807.959452501, 126.530000000]: Writing map occupancy data to map.pgm
[ INFO] [1418594808.997886519, 127.085000000]: Writing map occupancy data to map.yaml
[ INFO] [1418594808.998301431, 127.085000000]: Done
```

This command will create two files, `map.pgm` and `map.yaml`. The first one is the map in the `.pgm` format (the portable gray map format). The other is the configuration file for the map. If you open it, you will see the following output:

```
image: map.pgm
resolution: 0.050000
origin: [-100.000000, -100.000000, 0.000000]
negate: 0
occupied_thresh: 0.65
free_thresh: 0.196
```

Now, open the `.pgm` image file with your favorite viewer, and you will see the map being built before you:

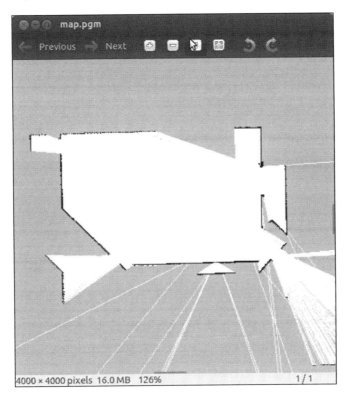

Loading the map using map_server

When you want to use the map built with your robot, it is necessary to load it with the map_server package. The following command will load the map:

```
$ rosrun map_server map_server map.yaml
```

But to make it easy, create another .launch file in chapter5_tutorials/launch with the name gazebo_map_robot.launch, and put in the following code:

```xml
<?xml version="1.0"?>
<launch>
  <param name="/use_sim_time" value="true" />
  <!-- start up wg world -->
  <include file="$(find
  gazebo_ros)/launch/willowgarage_world.launch"/>
  <arg name="model" />
  <param name="robot_description" command="$(find xacro)/xacro.py
  $(arg model)" />
  <node name="joint_state_publisher" pkg="joint_state_publisher"
  type="joint_state_publisher" ></node>
  <!-- start robot state publisher -->
  <node pkg="robot_state_publisher" type="robot_state_publisher"
  name="robot_state_publisher" output="screen" >
  <param name="publish_frequency" type="double" value="50.0" />
  </node>
  <node name="spawn_robot" pkg="gazebo_ros" type="spawn_model"
  args="-urdf -param robot_description -z 0.1 -model robot_model"
  respawn="false" output="screen" />
  <node name="map_server" pkg="map_server" type="map_server"
  args=" $(find chapter5_tutorials)/maps/map.yaml" />
  <node name="rviz" pkg="rviz" type="rviz" args="-d $(find
  chapter5_tutorials)/launch/mapping.rviz" />
</launch>
```

Now, launch the file using the following command and remember to put in the model of the robot that will be used:

```
$ roslaunch chapter5_tutorials gazebo_map_robot.launch model:="'rospack
find chapter5_tutorials'/urdf/robot1_base_04.xacro"
```

Then, you will see rviz with the robot and the map. The navigation stack, in order to know the localization of the robot, will use the map published by the map server and the laser readings. This will help it perform a scan matching algorithm that helps in estimating the robot's location using a particle filter implemented in the AMCL node.

We will see more about maps, as well as more useful tools, in the next chapter.

Summary

In this chapter, you worked on the steps required to configure your robot in order to use it with the navigation stack. Now you know that the robot must have a planar laser, must be a differential-wheeled robot, and it should satisfy some requirements for the base control and the geometry.

Keep in mind that we are working with Gazebo to demonstrate the examples and to explain how the navigation stack works with different configurations. It is more complex to explain all of this directly on a real, robotic platform because we do not know whether you have one or have access to one. In any case, depending on the platform, the instructions may vary and the hardware may fail, so it is safer and useful to run these algorithms in simulations; later, we can test them on a real robot, as long as it satisfies the requirements described thus far.

In the next chapter, you will learn how to configure the navigation stack, create the `.launch` files, and navigate autonomously in Gazebo with the robot that you created in the previous chapters.

In brief, what you will learn after this chapter will be extremely useful because it shows you how to configure everything correctly so you know how to use the navigation stack with other robots, either simulated or real.

6
The Navigation Stack – Beyond Setups

We have created packages, nodes, 3D models of robots, and more. In *Chapter 5, The Navigation Stack – Robot Setups*, you configured your robot in order to be used with the navigation stack, and in this chapter, we will finish the configuration for the navigation stack so that you learn how to use it with your robot.

All the work done in the previous chapters has been a preamble for this precise moment. This is when the fun begins and when the robots come alive.

In this chapter, we are going to learn how to do the following:

- Apply the knowledge of *Chapter 5, The Navigation Stack – Robot Setups* and the programs developed therein
- Understand the navigation stack and how it works
- Configure all the necessary files
- Create launch files to start the navigation stack

Let's begin!

Creating a package

The correct way to create a package is by adding the dependencies with the other packages created for your robot. For example, you could use the next command to create the package:

```
$ roscreate-pkg my_robot_name_2dnav move_base my_tf_configuration_dep my_odom_configuration_dep my_sensor_configuration_dep
```

But in our case, as we have everything in the same package, it is only necessary to execute the following:

```
$ catkin_create_pkg chapter6_tutorials roscpp tf
```

Remember that in the repository, you may find all the necessary files for the chapter.

Creating a robot configuration

To launch the entire robot, we are going to create a launch file with all the necessary files to activate all the systems. Anyway, here you have a launch file for a real robot that you can use as a template. The following script is present in configuration_template.launch:

```xml
<launch>
  <node pkg="sensor_node_pkg" type="sensor_node_type"
  name="sensor_node_name" output="screen">
    <param name="sensor_param" value="param_value" />
  </node>

  <node pkg="odom_node_pkg" type="odom_node_type" name="odom_node"
  output="screen">
    <param name="odom_param" value="param_value" />
  </node>

  <node pkg="transform_configuration_pkg"
  type="transform_configuration_type"
  name="transform_configuration_name" output="screen">
    <param name="transform_configuration_param"
    value="param_value" />
  </node>
</launch>
```

This launch file will launch three nodes that will start up the robot.

The first one is the node responsible for activating the sensors, for example, the **Laser Imaging, Detection, and Ranging (LIDAR)** system. The `sensor_param` parameter can be used to configure the sensor's port, for example, if the sensor uses a USB connection. If your sensor needs more parameters, you need to duplicate the line and add the necessary parameters. Some robots have more than one sensor to help in the navigation. In this case, you can add more nodes or create a launch file for the sensors, and include it in this launch file. This could be a good option for easily managing all the nodes in the same file.

The second node is to start the odometry, the base control, and all the necessary files to move the base and calculate the robot's position. Remember that in *Chapter 5*, *The Navigation Stack – Robot Setups*, we looked at these nodes in some detail. As in the other section, you can use the parameters to configure something in the odometry, or replicate the line to add more nodes.

The third part is meant to launch the node responsible for publishing and calculating the geometry of the robot, and the transform between the arms, sensors, and so on.

The previous file is for your real robot, but for our example, the next launch file is all we need.

Create a new file in `chapter6_tutorials/launch` with the name `chapter6_configuration_gazebo.launch`, and add the following code:

```xml
<?xml version="1.0"?>
<launch>
  <param name="/use_sim_time" value="true" />
  <remap from="robot/laser/scan" to="/scan" />
  <!-- start up wg world -->
  <include file="$(find
  gazebo_ros)/launch/willowgarage_world.launch"/>
  <arg name="model" default="$(find
  robot1_description)/urdf/robot1_base_04.xacro"/>
  <param name="robot_description" command="$(find xacro)/xacro.py
  $(arg model)" />
  <node name="joint_state_publisher" pkg="joint_state_publisher"
  type="joint_state_publisher" ></node>
  <!-- start robot state publisher -->
  <node pkg="robot_state_publisher" type="robot_state_publisher"
  name="robot_state_publisher" output="screen" />
  <node name="spawn_robot" pkg="gazebo_ros" type="spawn_model"
  args="-urdf -paramrobot_description -z 0.1 -model robot_model"
  respawn="false" output="screen" />
  <node name="rviz" pkg="rviz" type="rviz" args="-d $(find
  chapter6_tutorials)/launch/navigation.rviz" />
</launch>
```

This launch file is the same that we used in the previous chapters, so it does not need any additional explanation.

Now to launch this file, use the following command:

```
$ ros launch chapter6_tutorials chapter6_configuration_gazebo.launch
```

You will see the following window:

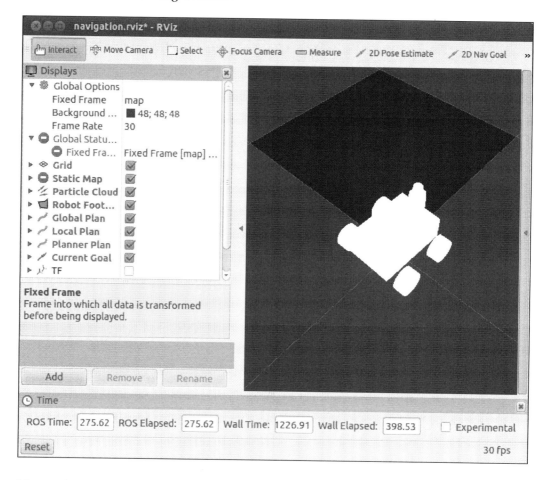

Notice that in the previous screenshot, there are some fields in red, blue, and yellow, without you having configured anything before. This is because in the launch file, a configuration file for the rviz layout is loaded along with rviz, and this file was configured in the previous chapter of this book.

In the upcoming sections, you will learn how to configure rviz to use it with the navigation stack and view all the topics.

Configuring the costmaps – global_ costmap and local_costmap

Okay, now we are going to start configuring the navigation stack and all the necessary files to start it. To start with the configuration, first we will learn what **costmaps** are and what they are used for. Our robot will move through the map using two types of navigation: global and local:

- The global navigation is used to create paths for a goal in the map or at a far-off distance
- The local navigation is used to create paths in the nearby distances and avoid obstacles, for example, a square window of 4 x 4 meters around the robot

These modules use costmaps to keep all the information of our map. The global costmap is used for global navigation and the local costmap for local navigation.

The costmaps have parameters to configure the behaviors, and they have common parameters as well, which are configured in a shared file.

The configuration basically consists of three files where we can set up different parameters. The files are as follows:

- costmap_common_params.yaml
- global_costmap_params.yaml
- local_costmap_params.yaml

Just by reading the names of these configuration files, you can instantly guess what they are used for. Now that you have a basic idea about the usage of costmaps, we are going to create the configuration files and explain the parameters that are configured in them.

Configuring the common parameters

Let's start with the common parameters. Create a new file in chapter6_tutorials/ launch with the name costmap_common_params.yaml, and add the following code.

The following script is present in costmap_common_params.yaml:

```
obstacle_range: 2.5
raytrace_range: 3.0
footprint: [[-0.2,-0.2],[-0.2,0.2], [0.2, 0.2], [0.2,-0.2]]
inflation_radius: 0.5
```

```
cost_scaling_factor: 10.0
observation_sources: scan
scan: {sensor_frame: base_link, observation_persistence: 0.0,
max_obstacle_height: 0.4, min_obstacle_height: 0.0, data_type:
LaserScan, topic: /scan, marking: true, clearing: true}
```

This file is used to configure common parameters. The parameters are used in `local_costmap` and `global_costmap`. Let's break the code and understand it.

The `obstacle_range` and `raytrace_range` attributes are used to indicate the maximum distance that the sensor will read and introduce new information in the costmaps. The first one is used for the obstacles. If the robot detects an obstacle closer than 2.5 meters in our case, it will put the obstacle in the costmap. The other one is used to clean/clear the costmap and update the free space in it when the robot moves. Note that we can only detect the echo of the laser or sonar with the obstacle; we cannot perceive the whole obstacle or object itself, but this simple approach will be enough to deal with these kinds of measurements, and we will be able to build a map and localize within it.

The `footprint` attribute is used to indicate the geometry of the robot to the navigation stack. It is used to keep the right distance between the obstacles and the robot, or to find out if the robot can go through a door. The `inflation_radius` attribute is the value given to keep a minimal distance between the geometry of the robot and the obstacles.

The `cost_scaling_factor` attribute modifies the behavior of the robot around the obstacles. You can make a behavior aggressive or conservative by changing the parameter.

With the `observation_sources` attribute, you can set the sensors used by the navigation stack to get the data from the real world and calculate the path.

In our case, we are using a simulated LIDAR in Gazebo, but we can use a point cloud to do the same.

The following line will configure the sensor's frame and the uses of the data:

```
scan: {sensor_frame: base_link, data_type: LaserScan, topic:
/scan, marking: true, clearing: true}
```

The laser configured in the previous line is used to add and clear obstacles in the costmap. For example, you could add a sensor with a wide range to find obstacles and another sensor to navigate and clear the obstacles. The topic's name is configured in this line. It is important to configure it well, because the navigation stack could wait for another topic and all this while, the robot is moving and could crash into a wall or an obstacle.

Configuring the global costmap

The next file to be configured is the `global` costmap configuration file. Create a new file in `chapter6_tutorials/launch` with the name `global_costmap_params.yaml`, and add the following code:

```
global_costmap:
  global_frame: /map
  robot_base_frame: /base_footprint
  update_frequency: 1.0
  static_map: true
```

The `global_frame` and the `robot_base_frame` attributes define the transformation between the map and the robot. This transformation is for the `global` costmap.

You can configure the frequency of updates for the costmap. In this case, it is 1 Hz. The `static_map` attribute is used for the `global` costmap to see whether a map or the map server is used to initialize the costmap. If you aren't using a static map, set this parameter to `false`.

Configuring the local costmap

The next file is for configuring the `local` costmap. Create a new file in `chapter6_tutorials/launch` with the name `local_costmap_params.yaml`, and add the following code:

```
local_costmap:
  global_frame: /map
  robot_base_frame: /base_footprint
  update_frequency: 5.0
  publish_frequency: 2.0
  static_map: false
  rolling_window: true
  width: 5.0
  height: 5.0
  resolution: 0.02
  transform_tolerance: 0.5
  planner_frequency: 1.0
  planner_patiente: 5.0
```

The `global_frame`, `robot_base_frame`, `update_frequency` and `static_map` parameters are the same as described in the previous section, configuring the `global` costmap. The `publish_frequency` parameter determines the frequency for publishing information. The `rolling_window` parameter is used to keep the costmap centered on the robot when it is moving around the world.

The `transform_tolerance` parameter configures the maximum latency for the transforms, in our case 0.5 seconds. With the `planner_frequency` parameter, we can configure the rate in Hz at which to run the planning loop. And the `planner_patiente` parameter configures how long the planner will wait in seconds in an attempt to find a valid plan, before space-clearing operations are performed.

You can configure the dimensions and the resolution of the costmap with the `width`, `height`, and `resolution` parameters. The values are given in meters.

Base local planner configuration

Once we have the costmaps configured, it is necessary to configure the base planner. The base planner is used to generate the velocity commands to move our robot. Create a new file in `chapter6_tutorials/launch` with the name `base_local_planner_params.yaml`, and add the following code:

```
TrajectoryPlannerROS:
  max_vel_x: 0.2
  min_vel_x: 0.05
  max_rotational_vel: 0.15
  min_in_place_rotational_vel: 0.01
  min_in_place_vel_theta: 0.01
  max_vel_theta: 0.15
  min_vel_theta: -0.15
  acc_lim_th: 3.2
  acc_lim_x: 2.5
  acc_lim_y: 2.5
  holonomic_robot: false
```

The `config` file will set the maximum and minimum velocities for your robot. The acceleration is also set.

The `holonomic_robot` parameter is `true` if you are using a holonomic platform. In our case, our robot is based on a non-holonomic platform and the parameter is set to `false`. A **holonomic vehicle** is one that can move in all the configured space from any position. In other words, if the places where the robot can go are defined by any x and y values in the environment, this means that the robot can move there from any position. For example, if the robot can move forward, backward, and laterally, it is holonomic. A typical case of a non-holonomic vehicle is a car, as it cannot move laterally, and from a given position, there are many other positions (or poses) that are not reachable. Also, a differential platform is non-holonomic.

Creating a launch file for the navigation stack

Now we have all the files created and the navigation stack is configured. To run everything, we are going to create a launch file. Create a new file in the `chapter6_tutorials/launch` folder, and put the following code in a file with the name `move_base.launch`:

```
<launch>
  <!-- Run the map server -->
  <node name="map_server" pkg="map_server" type="map_server"
  args="$(find chapter6_tutorials)/maps/map.yaml" output="screen"
  />
  <include file="$(find amcl)/examples/amcl_diff.launch" />
  <node pkg="move_base" type="move_base" respawn="false"
  name="move_base" output="screen">
    <rosparam file="$(find
    chapter6_tutorials)/launch/costmap_common_params.yaml"
    command="load" ns="global_costmap" />
    <rosparam file="$(find
    chapter6_tutorials)/launch/costmap_common_params.yaml"
    command="load" ns="local_costmap" />
    <rosparam file="$(find
    chapter6_tutorials)/launch/local_costmap_params.yaml"
    command="load" />
    <rosparam file="$(find
    chapter6_tutorials)/launch/global_costmap_params.yaml"
    command="load" />
    <rosparam file="$(find
    chapter6_tutorials)/launch/base_local_planner_params.yaml"
    command="load" />
  </node>
</launch>
```

Notice that in this file, we are launching all the files created earlier. We will launch a map server as well with a map that we created in *Chapter 5, The Navigation Stack – Robot Setups* and the `amcl` node.

The `amcl` node that we are going to use is for differential robots because our robot is also a differential robot. If you want to use `amcl` with holonomic robots, you will need to use the `amcl_omni.launch` file. If you want to use another map, go to *Chapter 5, The Navigation Stack – Robot Setups*, and create a new one.

Now launch the file and type the next command in a new shell. Recall that before you launch this file, you must launch the `chapter6_configuration_gazebo.launch` file:

```
$ roslaunch chapter6_tutorials move_base.launch
```

You will see the following window:

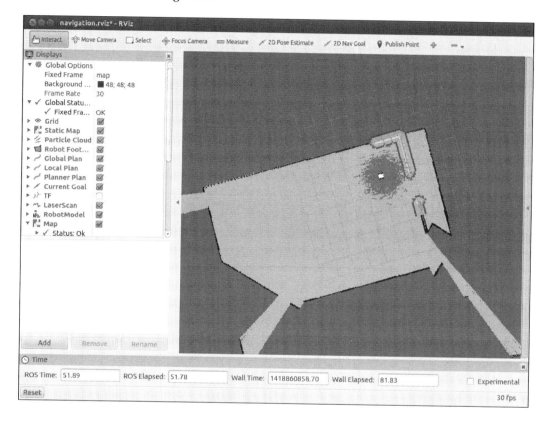

If you compare this image with the image that you saw when you launched the `chapter6_configuration_gazebo.launch` file, you will see that all the options are in blue; this is a good signal and it means that everything is okay.

As we said before, in the next section you will learn which options are necessary to visualize all the topics used in a navigation stack.

Setting up rviz for the navigation stack

It is good practice to visualize all possible data that the navigation stack does. In this section, we will show you the visualization topic that you must add to `rviz` to see the correct data sent by the navigation stack. Discussions on each visualization topic that the navigation stack publishes are given next.

The 2D pose estimate

The **2D pose estimate** (*P* shortcut) allows the user to initialize the localization system used by the navigation stack by setting the pose of the robot in the world.

The navigation stack waits for the new pose of a new topic with the name `initialpose`. This topic is sent using the `rviz` windows where we previously changed the name of the topic.

You can see in the following screenshot how you can use `initialpose`. Click on the **2D Pose Estimate** button, and click on the map to indicate the initial position of your robot. If you don't do this at the beginning, the robot will start the auto-localization process and try to set an initial pose:

- **Topic**: `initialpose`

- **Type**: `geometry_msgs/PoseWithCovarianceStamped`

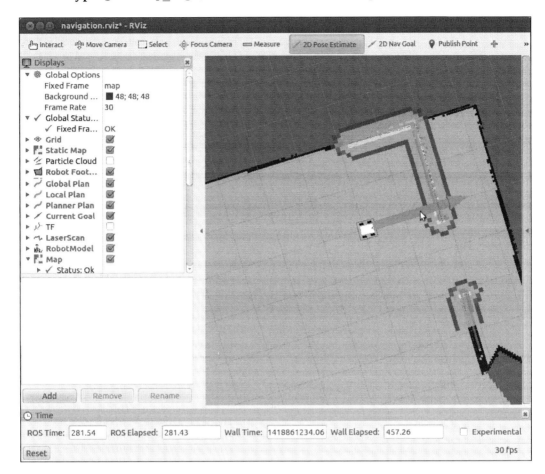

The 2D nav goal

The **2D nav goal** (*G* shortcut) allows the user to send a goal to the navigation by setting a desired pose for the robot to achieve. The navigation stack waits for a new goal with `/move_base_simple/goal` as the topic name; for this reason, you must change the topic's name in the `rviz` windows in **Tool Properties** in the **2D Nav Goal** menu. The new name that you must put in this textbox is `/move_base_simple/goal`. In the next window, you can see how to use it. Click on the **2D Nav Goal** button, and select the map and the goal for your robot. You can select the *x* and *y* position and the end orientation for the robot:

- **Topic**: `move_base_simple/goal`
- **Type**: `geometry_msgs/PoseStamped`

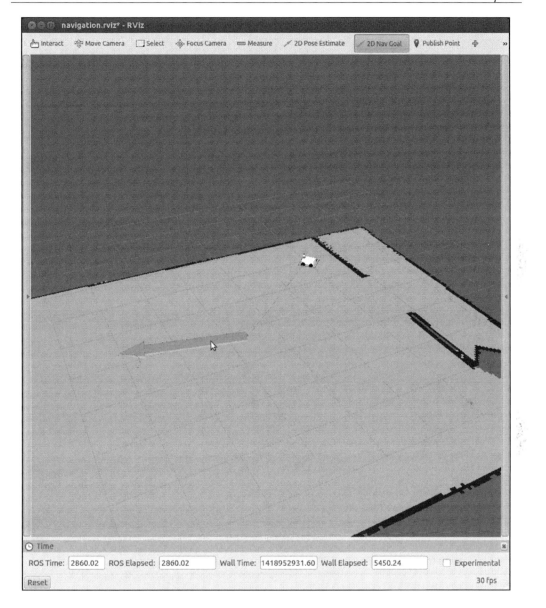

The static map

This displays the static map that is being served by `map_server`, if one exists.
When you add this visualization, you will see the map we captured in *Chapter 5,
The Navigation Stack – Robot Setups*, in the *Creating a map with ROS* section.

In the next window, you can see the display type that you need to select and the name that you must put in the display name:

- **Topic**: map
- **Type**: nav_msgs/GetMap

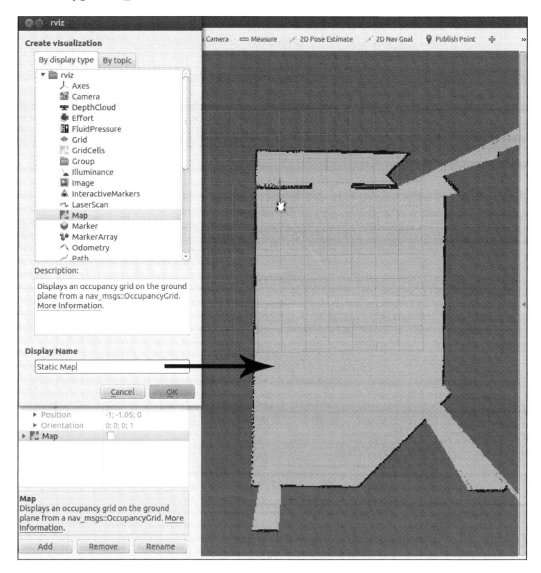

The particle cloud

This displays the particle cloud used by the robot's localization system. The spread of the cloud represents the localization system's uncertainty about the robot's pose. A cloud that spreads out a lot reflects high uncertainty, while a condensed cloud represents low uncertainty. In our case, you will obtain the following cloud for the robot:

- **Topic**: `particlecloud`
- **Type**: `geometry_msgs/PoseArray`

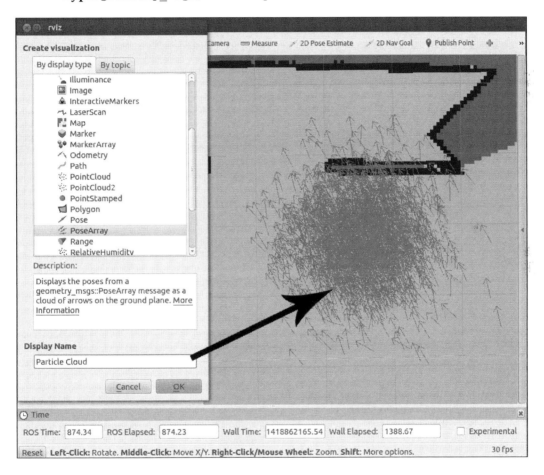

The robot's footprint

This shows the footprint of the robot; in our case, the robot has a footprint, which has a width of 0.4 meters and a height of 0.4 meters. Remember that this parameter is configured in the `costmap_common_params` file. This dimension is important because the navigation stack will move the robot in a safe mode using the values configured before:

- **Topic**: `local_costmap/robot_footprint`
- **Type**: `geometry_msgs/Polygon`

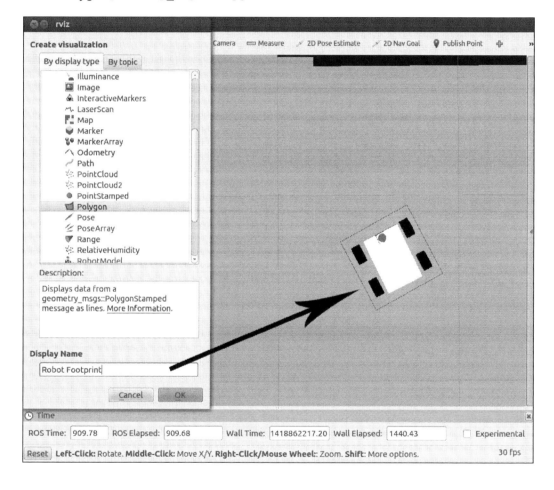

The local costmap

This shows the `local` costmap that the navigation stack uses for navigation. The yellow line is the detected obstacle. For the robot to avoid collision, the robot's footprint should never intersect with a cell that contains an obstacle. The blue zone is the inflated obstacle. To avoid collisions, the center point of the robot should never overlap with a cell that contains an inflated obstacle:

- **Topic**: `/move_base/local_costmap/costmap`
- **Type**: `nav_msgs/OccupancyGrid`

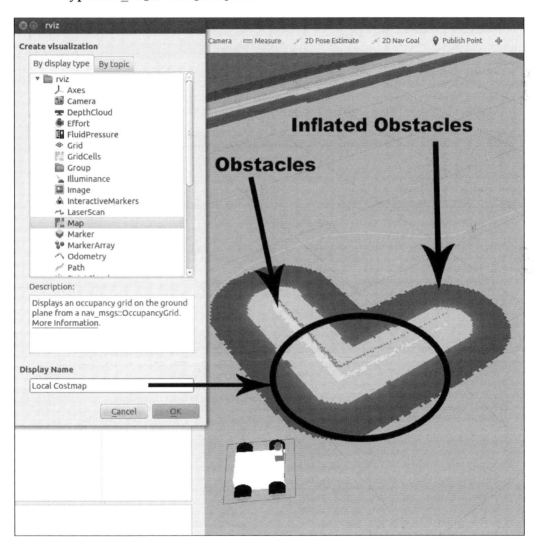

The global costmap

This shows the `global` costmap that the navigation stack uses for navigation. The yellow line is the detected obstacle. For the robot to avoid collision, the robot's footprint should never intersect with a cell that contains an obstacle. The blue zone is the inflated obstacle. To avoid collisions, the center point of the robot should never overlap with a cell that contains an inflated obstacle:

- **Topic**: `/move_base/global_costmap/costmap`
- **Type**: `nav_msgs/OccupancyGrid`

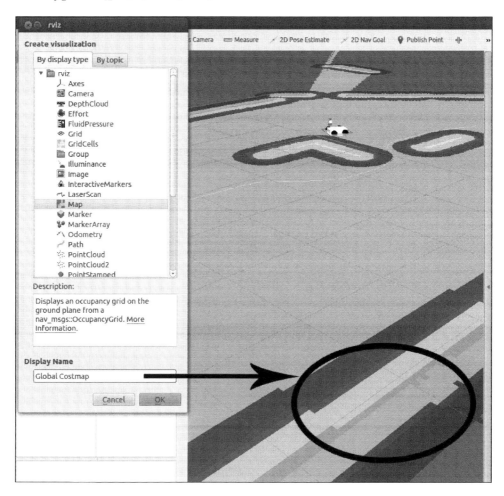

The global plan

This shows the portion of the global plan that the local planner is currently pursuing. You can see it in green in the next image. Perhaps the robot will find obstacles during its movement, and the navigation stack will recalculate a new path to avoid collisions and try to follow the global plan.

- **Topic**: `TrajectoryPlannerROS/global_plan`
- **Type**: `nav_msgs/Path`

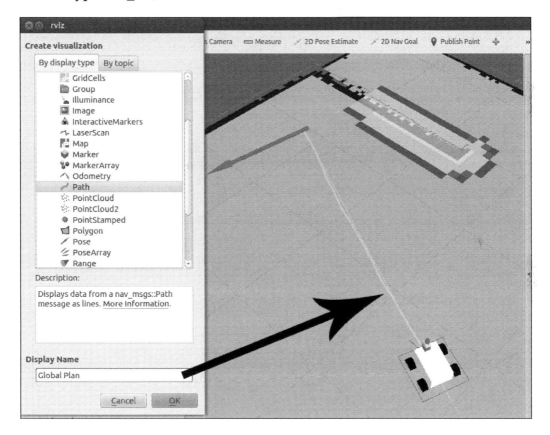

The local plan

This shows the trajectory associated with the velocity commands currently being commanded to the base by the local planner. You can see the trajectory in blue in front of the robot in the next image. You can use this display to see whether the robot is moving, and the approximate velocity from the length of the blue line:

- **Topic**: `TrajectoryPlannerROS/local_plan`
- **Type**: `nav_msgs/Path`

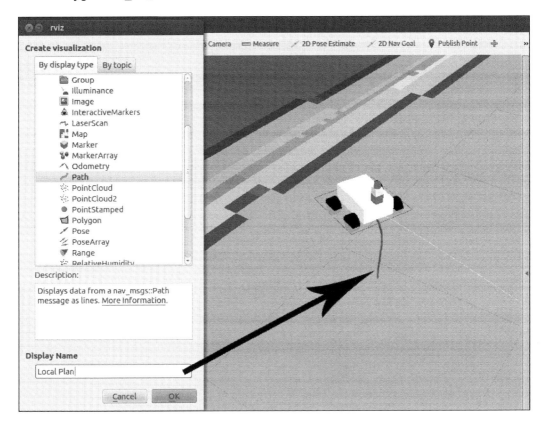

The planner plan

This displays the full plan for the robot computed by the global planner. You will see that it is similar to the global plan:

- **Topic**: NavfnROS/plan
- **Type**: nav_msgs/Path

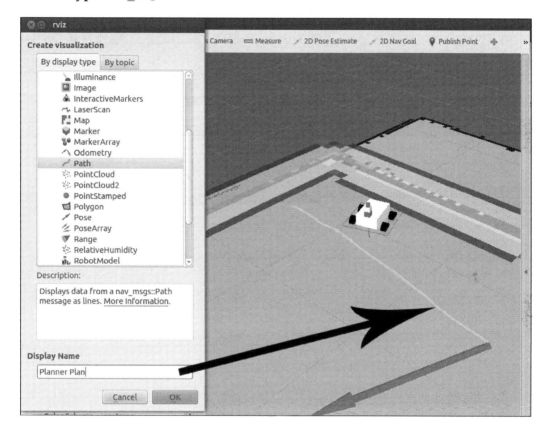

The current goal

This shows the goal pose that the navigation stack is attempting to achieve. You can see it as a red arrow, and it is displayed after you put in a new 2D nav goal. It can be used to find out the final position of the robot:

- **Topic**: current_goal
- **Type**: geometry_msgs/PoseStamped

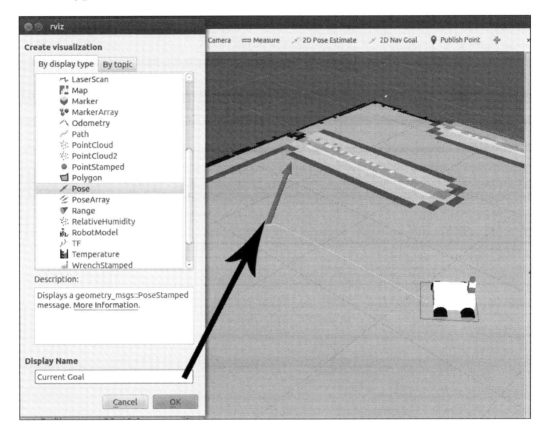

These visualizations are all you need to see the navigation stack in rviz. With this, you can notice whether the robot is doing something strange. Now we are going to see a general image of the system. Run rqt_graph to see whether all the nodes are running and to see the relations between them.

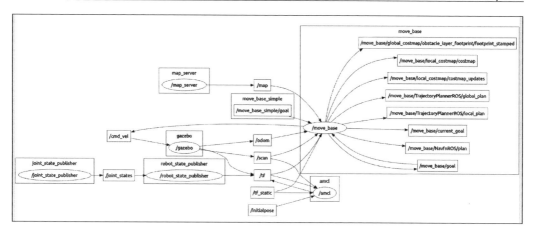

Adaptive Monte Carlo Localization

In this chapter, we are using the **Adaptive Monte Carlo Localization (AMCL)** algorithm for the localization. The AMCL algorithm is a probabilistic localization system for a robot moving in 2D. This system implements the adaptive Monte Carlo Localization approach, which uses a particle filter to track the pose of a robot against a known map.

The AMCL algorithm has many configuration options that will affect the performance of localization. For more information on AMCL, please refer to the AMCL documentation at http://wiki.ros.org/amcl and also at http://www. probabilistic-robotics.org/.

The amcl node works mainly with laser scans and laser maps, but it could be extended to work with other sensor data, such as a sonar or stereo vision. So for this chapter, it takes a laser-based map and laser scans, transforms messages, and generates a probabilistic pose. On startup, the amcl node initializes its particle filter according to the parameters provided in the setup. If you don't set the initial position, amcl will start at the origin of the coordinates. Anyway, you can set the initial position in rviz using the **2D Pose Estimate** button.

When we include the amcl_diff.launch file, we are starting the node with a series of configured parameters. This configuration is the default configuration and the minimum setting needed to make it work.

Next, we are going to see the content of the `amcl_diff.launch` launch file to explain some parameters:

```
<launch>
  <node pkg="amcl" type="amcl" name="amcl" output="screen">
    <!-- Publish scans from best pose at a max of 10 Hz -->
    <param name="odom_model_type" value="diff" />
    <param name="odom_alpha5" value="0.1" />
    <param name="transform_tolerance" value="0.2" />
    <param name="gui_publish_rate" value="10.0" />
    <param name="laser_max_beams" value="30" />
    <param name="min_particles" value="500" />
    <param name="max_particles" value="5000" />
    <param name="kld_err" value="0.05" />
    <param name="kld_z" value="0.99" />
    <param name="odom_alpha1" value="0.2" />
    <param name="odom_alpha2" value="0.2" />
    <!-- translation std dev, m -->
    <param name="odom_alpha3" value="0.8" />
    <param name="odom_alpha4" value="0.2" />
    <param name="laser_z_hit" value="0.5" />
    <param name="laser_z_short" value="0.05" />
    <param name="laser_z_max" value="0.05" />
    <param name="laser_z_rand" value="0.5" />
    <param name="laser_sigma_hit" value="0.2" />
    <param name="laser_lambda_short" value="0.1" />
    <param name="laser_lambda_short" value="0.1" />
    <param name="laser_model_type" value="likelihood_field" />
    <!--<param name="laser_model_type" value="beam"/> -->
    <param name="laser_likelihood_max_dist" value="2.0" />
    <param name="update_min_d" value="0.2" />
    <param name="update_min_a" value="0.5" />
    <param name="odom_frame_id" value="odom" />
    <param name="resample_interval" value="1" />
    <param name="transform_tolerance" value="0.1" />
    <param name="recovery_alpha_slow" value="0.0" />
    <param name="recovery_alpha_fast" value="0.0" />
  </node>
</launch>
```

The `min_particles` and `max_particles` parameters set the minimum and maximum number of particles that are allowed for the algorithm. With more particles, you get more accuracy, but this increases the use of the CPU.

The `laser_model_type` parameter is used to configure the laser type. In our case, we are using a `likelihood_field` parameter but the algorithm can also use beam lasers.

The `laser_likelihood_max_dist` parameter is used to set the maximum distance for obstacle inflation on the map, which is used in the `likelihood_field` model.

The `initial_pose_x`, `initial_pose_y`, and `initial_pose_a` parameters are not in the launch file, but they are interesting because they set the initial position of the robot when `amcl` starts; for example, if your robot always starts in the dock station and you want to set the position in the launch file.

Perhaps you should change some parameters to tune your robot and make it work fine. Visit `http://wiki.ros.org/amcl`, where you have a lot of information about the configuration and the parameters that you could change.

Modifying parameters with rqt_reconfigure

A good option for understanding all the parameters configured in this chapter, is by using `rqt_reconfigure` to change the values without restarting the simulation.

To launch `rqt_reconfigure`, use the following command:

```
$ rosrun rqt_reconfigure rqt_reconfigure
```

You will see the screen as follows:

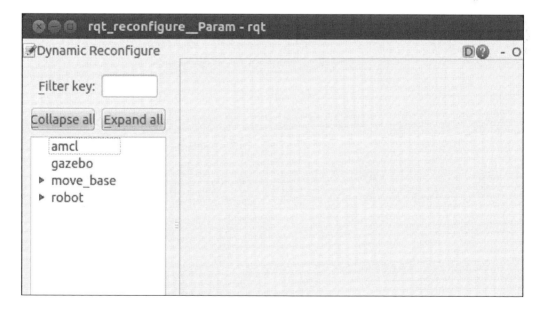

As an example, we are going to change the parameter `max_vel_x` configured in the file, `base_local_planner_params.yaml`. Click over the `move_base` menu and expand it. Then select `TrajectoryPlannerROS` in the menu tree. You will see a list of parameters. As you can see, the `max_vel_x` parameter has the same value that we assigned in the configuration file.

You can see a brief description for the parameter by hovering the mouse over the name for a few seconds. This is very useful for understanding the function of each parameter.

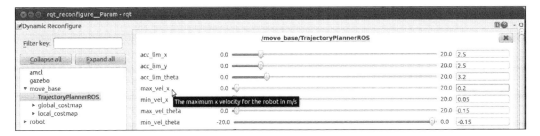

Avoiding obstacles

A great functionality of the navigation stack is the recalculation of the path if it finds obstacles during the movement. You can easily see this feature by adding an object in front of the robot in Gazebo. For example, in our simulation we added a big box in the middle of the path. The navigation stack detects the new obstacle, and automatically creates an alternative path.

In the next image, you can see the object that we added. Gazebo has some predefined 3D objects that you can use in the simulations with mobile robots, arms, humanoids, and so on.

To see the list, go to the **Insert model** section. Select one of the objects and then click at the location where you want to put it, as shown in the following screenshot:

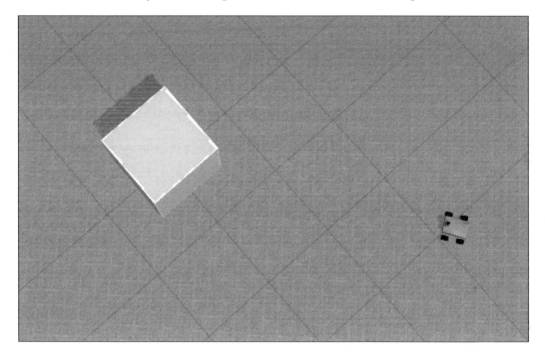

If you go to the `rviz` windows now, you will see a new global plan to avoid the obstacle. This feature is very interesting when you use the robot in real environments with people walking around the robot. If the robot detects a possible collision, it will change the direction, and it will try to arrive at the goal. Recall that the detection of such obstacles is reduced to the area covered by the local planner costmap (for example, 4 x 4 meters around the robot). You can see this feature in the next screenshot:

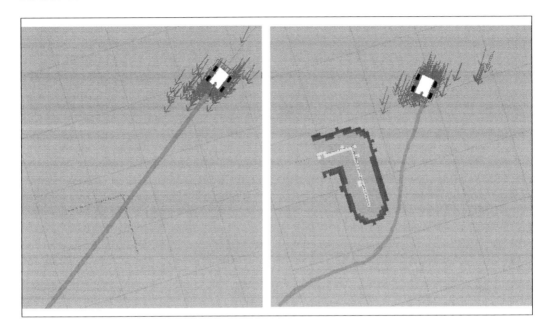

Sending goals

We are sure that you have been playing with the robot by moving it around the map a lot. This is funny but a little tedious, and it is not very functional.

Perhaps you were thinking that it would be a great idea to program a list of movements and send the robot to different positions with only a button, even when we are not in front of a computer with `rviz`.

Okay, now you are going to learn how to do it using `actionlib`.

The `actionlib` package provides a standardized interface for interfacing with tasks. For example, you can use it to send goals for the robot to detect something at a place, make scans with the laser, and so on. In this section, we will send a goal to the robot, and we will wait for this task to end.

It could look similar to services, but if you are doing a task that has a long duration, you might want the ability to cancel the request during the execution, or get periodic feedback about how the request is progressing. You cannot do this with services. Furthermore, `actionlib` creates messages (not services), and it also creates topics, so we can still send the goals through a topic without taking care of the feedback and the result, if we do not want to.

The following code is a simple example for sending a goal to move the robot. Create a new file in the `chapter6_tutorials/src` folder, and add the following code in a file with the name `sendGoals.cpp`:

```cpp
#include <ros/ros.h>
#include <move_base_msgs/MoveBaseAction.h>
#include <actionlib/client/simple_action_client.h>
#include <tf/transform_broadcaster.h>
#include <sstream>

typedefactionlib::SimpleActionClient<move_base_msgs::
MoveBaseAction>MoveBaseClient;

int main(int argc, char** argv){
  ros::init(argc, argv, "navigation_goals");

  MoveBaseClientac("move_base", true);

  while(!ac.waitForServer(ros::Duration(5.0))){
    ROS_INFO("Waiting for the move_base action server");
  }

  move_base_msgs::MoveBaseGoal goal;

  goal.target_pose.header.frame_id = "map";
  goal.target_pose.header.stamp = ros::Time::now();

  goal.target_pose.pose.position.x = 1.0;
  goal.target_pose.pose.position.y = 1.0;
  goal.target_pose.pose.orientation.w = 1.0;

  ROS_INFO("Sending goal");
  ac.sendGoal(goal);

  ac.waitForResult();
```

```
if(ac.getState() == actionlib::SimpleClientGoalState::SUCCEEDED)
ROS_INFO("You have arrived to the goal position");
else{
  ROS_INFO("The base failed for some reason");
}
return 0;
}
```

Add the next file in the `CMakeList.txt` file to generate the executable for our program:

```
add_executable(sendGoalssrc/sendGoals.cpp)
target_link_libraries(sendGoals ${catkin_LIBRARIES})
```

Now compile the package with the following command:

```
$ catkin_make
```

Now launch everything to test the new program. Use the following commands to launch all the nodes and the configurations:

```
$ roslaunch chapter6_tutorials chapter6_configuration_gazebo.launch
```

```
$ roslaunch chapter6_tutorials move_base.launch
```

Once you have configured the 2D pose estimate, run the `sendGoal` node with the next command in a new shell:

```
$ rosrun chapter6_tutorials sendGoals
```

If you go to the `rviz` screen, you will see a new global plan (green line) over the map. This means that the navigation stack has accepted the new goal and it will start to execute it.

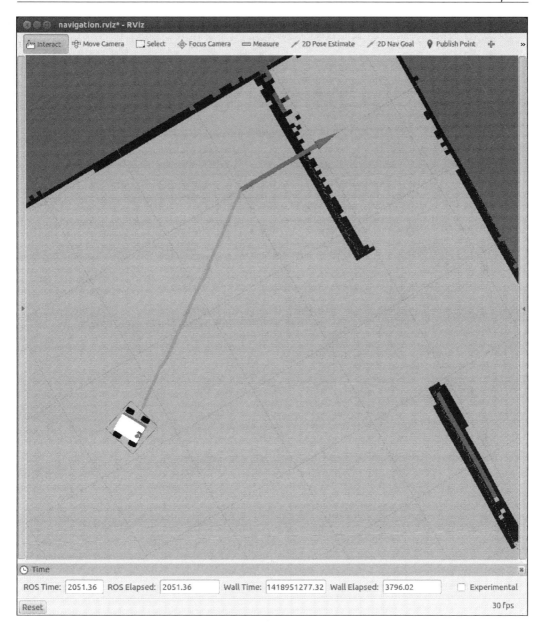

When the robot arrives at the goal, you will see the following message in the shell where you ran the node:

```
[ INFO ] [...,...]: You have arrived to the goal position
```

You can make a list of goals or waypoints, and create a route for the robot. This way you can program missions, guardian robots, or collect things from other rooms with your robot.

Summary

At the end of this chapter, you should have a robot-simulated or real-moving autonomously through the map (which models the environment), using the navigation stack. You can program the control and the localization of the robot by following the ROS philosophy of code reusability, so that you can have the robot completely configured without much effort. The most difficult part of this chapter is to understand all the parameters and learn how to use each one of them appropriately. The correct use of them will determine whether your robot works fine or not; for this reason, you must practice changing the parameters and look for the reaction of the robot.

In the next chapter, you will learn how to use MoveIt! with some tutorials and examples. If you don't know what MoveIt! is, it is a software for building mobile manipulation applications. With it, you can move your articulated robot in an easy way.

7
Manipulation with MoveIt!

MoveIt! is a set of tools for mobile manipulation in ROS. The main web page (`http://moveit.ros.org`) contains documentation, tutorials, and installation instructions as well as example demonstrations with several robotic arms (or robots) that use MoveIt! for manipulation tasks, such as grasping, picking and placing, or simple motion planning with inverse kinematics.

The library incorporates a fast inverse kinematics solver (as part of the motion planning primitives), state-of-the-art algorithms for manipulation, grasping 3D perception (usually in the form of point clouds), kinematics, control, and navigation. Apart from the backend, it provides an easy-to-use GUI to configure new robotic arms with the MoveIt! and **RViz** plugins to develop motion planning tasks in an intuitive way.

In this chapter, we will see how we can create a simple robotic arm in the URDF format and how we can define motion planning groups with the MoveIt! configuration tool. For a single arm, we will have a single group, so that later we can use the inverse kinematics solvers to perform manipulation tasks specified from the RViz interface. A pick and place task is used to illustrate the capabilities and tools of MoveIt!.

The first section explains the MoveIt! architecture, explaining the basic concepts used in the framework, such as joint groups and planning scene, and general concepts such as trajectory planning, (inverse) kinematics, and collision checking concerns. Then, we will show how you can integrate an arm into MoveIt!, creating the planning groups and scene. Next, we will show you how you can perform motion planning with collisions and how you can incorporate point clouds, which will allow you to avoid collisions with dynamic obstacles.

Finally, perception and object recognition tools will be explained and later used in a pick and place demonstration. For this demonstration, we will use the MoveIt! plugin for RViz.

The MoveIt! architecture

The architecture of MoveIt! is depicted in the following diagram taken from the concepts sections of its official documentation at `http://moveit.ros.org/documentation/concepts/`. Here, we describe the main concepts in brief.
In order to install MoveIt!, you only have to run this command:

```
$ sudo apt-get install ros-kinetic-moveit-full
```

Alternatively, you can install all the dependencies of the code that comes with this chapter by running the following command from a workspace that contains it:

```
$ rosdep install --from-paths src -iy
```

The following diagram shows the architecture of MoveIt!:

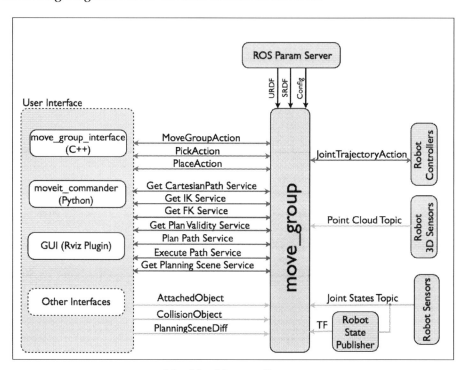

MoveIt! architecture diagram

In the center of the architecture, we have the `move_group` element. The main idea is that we have to define groups of joints and other elements to perform moving actions using motion planning algorithms. These algorithms consider a scene with objects to interact with and the joints characteristics of the group.

A group is defined using standard ROS tools and definition languages, such as YAML, URDF, and SDF. In brief, we have to define the joints that are part of a group with their joint limits. Similarly, we define the end effector tools, such as a gripper and perception sensors. The robot must expose `JointTrajectoryAction` controllers so that the output of the motion planning can be planned and executed on the robot hardware (or simulator). In order to monitor the execution, `/joint_states` is also needed by means of the robot state publisher. All this is provided by the ROS control as well as specific sensor drivers. Note that MoveIt! provides a GUI wizard to define the joint groups for a given robot that can be called directly as follows:

```
$ roslaunch moveit_setup_assistant setup_assistant.launch
```

Once `move_group` is configured properly, we can interface with it. MoveIt! provides a C++ and a Python API to do so, as well as an RViz plugin that integrates seamlessly and allows us to send motion goals, plan them, and send (execute) them on the robot, as shown in the following figure:

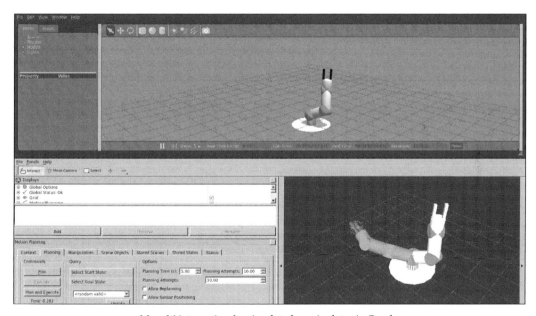

MoveIt! integration for simulated manipulator in Gazebo

Motion planning

Motion planning deals with the problem of moving the arm to a configuration, allowing you to reach a pose with the end effector without crashing the move group with any obstacle, that is, the links themselves or other objects perceived by sensors (usually as point clouds) or violating the joint limits. The MoveIt! user interface allows you to use different libraries for motion planning, such as OMPL (`http://ompl.kavrakilab.org`), using ROS actions, or services.

A motion plan request is sent to the motion planning module, which takes care of avoiding collisions (including self-collisions) and finds a trajectory for all the joints in the groups that move the arm so that it reaches the goal requested. Such a goal consists of a location in joint space or an end effector pose, which could include an object (for example, if the gripper picks up something) as well as kinematic constraints, such as position, orientation, visibility and user-specified constraints.

The result of the motion plan is a trajectory that moves the arm to the target goal location. This trajectory also avoids collisions and satisfies the velocity and acceleration constraints at the joint level.

Finally, MoveIt! has a motion planning pipeline made of motion planners and plan request adapters. The latter are components that allow the pre-processing and post-processing of the motion plan request. For example, pre-processing is useful when the initial state of the arm is outside joint limits; post-processing is useful to convert paths into time-parameterized trajectories.

The planning scene

The planning scene represents the world around the robot as well as the robot state. This is maintained by the planning scene monitor shown in the next diagram, taken from the concepts section of its official documentation at `http://moveit.ros.org/documentation/concepts/`. It is a subpart of `move_group`, which listens to `joint_states`, the sensor information (usually point clouds), and the world geometry, which is provided by the user input on the `planning_scene` topic.

This is shown in the following figure:

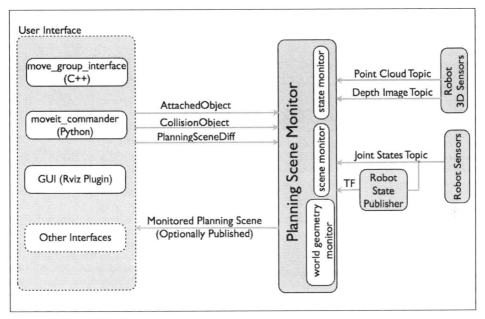

Movelt! planning scene diagram

World geometry monitor

As the name suggests, the world geometry monitor takes care of keeping track of the different aspects of what we consider to be the world. It uses an occupancy map monitor to build a 3D representation of the environment around the robot and augments it with the `plannin_scene` topic information, such as objects (for example, grasping objects); an octomap is used to register all this information. In order to generate the 3D representation, Movelt! supports different sensors to perceive the environment by means of plugins supplying two kinds of inputs: point clouds and depth images.

Kinematics

Forward kinematics and its Jacobians are integrated in the `RobotState` class. On the other hand, for inverse kinematics, Movelt! provides a default plugin that uses a numerical Jacobian-based solver that is automatically configured by the Setup Assistant. As with other components of Movelt!, users can write their own inverse kinematics plugins, such as **IKFast**.

Collision checking

The `CollisionWorld` object of the planning scene is used to configure collision checking using the **Flexible Collision Library** (**FCL**) package. The collision objects supported are meshes, primitive shapes (for example, boxes, cylinders, cones, spheres, and planes) and an octomap.

Integrating an arm in MoveIt!

In this section, we will go through the different steps required to get a robotic arm working with MoveIt! There are several elements that need to be provided beforehand, such as the arm description file (URDF), as well as the components required to make it work in Gazebo, although some of these will be covered in this chapter.

What's in the box?

In order to make it easier to understand how we can integrate a robotic arm with MoveIt!, we have provided a set of packages containing all of the necessary configurations, robot descriptions, launch scripts, and modules to integrate MoveIt! with ROS, Gazebo, and RViz. We will not cover the details of how to integrate a robot with Gazebo as that has been covered in other chapters, but an explanation on how to integrate MoveIt! with Gazebo will be provided. The following packages are provided in the repository for this chapter, in the `chapter7_tutorials` directory:

- `chapter7_tutorials`: This repository acts as a container for the rest of the packages that will be used in this chapter. This sort of structure usually requires a metapackage to let catkin know that the packages are loosely related; hence, this package is the metapackage of the repository.

- `rosbook_arm_bringup`: This package centralizes the launching of the controllers and MoveIt!. It brings up the robot—either the real one or in simulation.

- `rosbook_arm_controller_configuration`: This package contains the launch files to load the controllers required to move the arm. These are trajectory (`JointTrajectoryController`) controllers used to support the MoveIt! motion planning.

- `rosbook_arm_controller_configuration_gazebo`: This package contains the configuration for the joint trajectory controllers. This configuration also includes the PID values required to control the arm in Gazebo.

- `rosbook_arm_description`: This package contains all of the required elements to describe the robotic arm, including URDF files (actually Xacro), meshes, and configuration files.

- `rosbook_arm_gazebo`: This package is one of the most important packages, containing the launch files for Gazebo (which will take care of launching the simulation environment as well as MoveIt!) and the controllers, as well as taking care of running the launch files required (mainly calling the launch file in `rosbook_arm_bringup` but also all the previous packages). It also contains the world's descriptions in order to include objects to interact with.

- `rosbook_arm_hardware_gazebo`: This package uses the ROS Control plugin used to simulate the joints in Gazebo. This package uses the robot description to register the different joints and actuators, in order to be able to control their position. This package is completely independent of MoveIt!, but it is required for the integration with Gazebo.

- `rosbook_arm_moveit_config`: This package is generated through the MoveIt! Setup Assistant. This contains most of the launch files required for both MoveIt! and the RViz plugins as well as several configuration files for MoveIt!.

- `rosbook_arm_snippets`: Except for the pick and place example, this package contains all of the snippets used throughout the chapter.

- `rosbook_arm_pick_and_place`: This package is the biggest and most complex example in the book, containing a demonstration of how you can perform object picking and placing with MoveIt!.

Generating a MoveIt! package with the Setup Assistant

MoveIt! provides a user-friendly graphical interface for the purpose of integrating a new robotics arm into it. The **Setup Assistant** takes care of generating all of the configuration files and launch scripts based on the information provided by the user. In general, it is the easiest way to start using MoveIt! as it also generates several demonstration launch scripts, which can be used to run the system without a physical arm or simulation in place.

In order to launch the Setup Assistant, the following command needs to be executed in a terminal:

```
$ roslaunch moveit_setup_assistant setup_assistant.launch
```

Initial screen of MoveIt! setup assistant

Once the command has been executed, a window similar to the one shown above should appear; in this particular case, the goal is to generate a new configuration, so that's the button we should aim for. Once the button has been pressed, the assistant will request a URDF or COLLADA model of the robotic arm, which for our example arm can be found at `rosbook_arm_description/robots/rosbook_arm_base.urdf.xacro` inside the repository package.

Please note that the robot description provided is in the **XML Macros (Xacro)** format, which makes it easier to generate complex URDF files. Once the robot description has been loaded, the reader needs to go through each tab and add the required information. The first tab, as seen in following figure, is used to generate the self-collision matrix.

Fortunately for the user, this process is performed automatically by simply setting the sampling density (or using the default value), and clicking on the **Regenerate Default Collision Matrix** button. The collision matrix contains information about how and when links collide in order to improve the performance of the motion planner. The figure below shows this in detail:

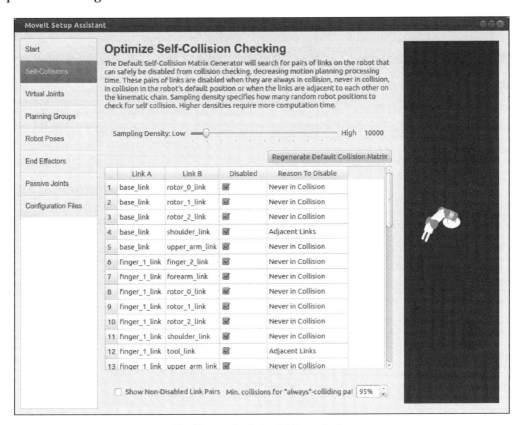

Self-collision tab of MoveIt! Setup Assistant

The second tab, as seen in the following figure, is used to assign virtual joints to the robot. A virtual joint is used to attach the robotic arm to the world as the pose of a robot can vary with respect to it, but in this particular case we won't need a virtual joint because the base of the arm does not move. We need virtual joints when the manipulator is not fixed in one place. For example, if the arm is on top of a mobile platform, we need a virtual joint for the odometry since `base_link` (base frame) moves with respect to the `odom` frame.

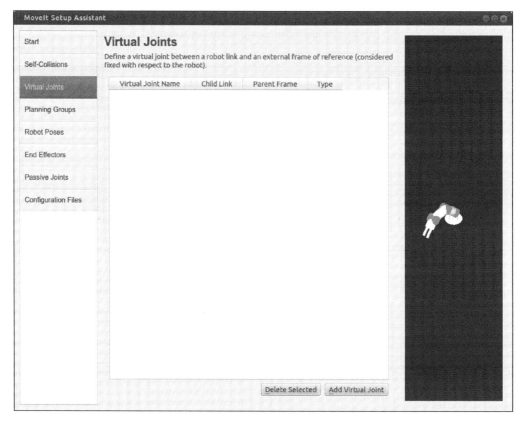

Virtual joints tab of MoveIt! Setup Assistant

In the third tab, which can be seen in the following figure, we need to define the planning groups of the robotic arm. Planning groups, as the name suggests, are sets of joints that need to be planned as a group in order to achieve a given goal on a specific link or end effector. In this particular case, we need to define two planning groups: one for the arm itself and another for the gripper. The planning will then be performed separately for the arm positioning and the gripper action.

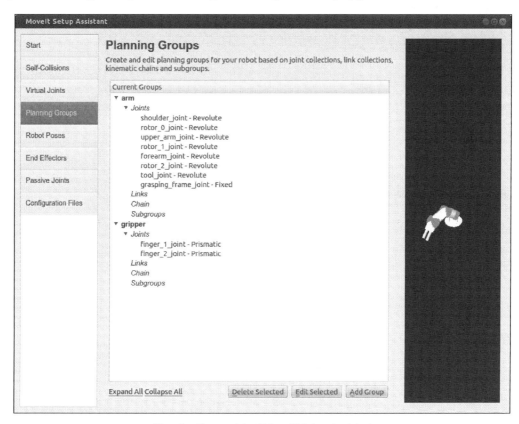

Planning Groups tab of MoveIt! Setup Assistant

The fourth tab, as shown in the next screenshot, gives us the ability to define known robot poses in order to be able to reference them later; these predefined poses are also referred to as group states. As we can see, we have set up two different poses: the home position, which corresponds to the *stored* position of the arm, and the grasping position, which, as the name suggests, should allow the robot to grasp elements in the scene. Setting known poses can have multiple benefits in a real-life situation; for example, it is common to have an initial position from which planning happens, a position where the arm is safe to be stored in a container, or even a set of known positions with which to compare the position accuracy over time.

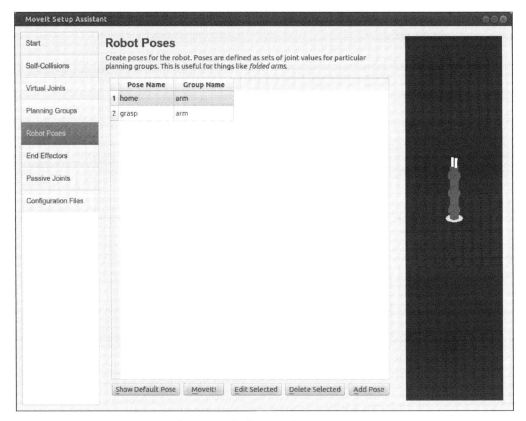

Robot Poses tab of MoveIt! Setup Assistant

The fifth tab is used to define the robotic arm's, can be seen in the following figure. As we discussed earlier, the robotic arm usually has an end effector, which is used to perform an action, such as a gripper or some other tool. In our case, the end effector is a gripper, which allows us to pick objects from the scene. In this tab, we need to define the gripper's end effector by assigning it a name, a planning group, and the parent link containing the end effector.

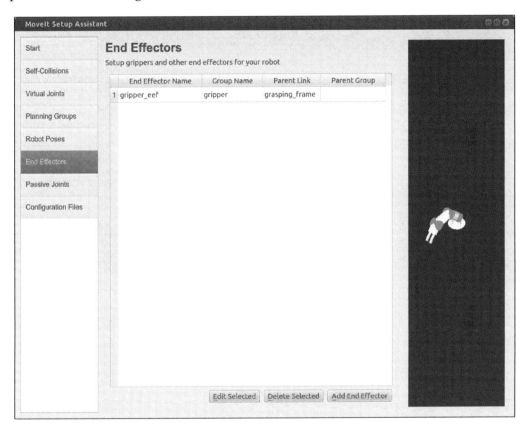

End Effectors tab of MoveIt! Setup Assistant

The sixth tab, shown in the following screenshot, is an optional configuration step, which allows us to define joints that cannot be actuated. An important feature of these joints is that MoveIt! doesn't need to plan for them and our modules don't need to publish information about them. An example of a passive joint in a robot could be a caster, but in this case, we'll skip this step as all of our passive joints have been defined as fixed joints, which will eventually produce the same effect on motion planning.

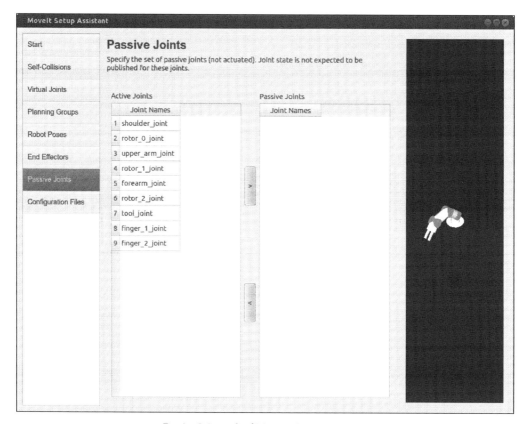

Passive Joints tab of MoveIt! Setup Assistant

Finally, as seen in the following diagram, the last step in the Setup Assistant is generating the configuration files. The only thing required in this step is to provide the path of the configuration package, which will be created by MoveIt!, and which will contain most of the launch and configuration files required to properly start controlling our robotic arm from MoveIt!

Generate Configuration Files tab of MoveIt! Setup Assistant

It is important to take into account that the configuration generated by the Setup Assistant has already been provided in the repository and that even though it is recommended that you go through the process, the result can be discarded in favor of the provided package, which is already being referenced by the rest of the launch scripts and configuration files in the repository.

Integration into RViz

MoveIt! provides a very useful and complete RViz plugin that gives the user the ability to perform several actions, such as plan different goals, add and remove objects to the scene, and so on. The Setup Assistant usually creates a number of launch files, among which there is one called `demo`, which takes care of launching MoveIt! as well as the fake controllers, RViz, and the plugin. In order to start the demonstration, run the following command:

```
$ roslaunch rosbook_arm_moveit_config demo.launch
```

Once RViz launches, a motion planning panel should appear as well as the visualization of the robotic arm. The important tabs we need to consider are the **Planning** tab and the **Scene objects** tab. In the **Planning** tab, the user will be able to plan different goal positions, execute them, and set some of the common planning options. In the latter, objects can be inserted and removed from the planning scene.

The following figure shows the **Planning** tab as well as a visualization of the robotic arm in both white and orange. The former is the current state of the arm, and the latter is the goal position defined by the user. In this particular case, the goal position has been generated using the tools in the **Query** panel. Once the user is happy with the goal state, the next step can be to either plan to visualize how the arm is going to move or plan to execute it to not only visualize the movement but also move the arm itself.

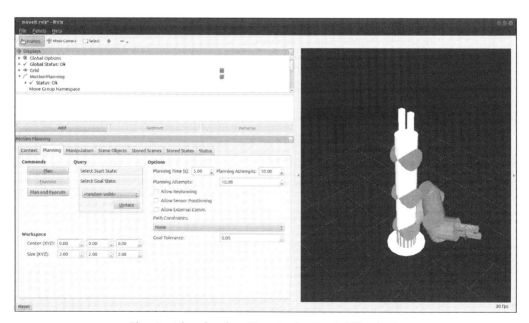

Planning tab and goal position visualization in RViz plugin

Other options, such as the planning time or the number of planning attempts, can be tweaked in order to account for complex goals, but for most of the cases in the demonstration, changing these parameters won't be required. Another important parameter is the goal tolerance, which defines how close to the goal position we require the robotic arm to be in order to consider the position as having been achieved.

Planning random goals might be of some interest, but another level of planning is provided by the RViz plugin. As illustrated in the following figure, the robotic arm visualization has a marker on the end effector. This marker allows us to position the end effector of the arm as well as rotate it on each axis. You can now make use of this marker to position the arm towards more interesting configurations.

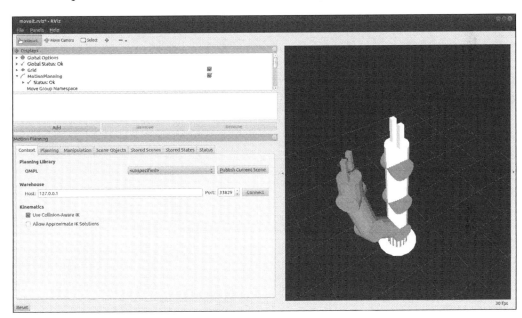

Using markers to set the goal position in RViz plugin

In many cases, planning by positioning the marker might produce no movement at all and show the robotic arm in the same position, but the marker and the end effector might be in other positions. An example of this behavior can be seen in the following figure, and it usually happens when the desired position is out of the range of motion of the robotic arm (when there are not enough degrees of freedom, too many constraints, and so on).

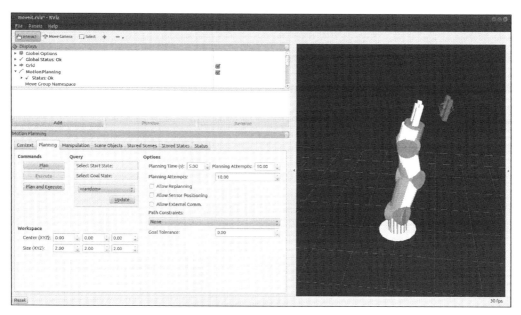

Markers out of bounds in RViz plugin

Similarly, when the arm is positioned in a state in which it collides with elements in the scene or with itself, the arm will show the collision zone in red. Finally, the following screenshot shows the different options provided by the MoveIt! plugin's visualization:

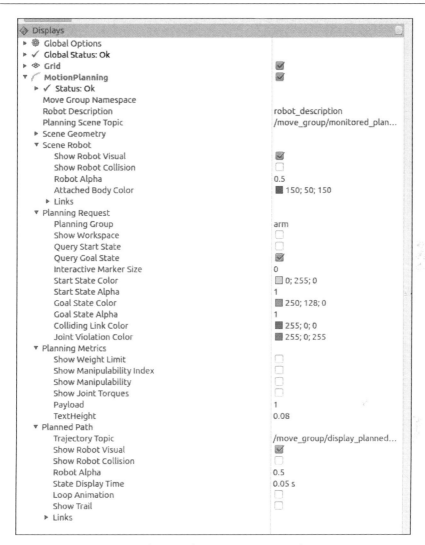

Motion planning plugin options in RViz plugin

As the names suggest, all of these options are meant to provide a way to tweak the visualization as well as add more information to it. Other interesting options that the user might want to modify are **Trajectory Topic**, which is the topic on which the visualization trajectory is published, and **Query Start State**, which will also show the state from which the arm is about to execute the plan. In most cases, the start state is usually the current state of the arm, but having a visualization cue can help spot issues in our algorithms.

Integration into Gazebo or a real robotic arm

The MoveIt! integration into Gazebo is a relatively straightforward process, which can be divided into two different steps: first of all, we need to provide all of the sensors required by MoveIt!, such as the RGB-D sensor, so that motion planning can take the environment into account, and secondly, we also need to provide a controller as well as the current joint states periodically.

When a sensor is created in Gazebo, it interacts with the system as a normal sensor would, by simply producing the required data. This data is then used by MoveIt! in exactly the same way that data produced by a real sensor would in order to generate collision artifacts in the planning scene. The process of making MoveIt! aware of those sensors will be explained later in this chapter.

As regards the manipulator's (arm and gripper) definition, a URDF description is provided using Xacro files as with any robot in ROS. In MoveIt!, we need to configure the controllers for the manipulator joints as `JointTrajectoryController` because the motion plans provide the output with messages for that type of controller. For the manipulator used in this chapter, we need two controllers of this type: one for the arm and another for the gripper. The controller configuration is organized in the `rosbook_arm_controller_configuration` and `rosbook_arm_controller_configuration_gazebo` packages with the `launch` and `config` YAML files, respectively.

This type of controller is provided by the ROS control. Consequently, we need a `RobotHardware` interface for our arm to actually move in Gazebo or in the real hardware. The implementation for Gazebo and the real arm is different, and here we only provide the first. The `rosbook_arm_hardware_gazebo` package has the C++ implementation of `RobotHardware` for the manipulator used in this chapter. This is done by implementing the interface, so we create a new class that inherits from it. Then, the joints are properly handled by writing the desired target positions (using position control) and reading the actual ones, along with the effort and velocity for each joint. For the sake of simplicity, we omit the explanation of the details of this implementation, which is not needed to understand MoveIt! However, if the number manipulator is drastically changed, the implementation must be changed although it is generic enough to detect the number of joints automatically from the robot description.

Simple motion planning

The RViz plugin provides a very interesting mechanism to interact with MoveIt! but it could be considered quite limited or even cumbersome due to the lack of automation. In order to fully make use of the capabilities included in MoveIt!, several APIs have been developed, which allow us to perform a range of operations over it, such as motion planning, accessing the model of our robot, and modifying the planning scene.

In the following section, we will cover a few examples on how to perform different sorts of simple motion planning. We will start by planning a single goal, continue with planning a random target, proceed with planning a predefined group state, and finally, explain how to improve the interaction of our snippets with RViz.

In order to simplify the explanations, a set of launch files have been provided to launch everything required. The most important one takes care of launching Gazebo, MoveIt!, and the arm controllers:

```
$ roslaunch rosbook_arm_gazebo rosbook_arm_empty_world.launch
```

Another interesting launch file has been provided by the Setup Assistant, which launches RViz and the motion planning plugin. This particular one is optional, but it is useful to have, as RViz will be used further in this section:

```
$ roslaunch rosbook_arm_moveit_config moveit_rviz.launch config:=true
```

A number of snippets have also been provided, which cover everything explained in this section. The snippets can be found in the `rosbook_arm_snippets` package. The snippets package doesn't contain anything other than code, and launching the snippets will be done by calling `rosrun` instead of the usual `roslaunch`.

Every snippet of code in this section follows the same pattern, starting with the typical ROS initialization, which won't be covered here. After the initialization, we need to define the planning group on which motion planning is going to be performed. In our case, we only have two planning groups, the arm and the gripper, but in this case, we only care about the arm. This will instantiate a planning group interface, which will take care of the interaction with MoveIt!:

```
moveit::planning_interface::MoveGroupplan_group("arm");
```

After the instantiation of the planning group interface, there is usually some code dedicated to deciding on the goal that will be specific to each of the types of goals covered in this section. After the goal has been decided, it needs to be conveyed to MoveIt! so that it gets executed. The following snippet of code takes care of creating a plan and using the planning group interface to request MoveIt! to perform motion planning and, if successful, also execute it:

```
moveit::planning_interface::MoveGroup::Plan goal_plan;
if (plan_group.plan(goal_plan))
{
   .plan_group.move();
}
```

Planning a single goal

To plan a single goal, we literally only need to provide MoveIt! with the goal itself. A goal is expressed by a `Pose` message from the `geometry_msgs` package. We need to specify both the orientation and the pose. For this particular example, this goal was obtained by performing manual planning and checking the state of the arm. In a real situation, goals will probably be set depending on the purpose of the robotic arm:

```
geometry_msgs::Pose goal;
goal.orientation.x = -0.000764819;
goal.orientation.y = 0.0366097;
goal.orientation.z = 0.00918912;
goal.orientation.w = 0.999287;
goal.position.x = 0.775884;
goal.position.y = 0.43172;
goal.position.z = 2.71809;
```

For this particular goal, we can also set the tolerance. We are aware that our PID is not incredibly accurate, which could lead to MoveIt! believing that the goal hasn't been achieved. Changing the goal tolerance makes the system achieve the waypoints with a higher margin of error in order to account for inaccuracies in the control:

```
plan_group.setGoalTolerance(0.2);
```

Finally, we just need to set the planning group target pose, which will then be planned and executed by the snippet of code shown at the beginning of this section:

```
plan_group.setPoseTarget(goal);
```

We can run this snippet of code with the following command; the arm should position itself without any issues:

```
$ rosrun rosbook_arm_snippets move_group_plan_single_target
```

Planning a random target

Planning a random target can be effectively performed in two steps: first of all, we need to create the random target itself and then check its validity. If the validity is confirmed, then we can proceed by requesting the goal as usual; otherwise, we will cancel (although we could retry until we find a valid random target). In order to verify the validity of the target, we need to perform a service call to a service provided by MoveIt! for this specific purpose. As usual, to perform a service call, we need a service client:

```
ros::ServiceClientvalidity_srv =
nh.serviceClient<moveit_msgs::GetStateValidity>("/check_state_vali
dity");
```

Once the service client is set up, we need to create the random target. To do so, we need to create a robot state object containing the random positions, but to simplify the process, we can start by acquiring the current robot state object:

```
robot_state::RobotStatecurrent_state =
*plan_group.getCurrentState();
```

We will then set the current robot state object to random positions, but to do so, we need to provide the joint model group for this robot state. The joint model group can be obtained using the already created robot state object as follows:

```
current_state.setToRandomPositions(current_state.getJointModelGrou
p("arm"));
```

Up to this point, we have a service client waiting to be used as well as a random robot state object, which we want to validate. We will create a pair of messages: one for the request and another for the response. Fill in the request message with the random robot state using one of the API conversion functions, and request the service call:

```
moveit_msgs::GetStateValidity::Request validity_request;
moveit_msgs::GetStateValidity::Response validity_response;

robot_state::robotStateToRobotStateMsg(current_state,
validity_request.robot_state);
validity_request.group_name = "arm";

validity_srv.call(validity_request, validity_response);
```

Once the service call is complete, we can check the response message. If the state appears to be invalid, we would simply stop running the module; otherwise, we will continue. As explained earlier, at this point, we could retry until we get a valid random state; this can be an easy exercise for the reader:

```
if (!validity_response.valid)
{
  ROS_INFO("Random state is not valid");
  ros::shutdown();
  return 1;
}
```

Finally, we will set the robot state we just created as the goal using the planning group interface, which will then be planned and executed as usual by MoveIt!:

```
plan_group.setJointValueTarget(current_state);
```

We can run this snippet of code with the following command, which should lead to the arm repositioning itself on a random configuration:

```
$ rosrun rosbook_arm_snippets move_group_plan_random_target
```

Planning a predefined group state

As we commented during the configuration generation step, when initially integrating our robotic arm, MoveIt! provides the concept of predefined group states, which can later be used to position the robot with a predefined pose. Accessing predefined group states requires creating a robot state object as a target; in order to do so, the best approach is to start by obtaining the current state of the robotic arm from the planning group interface:

```
robot_state::RobotStatecurrent_state =
*plan_group.getCurrentState();
```

Once we have obtained the current state, we can modify it by setting it to the predefined group state, with the following call, which takes the model group that needs to be modified and the name of the predefined group state:

```
current_state.setToDefaultValues(current_state.getJointModelGroup(
"arm"), "home");
```

Finally, we will use the new robot state of the robotic arm as our new goal and let MoveIt! take care of planning and execution as usual:

```
plan_group.setJointValueTarget(current_state);
```

We can run this snippet of code with the following command, which should lead to the arm repositioning itself to achieve the predefined group state:

```
$ rosrun rosbook_arm_snippets move_group_plan_group_state
```

Displaying the target motion

MoveIt! provides a set of messages that can be used to communicate visualization information, essentially providing it with the planned path in order to get a nice visualization of how the arm is going to move to achieve its goal. As usual, communication is performed through a topic, which needs to be advertised:

```
ros::Publisher display_pub =
nh.advertise<moveit_msgs::DisplayTrajectory>("/move_group/display_
planned_path", 1, true);
```

The message we need to publish requires the start state of the trajectory and the trajectory itself. In order to obtain such information, we always need to perform planning using the planning group interface first, and using the created plan, we can proceed to fill in the message:

```
moveit_msgs::DisplayTrajectorydisplay_msg;
display_msg.trajectory_start = goal_plan.start_state_;
display_msg.trajectory.push_back(goal_plan.trajectory_);
display_pub.publish(display_msg);
```

Once the message has been filled in, publishing it to the correct topic will cause the RViz visualization to show the trajectory that the arm is about to perform. It is important to take into account that, when performing a call to plan, it will also show the same type of visualization, so you shouldn't be confused if the trajectory is displayed twice.

Motion planning with collisions

It might be interesting for the reader to know that MoveIt! provides motion planning with collisions out of the box, so in this section we will cover how you can add elements to the planning scene that could potentially collide with our robotic arm. First, we will start by explaining how to add basic objects to the planning scene, which is quite interesting as it allows us to perform planning even if a real object doesn't exist in our scene. For completion, we will also explain how to remove those objects from the scene. Finally, we will explain how to add an RGBD sensor feed, which will produce point clouds based on real-life (or simulated) objects, thus making our motion planning much more interesting and realistic.

Adding objects to the planning scene

To start adding an object, we need to have a planning scene; this is only possible when MoveIt! is running, so the first step is to start Gazebo, MoveIt!, the controllers, and RViz. Since the planning scene only exists in MoveIt!, RViz is required to be able to visualize objects contained in it. In order to launch all of the required modules, we need to run the following commands:

```
$ roslaunch rosbook_arm_gazebo rosbook_arm_empty_world.launch
$ roslaunch rosbook_arm_moveit_config moveit_rviz.launch config:=true
```

The snippet of code then starts by instantiating the planning scene interface object, which can be used to perform actions on the planning scene itself:

```
moveit::planning_interface::PlanningSceneInterfacecurrent_scene;
```

The next step is to create the collision object message that we want to send through the planning scene interface. The first thing we need to provide for the collision object is a name, which will uniquely identify this object and will allow us to perform actions on it, such as removing it from the scene once we're done with it:

```
moveit_msgs::CollisionObject box;

box.id = "rosbook_box";
```

The next step is to provide the properties of the object itself. This is done through a solid primitive message, which specifies the type of object we are creating, and depending on the type of object, it also specifies its properties. In our case, we are simply creating a box, which essentially has three dimensions:

```
shape_msgs::SolidPrimitive primitive;
primitive.type = primitive.BOX;
primitive.dimensions.resize(3);
primitive.dimensions[0] = 0.2;
primitive.dimensions[1] = 0.2;
primitive.dimensions[2] = 0.2;
```

To continue, we need to provide the pose of the box in the planning scene. Since we want to produce a possible collision scenario, we have placed the box close to our robotic arm. The pose itself is specified with a pose message from the standard geometry messages package:

```
geometry_msgs::Pose pose;
pose.orientation.w = 1.0;
pose.position.x = 0.7;
pose.position.y = -0.5;
pose.position.z = 1.0;
```

We then add the primitive and the pose to the message and specify that the operation we want to perform is to add it to the planning scene:

```
box.primitives.push_back(primitive);
box.primitive_poses.push_back(pose);
box.operation = box.ADD;
```

Finally, we add the collision object to a vector of collision object messages and call the `addCollisionObjects` method from the planning scene interface. This will take care of sending the required messages through the appropriate topics, in order to ensure that the object is created in the current planning scene:

```
std::vector<moveit_msgs::CollisionObject>collision_objects;
collision_objects.push_back(box);

current_scene.addCollisionObjects(collision_objects);
```

We can test this snippet by running the following command in a terminal, as said earlier. Since the object is added to the planning scene, it is important to have the RViz visualization running; otherwise, the reader won't be able to see the object:

```
$ rosrun rosbook_arm_snippets move_group_add_object
```

The result can be seen in the following figure as a simple, green, squared box in between the arm's goal and the current position of the arm:

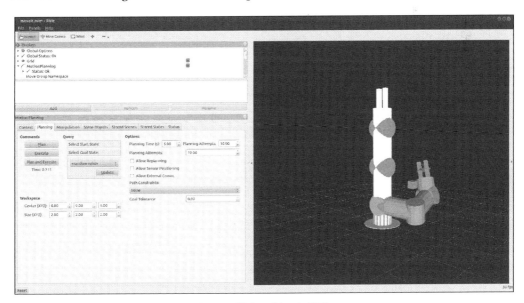

Scene collision object in RViz

Removing objects from the planning scene

Removing the added object from the planning scene is a very simple process. Following the same initialization as in the previous example, we only need to create a string vector containing the IDs of the objects we want to remove and call the removeCollisionObjects function from the planning scene interface:

```
std::vector<std::string>object_ids;
object_ids.push_back("rosbook_box");
current_scene.removeCollisionObjects(object_ids);
```

We can test this snippet by running the following command, which will remove the object created with the previous snippet from the planning scene:

```
$ rosrun rosbook_arm_snippets move_group_remove_object
```

Alternatively, we can also use the **Scene objects** tab in the RViz plugin to remove any objects from the scene.

Motion planning with point clouds

Motion planning with point clouds is much simpler than it would appear to be. The main thing to take into account is that we need to provide a point cloud feed as well as tell MoveIt! to take this into account when performing planning. The Gazebo simulation we have set up for this chapter already contains an RGBD sensor, which publishes a point cloud for us. To start with this example, let's launch the following commands:

```
$ roslaunch rosbook_arm_gazebo rosbook_arm_grasping_world.launch
$ roslaunch rosbook_arm_moveit_config moveit_rviz.launch config:=true
```

The user might have noticed that the Gazebo simulation now appears to include several objects in the world. Those objects are scanned by an RGBD sensor, and the resulting point cloud is published to the /rgbd_camera/depth/points topic. What we need to do in this case is tell MoveIt! where to get the information from and what the format of that information is. The first file we need to modify is the following one:

```
rosbook_arm_moveit_conifg/config/sensors_rgbd.yaml
```

This file will be used to store the information of the RGBD sensor. In this file, we need to tell MoveIt! which plugin it needs to use to manage the point cloud as well as some other parameters specific to the sensor plugin itself. In this particular case, the plugin to use is **Octomap Updater**, which will generate an octomap with the point cloud provided, downsample it, and publish the resulting cloud. With this first step we have set up a plugin which will provide MoveIt! with enough information to plan, while also taking into account possible collisions with the point cloud:

```
sensors:
- sensor_plugin: occupancy_map_monitor/PointCloudOctomapUpdater
  point_cloud_topic: /rgbd_camera/depth/points
  max_range: 10
  padding_offset: 0.01
  padding_scale: 1.0
  point_subsample: 1
  filtered_cloud_topic: output_cloud
```

As you might have suspected, the file itself is nothing more than a configuration file. The next step we need to perform is to load this configuration file into the environment so that MoveIt! is aware of the new sensor we have added. In order to do so, we will need to modify the following XML file:

```
$ rosbook_arm_moveit_config/launch/ rosbook_arm_moveit_sensor_manager.
launch.xml
```

In this XML file, we can potentially specify a few parameters that will be used by the sensor plugin, such as the cloud resolution and the frame of reference. It is important to take into account that some of these parameters might be redundant and can be omitted. Finally, we need to add a command to load the configuration file into the environment:

```
<launch>
  <rosparam command="load" file="$(find
  rosbook_arm_moveit_config)/config/sensors_rgbd.yaml" />
</launch>
```

The result of running the commands specified in the beginning with the new changes we have added can be seen in the following screenshot. In this particular case, we can see both the Gazebo simulation and the RViz visualization. The RViz simulation contains a point cloud, and we have already performed some manual motion planning, which successfully took the point cloud into account to avoid any collisions:

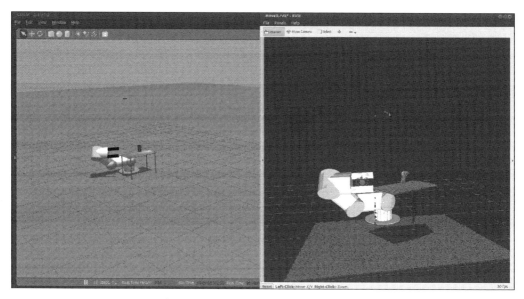

Gazebo simulation (left), point cloud in RViz (right)

The pick and place task

In this section, we are going to explain how to perform a very common application or task with a manipulator robot. A pick and place task consists of picking up a target object, which includes grasping it, and placing it somewhere else. Here, we assume that the object is initially on top of a supporting surface that is flat or planar, such as a table, but it is easy to generalize it to more complex environments. As regards the object to grasp, we will consider a cylinder that is approximated by a box, because the gripper we are going to use to grasp is very simple; for more complex objects, you will need a better gripper or even a hand.

In the further sections, we will start by describing how to set up the planning scene that MoveIt! needs in order to identify the objects that are there, apart from the arm itself. These objects are considered during motion planning to avoid obstacles, and they can also be targets for picking up or grasping. In order to simplify the problem, we will omit the perception part, but we will explain how it can be done and integrated. Once the planning scene is defined, we will describe how to perform the pick and place task using the MoveIt! API. Finally, we will explain how to run this task in demonstration mode using fake controllers so that we do not need the actual robot (either simulated on Gazebo or a real one). We will also show how you can actually see the motion on the simulated arm in Gazebo while it is interacting with the simulated objects in the environment.

The planning scene

The first thing we have to do is define the objects in the environment since MoveIt! needs this information to make the arm interact with an object without colliding with it, and to reference them to do certain actions. Here, we will consider the following scene:

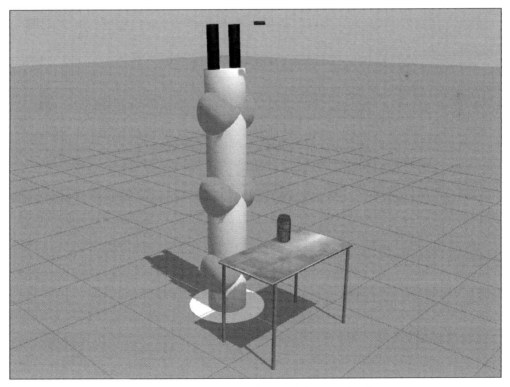

Environment with manipulator and objects in Gazebo

This scene has the arm with the gripper and the **RGB-D** sensor as the robotic manipulator. There is also a table and a can of Coke; the flat support surface and the cylindrical object, respectively. You can run this scene in Gazebo with the following command:

```
$ roslaunch rosbook_arm_gazebo rosbook_arm_grasping_world.launch
```

This scene is just a simple example that models a real use case. However, we still have to tell MoveIt! about the planning scene. At this moment, it only knows about the robotic manipulator. We have to tell it about the table and the can of Coke. This can be done either by using 3D perception algorithms, which take the point cloud of the RGB-D sensor, or programmatically, by specifying the pose and shape of the objects with some basic primitives. We will see how we can define the planning scene following the latter approach.

The code to perform the pick and place task is the `pick_and_place.py` Python program located in the scripts folder of the `rosbook_arm_pick_and_place` package. The important part to create the planning scene is in the `__init__` method of the `CokeCanPickAndPlace` class:

```
self._scene = PlanningSceneInterface()
```

In the following sections, we will add the table and the can of Coke to this planning scene.

The target object to grasp

In this case, the target object to grasp is the can of Coke. It is a cylindrical object that we can approximate as a box, which is one of the basic primitives in the MoveIt! planning scene API:

```
# Retrieve params:
self._grasp_object_name = rospy.get_param('~grasp_object_name',
'coke_can')

# Clean the scene:
self._scene.remove_world_object(self._grasp_object_name)

# Add table and Coke can objects to the planning scene:
self._pose_coke_can = self._add_coke_can(self._grasp_object_name)
```

The objects in the planning scene receive a unique identifier, which is a string. In this case, `coke_can` is the identifier for the can of Coke. We remove it from the scene to avoid having duplicate objects, and then we add to the scene. The `_add_coke_can` method does that by defining the `pose` and `shape` dimensions:

```python
def _add_coke_can(self, name):
    p = PoseStamped()
    p.header.frame_id = self._robot.get_planning_frame()
    p.header.stamp = rospy.Time.now()

    p.pose.position.x = 0.75 - 0.01
    p.pose.position.y = 0.25 - 0.01
    p.pose.position.z = 1.00 + (0.3 + 0.03) / 2.0

    q = quaternion_from_euler(0.0, 0.0, 0.0)
    p.pose.orientation = Quaternion(*q)

    self._scene.add_box(name, p, (0.15, 0.15, 0.3))

    returnp.pose
```

The important part here is the `add_box` method that adds a `box` object to the planning scene we created earlier. The box is given a name, its pose, and dimensions, which in this case are set to match the ones in the Gazebo world shown earlier, with the table and the can of Coke. We also have to set `frame_id` to the planning frame ID and the timestamp to `now`. In order to use the planning frame, we need `RobotCommander`, which is the MoveIt! interface to command the manipulator programmatically:

```python
self._robot = RobotCommander()
```

The support surface

We proceed similarly to create the object for the table, which is also approximated by a box. Therefore, we simply remove any previous object and add the table. In this case, the object name is `table`:

```python
# Retrieve params:
self._table_object_name = rospy.get_param('~table_object_name',
'table')
```

```
# Clean the scene:
self._scene.remove_world_object(self._table_object_name)

# Add table and Coke can objects to the planning scene:
self._pose_table = self._add_table(self._table_object_name)
```

The `_add_table` method adds the table to the planning scene:

```
def _add_table(self, name):
    p = PoseStamped()
    p.header.frame_id = self._robot.get_planning_frame()
    p.header.stamp = rospy.Time.now()

    p.pose.position.x = 1.0
    p.pose.position.y = 0.0
    p.pose.position.z = 1.0

    q = quaternion_from_euler(0.0, 0.0, numpy.deg2rad(90.0))
    p.pose.orientation = Quaternion(*q)

    self._scene.add_box(name, p, (1.5, 0.8, 0.03))

    returnp.pose
```

We can visualize the planning scene objects in RViz running the following commands:

```
$ roslaunch rosbook_arm_gazebo rosbook_arm_grasping_world.launch
$ roslaunch rosbook_arm_moveit_config moveit_rviz.launch config:=true
$ roslaunch rosbook_arm_pick_and_place grasp_generator_server.launch
$ rosrun rosbook_arm_pick_and_place pick_and_place.py
```

This actually runs the whole pick and place task, which we will continue to explain later. Right after starting the `pick_and_place.py` program, you will see the boxes that model the table and the can of Coke in green, matching perfectly with the point cloud seen by the RGB-D sensor, as shown in the following figure:

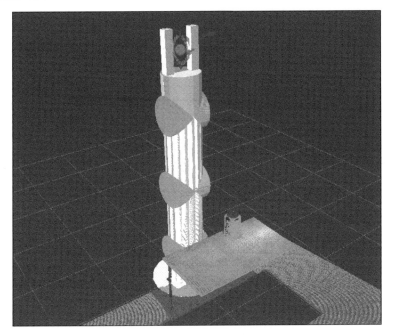

Point cloud seen by the RGB-D sensor of the environment

Perception

Adding the objects manually to the planning scenes can be avoided by perceiving the supporting surface. In this case, the table can be detected as a horizontal plane on the point cloud. Once the table is recognized, it can be subtracted from the original point cloud to obtain the target object, which can be approximated with a cylinder or a box. We will use the same method to add boxes to the planning scene as before, but in this case, the pose and dimensions (and the classification) of the objects will come from the output of the 3D perception and segmentation algorithm used.

This sort of perception and segmentation in the point cloud provided by the RGB-D sensor can be easily done using the concepts and algorithms. However, in some cases the accuracy will not be enough to grasp the object properly. The perception can be helped using fiducial markers placed on the object to grasp, such as **ArUco** (http://www.uco.es/investiga/grupos/ava/node/26) which has the ROS wrapper which can be found at https://github.com/pal-robotics/aruco_ros.

Here, we set the planning scene manually and leave the perception part to you. As we saw, the target object to grasp and the support surface is defined in the code manually, by comparing the correspondence with the point cloud in RViz until we have a good match.

Grasping

Now that we have the target object defined in the scene, we need to generate grasping poses to pick it up. To achieve this aim, we use the grasp generator server from the `moveit_simple_grasps` package, which can be found at `https://github. com/davetcoleman/moveit_simple_grasps`.

Unfortunately, there isn't a debian package available in Ubuntu for ROS Kinetic. Therefore, we need to run the following commands to add the `kinetic-devel` branch to our workspace (inside the `src` folder of the workspace):

```
$ wstool set moveit_simple_grasps --git https://github.com/davetcoleman/
moveit_simple_grasps.git -v kinetic-devel
$ wstool up moveit_simple_grasps
```

We can build this using the following commands:

```
$ cd ..
$ caktin_make
```

Now we can run the grasp generator server as follows (remember to source `devel/ setup.bash`):

```
$ roslaunch rosbook_arm_pick_and_place grasp_generator_server.launch
```

The grasp generator server needs the following grasp data configuration in our case:

```
    base_link: base_link

    gripper:
    end_effector_name: gripper

    # Default grasp params
    joints: [finger_1_joint, finger_2_joint]

    pregrasp_posture: [0.0, 0.0]
    pregrasp_time_from_start: &time_from_start 4.0
```

```
grasp_posture: [1.0, 1.0]
grasp_time_from_start: *time_from_start

postplace_time_from_start: *time_from_start

# Desired pose from end effector to grasp [x, y, z] + [R, P, Y]
grasp_pose_to_eef: [0.0, 0.0, 0.0]
grasp_pose_to_eef_rotation: [0.0, 0.0, 0.0]

end_effector_parent_link: tool_link
```

This defines the gripper we are going to use to grasp objects and the pre- and post-grasp postures, basically.

Now we need an action client to query for the grasp poses. This is done inside the `pick_and_place.py` program, right before we try to pick up the target object. So, we create an action client using the following code:

```
# Create grasp generator 'generate' action client:
self._grasps_ac =
SimpleActionClient('/moveit_simple_grasps_server/generate',
GenerateGraspsAction)
if not self._grasps_ac.wait_for_server(rospy.Duration(5.0)):
    rospy.logerr('Grasp generator action client not available!')
    rospy.signal_shutdown('Grasp generator action client not
    available!')
    return
```

Inside the `_pickup` method, we use the following code to obtain the grasp poses:

```
grasps = self._generate_grasps(self._pose_coke_can, width)
```

Here, the width argument specifies the width of the object to grasp. The `_generate_grasps` method does the following:

```
def _generate_grasps(self, pose, width):
    # Create goal:
    goal = GenerateGraspsGoal()

    goal.pose = pose
    goal.width = width

    # Send goal and wait for result:
    state = self._grasps_ac.send_goal_and_wait(goal)
```

```
if state != GoalStatus.SUCCEEDED:
    rospy.logerr('Grasp goal failed!: %s' %
    self._grasps_ac.get_goal_status_text())
    return None

grasps = self._grasps_ac.get_result().grasps

# Publish grasps (for debugging/visualization purposes):
self._publish_grasps(grasps)

return grasps
```

To summarize, it sends an `actionlib` goal to obtain a set of grasping poses for the target goal pose (usually at the object centroid). In the code provided with the book, there are some options commented upon, but they can be enabled to query only for particular types of grasps, such as some angles, or pointing up or down. The outputs of the function are all the grasping poses that the pickup action will try later. Having multiple grasping poses increases the possibility of a successful grasp.

The grasp poses provided by the grasp generation server are also published as `PoseArray` using the `_publish_grasps` method for visualization and debugging purposes. We can see them on RViz running the whole pick and place task as before:

```
$ roslaunch rosbook_arm_gazebo rosbook_arm_grasping_world.launch
$ roslaunch rosbook_arm_moveit_config moveit_rviz.launch config:=true
$ roslaunch rosbook_arm_pick_and_place grasp_generator_server.launch
$ rosrun rosbook_arm_pick_and_place pick_and_place.py
```

A few seconds after running the `pick_and_place.py` program, we will see multiple arrows on the target object which correspond to the grasp pose that will be tried in order to pick it up. This is shown in the following figure as follows:

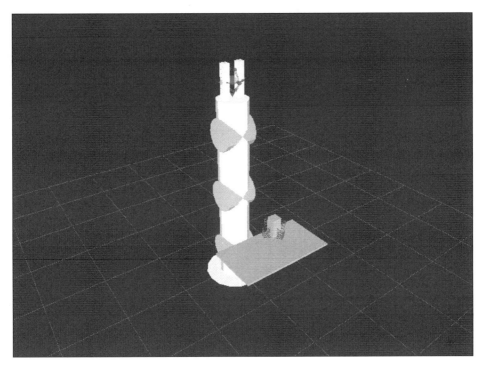

Visualization of grasping poses

The pickup action

Once we have the grasping poses, we can use the MoveIt! /pickup action server to send a goal passing all of them. As before, we will create an action client:

```
# Create move group 'pickup' action client:
self._pickup_ac = SimpleActionClient('/pickup', PickupAction)
if not self._pickup_ac.wait_for_server(rospy.Duration(5.0)):
    rospy.logerr('Pick up action client not available!')
    rospy.signal_shutdown('Pick up action client not available!')
    return
```

Then, we will try to pick up the can of Coke as many times as needed until we finally do it:

```
# Pick Coke can object:
while not self._pickup(self._arm_group, self._grasp_object_name,
self._grasp_object_width):
    rospy.logwarn('Pick up failed! Retrying ...')
    rospy.sleep(1.0)
```

Inside the _pickup method, we create a pickup goal for MoveIt!, right after generating the grasps poses, as explained earlier:

```
# Create and send Pickup goal:
goal = self._create_pickup_goal(group, target, grasps)

state = self._pickup_ac.send_goal_and_wait(goal)
if state != GoalStatus.SUCCEEDED:
    rospy.logerr('Pick up goal failed!: %s' %
    self._pickup_ac.get_goal_status_text())
    return None

result = self._pickup_ac.get_result()

# Check for error:
err = result.error_code.val
if err != MoveItErrorCodes.SUCCESS:
    rospy.logwarn('Group %s cannot pick up target %s!: %s' % (group,
    target, str(moveit_error_dict[err])))

    return False

return True
```

The goal is sent and the state is used to check whether the robot manipulator picks up the object or not. The pickup goal is created in the `_create_pickup_goal` method as follows:

```
def _create_pickup_goal(self, group, target, grasps):
    # Create goal:
    goal = PickupGoal()

    goal.group_name = group
    goal.target_name = target

    goal.possible_grasps.extend(grasps)

    # Configure goal planning options:
    goal.allowed_planning_time = 5.0

    goal.planning_options.planning_scene_diff.is_diff = True
    goal.planning_options.planning_scene_diff.robot_state.is_diff =
    True
    goal.planning_options.plan_only = False
    goal.planning_options.replan = True
    goal.planning_options.replan_attempts = 10

    return goal
```

The goal needs the planning group (`arm` in this case) and the target name (`coke_can` in this case). Then, all the possible grasps are set, and several planning options, including the allowed planning time, can be increased if needed.

When the target object is successfully picked up, we will see the box corresponding to it attached to the gripper's grasping frame with a purple color, as shown in the following figure (note that it might appear like a ghost gripper misplaced, but that is only a visualization artifact):

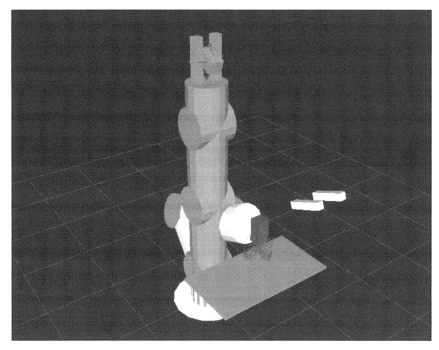

Arm picking up an object

The place action

Right after the object has been picked up, the manipulator will proceed with the place action. MoveIt! provides the /place action server, so the first step consists of creating an action client to send a place goal in the desired location, in order to place the object picked up:

```
# Create move group 'place' action client:
self._place_ac = SimpleActionClient('/place', PlaceAction)
if not self._place_ac.wait_for_server(rospy.Duration(5.0)):
    rospy.logerr('Place action client not available!')
    rospy.signal_shutdown('Place action client not available!')
    return
```

Then, we will try to place the object until we finally manage to do it:

```
# Place Coke can object on another place on the support surface
(table):
while not self._place(self._arm_group, self._grasp_object_name,
self._pose_place):
    rospy.logwarn('Place failed! Retrying ...')
    rospy.sleep(1.0)
```

The _place method uses the following code:

```
def _place(self, group, target, place):
    # Obtain possible places:
    places = self._generate_places(place)

    # Create and send Place goal:
    goal = self._create_place_goal(group, target, places)

    state = self._place_ac.send_goal_and_wait(goal)
    if state != GoalStatus.SUCCEEDED:
        rospy.logerr('Place goal failed!: ' %
        self._place_ac.get_goal_status_text())
        return None

    result = self._place_ac.get_result()

    # Check for error:
    err = result.error_code.val
    if err != MoveItErrorCodes.SUCCESS:
        rospy.logwarn('Group %s cannot place target %s!: %s' % (group,
        target, str(moveit_error_dict[err])))

        return False

    return True
```

The method generates multiple possible places to leave the object, creates the place goal, and sends it. Then, it checks the result to verify whether the object has been placed or not. To place an object, we can use a single place pose, but it is generally better to provide several options. In this case, we have the _generate_places method, which generates places with different angles at the position given.

When the places are generated, they are also published as `PoseArray` so we can see them with blue arrows, as shown in the following screenshot:

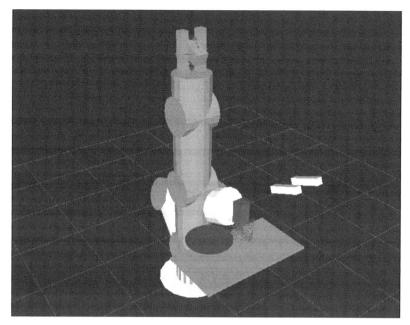

Visualization of place poses

Once the places are obtained, the `_create_place_goal` method creates a place goal as follows:

```
def _create_place_goal(self, group, target, places):
    # Create goal:
    goal = PlaceGoal()

    goal.group_name = group
    goal.attached_object_name = target

    goal.place_locations.extend(places)

    # Configure goal planning options:
    goal.allowed_planning_time = 5.0
```

```
goal.planning_options.planning_scene_diff.is_diff = True
goal.planning_options.planning_scene_diff.robot_state.is_diff =
True
goal.planning_options.plan_only = False
goal.planning_options.replan = True
goal.planning_options.replan_attempts = 10

return goal
```

In brief, the place goal has the group (`arm` in this case) and the target object (`coke_can` in this case), which are attached to the gripper and the place or places (poses). Additionally, several planning options are provided, along with the allowed planning time, which can be increased if needed. When the object is placed, we will see the box representing it in green again, and on top of the table. The arm will be up again, as shown in the following screenshot:

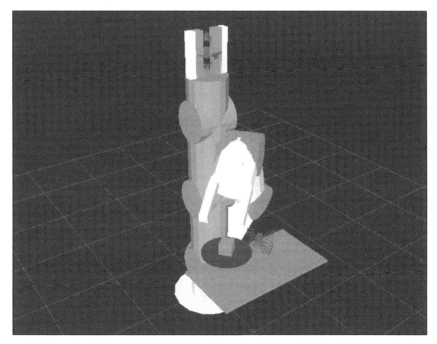

Arm after placing an object

The demo mode

We can do the whole *pick and place* task without perception in demo mode, that is, without actually actuating on the Gazebo simulation, or the real robotic arm. In this mode, we will use fake controllers to move the arm once the motion plan has been found by MoveIt! to do the pick and place actions, including grasping the object. The same code can be used directly on the actual controllers.

In order to run pick and place in the demo mode, run the following commands:

```
$ roslaunch rosbook_arm_moveit_config demo.launch
$ roslaunch rosbook_arm_pick_and_place grasp_generator_server.launch
$ rosrunros book_arm_pick_and_place pick_and_place.py
```

The special part is the first launch file, which simply opens RViz and loads fake controllers instead of spawning the robotic manipulator on Gazebo. The following figure shows several snapshots of the arm moving and doing the pick and place after running the preceding commands:

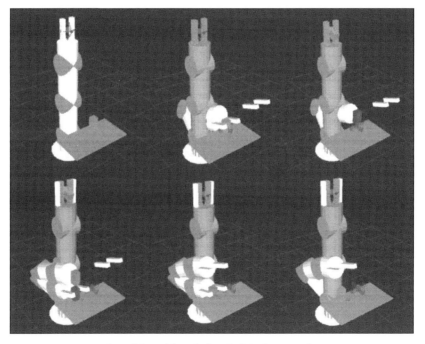

Arm doing pick and place task in demo mode

Simulation in Gazebo

Using the same code as in demo mode, we can actually move the real controllers, either in simulation (Gazebo) or using the real hardware. The interface is the same, so using a real arm or Gazebo is exactly the same. In these cases, the joints will actually move and the grasping will actually make the gripper come in contact with the grasping object (the can of Coke). This requires a proper definition of the objects and the gripper in Gazebo to work properly.

The commands to run the pick and place in this case (as shown previously) are:

```
$ roslaunch rosbook_arm_gazebo rosbook_arm_grasping_world.launch
$ roslaunch rosbook_arm_moveit_config moveit_rviz.launch config:=true
$ roslaunch rosbook_arm_pick_and_place grasp_generator_server.launch
$ rosrun rosbook_arm_pick_and_place pick_and_place.py
```

It is only the first part, to launch files, that changes with respect to the demo mode; it replaces demo.launch in the demo mode. In this case, we spawn the robotic manipulator in Gazebo with the environment containing the table and the can of Coke as well as the RGB-D camera. Then, the moveit_rviz.launch file opens RViz with the MoveIt! plugin providing the same interface as with demo.launch. However, in this case, when the pick_and_place.py program is run, the arm in Gazebo is moved.

Summary

In this chapter, we have covered most of the aspects involved in integrating a robotic arm with MoveIt! and Gazebo, which gives us a realistic view of how a robotic arm could be used in a real-life environment. MoveIt! provides us with very simple and concise tools for motion planning with robotic arms using an Inverse Kinematics (IK) solver as well as ample documentation in order to facilitate this process, but given the complexity of the architecture, it can only be done properly once all of the different interactions between MoveIt!, the sensors, and the actuators in our robot have been properly understood.

We have glanced through the different high-level elements in the MoveIt! API, which, to cover in detail, would require an entire book of their own. In an attempt to avoid the cost of understanding a full API to perform very simple actions, the approach taken in this book has been to limit ourselves to very simple motion planning and interacting with both artificially created objects in the planning scene and RGB-D sensors that generate a point cloud.

Finally, a very detailed explanation has been provided for how to perform an object pick and place task. Although not being the sole purpose of a robotic arm, this is one that you might enjoy experimenting with as it is very common in industrial robots, but using MoveIt! motion planning and 3D perception allows you to do so in complex and dynamic environments. For this particular purpose of the robotic arm, a deeper look at the APIs and enhanced understanding of the MoveIt! architecture was required, giving you much more depth and understanding as to the possibilities of MoveIt!

8
Using Sensors and Actuators with ROS

When you think of a robot, you would probably think of a human-sized one with arms, a lot of sensors, and a wide field of locomotion systems.

Now that we know how to write programs in ROS and that we know how to create robot models and simulate their behavior, we are going to work with real sensors and actuators—things that can interact with the real world. In the first section, we are going to learn how to control a DIY robot platform using ROS. Then, we are going to see how to interface different sensors and actuators that you can typically find in robotics laboratories.

 You can find a wide list of devices supported by ROS at http://www.ros.org/wiki/Sensors.

Sensors and actuators can be organized into different categories: rangefinders, cameras, pose estimation devices, and so on. They will help you find what you are looking for more quickly.

In this chapter, we will deal with the following topics:

- Cheap and common actuators and sensors for your projects
- Using Arduino to connect them
- 2D laser rangefinders, Kinect 3D sensors, GPS, or servomotors

We know that it is impossible to explain all the types of sensors in this chapter. For this reason, we have selected some of the most commonly used sensors that are affordable to most users—regular, sporadic, or amateur. With them, we are going to connect all the elements needed to have a small robot platform working.

Using a joystick or a gamepad

I am sure that, at one point or another, you have used a joystick or a gamepad of a video console.

A joystick is nothing more than a series of buttons and potentiometers. With this device, you can perform or control a wide range of actions.

In ROS, a joystick is used to telecontrol a robot to change its velocity or direction.

Before we start, we are going to install some packages. To install these packages in Ubuntu, execute the following command:

```
$ sudo apt-get install ros-kinetic-joystick-drivers
$ rosstack profile & rospack profile
```

In these packages, you will find code to learn how to use the joystick and a guide to create our packages.

First of all, connect your joystick to your computer. Now, we are going to check whether the joystick is recognized using the following command:

```
$ ls /dev/input/
```

We will see the following output:

```
by-id event0 event2 event4 event6 event8 js0 mouse0
by-path event1 event3 event5 event7 event9 mice
```

The port created is js0; with the jstest command, we can check whether it is working, using the following code:

```
$ sudo jstest /dev/input/js0
```

```
Axes: 0: 0 1: 0 2: 0 Buttons: 0:off 1:off 2:off 3:off 4:off 5:off 6:off
7:off 8:off 9:off 10:off
```

Our joystick, *Logitech F710*, has 8 axes and 11 buttons, and if we move the joystick, the values change.

Once you have checked the joystick, we are going to test it in ROS. To do this, you can use the joy and joy_node packages:

```
$ rosrun joy joy_node
```

If everything is OK, you will see the following output:

```
[ INFO] [1357571588.441808789]: Opened joystick: /dev/input/js0.
deadzone_: 0.050000.
```

How does joy_node send joystick movements?

With the joy_node package active, we are going to see the messages sent by this node. This will help us understand how it sends information about axes and buttons.

To see the messages sent by the node, we can use this command:

```
$ rostopic echo /joy
```

And then, we can see each message sent as follows:

```
header:
  seq: 33
  stamp:
    secs: 1480289803
    nsecs: 599782892
  frame_id: ''
axes: [-0.0, -0.2219386249780655, 0.0, 0.0, 0.0, 0.0, 0.0, 0.0]
buttons: [0, 0, 0, 0, 0, 0, 0, 0, 0, 0, 0]
```

You will see two main vectors: one for axes and the other for buttons. Obviously, these vectors are used to publish the states of the buttons and axes of the real hardware.

If you want to know the message type, type the following command line in a shell:

```
$ rostopic type /joy
```

You will then obtain the type used by the message; in this case, it is sensor_msgs/Joy.

Now, to see the fields used in the message, use the following command line:

```
$ rosmsg show sensor_msgs/Joy
```

You will see the following output:

```
std_msgs/Header header
  uint32 seq
  time stamp
  string frame_id
float32[] axes
int32[] buttons
```

This is the message structure that you must use if you want to use a joystick with your developments. In the next section, you will learn how to write a node that subscribes to the joystick topic and how to generate moving commands to move a robot model.

Using joystick data to move our robot model

Now, we are going to create a node that gets data from joy_node and published topics to control a robot model.

Now, it is necessary to create a robot 3D model like we have seen in the previous chapters and a node with the odometry. In the repository, you can check the urdf model in the chapter8_tutorials/urdf folder and you can check the code for odometry in the /src folder where the file is named c8_odom.cpp.

In this code, odometry is calculated using an initial position 0,0,0 and using velocity information from a geometry_msgs::Twist. The velocity of each wheel is calculated, and the position is updated using differential drive kinematics. You can run the odometry node after a roscore command typing the following in a terminal:

```
$ rosrun chapter8_tutorials c8_odom
```

To understand the topics used in this node, we can display the topic list; use the following command line:

```
$ rosnode info /odom
```

You will then see the following output, where /cmd_vel is the topic published by the node:

```
-----------------------------------------------
Node [/odom]
Publications:
 * /odom [nav_msgs/Odometry]
 * /rosout [rosgraph_msgs/Log]
 * /tf [tf2_msgs/TFMessage]

Subscriptions:
 * /cmd_vel [unknown type]

Services:
 * /odom/get_loggers
 * /odom/set_logger_level


contacting node http://daneel:35582/ ...
Pid: 30375
Connections:
 * topic: /rosout
    * to: /rosout
     * direction: outbound
     * transport: TCPROS
```

We can check the topic type of /cmd_vel. Use the following command line to know it:

```
$ rostopic type /cmd_vel
```

You will see this output:

```
geometry_msgs/Twist
```

To know the contents of this message, execute the following command line:

```
$ rosmsg show geometry_msgs/Twist
```

You will then see the two fields that are used to send the velocity:

```
geometry_msgs/Vector3 linear
    float64 x
    float64 y
    float64 z
geometry_msgs/Vector3 angular
    float64 x
    float64 y
    float64 z
```

OK, now that we have localized the topic and the structure to use, it is time to create a program to generate velocity commands using data from the joystick.

Create a new file, c8_teleop_joy.cpp, in the chapter8_tutorials/src directory and type in the following code snippet:

```cpp
#include<ros/ros.h>
#include<geometry_msgs/Twist.h>
#include<sensor_msgs/Joy.h>
#include<iostream>

using namespace std;
float max_linear_vel = 0.2;
float max_angular_vel = 1.5707;

class TeleopJoy{
  public:
  TeleopJoy();
  private:
```

```
    void callBack(const sensor_msgs::Joy::ConstPtr& joy);
    ros::NodeHandle n;
    ros::Publisher pub;
    ros::Subscriber sub;
    int i_velLinear , i_velAngular;
};

TeleopJoy::TeleopJoy()
{ i_velLinear = 1;
  i_velAngular = 0;
  n.param("axis_linear",i_velLinear,i_velLinear);
  n.param("axis_angular",i_velAngular,i_velAngular);
  pub = n.advertise<geometry_msgs::Twist>("/cmd_vel",1);
  sub = n.subscribe<sensor_msgs::Joy>("joy", 10,
  &TeleopJoy::callBack, this);
}

void TeleopJoy::callBack(const sensor_msgs::Joy::ConstPtr& joy)
{
  geometry_msgs::Twist vel;
  vel.angular.z = max_angular_vel*joy->axes[0];
  vel.linear.x = max_linear_vel*joy->axes[1];
  pub.publish(vel);
}

int main(int argc, char** argv)
{
  ros::init(argc, argv, "c8_teleop_joy");
  TeleopJoy teleop_joy;
  ros::spin();
}
```

Now, we are going to break the code to explain how it works. In the `main` function, we create an instance of the `TeleopJoy` class:

```
int main(int argc, char** argv)
{

  TeleopJoy teleop_joy;
}
```

In the constructor, four variables are initialized. The first two variables are filled using data from Parameter Server. These variables are joystick axes. The next two variables are the advertiser and the subscriber. The advertiser will publish a topic with the `geometry_msgs::Twist` type. The subscriber will get data from the topic with the name `Joy`. The node that is handling the joystick sends this topic:

```
TeleopJoy::TeleopJoy()
{ i_velLinear = 1;
  i_velAngular = 0;
  n.param("axis_linear",i_velLinear,i_velLinear);
  n.param("axis_angular",i_velAngular,i_velAngular);
  pub = n.advertise<geometry_msgs::Twist>("/cmd_vel",1);
  sub = n.subscribe<sensor_msgs::Joy>("joy", 10,
  &TeleopJoy::callBack, this);
}
```

Each time the node receives a message, the `callBack()` function is called. We create a new variable with the name `vel`, which will be used to publish data. The values of the axes of the joystick are assigned to the `vel` variable using coefficients to assign the maximum velocities. In this part, you can create a process with the data received before publishing it:

```
void TeleopJoy::callBack(const sensor_msgs::Joy::ConstPtr& joy)
{
  geometry_msgs::Twist vel;
  vel.angular.z = max_angular_vel*joy->axes[0];
  vel.linear.x = max_linear_vel*joy->axes[1];
  pub.publish(vel);
}
```

Finally, the topic is published using `pub.publish(vel)`.

We are going to create a launch file for this example. In the launch file, we declare data for Parameter Server and launch the `joy` and `c8_teleoop_joy` nodes:

```
<?xml version="1.0" ?>
<launch>
  <node pkg="chapter8_tutorials" type="c8_teleop_joy"
  name="c8_teleop_joy" />
  <param name="axis_linear" value="1" type="int" />
  <param name="axis_angular" value="0" type="int" />
  <node respawn="true" pkg="joy" type="joy_node" name="joy_node">
    <param name="dev" type="string" value="/dev/input/js0" />
    <param name="deadzone" value="0.12" />
  </node>
</launch>
```

There are four parameters in the launch file; these parameters will add data to Parameter Server, and it will be used by our node. The `axis_linear` and `axis_angular` parameters will be used to configure the axes of the joystick. If you want to change the axes configuration, you only need to change the value and put the number of the axes you want to use. The `dev` and `deadzone` parameters will be used to configure the port where the joystick is connected, and the dead zone is the region of movement that is not recognized by the device.

```
$ roslaunch chapter8_tutorials chapter8_teleop_joy.launch
```

You can check that the code is working using `rostopic echo` that `/cmd_vel` topic is published when you move the joystick axes.

Now, we are going to prepare a larger launch to visualize a robot model that moves with the joystick. Copy the following code step to a new file, `chapter8_tutorials_robot_model.launch`, in the `chapter8_tutorials/launch` directory:

```xml
<?xml version="1.0"?>
<launch>
  <arg name="model" />
  <arg name="gui" default="False" />
  <param name="robot_description" textfile="$(find
  chapter8_tutorials)/urdf/robot2.urdf" />
  <param name="use_gui" value="$(arg gui)" />
  <node name="joint_state_publisher" pkg="joint_state_publisher"
  type="joint_state_publisher" />
  <node name="robot_state_publisher" pkg="robot_state_publisher"
  type="state_publisher" />
  <node name="rviz" pkg="rviz" type="rviz" args="-d $(find
  chapter8_tutorials)/config/config.rviz" />
  <node name="c8_odom" pkg="chapter8_tutorials" type="c8_odom" />
  <node name="joy_node" pkg="joy" type="joy_node" />
  <node name="c8_teleop_joy" pkg="chapter8_tutorials"
  type="c8_teleop_joy" />
</launch>
```

You will note that, in the launch file, there are four different nodes: `c8_teleop_joy`, `joy_node`, `c8_odom`, `joint_state_publisher`, and `rviz`. You can note in the launch file that the robot model is named `robot2.urdf` and you can find it in `chapter8_tutorials/urdf`.

To launch the example, use the following command line:

```
$ roslaunch chapter8_tutorials chapter8_robot_model.launch
```

You can see whether everything is fine by checking the running nodes and the topic list using the `rosnode` and `rostopic` lists. If you want to see it graphically, use `rqt_graph`.

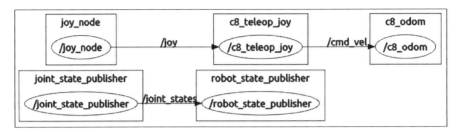

If all has been successful, you should see in the RViz visualizer a robot model that you can control with the joystick!

In the next sections, we will learn how to use Arduino with ROS. Then, we will connect the joystick example nodes to Arduino node to control real robot motors.

Using Arduino to add sensors and actuators

Arduino is an open source electronics prototyping platform based on flexible, easy-to-use hardware and software. It's intended for artists, designers, hobbyists, and anyone interested in creating interactive objects or environments.

The following image shows how an Arduino board looks:

ROS can use this type of device with the `rosserial` package. Basically, Arduino is connected to the computer using a serial connection, and data is transmitted using this port. With `rosserial`, you can also use a lot of devices controlled by a serial connection, for example, GPS and servo controllers.

First, we need to install the packages. To do this, we use the following command lines:

```
$ sudo apt-get install ros-kinect-rosserial-arduino
$ sudo apt-get install ros-kinect-rosserial
```

Then, for the `catkin` workspace, we need to clone the `rosserial` repository into the workspace. The `rosserial` messages are created, and `ros_lib` is compiled with the following command lines:

```
$ cd dev/catkin_ws/src/
$ git clone https://github.com/ros-drivers/rosserial.git
$ cd dev/catkin_ws/
$ catkin_make
$ catkin_make install
$ source install/setup.bash
```

OK, we assume that you have the Arduino IDE installed. If not, just follow the steps described at `http://arduino.cc/en/Main/Software`. For ROS Kinetic, Arduino core is installed with the `rosserial_arduino` package. You can download new versions of Arduino IDE from `www.arduino.cc`.

n the new versions of Arduino IDE, the `sketchbook` folder is now named `Arduino` and is in your home folder.

Once you have the package and the IDE installed, it is necessary to copy `ros_lib` from the `rosserial` package to the `sketchbook/libraries` folder, which is created on your computer after running the Arduino IDE. Then, you have to run `make_libraries.py`:

```
$ cd ~/Arduino/libraries
$ sudo rm -r roslib
$ rosrun rosserial_arduino make_libraries.py .
```

Creating an example program to use Arduino

Now, we are going to upload an example program from the IDE to Arduino. Select the `Hello World` sample and upload the sketch:

Arduino IDE with roslib examples

The code in the preceding screenshot is very similar to the following code. In the following code, you can see an include line with the `ros.h` library. This library is the `rosserial` library, which we have installed before. Also, you can see a library with the message to send with a topic; in this case, it is the `std_msgs/String` type.

The following code snippet is present in the `c8_arduino_string.ino` file:

```
#include <ros.h>
#include <std_msgs/String.h>

ros::NodeHandle nh;

std_msgs::String str_msg;
ros::Publisher chatter("chatter", &str_msg);
char hello[19] = "chapter8_tutorials";

void setup()
{
  nh.initNode();
  nh.advertise(chatter);
}

void loop()
{
  str_msg.data = hello;
  chatter.publish( &str_msg );
  nh.spinOnce();
  delay(1000);
}
```

The Arduino code is divided into two functions: `setup()` and `loop()`. The `setup()` function is executed once and is usually used to set up the board. After `setup()`, the `loop()` function runs continuously. In the `setup()` function, the name of the topic is set; in this case, it is named `chatter`. Now, we need to start a node to hear the port and publish the topics sent by Arduino on the ROS network. Type the following command in a shell and remember to run `roscore`:

```
$ rosrun rosserial_python serial_node.py /dev/ttyACM0
```

Now, you can see the messages sent by Arduino with the `rostopic echo` command:

```
$ rostopic echo chatter
```

You will see the following data in the shell:

```
data: chapter8_tutorials
```

The last example is about the data sent from Arduino to the computer. Now, we are going to use an example where Arduino will subscribe to a topic and will change the LED state connected to the pin number 13. The name of the example that we are going to use is blink; you can find this in the Arduino IDE by navigating to **File** | **Examples** | ros_lib | **Blink**.

The following code snippet is present in the c8_arduino_led.ino file:

```cpp
#include <ros.h>
#include <std_msgs/Empty.h>

ros::NodeHandle nh;
void messageCb( const std_msgs::Empty& toggle_msg){
  digitalWrite(13, HIGH-digitalRead(13)); // blink the led
}

ros::Subscriber<std_msgs::Empty> sub("toggle_led", &messageCb );
void setup()
{
  pinMode(13, OUTPUT);
  nh.initNode();
  nh.subscribe(sub);
}

void loop()
{
  nh.spinOnce();
  delay(1);
}
```

Remember to launch the node to communicate with the Arduino board:

```
$ rosrun rosserial_python serial_node.py /dev/ttyACM0
```

Now, if you want to change the LED status, you can use the rostopic pub command to publish the new state:

```
$ rostopic pub /toggle_led std_msgs/Empty "{}" -once


publishing and latching message for 3.0 seconds
```

You will note that the LED has changed its status; if the LED was on, it will now turn off. To change the status again, you only have to publish the topic once more:

```
$ rostopic pub /toggle_led std_msgs/Empty "{}" –once
```

```
publishing and latching message for 3.0 seconds
```

Now, you can use all the devices available to Arduino on ROS. This is very useful because you have access to cheap sensors and actuators to implement your robots.

> When we were writing the chapter, we noted that Arduino does not work with `rosserial`, for instance, in the case of Arduino Leonardo. So, be careful with the selection of the device to use with this package.
>
> We didn't face any problems while working with Arduino UNO R3, Genuino, Mega, Arduino Duemilanove, or Arduino Nano.

Robot platform controlled by ROS and Arduino

Now, we have understood how to use Arduino with ROS. In this section, we are prepared to connect our first actuators to ROS. There are a lot of low-cost kits for Arduino users that we can choose to make a robot controlled by ROS. During this section, we are going to use a 4 x 4 robot kit chassis.

4 x 4 robot platform with Odroid C1, Arduino, 9 DOF Razor IMU, and joystick

In order to have ROS in our robot, not only an Arduino is needed, but we will also need an embedded computer with ROS installed. There is a lot of ARM based-boards compatible with ROS, such as Dragonboard, Raspberry Pi, or BeagleBone Black. In this case, there is an Odroid C1 with Ubuntu Xenial and ROS Kinetic. During the chapter, we are going to learn how to connect different sensors to the platform such as an **Inertial Measurement Unit (IMU)** or some wheel encoders to calculate the odometry.

The robot platform has four motors that have to be controlled. For this purpose, we are going to use an Arduino with a motor controller. There is a lot of motor controllers that can be interfaced with Arduino. In this case, we are going to use a very common board based on L298N dual motor driver. A kit of two wheels, two motors, and two magnetic encoders are shown in the figure:

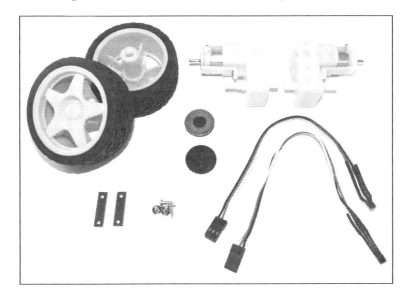

Connecting your robot motors to ROS using Arduino

As we have four motors, we will connect the motors from the same side of the platform to the same output. We will connect digital signals to the L298N board to control the motors' behavior.

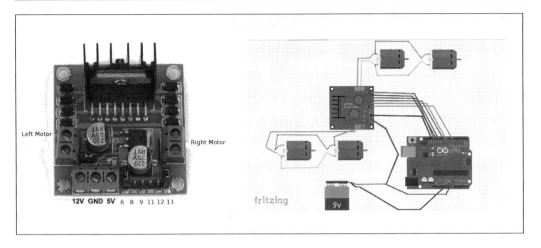

Each channel needs three signals to be controlled. **IN1** and **IN2** are digital signals used to set the rotation sense of the motor. **ENA** is used to control the intensity of the motor using Arduino **Pulse Width Modulation (PWM)** signal. This signal will control the left motor. For the right motor, **IN3, IN4**, and **ENB** will be the control signals. In the figure mentioned earlier, you have a diagram of the connection. Be careful connecting the wires from Arduino to L298N and programming INx signals. Once you have connected the motors to the L298N motor controller and the control signals to Arduino.

We can start a program to control the motors; you can find the entire code in `chapter8_tutorials/src/robot_motors.ino`. We are going to use Arduino IDE to code the sketch. First, we are going to declare the dependencies and define the Arduino pins connected to the L298N motor controller:

```
#include <ros.h>
#include <std_msgs/Int16.h>

#define ENA 6
#define ENB 11
#define IN1 8
#define IN2 9
#define IN3 12
#define IN4 13
```

Then, we are going to declare two callback functions to activate each motor. When a command message for the left wheel is received, the direction of the motors is set depending of the sign of the command. Digital signals IN1 and IN2 set the motor direction forward or backward. ENA is a PWM signal that controls the motor voltage; this signal is able to regulate the speed of the motor. The callback for the right wheel command is similar to the first callback:

```
void cmdLeftWheelCB( const std_msgs::Int16& msg)
{
  if(msg.data >= 0)
  {
    analogWrite(ENA,msg.data);
    digitalWrite(IN1, LOW);
    digitalWrite(IN2, HIGH);
  }
  else
  {
    analogWrite(ENA,-msg.data);
    digitalWrite(IN1, HIGH);
    digitalWrite(IN2, LOW);
  }
}

void cmdRightWheelCB( const std_msgs::Int16& msg)
{
  if(msg.data >= 0)
    {
    analogWrite(ENB,msg.data);
    digitalWrite(IN3, LOW);
    digitalWrite(IN4, HIGH);
  }
  else
  {
    analogWrite(ENB,-msg.data);
    digitalWrite(IN3, HIGH);
    digitalWrite(IN4, LOW);
  }
}
```

Then, two subscribers are declared, the topics are named `cmd_left_wheel`, we are using `std::msgs::Int16` topic type, and we have just seen the callback functions:

```
ros::Subscriber<std_msgs::Int16> subCmdLeft("cmd_left_wheel",
cmdLeftWheelCB );
ros::Subscriber<std_msgs::Int16>
subCmdRight("cmd_right_wheel",cmdRightWheelCB );
```

In the Arduino `setup()` function, the pins are declared as outputs and `nh` node is initialized and subscription to the topics starts:

```
void setup() {
  // put your setup code here, to run once:
  pinMode(ENA, OUTPUT);
  pinMode(ENB, OUTPUT);
  pinMode(IN1, OUTPUT);
  pinMode(IN2, OUTPUT);
  pinMode(IN3, OUTPUT);
  pinMode(IN4, OUTPUT);
  analogWrite(ENA,0);
  analogWrite(ENB, 0);
  digitalWrite(IN1, LOW);
  digitalWrite(IN2, HIGH);
  digitalWrite(IN3, LOW);
  digitalWrite(IN4, HIGH);

  nh.initNode();
  nh.subscribe(subCmdRight);
  nh.subscribe(subCmdLeft);
}
```

The `loop` function is as follows:

```
void loop()
{
  nh.spinOnce();
}
```

You can upload now the code to the board, and run the Arduino node from terminal:

```
$ roscore
$ rosrun rosserial_python serial_node.py /dev/ttyACM0
```

In other terminal, you can publish manually some commands to the left and the right motor:

```
$ rostopic pub /cmd_right_wheel std_msgs/Int16 "data: 190"
$ rostopic pub /cmd_left_wheel std_msgs/Int16 "data: -100"
```

The command signals are expected to be between `-255` and `255`, and motors should stop with a zero value.

Now that we have our robot motor connected to ROS, it is time to control them with a joystick. We can unify the velocity topics, using differential drive kinematics equations and ROS `geometry_msgs::Twist` topic. By this way, we can send a standard message to the odometry nodes that is independent of the type of robot that we are using. As we have prepared `c8_teleop_joy` node to send this type of topics, we will be able to control the wheels with the joystick.

We are going to create a new sketch name `robot_motors_with_twist.ino`. We are going to copy the previous sketch, and we will have to add a new include at the beginning of the sketch to use `geometry_msgs::Twist`:

```
#include <geometry_msgs/Twist.h>
float L = 0.1; //distance between wheels
```

Then, we will include a new subscriber and its callback function:

```
void cmdVelCB( const geometry_msgs::Twist& twist)
{
  int gain = 4000;
  float left_wheel_data = gain*(twist.linear.x -
  twist.angular.z*L);
  float right_wheel_data = gain*(twist.linear.x +
  twist.angular.z*L);
  {
    analogWrite(ENA,abs(left_wheel_data));
    digitalWrite(IN1, LOW);
    digitalWrite(IN2, HIGH);
  }
  else
  {
    analogWrite(ENA,abs(left_wheel_data));
    digitalWrite(IN1, HIGH);
    digitalWrite(IN2, LOW);
  }
  if(right_wheel_data >= 0)
  {
```

```
      analogWrite(ENB,abs(left_wheel_data));
      digitalWrite(IN3, LOW);
      digitalWrite(IN4, HIGH);
    }
    else
    {
      analogWrite(ENB,abs(left_wheel_data));
      digitalWrite(IN3, HIGH);
      digitalWrite(IN4, LOW);
    }
  }
  ros::Subscriber<geometry_msgs::Twist> subCmdVel("cmd_vel",
  cmdVelCB);
```

Now, you can upload the code to the Arduino board. In order to make easier to run all the nodes, we are going to create a launch file that manages the joystick, the robot model in the RViz visualizer, and the Arduino node.

You can launch the example with the following command in terminals:

```
$ roslaunch chapter8_tutorials chapter8_tutorials robot_model_with_
motors.launch
```

```
$ rosrun rosserial_python serial_node.py /dev/ttyACM0
```

Now, you can control the robot with the joystick; also you can see in the RViz visualizer the robot model moving. If you are testing the code on an embedded ARM computer without display, you can comment the `rviz` node in the launch file.

Connecting encoders to your robot

Dagu encoders are composed of two parts for each wheel. A magnetic disk with eight poles: four north poles and four south poles and a Hall effect sensor. The magnet disk is placed in a shaft of a wheel and the Hall effect must face it at a maximum distance of 3 mm.

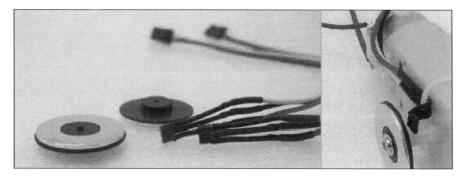

Dagu encoders: sensors and magnet, example of installation

nce you have placed the encoder on the wheel, you can connect it to the Arduino. The Hall effect sensor is directly soldered to three wires: black, ground, and white.

The black wire is the ground of the sensor and must be connected to Arduino ground; the red one is for power supply and should be connected to 5V. The white wire is the signal; the signal is binary and changes his values from high level to low level once the magnet disk turns and a different pole faces the sensor.

So, it is logical to think in connecting signal wire to an Arduino digital pin. But furthermore, encoders' signals can change very quickly depending on the revolutions of the motor and the number of poles/steps of your encoder. It is recommended to connect encoder signals to Arduino interruption pins to achieve a faster reading of the signal changes

For *Arduino/Genuino Uno*, interruption pins are digital pin 2 and digital pin 3. We will connect the encoders to this pin. For checking how the encoder works and learning how you can use Arduino interruptions, we will use the following code:

```
#include <std_msgs/Float32.h>
#include <TimerOne.h>
#define LOOP_TIME 200000
#define left_encoder_pin 3
#define right_encoder_pin 2
```

We declare new variables to count each tick of the encoders and create topics in order to publish the wheel velocities:

```
unsigned int counter_left=0;
unsigned int counter_right = 0;

ros::NodeHandle nh;
std_msgs::Float32 left_wheel_vel;
ros::Publisher left_wheel_vel_pub("/left_wheel_velocity",
&left_wheel_vel);

std_msgs::Float32 right_wheel_vel;
ros::Publisher right_wheel_vel_pub("/right_wheel_velocity",
&right_wheel_vel);
```

We have to create two functions to handle encoders' interruptions. Each time a change is detected in the right or left encoder pin, a count is increased:

```
void docount_left() // counts from the speed sensor
{
```

```
    counter_left++; // increase +1 the counter value
}

void docount_right() // counts from the speed sensor
{
    counter_right++; // increase +1 the counter value
}
```

A timer is used to publish the velocity of each wheel. We use the encoder counters, the wheel radius and the timer duration to calculate `speed:void timerIsr():`

```
{
    Timer1.detachInterrupt(); //stop the timer
    //Left Motor Speed
    left_wheel_vel.data = counter_left;
    left_wheel_vel_pub.publish(&left_wheel_vel);
    right_wheel_vel.data = counter_right;
    right_wheel_vel_pub.publish(&right_wheel_vel);
    counter_right=0;
    counter_left=0;
    Timer1.attachInterrupt( timerIsr ); //enable the timer
}
```

Finally, in the setup functions, the encoder pins are declared as INPUT_PULLUP. This means that Arduino will treat them as inputs and it will connect internally a pull-up resistor to these pins:

```
//Setup for encoders
pinMode(right_encoder_pin, INPUT_PULLUP);
pinMode(left_encoder_pin, INPUT_PULLUP);
Timer1.initialize(LOOP_TIME);
attachInterrupt(digitalPinToInterrupt(left_encoder_pin),
docount_left, CHANGE); // increase counter when speed sensor pin
goes High
attachInterrupt(digitalPinToInterrupt(right_encoder_pin),
docount_right, CHANGE); // increase counter when speed sensor pin
goes High
```

Also, the messages that will be published have been advertised in the setup:

```
nh.advertise(left_wheel_vel_pub);
nh.advertise(right_wheel_vel_pub);
Timer1.attachInterrupt( timerIsr ); // enable the timer
```

You can upload now the code to the board, and run the Arduino node:

```
$ roscore
$ rosrun rosserial_python serial_node.py /dev/ttyACM0
```

When you type the following in another terminal:

```
$ rostopic list
```

You will see:

```
/cmd_left_wheel
/cmd_right_wheel
/diagnostics
/left_wheel_velocity
/right_wheel_velocity
/rosout
/rosout_agg
```

You can now make an echo of the topic and turn the wheels or you can run `rqt_graph`. Also, you can check the frequency of each publications with `rostopic hz`:

```
subscribed to [/left_wheel_velocity]
average rate: 5.008
        min: 0.198s max: 0.201s std dev: 0.00127s window: 5
average rate: 5.004
        min: 0.197s max: 0.201s std dev: 0.00146s window: 10
^Caverage rate: 5.006
        min: 0.197s max: 0.201s std dev: 0.00156s window: 14
luis@daneel:~$ rostopic hz /right_wheel_velocity
subscribed to [/right_wheel_velocity]
average rate: 5.007
        min: 0.198s max: 0.201s std dev: 0.00095s window: 5
average rate: 5.011
        min: 0.198s max: 0.201s std dev: 0.00083s window: 10
average rate: 5.009
        min: 0.198s max: 0.201s std dev: 0.00078s window: 15
^Caverage rate: 5.007
        min: 0.198s max: 0.201s std dev: 0.00081s window: 16
```

OK, now we can unify these two topics in `geometry msgs::Twist` as we have done with `/cmd_vel` previously. We have to create a new `geometry_msgs::Twist` to send the velocity of the platform and a topic publisher for this message:

```
geometry_msgs::Twist sensor_vel;
ros::Publisher sensor_vel_pub("/sensor_velocity", &sensor_vel);
```

And in the `timerISR()` function, we calculate the linear and angular velocities using kinematics equations:

```
sensor_vel.linear.x = radius*(left_wheel_vel.data +
right_wheel_vel.data)/2;
sensor_vel.linear.y = 0;
sensor_vel.linear.z = 0;
sensor_vel.angular.x = 0;
sensor_vel.angular.y = 0;
sensor_vel.angular.z = radius*(left_wheel_vel.data +
right_wheel_vel.data)/L;
sensor_vel_pub.publish(&sensor_vel);
```

After that, we can modify the odometry node to subscribe to the real odometry data from our encoder sensors published in the topic `/sensor_vel`:

You can check the example with the following command:

```
$ roslaunch chapter8_tutorials chapter8_robot_encoders.launch
$ rosrun rosserial_python serial_node.py /dev/ttyACM0
```

Controlling the wheel velocity

Now, we can command the wheels of our robot using a joystick, publishing manually /cmd_vel topics or using navigation algorithms. Also, we can calculate the odometry of the vehicle and estimate its position; thanks to the encoder data. But have you checked whether your /sensor_velocity data is close to /cmd_vel command?

If you check our /cmd_vel command and the data from /sensor_velocity, you will see that they are not equal. You can try to set different gains in your /cmd_vel command functions to adjust the velocity command with your real velocity, but it is not the best way to do that. This solution will depend on your power supply, the weight of the vehicle, or the floor surface where you are driving the robot among others.

It is time to go deeper and explore control algorithms. As we have a desired velocity for our robot, /cmd_vel and feedback from our encoder sensors, we can implement close-loop control algorithms to reach our /cmd_vel in our robot platform. For example, PID algorithms are commonly applied in these situations. So, try to do your own platform control algorithm in Arduino. If you have arrived here, you will be able to do it.

Wheel, motor, and encoders mounted in the platform

In the code repository, you will find an example of close-loop control algorithm with PID, just in case you want to try it without developing your own control algorithm.

Using a low-cost IMU – 9 degrees of freedom

"An inertial measurement unit, or IMU, is an electronic device that measures and reports on a craft's velocity, orientation, and gravitational forces, using a combination of accelerometers and gyroscopes, sometimes also magnetometers. IMUs are typically used to manoeuvre aircraft, including unmanned aerial vehicles (UAVs), among many others, and spacecraft, including satellites and landers."

– Wikipedia

In this section, we will learn to use a low-cost sensor with 9 **Degree of Freedom (DoF)**. This sensor has an accelerometer (x3), a magnetometer (x3), a barometer (x1), and a gyroscope (x3). 9DoF Razor IMU and the 9DoF sensor stick are low-cost IMU that can be used in your robotics projects. The two boards have an HMCL5883 magnetometer, an ADXL345, and ITG3200 gyroscope. The old version has different magnetometer. The main difference between the two boards are that the Razor IMU contains an **ATMega328** microcontroller, so the pitch, roll, and yaw are calculated from raw data and transmitted by TTL. For connecting the Razor IMU, you will need a 3.3V TTL to USB converter. The sensor stick has only the three sensors, and it has I2C communication.

Note that the 9DoF Razor IMU is based on an ATMega328, the same microcontroller used by that Arduino UNO, so you can update the firmware or developing your own code easily using Arduino IDE. You can use your own Arduino to control the sensor stick using I2C.

The sensor explained in this section had an approximate cost of $70. The low price of this sensor permits its usage in a lot of projects. Now, Sparkfun has upgraded it to a new 9DoF Razor IMU M0 with a cost around 50$, you can check it in the link `https://www.sparkfun.com/products/14001`.

You can see the 9DoF Razor IMU sensor in the following image. It is small, and it has the following main components:

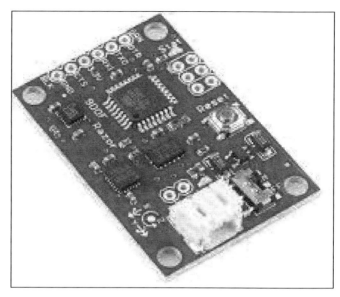

9DoF Razor IMU

This board has the following sensors:

- **ADXL345**: This is a three-axis accelerometer with a high resolution (13-bit) measurement of up to ±16 g. This sensor is widely used in mobile device applications. It measures the static acceleration of gravity in tilt-sensing applications as well as the dynamic acceleration resulting from motion or shock.

- **HMC5883L**: This sensor is designed for low-field magnetic sensing with a digital interface for devices such as low-cost compasses and magnetometers.

- **BMP085**: This is a high-precision barometric pressure sensor used in advanced mobile applications. It offers superior performance with an absolute accuracy up to 0.03 hPa and has very low power consumption, 3 μA.

- **L3G4200D**: This is a three-axis gyroscope with a very high resolution (16-bit) measurement of up to 2,000 **degrees per second** (**dps**).This gyroscope measures how much the device is rotating around all three axes.

As we have said earlier, the sensor stick is controlled using the I2C protocol, and we will use Arduino to control it. In the following image, you can see the way to connect both the boards:

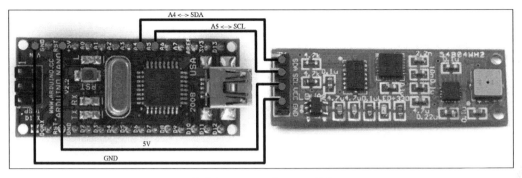

Arduino nano and sensor stick

For Arduino UNO, the pins connected are the same that for the Arduino Nano of the image. The only thing necessary to make it work is to connect the four wires. Connect **GND** and **VCC** from the sensor to **GND** and **5V** in Arduino.

The **Serial Data Line (SDL)** must be connected to the analog pin 4, and the **Serial Clock (SCK)** must be connected to the analog pin 5. If you connect these pins wrongly, Arduino will not be able to communicate with the sensor.

Installing Razor IMU ROS library

In order to install the Razor IMU library for ROS, we have to install visual python with the following command:

```
$ sudo apt-get install python-visual
```

Then, we have to go to our workspace /src folder and clone from GitHub the razor_imu_9dof repository from *Kristof Robot* and compile it:

```
$ cd ~/dev/catkin_ws/src
$ git clone https://github.com/KristofRobot/razor_imu_9dof.git
$ cd ..
$ catkin_make
```

You need to have Arduino IDE installed; this is explained previously in the Arduino section of this chapter. Open your Arduino IDE—/dev/catkin_ws/src/Razor_AHRS/Razor_AHRS.ino. Now, you have to select your hardware options. Search in the code this section and uncomment the right line for you:

```
/*****************************************************************/
/*********** USER SETUP AREA! Set your options here! ************/
/*****************************************************************/

// HARDWARE OPTIONS
/*****************************************************************/
// Select your hardware here by uncommenting one line!
//#define HW__VERSION_CODE 10125 // SparkFun "9DOF Razor IMU"
version "SEN-10125" (HMC5843 magnetometer)
#define HW__VERSION_CODE 10736 // SparkFun "9DOF Razor IMU"
version "SEN-10736" (HMC5883L magnetometer)
//#define HW__VERSION_CODE 10183 // SparkFun "9DOF Sensor Stick"
version "SEN-10183" (HMC5843 magnetometer)
//#define HW__VERSION_CODE 10321 // SparkFun "9DOF Sensor Stick"
version "SEN-10321" (HMC5843 magnetometer)
//#define HW__VERSION_CODE 10724 // SparkFun "9DOF Sensor Stick"
version "SEN-10724" (HMC5883L magnetometer)
```

In my case, I'm using 9DoF Razor IMU version SEN-10736. Now, you can save and upload the code. Take care to choose the right processor in the Arduino IDE. For my razor IMU, an Arduino Pro or Pro Mini has to be chosen and an ATMega 3.3V 8 MHz must be selected as processor.

In the razor_imu package, you have to prepare a config file named my_razor.yaml. You can copy the default to my_razor.yaml configuration doing:

```
$ roscd razor_imu_9dof/config
$ cp razor.yaml my_razor.yaml
```

You can open the file and check whether the configuration matches with yours. Now the most important thing is setting up your port correctly; check it whether you are using the sensor stick and your Arduino. In my case, it is by default:

```
port: /dev/ttyUSB0
```

Note that if you calibrate your IMU, you can include all the calibration parameter in this file to have a correct orientation measurement.

You can use now your razor_imu or stick with the following launch command:

```
$ roslaunch razor_imu_9dof razor-pub-and-display.launch
```

Two windows must appear, one with a 3D figure that represents the pose of the IMU and a 2D figure with the **Roll**, **Pitch**, and **Yaw**.

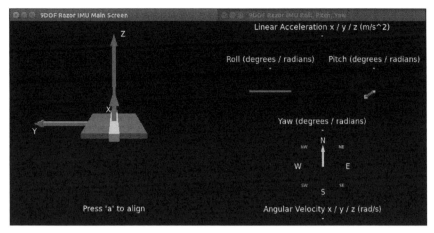

Razor IMU display

After some seconds, sensor `msgs::IMU` start to be transmitted and you will see how the parameters will change if you move your sensor.

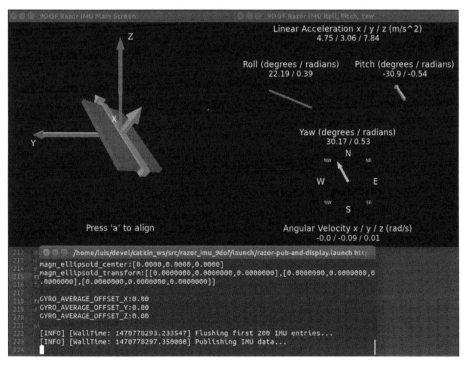

Razor IMU with different orientation

How does Razor send data in ROS?

If everything is fine, you can see the topic list using the `rostopic` command:

```
$ rostopic list
```

The node will publish three topics. We will work with /imu/data in this section. First of all, we are going to see the type and the data sent by this topic. To see the type and the fields, use the following command lines:

```
$ rostopic type /imu
$ rosmsg show sensor_msgs/Imu
```

```
std_msgs/Header header
  uint32 seq
  time stamp
  string frame_id
geometry_msgs/Quaternion orientation
  float64 x
  float64 y
  float64 z
  float64 w
float64[9] orientation_covariance
geometry_msgs/Vector3 angular_velocity
  float64 x
  float64 y
  float64 z
float64[9] angular_velocity_covariance
geometry_msgs/Vector3 linear_acceleration
  float64 x
  float64 y
  float64 z
float64[9] linear_acceleration_covariance
```

The /imu topic is sensor_msg/Imu. The fields are used to indicate the orientation, acceleration, and velocity. In our example, we will use the orientation field. Check a message to see a real example of the data sent. You can do it with the following command:

```
$ rostopic echo /imu
```

You will see something similar to the following output:

```
header:
  seq: 43264
  stamp:
    secs: 1480621387
    nsecs: 926049947
  frame_id: base_imu_link
orientation:
  x: -0.664401936806
  y: 0.459286679427
  z: -0.562455021343
  w: 0.176833711254
orientation_covariance: [0.0025, 0.0, 0.0, 0.0, 0.0025, 0.0, 0.0, 0.0, 0.0025]
angular_velocity:
  x: -0.02
  y: -0.04
  z: -0.0
angular_velocity_covariance: [0.02, 0.0, 0.0, 0.0, 0.02, 0.0, 0.0, 0.0, 0.02]
linear_acceleration:
  x: 5.8836
  y: -7.60960921875
  z: -2.98087078125
linear_acceleration_covariance: [0.04, 0.0, 0.0, 0.0, 0.04, 0.0, 0.0, 0.0, 0.04]
---
```

If you observe the orientation field, you will see four variables instead of three, as you would probably expect. This is because in ROS, the spatial orientation is represented using quaternions. You can find a lot of literature on the Internet about this concise and unambiguous orientation representation.

Creating an ROS node to use data from the 9DoF sensor in our robot

Now that we have our low-cost IMU working in ROS, we are going to create a new node that subscribes to the `imu/data` topics from the Razor IMU. For example, we can see in our robot model the pitch, roll, and heading depending on the IMU data. So, let's create a new node based on our `c8_odom.cpp`. We will name this file `c8_odom_with_imu.cpp`.

Now, we are going to make some modifications. First, we will include `sensor_msgs/Imu` to be able to subscribe to IMU topics:

```
#include <sensor_msgs/Imu.h>
```

Also, we need a global variable to store IMU data:

```
sensor_msgs::Imu imu;
```

Then, we are going to create a callback function to obtain IMU data:

```
void imuCallback(const sensor_msgs::Imu &imu_msg)
{
  imu = imu_msg;
}
```

In the `main` function, we need to declare a subscriber to `/imu_data` topic:

```
ros::Subscriber imu_sub = n.subscribe("imu_data", 10,
imuCallback);
```

And we have to assign each `odom` transform to the right IMU orientation data:

```
odom_trans.transform.rotation.x = imu.orientation.x;
odom_trans.transform.rotation.y = imu.orientation.y;
odom_trans.transform.rotation.z = imu.orientation.z;
odom_trans.transform.rotation.w = imu.orientation.w;
```

Also, we have to assign the pose of the robot to the orientation obtained by the IMU:

```
odom.pose.pose.orientation.x = imu.orientation.x;
odom.pose.pose.orientation.y = imu.orientation.y;
odom.pose.pose.orientation.z = imu.orientation.z;
odom.pose.pose.orientation.w = imu.orientation.w;
```

Once we have created this file and compile it, we are able to run this example:

```
$ roslaunch razor_imu_9dof razor-pub-and-display.launch
$ roslaunch chapter8_tutorials chapter8_robot_imu.launch
```

You will see the Razor IMU display and the robot model in the RViz visualizer. The robot model will have the pose and orientation of the Razor IMU.

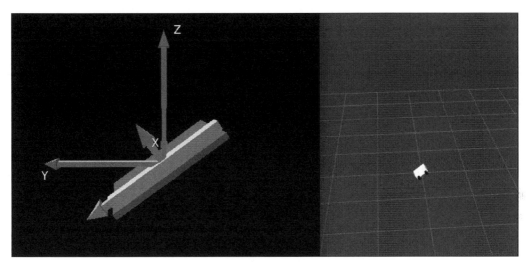

Razor IMU display and robot model in Rviz

Using robot localization to fuse sensor data in your robot

Now, we have our robot and we have different sources that can be used to localize the robot such as the wheel encoders and the 9DoF Razor IMU. We are going to install a new package to combine the data from these sensors to improve our robot position estimation. The package `robot_localization` use an **Extended Kalman Filter (EKF)** to calculate the new estimation using data from multiple sensors.

To install this package, we will type the following command in a terminal:

```
$ sudo apt-get install ros-kinetic-robot-localization
```

Once we have installed this package, the next step is learning how to use it. So, we are going to explore inside the package, a launch file named `ekf_template.launch`:

```
$ rosed robot_localization ekf_template.launch
```

When the file is opened, we will see the following code:

```
<launch>
  <node pkg="robot_localization" type="ekf_localization_node"
  name="ekf_se" clear_params="true">
    <rosparam command="load" file="$(find
    robot_localization)/params/ekf_template.yaml" />
    <!-- Placeholder for output topic remapping
<remap from="odometry/filtered" to=""/>
-->
  </node>
</launch>
```

And we will see the code in order to launch the `ekf_localization_node` and load some parameters that are saved in `ekf_template.yaml`. The `yaml` file is similar to this format:

```
#Configuration for robot odometry EKF
#
frequency: 50

odom0: /odom
odom0_config: [false, false, false,
false, false, false,
true, true, true,
false, false, true,
false, false, false]
odom0_differential: false

imu0: /imu_data
imu0_config: [false, false, false,
false, false, true,
false, false, false,
false, false, true,
true, false, false]
imu0_differential: false

odom_frame: odom
base_link_frame: base_footprint
world_frame: odom
```

In this file, we define the name of our IMU topic, our odometry topic, also the `base_link_frame`. The EKF filter uses only data from the IMU and odometry topics that are selected by a 6 x 3 matrix filled with true or false.

We are going to save this `yaml` file in `chapter8_tutorials/config` with the name `robot_localization.yaml`, and we are going to create a new launch file in the launch folder of the chapter named `robot_localization.yaml`:

```
<launch>
  <node pkg="robot_localization" type="ekf_localization_node"
  name="ekf_localization">
    <rosparam command="load" file="$(find
    chapter8_tutorials)/config/robot_localization.yaml" />
  </node>
</launch>
```

Now, we have finished the code of our robot and we can test all the parts:

```
$ roscore
```

```
$ rosrun rosserial_python serial_node.py /dev/ttyACM0
```

```
$ roslaunch razor_imu_9dof razor-pub-and-display.launch
```

```
$ roslaunch chapter8_tutorials chapter8_robot_encoders.launch
```

```
$ roslaunch chapter8_tutorials robot_localization
```

Using the IMU – Xsens MTi

In the following image, you can see the Xsens MTi, which is the sensor used in this section:

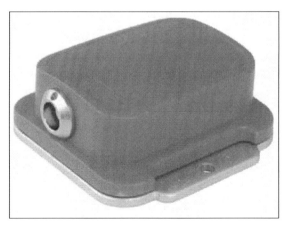

Xsens Mti

Xsens IMU is a typical inertial sensor that you can find in a robot. In this section, you will learn how to use it in ROS and how to use the topics published by the sensor.

You can use a lot of IMU devices with ROS such as the Razor IMU that we have used before. In this section, we will use the Xsens IMU, which is necessary to install the right drivers. But if you want to use MicroStrain 3DM-GX2 or Wiimote with Wii Motion Plus, you need to download the following drivers:

> The drivers for the MicroStrain 3DM-GX2 IMU are available at
> `http://www.ros.org/wiki/microstrain_3dmgx2_imu`.
> The drivers for Wiimote with Wii Motion Plus are available at
> `http://www.ros.org/wiki/wiimote`.

To use our device, we are going to use `xsens_driver`. You can install it using the following command:

```
$ sudo apt-get install ros-kinect-xsens-driver
```

Using the following commands, we also need to install two packages because the driver depends on them:

```
$ rosstack profile
```

```
$ rospack profile
```

Now, we are going to start IMU and see how it works. In a shell, launch the following command:

```
$ roslaunch xsens_driver xsens_driver.launch
```

This driver detects the USB port and the baud rate directly without any changes.

How does Xsens send data in ROS?

If everything is fine, you can see the topic list by using the `rostopic` command:

```
$ rostopic list
```

The node will publish three topics. We will work with /imu/data in this section. First of all, we are going to see the type and the data sent by this topic. To see the type and the fields, use the following command lines:

```
$ rostopic type /imu/data
$ rostopic type /imu/data | rosmsg show
```

The /imu/data topic is sensor_msg/Imu. The fields are used to indicate the orientation, acceleration, and velocity. In our example, we will use the orientation field. Check a message to see a real example of the data sent. You can do it with the following command:

```
$ rostopic echo /imu/data
```

You will see something similar to the following output:

```
---
header:
seq: 288
stamp:
secs: 1330631562
nsecs: 789304161
frame_id: xsens_mti_imu
orientation:
x:  0.00401890464127
y: -0.00402884092182
z:  0.679586052895
w:  0.73357373476
---
```

If you observe the orientation field, you will see four variables instead of three, as you would probably expect. This is because in ROS, the spatial orientation is represented using quaternions. You can find a lot of literature on the Internet about this concise and nonambiguous orientation representation.

We can observe the IMU orientation in the rviz run and add the imu display type:

```
$ rosrun rviz rviz
```

Using a GPS system

The **Global Positioning System (GPS)** is a space-based satellite system that provides information on the position and time for any weather and any place on the face of the earth and its vicinity. You must have an unobstructed direct path with four GPS satellites to obtain valid data.

The data received from the GPS conforms to the standards of communication set up by **National Maritime Electronics Association (NMEA)** and follows a protocol with different types of sentences. In them, we can find all the information about the position of the receiver.

To read more about all the types of NMEA messages, you can visit http://www.gpsinformation.org/dale/nmea.htm.

One of the most interesting pieces of information about GPS is contained in GGA sentences. They provide the current fix data with the 3D location of the GPS. An example of this sentence and an explanation of each field is given here:

```
$GPGGA,123519,4807.038,N,01131.000,E,1,08,0.9,545.4,M,46.9,M,,*47
Where:
GGA Global Positioning System Fix Data
123519 Fix taken at 12:35:19 UTC
4807.038,N Latitude 48 deg 07.038' N
01131.000,E Longitude 11 deg 31.000' E
1 Fix quality: 0 = invalid
1 = GPS fix (SPS)
2 = DGPS fix
3 = PPS fix
4 = Real Time Kinematic
5 = Float RTK
6 = estimated (dead reckoning) (2.3 feature)
7 = Manual input mode
8 = Simulation mode
08 Number of satellites being tracked
0.9 Horizontal dilution of position
545.4,M Altitude, Meters, above mean sea level
46.9,M Height of geoid (mean sea level) above WGS84
ellipsoid
(empty field) time in seconds since last DGPS update
(empty field) DGPS station ID number
*47 the checksum data, always begins with *
```

Depending on the GPS receiver, we can find different performances and precisions. We have a simple GPS at a low cost that is commonly used in different applications, such as UAV. They have an error that can be in the range of a few meters. Also, we can find expensive GPS devices that can be configured as differential GPS or can work in the **Real Time Kinematics (RTK)** mode, where a second GPS at a known location sends corrections to the first GPS. This GPS can achieve great results in terms of precision, with location errors less than 10 cm.

In general, GPS uses serial protocols to transmit the data received to a computer or a microcontroller, such as Arduino. We can find devices that use TTL or RS232, and they are easy to connect to the computer with a USB adapter. In this section, we will use a low-cost NEO-Bloc 6 M and a really accurate system, such as GR-3 Topcon in the RTK mode. We will see that, with the same drivers, we can obtain the latitude, longitude, and altitude from both devices:

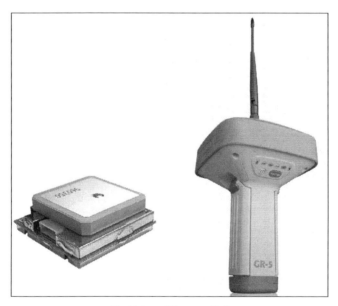

Em406a and Topcon GPS

In order to control a GPS sensor with ROS, we will install the NMEA GPS driver package by using the following command line (don't forget to run the `rosstack` and `rospack` profiles after that):

```
$ sudo apt-get install ros-kinetic-nmea-gps-driver
$ rosstack profile & rospack profile
```

To execute the GPS driver, we will run the `nmea_gpst_driver.py` file. To do that, we have to indicate two arguments: the port that is connected to the GPS and the baud rate:

```
$ rosrun nmea_gps_driver nmea_gps_driver.py _port:=/dev/ttyUSB0 _
baud:=4800
```

In the case of the EM-406a GPS, the default baud rate is 4800 Hz as indicated in the preceding command line. For Topcon GR-3, the baud rate is higher; it's about 1,15,200 Hz. If we want to use it with ROS, we will modify the `_baud` argument, as shown in the following command:

```
$ rosrun nmea_gps_driver nmea_gps_driver.py _port:=/dev/ttyUSB0 _
baud:=115200
```

How GPS sends messages

If everything is OK, we will see a topic named `/fix` in the topic list by typing this:

```
$ rostopic list
```

To know which kind of data we will use, we typed the `rostopic` command. The NMEA GPS driver uses the `sensor_msgs/NavSatFix` message to send the GPS status information:

```
$ rostopic type /fix
```

```
sensor_msgs/NavSatFix
```

The `/fix` topic is `sensor_msg/NavSatFix`. The fields are used to indicate the latitude, longitude, altitude, status, quality of the service, and the covariance matrix. In our example, we will use the latitude and the longitude to project them to a 2D Cartesian coordinate system named **Universal Transverse Mercator (UTM)**.

Check a message to see a real example of the data sent. You can do it with the following command:

```
$ rostopic echo /fix
```

You will see something that looks similar to the following output:

```
---
header:
seq: 3
stamp:
```

```
secs: 1404993925
nsecs: 255094051
frame_id: /gps
status:
status: 0
service: 1
latitude: 28.0800916667
longitude: -15.451595
altitude: 315.3
position_covariance: [3.24, 0.0, 0.0, 0.0, 3.24, 0.0, 0.0, 0.0, 12.96]
position_covariance_type: 1
---
```

Creating an example project to use GPS

In this example, we are going to project the latitude and the longitude of GPS to a 2D Cartesian space. For this, we will use a function written by *Chuck Gantz* that converts latitudes and longitudes into UTM coordinates. The node will subscribe to the /fix topic where GPS data is sent. You can find the code in chapter8_tutorials in the c8_fixtoUTM.cpp file:

```cpp
#include <ros/ros.h>
#include <tf/transform_broadcaster.h>
#include <nav_msgs/Odometry.h>
#include <stdio.h>
#include <iostream>
#include <sensor_msgs/NavSatFix.h>
geometry_msgs::Point global_position;
ros::Publisher position_pub;
void gpsCallBack(const sensor_msgs::NavSatFixConstPtr& gps)
{
  double northing, easting;
  char zone;
  LLtoUTM(gps->latitude, gps->longitude, northing, easting ,
  &zone);
  global_position.x = easting;
  global_position.y = northing;
  global_position.z = gps->altitude;
}
```

```
int main(int argc, char** argv){
  ros::init(argc,argv, "fixtoUTM");
  ros::NodeHandle n;
  ros::Subscriber gps_sub = n.subscribe("fix",10, gpsCallBack);
  position_pub = n.advertise<geometry_msgs::Point>
  ("global_position", 1);
  ros::Rate loop_rate(10);
  while(n.ok())
  {
    ros::spinOnce();
    loop_rate.sleep();
  }
}
```

First, you should declare the `NavSatFix` message using `#include <sensor_msgs/NavSatFix.h>`.

This way, we can subscribe to the `/fix` topic in the `ros::Subscriber gps_sub = n.subscribe("fix",10, gpsCallBack)` main function.

All the action happens in the `gpsCallBack()` function. We will use the `LltoUTM()` function to make the conversion from latitudes and longitudes to the UTM space. We will publish a `geometry_msg/Point` topic named `/global_position` with the UTM northing and easting coordinates and the altitude from the GPS.

To try this code, after running the GPS driver, you can use the following command:

```
$ rosrun chapter8_tutorials c8_fixtoUTM
```

You can use GPS data to improve your robot localization using *Kalman* filters to fuse odometry and IMU with `NavSatFix` data.

Using a laser rangefinder – Hokuyo URG-04lx

In mobile robotics, it is very important to know where the obstacles are, the outline of a room, and so on. Robots use maps to navigate and move across unknown spaces. The sensor used for these purposes is LIDAR. This sensor is used to measure distances between the robot and objects.

In this section, you will learn how to use a low-cost version of LIDAR that is widely used in robotics. This sensor is the Hokuyo URG-04lx rangefinder. You can obtain more information about it at `http://www.hokuyo-aut.jp/`. The Hokuyo rangefinder is a device used to navigate and build maps in real time:

Hokuyo URG-041x

The Hokuyo URG-04lx model is a low-cost rangefinder commonly used in robotics. It has a very good resolution and is very easy to use. To start with, we are going to install the drivers for the laser:

```
$ sudo apt-get install ros-kinetic-hokuyo-node
$ rosstack profile && rospack profile
```

Once installed, we are going to check whether everything is OK. Connect your laser and check whether the system can detect it and whether it is configured correctly:

```
$ ls -l /dev/ttyACM0
```

When the laser is connected, the system sees it, so the result of the preceding command line is the following output:

```
crw-rw---- 1 root dialout 166, 0 Jan 13 11:09 /dev/ttyACM0
```

In our case, we need to reconfigure the laser device to give ROS the access to use it; that is, we need to give the appropriate permissions:

```
$ sudo chmod a+rw /dev/ttyACM0
```

Check the reconfiguration with the following command line:

```
$ ls -l /dev/ttyACM0
crw-rw-rw- 1 root dialout 166, 0 Jan 13 11:09 /dev/ttyACM0
```

Once everything is OK, we are going to switch on the laser. Start roscore in one shell, and in another shell, execute the following command:

```
$ rosrun hokuyo_node hokuyo_node
```

If everything is fine, you will see the following output:

```
[ INFO] [1358076340.184643618]: Connected to device with ID: H1000484
```

Understanding how the laser sends data in ROS

To check whether the node is sending data, use rostopic, as shown here:

```
$ rostopic list
```

You will see the following topics as the output:

```
/diagnostics
/hokuyo_node/parameter_descriptions
/hokuyo_node/parameter_updates
/rosout
/rosout_agg
/scan
```

The /scan topic is the topic where the node is publishing. The type of data used by the node is shown here:

```
$ rostopic type /scan
```

You will then see the message type used to send information about the laser:

```
sensor_msgs/LaserScan
```

You can see the structure of the message using the following command:

```
$ rosmsg show sensor_msgs/LaserScan
```

To learn a little bit more about how the laser works and what data it is sending, we are going to use the rostopic command to see a real message:

```
$ rostopic echo /scan
```

Then, you will see the following message sent by the laser:

```
---
header:
seq: 3895
stamp:
secs: 1358076731
nsecs: 284896750
frame_id: laser
...
ranges: [1.1119999885559082, 1.1119999885559082, 1.1109999418258667, ...]
intensities: []
---
```

This data is difficult to understand for humans. If you want to see the data in a more friendly and graphical way, it is possible to do so using `rviz`. Type the following command line in a shell to launch `rviz` with the correct configuration file:

```
$ rosrun rviz rviz -d 'rospack find chapter8_tutorials'/config/laser.rviz
```

The following screenshot shows a graphical representation of the message:

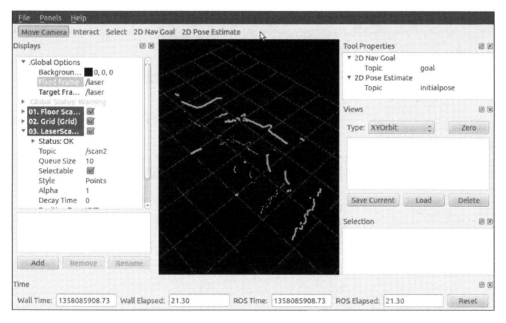

Laser visualization in Rviz

You will see the contour on the screen. If you move the laser sensor, you will see the contour changing.

Accessing the laser data and modifying it

Now, we are going to make a node get the laser data, do something with it, and publish the new data. Perhaps, this will be useful at a later date, and with this example, you will learn how to do it.

Copy the following code snippet to the `c8_laserscan.cpp` file in your `/chapter8_tutorials/src` directory:

```cpp
#include <ros/ros.h>
#include "std_msgs/String.h"
#include <sensor_msgs/LaserScan.h>

#include<stdio.h>
using namespace std;
class Scan2{
  public:
  Scan2();
  private:
  ros::NodeHandle n;
  ros::Publisher scan_pub;
  ros::Subscriber scan_sub;
  void scanCallBack(const sensor_msgs::LaserScan::ConstPtr&
  scan2);
};
Scan2::Scan2()
{
  scan_pub = n.advertise<sensor_msgs::LaserScan>("/scan2",1);
  scan_sub = n.subscribe<sensor_msgs::LaserScan>("/scan",1,
  &Scan2::scanCallBack, this);
}

void Scan2::scanCallBack(const sensor_msgs::LaserScan::ConstPtr&
scan2)
{
  int ranges = scan2->ranges.size();
  //populate the LaserScan message
  sensor_msgs::LaserScan scan;
  scan.header.stamp = scan2->header.stamp;
  scan.header.frame_id = scan2->header.frame_id;
  scan.angle_min = scan2->angle_min;
  scan.angle_max = scan2->angle_max;
```

```
   scan.angle_increment = scan2->angle_increment;
   scan.time_increment = scan2->time_increment;
   scan.range_min = 0.0;
   scan.range_max = 100.0;
   scan.ranges.resize(ranges);
   for(int i = 0; i < ranges; ++i)
   {
      scan.ranges[i] = scan2->ranges[i] + 1;
   }
   scan_pub.publish(scan);
}
int main(int argc, char** argv)
{
   ros::init(argc, argv, "laser_scan_publisher");
   Scan2 scan2;
   ros::spin();
}
```

We are going to break the code and see what it is doing.

In the `main` function, we initialize the node with the name `example2_laser_scan_publisher` and create an instance of the class that we have created in the file.

In the constructor, we will create two topics: one of them will subscribe to the other topic, which is the original data from the laser. The second topic will publish the newly modified data from the laser.

This example is very simple; we are only going to add one unit to the data received from the laser topic and publish it again. We do that in the `scanCallBack()` function. Take the input message and copy all the fields to another variable. Then, take the field where the data is stored and add the one unit. Once the new value is stored, publish the new topic:

```
void Scan2::scanCallBack(const sensor_msgs::LaserScan::ConstPtr&
scan2)
{
   ...
   sensor_msgs::LaserScan scan;
   scan.header.stamp = scan2->header.stamp;
   ...
   ...
   scan.range_max = 100.0;
   scan.ranges.resize(ranges);
```

```
for(int i = 0; i < ranges; ++i){
    scan.ranges[i] = scan2->ranges[i] + 1;
}

scan_pub.publish(scan);
}
```

Creating a launch file

To launch everything, we are going to create a launch file, `chapter8_laserscan.launch`:

```
<launch>
  <node pkg="hokuyo_node" type="hokuyo_node" name="hokuyo_node"/>
  <node pkg="rviz" type="rviz" name="rviz"
  args="-d $(find chapter8_tutorials)/config/laser.rviz"/>

  <node pkg="chapter8_tutorials" type="c8_laserscan"
  name="c8_laserscan" />
</launch>
```

Now, if you launch the `chapter8_laserscan.launch` file, three nodes will start: `hokuyo_node`, `rviz`, and `c8_laserscan`. You will see the RViz visualizer screen with the two-laser contour. The green contour is the new data, as shown in the following screenshot:

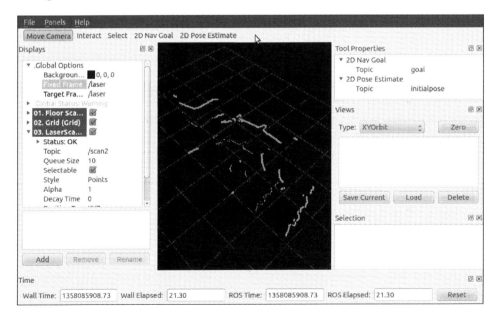

Using the Kinect sensor to view objects in 3D

The Kinect sensor is a flat, black box that sits on a small platform when placed on a table or shelf near the television you're using with your Xbox 360. This device has the following three sensors that we can use for vision and robotics tasks:

- A color VGA video camera to see the world in color

- A depth sensor, which is an infrared projector and a monochrome CMOS sensor working together, to see objects in 3D

- A multiarray microphone that is used to isolate the voices of the players from the noise in the room

Kinect

In ROS, we are going to use two of these sensors: the RGB camera and the depth sensor. In the latest version of ROS, you can even use three.

Before we start using it, we need to install the packages and drivers. Use the following command lines to install them:

```
$ sudo apt-get install ros-kinetic-openni-camera ros-kinetickinetic-openni-launch
$ rosstack profile && rospack profile
```

Once the packages and drivers are installed, plug in the Kinect sensor, and we will run the nodes to start using it. In a shell, start `roscore`. In another shell, run the following command lines:

```
$ rosrun openni_camera openni_node
$ roslaunch openni_launch openni.launch
```

If everything goes well, you will not see any error messages.

How does Kinect send data from the sensors, and how do we see it?

Now, we are going to see what we can do with these nodes. List the topics that you have created using this command:

```
$ rostopic list
```

Then, you will see a lot of topics, but the most important ones for us are the following:

```
...
/camera/rgb/image_color
/camera/rgb/image_mono
/camera/rgb/image_raw
/camera/rgb/image_rect
/camera/rgb/image_rect_color
...
```

We will see a lot of topics created by nodes. If you want to see one of the sensors, for example, the RGB camera, you can use the `/camera/rgb/image_color` topic. To see the image from the sensor, we are going to use the `image_view` package. Type the following command in a shell:

```
$ rosrun image_view image_view image:=/camera/rgb/image_color
```

Note that we need to rename (remap) the image topic to `/camera/rgb/image_color` using the parameter's image. If everything is fine, a new window appears that shows the image from Kinect.

If you want to see the depth sensor, you can do so just by changing the topic in the last command line:

```
$ rosrun image_view image_view image:=/camera/depth/image
```

You will then see an image similar to the following screenshot:

RGB and depth image from Kinect

Another important topic is the one that sends the point cloud data. This kind of data is a 3D representation of the depth image. You can find this data in /camera/depth/ points, /camera/depth_registered/points and other topics.

We are going to see the type of message this is. To do this, use rostopic type. To see the fields of a message, we can use rostopic type /topic_name | rosmsg show. In this case, we are going to use the /camera/depth/points topic:

$ rostopic type /camera/depth/points | rosmsg show

> To see the official specification of the message, visit http://ros.org/ doc/api/sensor_msgs/html/msg/PointCloud2.html.

If you want to visualize this type of data, run rviz in a new shell and add a new PointCloud2 data visualization, as shown here:

$ rosrun rviz rviz

Click on **Add**, order topics by display type, and select PointCloud2. Once you have added a PointCloud2 display type, you have to select the name of the camera/ depth/points topic.

On your computer, you will see a 3D image in real time; if you move in front of the sensor, you will see yourself moving in 3D, as you can see in the following screenshot:

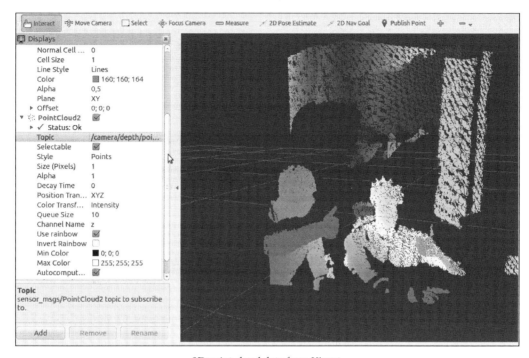

3D point cloud data from Kinect

Creating an example to use Kinect

Now, we are going to implement a program to generate a node that filters the point cloud from the Kinect sensor. This node will apply a filter to reduce the number of points in the original data. It will make a down sampling of the data.

Create a new file, c8_kinect.cpp, in your chapter8_tutorials/src directory and type in the following code snippet:

```
#include <ros/ros.h>
#include <sensor_msgs/PointCloud2.h>
// PCL specific includes
#include <pcl_conversions/pcl_conversions.h>
#include <pcl/point_cloud.h>
```

```
#include <pcl/point_types.h>
#include <pcl/filters/voxel_grid.h>

#include <pcl/io/pcd_io.h>

ros::Publisher pub;
void cloud_cb (const pcl::PCLPointCloud2ConstPtr& input)
{
  pcl::PCLPointCloud2 cloud_filtered;
  pcl::VoxelGrid<pcl::PCLPointCloud2> sor;
  sor.setInputCloud (input);
  sor.setLeafSize (0.01, 0.01, 0.01);
  sor.filter (cloud_filtered);
  // Publish the dataSize
  pub.publish (cloud_filtered);
}

int main (int argc, char** argv)
{
  // Initialize ROS
  ros::init (argc, argv, "c8_kinect");
  ros::NodeHandle nh;
  // Create a ROS subscriber for the input point cloud
  ros::Subscriber sub = nh.subscribe ("/camera/depth/points", 1,
  cloud_cb);
  // Create a ROS publisher for the output point cloud
  pub = nh.advertise<sensor_msgs::PointCloud2> ("output", 1);
  // Spin
  ros::spin ();
}
```

This sample is based on the tutorial of **Point Cloud Library (PCL)**.

You can see it at http://pointclouds.org/documentation/
tutorials/voxel_grid.php#voxelgrid.

All the work is done in the `cb()` function. This function is called when a message arrives. We create a `sor` variable with the `VoxelGrid` type, and the range of the grid is changed in `sor.setLeafSize()`. These values will change the grid used for the filter. If you increment the value, you will obtain less resolution and fewer points on the point cloud:

```
cloud_cb (const sensor_msgs::PointCloud2ConstPtr& input)
{
  ...
  pcl::VoxelGrid<sensor_msgs::PointCloud2> sor;
  ...
  sor.setLeafSize(0.01f,0.01f,0.01f);
  ...
}
```

If we open `rviz` now with the new node running, we will see the new point cloud in the window, and you will directly notice that the resolution is less than that of the original data, as shown in the following screenshot:

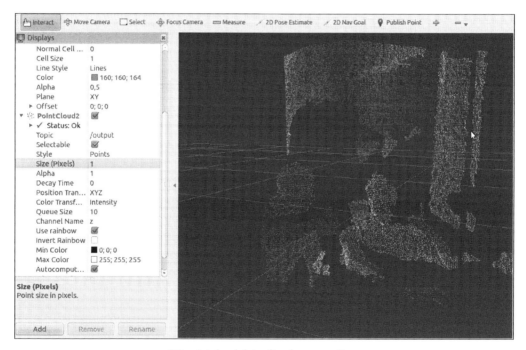

3D point cloud data after downsampling

On `rviz`, you can see the number of points that a message has. For original data, we can see that the number of points is **2,19,075**. With the new point cloud, we obtain **16,981** points. As you can see, it is a huge reduction of data.

At `http://pointclouds.org/`, you will find more filters and tutorials on how you can use this kind of data.

Using servomotors – Dynamixel

In mobile robots, servomotors are widely used. This kind of actuator is used to move sensors, wheels, and robotic arms. A low-cost solution is to use RC servomotors. It provides a movement range of 180 degrees and a high torque for the existing servomotors.

The servomotor that we will explain in this section is a new type of servomotor designed and used for robotics. This is the **Dynamixel servomotor**.

Dynamixel is a lineup, high-performance, networked actuator for robots developed by *ROBOTIS*, a Korean manufacturer. ROBOTIS is also the developer and manufacturer of OLLO, Bioloid, and DARwIn-OP DXL. These robots are used by numerous companies, universities, and hobbyists due to their versatile expansion capability, powerful feedback functions, position, speed, internal temperature, input voltage, and their simple daisy chain topology for simplified wiring connections.

In the following image, you can see Dynamixel AX-12 and the USB interface. Both are used in this example.

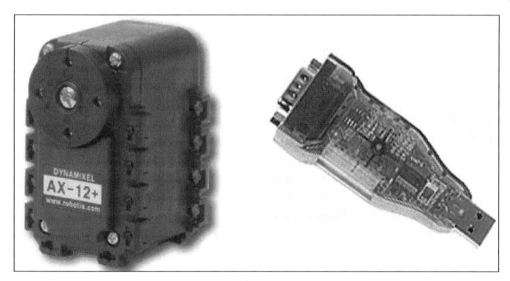

Dynamixel AX-12+ motor

First, we are going to install the necessary packages and drivers. Type the following command line in a shell:

```
$ sudo apt-get install ros-kinetic-dynamixel-motor
$ rosstack profile && rospack profile
```

Once the necessary packages and drivers are installed, connect the dongle to the computer and check whether it is detected. Normally, it will create a new port with the name `ttyUSBX` inside your `/dev/` folder. If you see this port, everything is OK, and now we can let the nodes play a little with the servomotor.

In a shell, start `roscore`, and in another shell, type the following command line:

```
$ roslaunch dynamixel_tutorials controller_manager.launch
```

If the motors are connected, you will see the motors detected by the driver. In our case, a motor with the ID 6 is detected and configured:

```
process[dynamixel_manager-1]: started with pid [3966]

[INFO] [WallTime: 1359377042.681841] pan_tilt_port: Pinging motor IDs 1
through 25...

[INFO] [WallTime: 1359377044.846779] pan_tilt_port: Found 1 motors - 1
AX-12 [6], initialization complete.
```

How does Dynamixel send and receive commands for the movements?

Once you have launched the `controller_manager.launch` file, you will see a list of topics. Remember to use the following command line to see these topics:

```
$ rostopic list
```

These topics will show the state of the motors configured, as follows:

```
/diagnostics
/motor_states/pan_tilt_port
/rosout
/rosout_agg
```

If you see `/motor_states/pan_tilt_port` with the `rostopic` echo command, you will see the state of all the motors, which, in our case, is only the motor with the ID 6; however, we cannot move the motors with these topics, so we need to run the next launch file to do it.

This launch file will create the necessary topics to move the motors, as follows:

```
$ roslaunch dynamixel_tutorials controller_spawner.launch
```

The topic list will have two new topics added to the list. One of the new topics will be used to move the servomotor, as follows:

```
/diagnostics
/motor_states/pan_tilt_port
/rosout
/rosout_agg
/tilt_controller/command
/tilt_controller/state
```

To move the motor, we are going to use the /tilt_controller/command that will publish a topic with the rostopic pub command. First, you need to see the fields of the topic and the type. To do this, use the following command lines:

```
$ rostopic type /tilt_controller/command
```

```
std_msgs/Float64
```

As you can see, it is a Float64 variable. This variable is used to move the motor to a position measured in radians. So, to publish a topic, use the following commands:

```
$ rostopic pub /tilt_controller/command std_msgs/Float64 -- 0.5
```

Once the command is executed, you will see the motor moving, and it will stop at 0.5 radians or 28.6478898 degrees.

Creating an example to use the servomotor

Now, we are going to show you how you can move the motor using a node. Create a new file, c8_dynamixel.cpp, in your /c_tutorials/src directory with the following code snippet:

```cpp
#include<ros/ros.h>
#include<std_msgs/Float64.h>
#include<stdio.h>

using namespace std;
```

```
class Dynamixel{
  private:
  ros::NodeHandle n;
  ros::Publisher pub_n;
  public:
  Dynamixel();
  int moveMotor(double position);
};

Dynamixel::Dynamixel(){
  pub_n = n.advertise<std_msgs::Float64>
  ("/tilt_controller/command",1);
}
int Dynamixel::moveMotor(double position)
{
  std_msgs::Float64 aux;
  aux.data = position;
  pub_n.publish(aux);
  return 1;
}

int main(int argc,char** argv)
{
  ros::init(argc, argv, "c8_dynamixel");
  Dynamixel motors;

  float counter = -180;
  ros::Rate loop_rate(100);
  while(ros::ok())
  {
    if(counter < 180)
    {
      motors.moveMotor(counter*3.14/180);
      counter++;
    }else{
      counter = -180;
    }
    loop_rate.sleep();
  }
}
```

This node will move the motor continuously from -180 to 180 degrees. It is a simple example, but you can use it to make complex movements or control more motors. We assume that you understand the code and that it is not necessary to explain it. Note that you are publishing data to the /tilt_controller/command topic; this is the name of the motor.

Summary

The use of sensors and actuators in robotics is very important since this is the only way to interact with the real world. In this chapter, you learned how to use, configure, and investigate further how certain common sensors and actuators work, which are used by a number of people in the world of robotics. We are sure that if you wish to use another type of sensor, you will find information on the Internet and in the ROS documentation about how to use it without problems.

In our opinion, Arduino is a very interesting device because you can build your own robots, add more devices and cheap sensors to your computer with it, and use them within the ROS framework easily and transparently. Arduino has a large community, and you can find information on many sensors, which cover the spectrum of applications you can imagine.

Finally, we must mention that the range laser will be a very useful sensor for the navigation algorithms as you saw in the simulation chapters. The reason is that it is a mandatory device to implement the navigation stack, which relies on the range readings it provides at a high frequency and with good precision.

9
Computer Vision

ROS provides basic support for **Computer Vision**. First, drivers are available for different cameras and protocols, especially for FireWire (IEEE1394a or IEEE1394b) cameras. An image pipeline helps with the camera calibration process, distortion rectification, color decoding, and other low-level operations. For more complex tasks, you can use **OpenCV** and the `cv_bridge` and `image_transport` libraries to interface with it and subscribe and publish images on topics. Finally, there are several packages that implement algorithms for object recognition, augmented reality, visual odometry, and so on.

Although FireWire cameras are best integrated in ROS, it is not difficult to support other protocols, such as USB and Gigabit Ethernet. Since USB cameras are usually less expensive and easier to find, in this chapter we discuss several available options, and we will also provide a driver that integrates seamlessly in the image pipeline, using the OpenCV video capture API.

The camera calibration and the result integration in the image pipeline will be explained in detail. ROS provides GUIs to help with the camera calibration process using a calibration pattern. Furthermore, we will cover stereo cameras and explain how we can manage rigs of two or more cameras, with more complex setups than a binocular camera. Stereo vision will also let us obtain depth information from the world, up to a certain extent and depending on certain conditions. Hence, we will also see how to inspect that information as point clouds and how to improve its quality to the best possible extent for our camera's quality and its setup.

We will also explain the **ROS image pipeline**, which simplifies the process of converting the RAW images acquired by the camera into monochrome (grayscale) and color images; this sometimes requires you to *debayer* the RAW images if they are codified as a Bayer pattern. If the camera has been calibrated, the calibration information is used to rectify the images, that is, to correct the distortion.

For stereo images, since we have the baseline the left and right cameras, we can compute the disparity image, which allows us to obtain depth information and a 3D point cloud once it has been fine-tuned; here, we will also give you tuning advice, as this can be be quite difficult for low-quality cameras that sometimes require good calibration results beforehand. Finally, by using OpenCV inside ROS, even though it's only version 2.x (version 3.x is not yet supported), we have the ability to implement a wide range of Computer Vision and machine learning algorithms, or we can even run some algorithms or examples already present in this library. However, we will not cover the OpenCV API, which is outside the scope of this book. We advise the reader to check the online documentation (`http://docs.opencv.org`) or any book about OpenCV and Computer Vision. We will also simply show you how you can use OpenCV in your nodes, with examples of feature detection, descriptor extraction, and matching to compute the homography between two images. Additionally, this chapter will finish with a tutorial that will show you how to set up and run a visual odometry implementation integrated into ROS, the `viso2_ros` wrapper of the `libviso2` visual odometry library, using a stereo pair built with two cheap webcams attached to a supporting bar. Other visual odometry libraries will be mentioned, for example, `fovis`, along with some advice on how to start working with them and how to improve the results with RGBD sensors (such as Kinect), sensor fusion, and additional information on monocular vision.

ROS camera drivers support

The different camera drivers available and the different ways to use cameras on ROS are explained in the following sections. In essence, they distinguish between FireWire and USB cameras.

The first few steps that we must perform are connecting the camera to the computer, running the driver, and seeing the images it acquires in ROS. Before we get into ROS, it is always a good idea to use external tools to check that the camera is actually recognized by our system, which, in our case, is an Ubuntu distribution. We will start with FireWire cameras since they are better supported in ROS, and later we will look at USB cameras.

FireWire IEEE1394 cameras

Connect your camera to the computer, which should have a FireWire IEEE1394a or IEEE1394b slot. Then, in Ubuntu, you only need `coriander` to check that the camera is recognized and working. If it is not already installed, just install `coriander`. Then, run it (in old Ubuntu distributions, you may have to run it as `sudo`):

```
$ coriander
```

It will automatically detect all your FireWire cameras, as shown in the following screenshot:

The great thing about `coriander` is that it also allows us to view the image and configure the camera. Indeed, our advice is to use the `coriander` package's camera configuration interface and then take those values into ROS, as we will see later. The advantage of this approach is that `coriander` gives us the dimensional values of some parameters. In ROS, there are certain parameters that sometimes fail to set, that is, gamma, and they may need to be set beforehand in `coriander` as a workaround.

Now that we know that the camera is working, we can close `coriander` and run the ROS FireWire camera driver (with `roscore` running). The camera driver package can be installed with:

```
$ sudo apt-get install ros-kinetic-camera1394
```

If it is not available yet on ROS Kinetic, build it from source on a workspace. It can be obtained from: `https://github.com/ros-drivers/camera1394`; simply clone the repository into a workspace and build it.

The camera driver is run with:

```
$ rosrun camera1394 camera1394_node
```

Simply run `roscore` and the previous command. It will start the first camera on the bus, but note that you can select the camera by its GUID, which you can see in the `coriander` package's GUI.

The FireWire camera's supported parameters are listed and assigned sensible values in the `camera1394/config/firewire_camera/format7_mode0.yaml` file, as shown in the following code:

```
guid: 00b09d0100ab1324 # (defaults to first camera on bus)
iso_speed: 800 # IEEE1394b
video_mode: format7_mode0 # 1384x1036 @ 30fpsbayer pattern
# Note that frame_rate is overwritten by frame_rate_feature; some
useful values:
# 21fps (480)
frame_rate: 21 # max fps (Hz)
auto_frame_rate_feature: 3 # Manual (3)
frame_rate_feature: 480
format7_color_coding: raw8 # for bayer
bayer_pattern: rggb
bayer_method: HQ
auto_brightness: 3 # Manual (3)
brightness: 0
auto_exposure: 3 # Manual (3)
exposure: 350
auto_gain: 3 # Manual (3)
gain: 700
# We cannot set gamma manually in ROS, so we switch it off
auto_gamma: 0 # Off (0)
#gamma: 1024 # gamma 1
auto_saturation: 3 # Manual (3)
saturation: 1000
auto_sharpness: 3 # Manual (3)
sharpness: 1000
auto_shutter: 3 # Manual (3)
#shutter: 1000 # = 10ms
shutter: 1512 # = 20ms (1/50Hz), max. in30fps
auto_white_balance: 3 # Manual (3)
white_balance_BU: 820
white_balance_RV: 520
```

```
frame_id: firewire_camera
camera_info_url:
package://chapter5_tutorials/calibration/firewire_camera/
calibration_firewire_camera.yaml
```

The values must be tuned by watching the images acquired, for example in coriander, and setting the values that give better images. The GUID parameter is used to select the camera, which is a unique value. You should set the shutter speed to a frequency equal to, or a multiple of, the electric light you have in the room to avoid flickering. If outside in sunlight, you only have to worry about setting a value that gives you an appropriate amount of light. You can use a high gain, but it will introduce noise. However, in general, it is better to have salt-and-pepper noise such as that of a low shutter speed (to receive most light), because with a low shutter speed, we have motion blur and most algorithms perform badly with it. As you can see, the configuration depends on the lighting conditions of the environment, and you may have to adapt the configuration to them. That is quite easy using coriander or the rqt_reconfigure interface (see the following screenshots and the upcoming code, for instance):

```
$ rosrun rqt_reconfigure rqt_reconfigure /camera
```

```
$ coriander
```

In order to better understand how to properly set the parameters of the camera to obtain high-quality images, which are also algorithm-friendly, you are encouraged to find out more about the basic concepts of photography, such as the exposure triangle, which is a combination of shutter speed, ISO, and aperture.

Here, the camera's namespace is /camera. Then, we can change all the parameters that are specified in the camera1394 dynamic reconfigure .cfg file, as shown in *Chapter 3*, *Visualization and Debugging Tools*. Here, for your convenience, you can create a launch file, which is also in launch/firewire_camera.launch:

```
<launch>
  <!-- Arguments -->
  <!-- Show video output (both RAW and rectified) -->
  <arg name="view" default="false" />
  <!-- Camera params (config) -->
  <arg name="params" default="$(find
  chapter5_tutorials)/config/firewire_camera/format7_mode0.yaml"
  />
  <!-- Camera driver -->
  <node pkg="camera1394" type="camera1394_node"
  name="camera1394_node">
    <rosparam file="$(argparams)" />
  </node>
```

```
<!-- Camera image processing (color + rectification) -->
<node ns="camera" pkg="image_proc" type="image_proc"
name="image_proc" />
<!-- Show video output -->
<group if="$(arg view)">
  <!-- Image viewer (non-rectified image) -->
  <node pkg="image_view" type="image_view"
  name="non_rectified_image">
    <remap from="image" to="camera/image_color" />
  </node>
  <!-- Image viewer (rectified image) -->
  <node pkg="image_view" type="image_view"
  name="rectified_image">
    <remap from="image" to="camera/image_rect_color" />
  </node>
</group>
</launch>
```

The `camera1394` driver is started with the parameters shown so far. It also runs the image pipeline that we will see in the sequel in order to obtain the color-rectified images using the **Debayer algorithm** and the calibration parameters (once the camera has been calibrated). We have a conditional group to visualize the color and color-rectified images using `image_view` (or `rqt_image_view`).

In sum, in order to run a FireWire camera in ROS and view the images, once you have set its GUID in the parameters file, simply run the following command:

```
$ roslaunch chapter5_tutorials firewire_camera.launch view:=true
```

Then, you can also configure it dynamically with `rqt_reconfigure`.

USB cameras

Now we are going to do the same thing with USB cameras. The only problem is that, surprisingly, they are not inherently supported by ROS. First of all, once you have connected the camera to the computer, test it with a chat or video meeting program, for example Skype or Cheese. The camera resource should appear in `/dev/video?`, where `?` should be a number starting with `0` (that may be your internal webcam if you are using a laptop).

There are two main options that deserve to be mentioned as possible USB camera drivers for ROS. First, we have `usb_cam`. To install it, use the following command:

```
$ sudo apt-get install ros-kinetic-usb-cam
```

Then, run the following command:

```
$ roslaunch chapter5_tutorials usb_cam.launch view:=true
```

It simply does `rosrun usb_cam usb_cam_node` and shows the camera images with `image_view` (or `rqt_image_view`), so you should see something similar to the following screenshot. It has the RAW image of the USB camera, which is already in color:

Similarly, another good option is `gscam`, which is installed as follows:

```
$ sudo apt-get install ros-kinetic-gscam
```

Then, run the following command:

```
$ roslaunch chapter5_tuturials gscam.launch view:=true
```

As for `usb_cam`, this launch file performs a `rosrun gscam` and also sets the camera's parameters. It also visualizes the camera's images with `image_view` (or `rqt_image_view`), as shown in the following screenshot:

The parameters required by `gscam` are as follows (see `config/gscam/logitech.yaml`):

```
gscam_config: v4l2src device=/dev/video0 !video/x-raw-
rgb,framerate=30/1 ! ffmpegcolorspace
frame_id: gscam
camera_info_url:
package://chapter5_tutorials/calibration/gscam/
calibration_gscam.yaml
```

The `gscam_config` parameter invokes the `v4l2src` command with the appropriate arguments to run the camera. The rest of the parameters will be useful once the camera is calibrated and used in the ROS image pipeline.

Making your own USB camera driver with OpenCV

Although we have the two previous options, this book comes with its own USB camera driver implemented on top of OpenCV using the `cv::VideoCapture` class. It runs the camera and also allows you to change some of its parameters as long as they are supported by the camera's firmware. It also allows us to set the calibration information in the same way as with the FireWire cameras. With `usb_cam`, this is not possible because the `CameraInfo` message is not available. With regards to `gscam`, we have more control; we can change the camera configuration and see how to publish the camera's images and information in ROS. In order to implement a camera driver using OpenCV, we have two options on how we read images from the camera. First, we can poll with a target **Frames Per Second** (FPS); secondly, we can set a timer for the period of such FPS and, in the timer callback, we perform the actual reading. Depending on the FPS, one solution may be better than the other in terms of CPU consumption. Note that polling does not block anything, as the OpenCV reading function waits until an image is ready; meanwhile, other processes take the CPU. In general, for fast FPS, it is better to use polling so that we do not incur the time penalty of using the timer and its callback. For low FPS, the timer should be similar to polling and the code should be cleaner. We invite the reader to compare both implementations in the `src/camera_polling.cpp` and `src/camera_timer.cpp` files. For the sake of space, here we will only show you the timer-based approach. Indeed, the final driver in `src/camera.cpp` uses a timer. Note that the final driver also includes camera information management, which we will see in the sequel.

In the package, we must set the dependency with OpenCV, the ROS image message libraries, and related. They are the following packages:

```
<depend package="sensor_msgs"/>
<depend package="opencv2"/>
<depend package="cv_bridge"/>
<depend package="image_transport"/>
```

Consequently, in `src/camera_timer.cpp`, we have the following headers:

```
#include <ros/ros.h>
#include <image_transport/image_transport.h>
#include <cv_bridge/cv_bridge.h>
#include <sensor_msgs/image_encodings.h>
#include <opencv2/highgui/highgui.hpp>
```

The `image_transport` API allows the publishing of images using several transport formats seamlessly, which can be compressed images, with different codecs, based on the plugins installed in the ROS system, for example `compressed` and `theora`. The `cv_bridge` is used to convert OpenCV images to ROS image messages, for which we may need the image encoding of `sensor_msgs` in the case of grayscale/color conversion. Finally, we need the `highgui` API of OpenCV (`opencv2`) in order to use `cv::VideoCapture`.

Here, we will explain the main parts of the code in `src/camera_timer.cpp`, which has a class that implements the camera driver. Its attributes are as follows:

```
ros::NodeHandle nh;
image_transport::ImageTransport it;
image_transport::Publisher pub_image_raw;

cv::VideoCapture camera;
cv::Mat image;
cv_bridge::CvImagePtr frame;

ros::Timer timer;

intcamera_index;
int fps;
```

As usual, we need the node handle. Then, we need `ImageTransport`, which is used to send the images in all available formats in a seamless way. In the code, we only need to use `Publisher` (only one), but note that it must be a specialization of the `image_transport` library.

Then, we have the OpenCV stuff to capture images/frames. In the case of the frame, we directly use the `cv_brigde` frame, which is `CvImagePtr`, because we can access the image field it has.

Finally, we have the timer and the basic camera parameters for the driver to work. This is the most basic driver possible. These parameters are the camera index, that is, the number for the `/dev/video?` device, for example `0` for `/dev/video0`; the camera index is then passed to `cv::VideoCapture`. The `fps` parameter sets the camera FPS (if possible) and the timer. Here, we use an `int` value, but it will be a double in the final version, `src/camera.cpp`.

The driver uses the class constructor for the setup or initialization of the node, the camera, and the timer:

```
nh.param<int>( "camera_index", camera_index, DEFAULT_CAMERA_INDEX
);

if ( not camera.isOpened() )
{
  ROS_ERROR_STREAM( "Failed to open camera device!" );
  ros::shutdown();
}

nh.param<int>( "fps", fps, DEFAULT_FPS );
ros::Duration period = ros::Duration( 1. / fps );

pub_image_raw = it.advertise( "image_raw", 1 );

frame = boost::make_shared<cv_bridge::CvImage>();
frame->encoding = sensor_msgs::image_encodings::BGR8;

timer = nh.createTimer( period, &CameraDriver::capture, this );
```

First, we open the camera and abort it if it does not open. Note that we must do this in the attribute constructor, shown as follows, where `camera_index` is passed by the parameter:

```
camera(camera_index )
```

Then, we read the `fps` parameter and compute the timer period, which is used to create the timer and set the `capture` callback at the end. We advertise the image publisher using the image transport API, for `image_raw` (RAW images), and initialize the `frame` variable.

The `capture` callback method reads and publishes images as follows:

```
camera>> frame->image;
if( not frame->image.empty() )
{
  frame->header.stamp = ros::Time::now();
  pub_image_raw.publish( frame->toImageMsg() );
}
```

The preceding method captures the images, checks whether a frame was actually captured, and in that case sets the timestamp and publishes the image, which is converted to a ROS image.

You can run this node with the following command:

```
$ rosrun chapter9_tutorials camera_timer _camera_index:=0 _fps:=15
```

This will open the `/dev/video0` camera at `15` fps.

Then, you can use `image_viewer rqt_image_view` to see the images. Similarly, for the polling implementation, you have the following command:

```
$ roslaunch chapter5_tutorials camera_polling.launch camera_index:=0
fps:=15 view:=true
```

With the previous command, you will see the `/camera/image_raw` topic images.

For the timer implementation, we also have the `camera.launch` file, which runs the final version and provides more options, which we will see throughout this entire chapter. The main contributions of the final version are support for dynamic reconfiguration parameters and the provision of camera information, which includes camera calibration. We are going to show you how to do this in brief, and we advise that you look at the source code for a more detailed understanding.

As with the FireWire cameras, we can give support for the dynamic reconfiguration of the camera's parameters. However, most USB cameras do not support changing certain parameters. What we do is expose all OpenCV supported parameters and warn in case of error (or disable a few of them). The configuration file is in `cfg/Camera.cfg`; check it for details. It supports the following parameters:

- `camera_index`: This parameter is used to select the `/dev/video?` device
- `frame_width` and `frame_height`: These parameters give the image resolution
- `fps`: This parameter sets the camera FPS
- `fourcc`: This parameter specifies the camera pixel format in the **FOURCC** format (`http://www.fourcc.org`); the file format is typically **YUYV** or **MJPEG**, but they fail to change in most USB cameras with OpenCV
- `brightness`, `contrast`, `saturation`, and `hue`: These parameters set the camera's properties; in digital cameras, this is done by software during the acquisition process in the sensor or simply on the resulting image
- `gain`: This parameter sets the gain of the **Analog-to-Digital Converter** (ADC) of the sensor; it introduces salt-and-pepper noise into the image but increases the lightness in dark environments

- exposure: This parameter sets the lightness of the images, usually by adapting the gain and shutter speed (in low-cost cameras, this is simply the integration time of the light that enters the sensor)

- frame_id: This parameter is the camera frame and is useful if we use it for navigation, as we will see in the *Using visual odometry with viso2* section

- camera_info_url: This parameter provides the path to the camera's information, which is basically its calibration

Then, in the following line of code in the driver, we use a dynamic reconfigure server:

```
#include <dynamic_reconfigure/server.h>
```

We set a callback in the constructor:

```
server.setCallback( boost::bind( &CameraDriver::reconfig, this,
_1, _2 ) );
```

The setCallback constructor reconfigures the camera. We even allow it to change the camera and stop the current one when the camera_index changes. Then, we use the OpenCV cv::VideoCapture class to set the camera's properties, which are part of the parameters shown in the preceding line. As an example, in the case of frame_width, we use the following commands:

```
newconfig.frame_width = setProperty( camera,
CV_CAP_PROP_FRAME_WIDTH, newconfig.frame_width );
```

This relies on a private method named setProperty, which calls the set method of cv::VideoCapture and controls the cases in which it fails to print a ROS warning message. Note that the FPS has changed in the timer itself and cannot usually be modified in the camera. Finally, it is important to note that all this reconfiguration is done within a locked mutex to avoid acquiring any images while reconfiguring the driver.

In order to set the camera's information, ROS has a camera_info_manager library that helps us to do so, as shown in the following line:

```
#include <camera_info_manager/camera_info_manager.h>
```

We use the library to obtain the `CameraInfo` message. In the `capture` callback of the timer, we use `image_transport::CameraPublisher`, and not only for images. The code is as follows:

```
camera>> frame->image;
if( not frame->image.empty() )
{
  frame->header.stamp = ros::Time::now();

  *camera_info = camera_info_manager.getCameraInfo();
  camera_info->header = frame->header;

  camera_pub.publish( frame->toImageMsg(), camera_info );
}
```

This is run within the mutex mentioned previously for the reconfiguration method. We do the same as for the first version of the driver but also retrieve the camera information from the manager, which is set with the node handler, the camera name, and `camera_info_url` in the reconfiguration method (which is always called once on loading). Then, we publish both the image/frame (ROS image) and the `CameraImage` messages.

In order to use this driver, use the following command:

$ roslaunch chapter5_tutorials camera.launch view:=true

The command will use the `config/camera/webcam.yaml` parameter as default, which sets all the dynamic reconfiguration parameters seen so far.

You can check that the camera is working with `rostopic list` and `rostopic hz/ camera/image_raw`; you can also check with `image_view` or `rqt_image_view`.

With the implementation of this driver, we have used all the resources available in ROS to work with cameras, images, and Computer Vision. In the following sections, for the sake of clarity, we will explain each of them separately.

ROS images

ROS provide the `sensor_msgs::Image` message to send images between nodes. However, we usually need a data type or object to manipulate the images in order to do some useful work. The most common library for that is OpenCV, so ROS offers a bridge class to transform ROS images back and forth from OpenCV.

If we have an OpenCV image, that is, `cv::Mat` image, we need the `cv_bridge` library to convert it into a ROS image message and publish it. We have the option to share or copy the image with `CvShare` or `CvCopy`, respectively. However, if possible, it is easier to use the OpenCV image field inside the `CvImage` class provided by `cv_bridge`. That is exactly what we do in the camera driver as a pointer:

```
cv_bridge::CvImagePtr frame;
```

Being a pointer, we initialize it in the following way:

```
frame = boost::make_shared<cv_bridge::CvImage>();
```

If we know the image encoding beforehand, we can use the following code:

```
frame->encoding = sensor_msgs::image_encodings::BGR8;
```

Later, we set the OpenCV image at some point, for example, capturing it from a camera:

```
camera>> frame->image;
```

It is also common to set the timestamp of the message at this point:

```
frame->header.stamp = ros::Time::now();
```

Now we only have to publish it. To do so, we need a publisher and it must use the `image_transport` API of ROS. This is shown in the following section.

Publishing images with ImageTransport

We can publish single images with `ros::Publisher`, but it is better to use an `image_transport` publisher. It can publish images with their corresponding camera information. That is exactly what we did for the camera driver previously. The `image_transport` API is useful for providing different transport formats in a seamless way. The images you publish actually appear in several topics. Apart from the basic, uncompressed one, you will see a compressed one or even more. The number of supported transports depends on the plugins installed in your system; you will usually have the `compressed` and `theora` transports.

You can see this with `rostopic info`. In order to install all the plugins, use the following command:

```
$ sudo apt-get install ros-kinetic-image-transport-plugins
```

In your code, you need the node handle to create the image transport and then the publisher. In this example, we will use a simple image publisher; please check the final USB camera driver for the `CameraPublisher` usage:

```
ros::NodeHandle nh;
image_transport::ImageTransport it;
image_transport::Publisher pub_image_raw;
```

The node handle and the image transport are constructed with (in the attribute constructors of a class) the following code:

```
nh( "~" ),
it( nh )
```

For an `image_raw` topic, the publisher is created this way within the node namespace:

```
pub_image_raw = it.advertise( "image_raw", 1 );
```

Hence, now the frame shown in the previous section can be published with the following code:

```
pub_image_raw.publish( frame->toImageMsg() );
```

OpenCV in ROS

ROS provides a very simple integration with OpenCV, the most widely used open source Computer Vision library. However, it does not ship a specific Debian for ROS kinetic because that would force users to use a single version. Instead of that, it allows you to use the latest OpenCV library on the system and provides additional integration tools to use OpenCV in ROS. In the following sections we will explain how to install OpenCV and those additional tools.

Installing OpenCV 3.0

In ROS Kinetic we can start using OpenCV 3.0, in contrast to previous versions where some packages had some dependencies on OpenCV 2.* or compatibility issues with 3.0.

The installation follows the standard workflow of installing Ubuntu packages, so you only have to do the following:

```
$ sudo apt-get install libopencv-dev
```

Alternatively, you can also install an ROS package that installs the library too:

```
$ sudo apt-get install ros-kinetic-opencv3
```

Using OpenCV in ROS

ROS uses the standalone OpenCV library installed on your system. However, you must specify a build and running dependency with an `opencv2` package in the `package.xml` file:

```
<build_depend>opencv2</build_depend>
<run_depend>opencv2</run_depend>
```

In `CMakeLists.xml`, we have to insert the following lines:

```
find_package(OpenCV)
include_directories(${catkin_INCLUDE_DIRS} ${OpenCV_INCLUDE_DIRS})
```

Then, for each library or executable that uses OpenCV, we must add `${OpenCV_LIBS}` to `target_link_libraries` (see `CMakeLists.txt` provided for the `chapter5_tutorials` package).

In our node `.cpp` file, we include any of the OpenCV libraries we need. For example, for `highgui.hpp`, we use the following line:

```
#include <opencv2/highgui/highgui.hpp>
```

Now you can use any of the OpenCV API classes, functions, and so on in your code, as usual. Simply use its `cv` namespace and follow any OpenCV tutorial if you are starting with it. Note that this book is not about OpenCV—just how we can do Computer Vision inside ROS.

Visualizing the camera input images with rqt_image_view

In *Chapter 3*, *Visualization and Debugging Tools*, we explained how to visualize any image published in the ROS framework by using the `image_view` node of the `image_view` package or `rqt_image_view`. The following code encapsulates this discussion:

```
$ rosrun image_view image_view image:=/camera/image_raw
```

What is important here is the fact that by using the image transport, we can select different topics for viewing images using compressed formats if required. Also, in the case of stereo vision, as we will see later, we can use `rqt rviz` to see the point cloud obtained with the disparity image.

Camera calibration

Most cameras, especially wide-angle ones, exhibit large distortions. We can model such distortions as radial or tangential and compute the coefficients of that model using calibration algorithms. The camera calibration algorithms also obtain a calibration matrix that contains the focal distance and principle point of the lens and, hence, provide a way to measure distances in the world using the images acquired. In the case of stereo vision, it is also possible to retrieve depth information, that is, the distance of the pixels to the camera, as we will see later. Consequently, we have 3D information of the world up to a certain extent.

The calibration is done by showing several views of a known image called a calibration pattern, which is typically a chessboard/checkerboard. It can also be an array of circles or an asymmetric pattern of circles; note that circles are seen as ellipses by the camera for skew views. A detection algorithm obtains the inner corner point of the cells in the chessboard and uses them to estimate the camera's intrinsic and extrinsic parameters. In brief, the extrinsic parameters are the pose of the camera or, in other words, the pose of the pattern with respect to the camera if we left the camera in a fixed position. What we want are the intrinsic parameters because they do not change, can be used later for the camera in any pose, allow the measuring of distances in the images, and allow correcting the image distortion, that is, rectifying the image.

How to calibrate a camera

With our camera driver running, we can use the calibration tool of ROS to calibrate it. It is important that the camera driver provides `CameraInfo` messages and has the `camera_info_set` service, which allows you to set the path to the calibration results file. Later, this calibration information is loaded by the image pipeline when using the camera. One camera driver that satisfies these prerequisites is the `camera1394` driver for the FireWire cameras. In order to calibrate your FireWire camera, use the following command:

```
$ roslaunch chapter5_tutorialscalibration_firewire_camera_ chessboard.
launch
```

This will open a GUI that automatically selects the views of our calibration pattern and provides bars to inform users how each axis is covered by the views retrieved. It comprises the x and y axes, meaning how close the pattern has been shown to each extreme of these axes in the image plane, that is, the horizontal and vertical axes, respectively. Then, the scale goes from close to far (up to the distance at which the detection works). Finally, skew requires that views of the pattern tilt in both the x and y axes. The three buttons below these bars are disabled by default, as shown in the following screenshot:

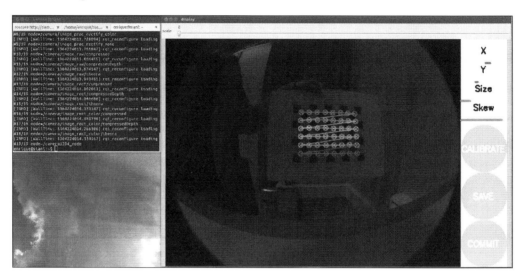

You will see the points detected overlaid over the pattern every time the detector finds them. The views are automatically selected to cover a representative number of different views, so you must show views to make the bars become green from one side to the other, following the instructions given in the following section. In theory, two views are enough, but in practice around ten are usually needed. In fact, this interface captures even more (30 to 40). You should avoid fast movements because blurry images are bad for detection. Once the tool has enough views, it will allow you to calibrate, that is, to start the optimizer which, given the points detected in the calibration pattern views, solves the system of the pinhole camera model.

This is shown in the following screenshot:

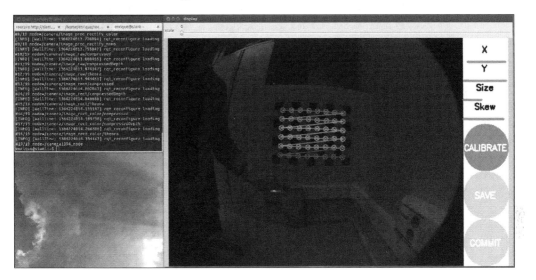

Then, you can save the calibration data and commit the calibration results to the camera, that is, it uses the `camera_info_set` service to commit the calibration to the camera, so later it is detected automatically by the ROS image pipeline.

The launch file provided for the calibration simply uses `cameracalibrator.py` of the `camera_calibration` package:

```
<node pkg="camera_calibration" type="cameracalibrator.py"
name="cameracalibrator" args="--size 8x6 --square 0.030"
output="screen">
  <remap from="image" to="camera/image_colour" />
  <remap from="camera" to="camera" />
</node>
```

The calibration tool only needs the pattern's characteristics (the number of squares and their size, `--size 8x6` and `--square 0.030` in this case), the `image` topic, and the `camera` namespace.

The launch file also runs the image pipeline, but it is not required. In fact, instead of the `image_color` topic, we could have used the `image_raw` one.

Once you have saved the calibration (**Save** button), a file is created in your `/tmp` directory. It contains the calibration pattern views used for the calibration. You can find it at `/tmp/calibrationdata.tar.gz`; the ones used for calibration in the book can be found in the `calibration` directory and the `firewire_camera` subfolder for the FireWire camera. Similarly, on the terminal (`stdout` output), you will see information regarding the views taken and the calibration results. The ones obtained for the book are in the same folder as the calibration data. The calibration results can also be consulted in the `ost.txt` file inside the `calibrationdata.tar.gz` ZIP file. Remember that after the commit, the calibration file is updated with the calibration matrix and the coefficients of the distortion model. A good way to do so consists of creating a dummy calibration file before the calibration. In our package, that file is in `calibration/firewire_camera/calibration_firewire_camera.yaml`, which is referenced by the parameters file:

```
camera_info_url:
package://chapter5_tutorials/calibration/firewire_camera/calibrati
on_firewire_camera.yaml
```

Now, we can use our camera again with the image pipeline, and the rectified images will have the distortion corrected as a clear sign that the camera is calibrated correctly. Since ROS uses the Zhang calibration method implemented in OpenCV, our advice is that you consult its documentation at `http://docs.opencv.org/doc/tutorials/calib3d/camera_calibration/camera_calibration.html`.

Finally, you can also play with different calibration patterns using the following launch files for circles and asymmetric circles (`https://raw.githubusercontent.com/opencv/opencv/05b15943d6a42c99e5f921b7dbaa8323f3c042c6/doc/acircles_pattern.png`), prepared for FireWire cameras, as an example:

```
roslaunchchapter5_tutorialscalibration_firewire_camera_circles.lau
nch
roslaunchchapter5_tutorialscalibration_firewire_camera_acircles.la
unch
```

You can also use multiple chessboard patterns for a single calibration using patterns of different sizes. However, we think it is enough to use a single chessboard pattern printed with good quality. Indeed, for the USB camera driver we only use that.

In the case of the USB camera driver, we have a more powerful launch file that integrates the camera calibration node; there is also a standalone one for FireWire cameras. In order to calibrate your camera, use the following action:

```
$ roslaunch chapter5_tutorials camera.launch calibrate:=true
```

In the following screenshots, you will see the steps of the calibration process in the GUI, identical to the case of FireWire cameras. That means we have an operating `camera_info_set` service.

After pressing the **CALIBRATE** button, the calibration optimization algorithm will take a while to find the best intrinsic and extrinsic parameters. Once it is done, **SAVE** and **COMMIT** will be enabled. The following screenshot shows this:

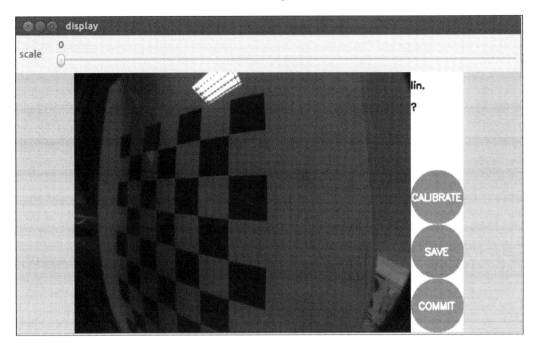

Stereo calibration

The next step consists of working with stereo cameras. One option is to run two monocular camera nodes, but in general it is better to consider the whole stereo pair as a single sensor because the images must be synchronized. In ROS, there is no driver for FireWire stereo cameras, but we can use an extension to stereo using the following command line:

```
$ git clone git://github.com/srv/camera1394stereo.git
```

However, FireWire stereo pairs are quite expensive. For this reason, we provide a stereo camera driver for USB cameras. We use the Logitech C120 USB webcam, which is very cheap. It is also noisy, but we will see that we can do great things with it after calibration. It is important that in the stereo pair, the cameras are similar, but you can try with different cameras as well. Our setup for the cameras is shown in the images. You only need the two cameras on the same plane, pointing in parallel directions.

We have a baseline of approximately 12 cm, which will also be computed in the stereo calibration process. As you can see in the following screenshot, you only need a rod to attach the cameras to, with zip ties:

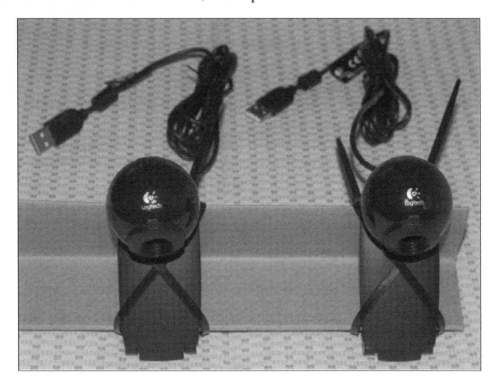

Now, connect the cameras to your USB slots. It is good practice to connect the left-hand side camera first and then the right-hand side one. This way, they are assigned to the /dev/video0 and /dev/video1 devices, or 1 and 2 if 0 was already taken. Alternatively, you can create a udev rule.

Then, you can test each camera individually, as we would for a single camera. Some tools you will find useful are the video4linux control panels for cameras:

```
$ sudo apt-get install v4l-utils qv4l2
```

You might experience the following problem:

```
In case of problems with stereo:
libv4l2: error turning on stream: No space left on device
```

This happens because you have to connect each camera to a different USB controller; note that certain USB slots are managed by the same controller, and hence it cannot deal with the bandwidth of more than a single camera. If you only have a USB controller, there are other options you can try. First, try to use a compressed pixel format, such as MJPEG in both cameras. You can check whether or not it is supported by your by using the following command:

```
$ v4l2-ctl -d /dev/video2 --list-formats
```

The command will generate something similar to the following output:

```
ioctl: VIDIOC_ENUM_FMT
Index : 0
Type : Video Capture
Pixel Format: 'YUYV'
Name : YUV 4:2:2 (YUYV)

Index : 1
Type : Video Capture
Pixel Format: 'MJPG' (compressed)
Name : MJPEGioctl: VIDIOC_ENUM_FMT
Index : 0
Type : Video Capture
Pixel Format: 'YUYV'
Name : YUV 4:2:2 (YUYV)

Index : 1
Type : Video Capture
Pixel Format: 'MJPG' (compressed)
```

If MJPEG is supported, we can use more than one camera in the same USB controller; otherwise, with uncompressed pixel formats, we must use different USB controllers or reduce the resolution to 320 x 240 or lower. Similarly, with the GUI of qv4l2, you can check this and test your camera. You can also check whether it is possible to set the desired pixel format. In fact, this does not work for our USB cameras using the OpenCV set method, so we use a USB slot managed by a different USB controller.

The USB stereo camera driver that comes with this book is based on the USB camera discussed so far. Basically, the driver extends the camera to support camera publishers, which send the left-hand side and right-hand side images and the camera information as well. You can run it and view the images by using the following command:

```
$ roslaunch chapter5_tutorials camera_stereo.launch view:=true
```

It also shows the disparity image of the left-hand side and right-hand side cameras, which will be useful once the cameras are calibrated as it is used by the ROS image pipeline. In order to calibrate the cameras, use the following command:

```
$ roslaunch chapter5_tutorials camera_stereo.launch calibrate:=true
```

You will see a GUI for monocular cameras similar to the following screenshot:

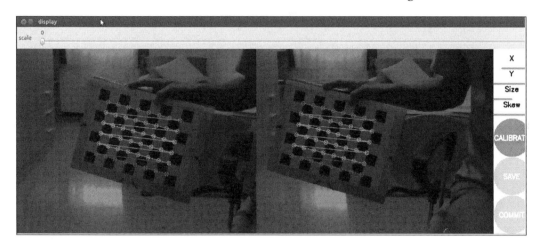

At the time the preceding image was taken, we had shown enough views to start the calibration. Note that the calibration pattern must be detected by both cameras simultaneously to be included in the calibration optimization step. Depending on the setup, this may be quite tricky, so you should put the pattern at an appropriate distance from the camera. You will see the setup used for the calibration of this book in the following image:

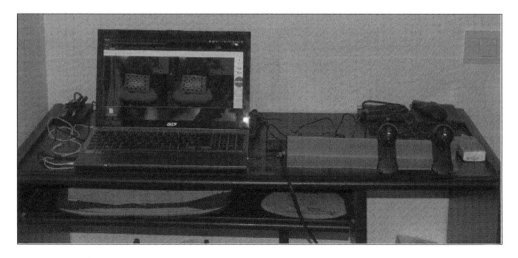

The calibration is done by the same `cameracalibrator.py` node used for monocular cameras. We pass the left-hand side and right-hand side cameras and images, so the tool knows that we are going to perform stereo calibration. The following is the node in the launch file:

```
<node ns="$(arg camera)" name="cameracalibrator"
pkg="camera_calibration" type="cameracalibrator.py"
args="--size 8x6 --square 0.030" output="screen">
  <remap from="left" to="left/image_raw"/>
  <remap from="right" to="right/image_raw"/>
  <remap from="left_camera" to="left"/>
  <remap from="right_camera" to="right"/>
</node>
```

The result of the calibration is the same as for monocular cameras, but in this case we have two calibration files, one for each camera. In accordance with the parameters file in `config/camera_stereo/logitech_c120.yaml`, we have the following code:

```
camera_info_url_left:
package://chapter5_tutorials/calibration/camera_stereo/
${NAME}.yaml
camera_info_url_right:
package://chapter5_tutorials/calibration/camera_stereo/
${NAME}.yaml
```

`${NAME}` is the name of the camera, which resolved to `logitech_c120_left` and `logitech_c120_right` for the left-hand side and right-hand side cameras, respectively. After the commit of the calibration, those files are updated with the calibration of each camera. They contain the calibration matrix, the distortion model coefficients, and the rectification and projection matrix, which includes the baseline, that is, the separation between each camera in the x axis of the image plane. In the parameters file, you can also see values for the camera properties that have been set for indoor environments with artificial light; the camera model used has some auto correction, so sometimes the images may be bad, but these values seem to work well in most cases.

The ROS image pipeline

The ROS image pipeline is run with the `image_proc` package. It provides all the conversion utilities for obtaining monochrome and color images from the RAW images acquired from the camera. In the case of FireWire cameras, which may use a Bayer pattern to code the images (actually in the sensor itself), it *debayers* them to obtain the color images. Once you have calibrated the camera, the image pipeline takes the `CameraInfo` messages, which contain that information, and rectifies the images. Here, rectification means to un-distort the images, so it takes the coefficients of the distortion model to correct the radial and tangential distortion.

As a result, you will see more topics for your camera in its namespace. In the following screenshots, you can see the `image_raw`, `image_mono`, and `image_colour` topics, which display the RAW, monochrome, and color images, respectively:

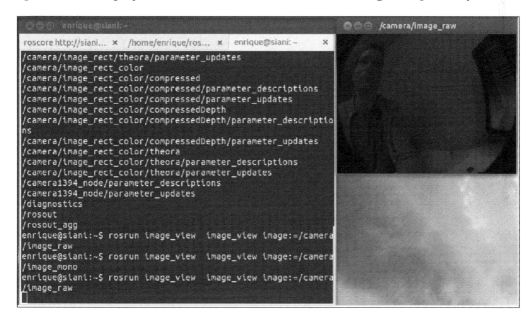

The mono color, in this case, is equivalent to the following raw image. Note that for good cameras the raw image usually employs a Bayer pattern for the cells on the camera sensor, so it will not be equivalent to the mono color one.

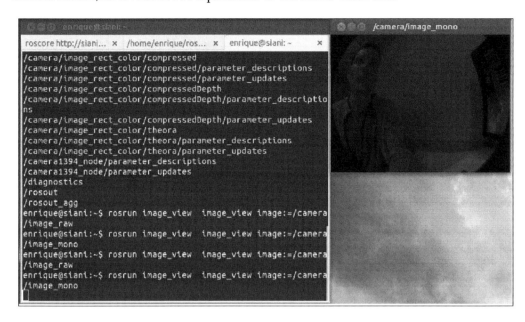

Finally, the following color image is shown, which is only different from the mono color one if the camera actually supports colors; otherwise it will be mono color too:

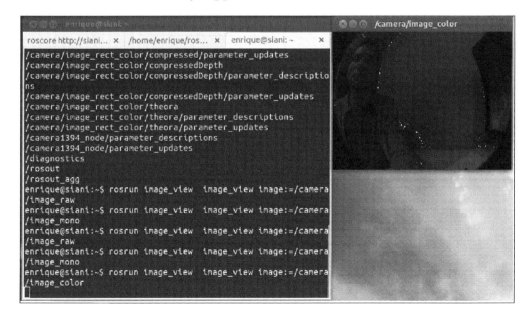

The rectified images are provided in monochrome and color in the `image_rect` and `image_rect_color` topics. In the following image, we compare the uncalibrated, distorted RAW images with the rectified ones. You can see the correction because the pattern shown in the screenshots has straight lines only in the rectified images, particularly in areas far from the center (principle point) of the image (sensor):

You can see all the topics available with `rostopic list` or `rqt_graph`, which include the `image_transport` topics as well.

You can view the `image_raw` topic of a monocular camera directly with the following command:

```
$ roslaunch chapter5_tutorials camera.launch view:=true
```

It can be changed to see other topics, but for these cameras the RAW images are already in color. However, in order to see the rectified images, use `image_rect_color` with `image_view` or `rqt_image_view` or change the launch file. The `image_proc` node is used to make all these topics available. The following code shows this:

```
<node ns="$(arg camera)" pkg="image_proc" type="image_proc"
name="image_proc"/>
```

Image pipeline for stereo cameras

In the case of stereo cameras, we have the same for the left-hand side and right-hand side cameras. However, there are specific visualization tools for them because we can use the left-hand side and right-hand side images to compute and see the disparity image. An algorithm uses stereo calibration and the texture of both images to estimate the depth of each pixel, which is the disparity image. To obtain good results, we must tune the algorithm that computes such an image. In the following screenshot, we will see the left-hand side, right-hand side, and disparity images as well as `rqt_reconfiguire` for `stereo_image_proc`, which is the node that builds the image pipeline for stereo images; in the launch file, we only need the following lines:

```
<node ns="$(arg camera)" pkg="stereo_image_proc"
      type="stereo_image_proc"
      name="stereo_image_proc" output="screen">
  <rosparam file="$(argparams_disparity)"/>
</node>
```

It requires the disparity parameters, which can be set with `rqt_reconfigure`, as shown in the following screenshot, and saved with `rosparam dump/stereo/stereo_image_proc`:

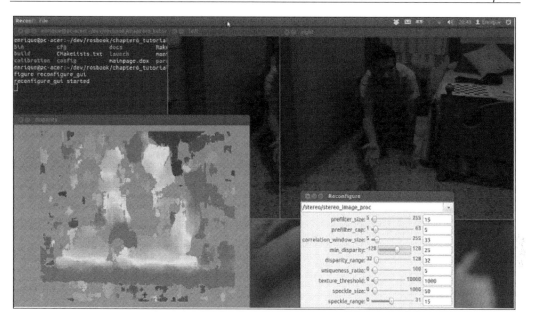

We have good values for the environment used in this book's demonstration in the `config/camera_stereo/disparity.yaml` parameters file. This is shown in the following code:

```
{correlation_window_size: 33, disparity_range: 32, min_disparity:
25, prefilter_cap: 5,
prefilter_size: 15, speckle_range: 15, speckle_size: 50,
texture_threshold: 1000,
uniqueness_ratio: 5.0}
```

However, these parameters depend a lot on the calibration quality and the environment. You should adjust it to your experiment. It takes time and it is quite tricky, but you can follow the next guidelines. You start by setting a `disparity_range` value that makes enough blobs appear. You also have to set `min_disparity`, so you can see areas covering the whole range of depths (from red to blue/purple). Then, you can fine-tune the result, setting `speckle_size` to remove small, noisy blobs. You can also modify `uniqueness_ratio` and `texture_threshold` to have larger blobs. The `correlation_window_size` is also important as it affects the detection of initial blobs.

If it becomes difficult to obtain good results, you might have to recalibrate or use better cameras for your environment and lighting conditions. You can also try it in another environment or with more light. It is important that you have texture in the environment; for example, against a flat, white wall, you cannot find any disparity. Also, depending on the baseline, you cannot retrieve depth information very close to the camera. For stereo navigation, it is better to have a large baseline, say 12 cm or more. We use it here because we are trying visual odometry later. With this setup, we only have depth information one meter away from the cameras. With a smaller baseline, we can obtain depth information from closer objects. This is bad for navigation because we lose resolution far away, but it is good for perception and grasping.

As far as calibration problems go, you can check your calibration results with the `cameracheck.py` node, which is integrated in both the monocular and stereo camera launch files:

```
$ roslaunch chapter5_tutorials camera.launch view:=true check:=true
$ roslaunch chapter5_tutorials camera_stereo.launch view:=true
check:=true
```

For the monocular camera, our calibration yields this RMS error (see more in `calibration/camera/cameracheck-stdout.log`):

```
Linearity RMS Error: 1.319 Pixels ReprojectionRMS Error: 1.278
Pixels
Linearity RMS Error: 1.542 Pixels ReprojectionRMS Error: 1.368
Pixels
Linearity RMS Error: 1.437 Pixels ReprojectionRMS Error: 1.112
Pixels
Linearity RMS Error: 1.455 Pixels ReprojectionRMS Error: 1.035
Pixels
Linearity RMS Error: 2.210 Pixels ReprojectionRMS Error: 1.584
Pixels
Linearity RMS Error: 2.604 Pixels ReprojectionRMS Error: 2.286
Pixels
Linearity RMS Error: 0.611 Pixels ReprojectionRMS Error: 0.349
Pixels
```

For the stereo camera, we have `epipolar error` and the estimation of the cell size of the calibration pattern (see more in `calibration/camera_stereo/cameracheck-stdout.log`):

```
epipolar error: 0.738753 pixels dimension: 0.033301 m
epipolar error: 1.145886 pixels dimension: 0.033356 m
epipolar error: 1.810118 pixels dimension: 0.033636 m
epipolar error: 2.071419 pixels dimension: 0.033772 m
epipolar error: 2.193602 pixels dimension: 0.033635 m
epipolar error: 2.822543 pixels dimension: 0.033535 m
```

To obtain these results, you only have to show the calibration pattern to the camera; that is the reason we also pass `view:=true` to the launch files. An RMS error greater than 2 pixels is quite large; we have something around it, but remember that these are very low-cost cameras. Something below a 1 pixel error is desirable. For the stereo pair, the `epipolar error` should also be lower than 1 pixel; in our case, it is still quite large (usually greater than 3 pixels), but we still can do many things. Indeed, the disparity image is just a representation of the depth of each pixel shown with the `stereo_view` node. We also have a 3D point cloud that can be visualized and texturized with `rviz`. We will see this in the following demonstrations on visual odometry.

ROS packages useful for Computer Vision tasks

The great advantage of doing Computer Vision in ROS is the fact that we do not have to re-invent the wheel. A lot of third-party software is available, and we can also connect our vision stuff to the real robots or perform simulations. Here, we are going to enumerate interesting Computer Vision tools for the most common visual tasks, but we will only explain one of them in detail, including all the steps to set it up.

We will do this for visual odometry, but other packages are also easy to install and it is also easy to start playing with them; simply follow the tutorials or manuals in the links provided here:

- **Visual Servoing**: Also known as **Vision-based Robot Control**, this is a technique that uses feedback information obtained from a vision sensor to control the motion of a robot, typically an arm used for grasping. In ROS, we have a wrapper of the **Visual Servoing Platform** (**ViSP**) software (`http://www.irisa.fr/lagadic/visp/visp.html` and `http://www.ros.org/wiki/vision_visp`). ViSP is a complete cross-platform library that allows you to prototype and develop applications in visual tracking and visual serving. The ROS wrapper provides a tracker that can be run with the `visp_tracker` (moving edge tracker) node as well as `visp_auto_tracker` (a model-based tracker). It also helps to calibrate the camera and perform hand-to-eye calibration, which is crucial for visual serving in grasping tasks.

- **Augmented Reality**: An **Augmented Reality** (**AR**) application involves overlaying virtual imagery on the real world. A well-known library for this purpose is ARToolkit (`https://www.hitl.washington.edu/artoolkit/`). The main problem in this application is tracking the user's viewpoint to draw the virtual imagery on the viewpoint where the user is looking in the real world. **ARToolkit** video tracking libraries calculate the real camera position and orientation relative to physical markers in real time. In ROS, we have a wrapper named `ar_pose` (`http://www.ros.org/wiki/ar_pose`). It allows us to track single or multiple markers where we can render our virtual imagery (for example, a 3D model).

- **Perception and object recognition**: Most basic perception and object recognition is possible with the OpenCV libraries. However, there are several packages that provide an object recognition pipeline, such as the `object_recognition` stack, which provides `tabletop_object_detector` to detect objects on a table; for example a more general solution provided by **Object Recognition Kitchen** (**ORK**) can be found at `http://wg-perception.github.io/object_recognition_core`. It is also worth mentioning a tool called **RoboEarth** (`http://www.roboearth.org`), which allows you to detect and build 3D models of physical objects and store them in a global database accessible for any robot (or human) worldwide. The models stored can be 2D or 3D and can be used to recognize similar objects and their viewpoint, that is, to identify what the camera/robot is watching. The RoboEarth project is integrated into ROS, and many tutorials are provided to have a running system (`http://www.ros.org/wiki/roboearth`), although it does not support officially the latest versions of ROS.

- **Visual odometry**: A visual odometer is an algorithm that uses the images of the environment to track features and estimate the robot's movement, assuming a static environment. It can solve the six DoF poses of the robot with a monocular or stereo system, but it may require additional information in the monocular case. There are two main libraries for visual odometry: `libviso2` (`http://www.cvlibs.net/software/libviso2.html`) and `libfovis` (`http://www.ros.org/wiki/fovis_ros`), both of which have wrappers for ROS. The wrappers just expose these libraries to ROS. They are the `viso2` and `fovis` packages, respectively. In the following section, we will see how we can do visual odometry with our homemade stereo camera using the `viso2_ros` node of `viso2`. We also show how to install them, which at the moment needs to be done from source because these packages do not support ROS Kinetic officially; however, there is no other alternative for them integrated in ROS. The `libviso2` library allows us to do monocular and stereo visual odometry. However, for monocular odometry, we also need the pitch and heading for the ground plane estimation. You can try the monocular case with one camera and an IMU (see *Chapter 4*, *3D Modeling and Simulation*), but you will always have better results with a good stereo pair, correctly calibrated, as seen so far in this chapter. Finally, `libfovis` does not allow the monocular case, but it does support RGBD cameras, such as the Kinect sensor (see *Chapter 6*, *The Navigation Stack – Beyond Setups*). In regards the stereo case, it is possible to try both libraries and see which one works better in your case. Here, we will give you a step-by-step tutorial on how to install and run `viso2` in ROS and `fovis` with Kinect.

Visual odometry

Visual odometry is the name used for algorithms that use vision to estimate the relative displacement of a mobile robot or sensor. Odometry accumulates the consecutive relative displacement to give a global estimation of the robot or sensor pose in the environment in respect to the initial pose, but bear in mind that it accumulates drift because the error on each relative displacement accumulates and grows without bounds. To solve this problem, a global localization or loop closure detection algorithm is needed. This is one of the components of a Visual SLAM system, but it also needs visual odometry to create a reference guess for the pose estimation.

Using visual odometry with viso2

In order to use `viso2`, go to your `catkin` workspace (`~/catkin_ws`) and use the following commands:

```
$ cdsrc
$ wstoolinit
$ wstool set viso2 --git git://github.com/srv/viso2.git
$ wstool update
```

Now, to build it, run the following command:

```
$ cd ..
$ catkin_make
```

Once it is built, we set up our environment by using the following command:

```
$ sourcedevel/setup.bash
```

Now we can run `viso2_ros` nodes, such as `stereo_odometer`, which is the one we are going to use here. But before that, we need to publish the frame transformation between our camera and the robot or its base link. The stereo camera driver is already prepared for that, but we will explain how it is done in the following sections.

Camera pose calibration

In order to set the transformation between the different frames in our robot system, we must publish the `tf` message of such transforms. The most appropriate and generic way to do so consists of using the `camera_pose` stack; we will use the latest version from this repository, which can be found at `https://github.com/jbohren-forks/camera_pose`. This stack offers a series of launch files that calibrate the camera poses in respect to each other. It comes with launch files for two, three, or more cameras. In our case, we only have two cameras (stereo), so we proceed this way. First, we extend `camera_stereo.launch` with the `calibrate_pose` argument that calls `calibration_tf_publisher.launch` from `camera_pose`:

```
<include file="$(find
camera_pose_calibration)/blocks/calibration_tf_publisher.launch">
  <arg name="cache_file"
  value="/tmp/camera_pose_calibration_cache.bag"/>
</include>
```

Now, run the following command:

```
$ roslaunch chapter5_tutorials camera_stereo.launch calibrate_pose:=true
```

The `calibration_tf_publisher` will publish the frame transforms (`tf`) as soon as the calibration has been done correctly. The calibration is similar to the one we have seen so far but uses the specific tools from `camera_pose`, which are run using the following command:

```
$ roslaunch camera_pose_calibration calibrate_2_ camera.launch camera1_
ns:=/stereo/left camera2_ns:=/stereo/right checker_rows:=6 checker_
cols:=8 checker_size:=0.03
```

With this call, we can use the same calibration pattern we used with our previous calibration tools. However, this requires the images to be static; some bars can move from one side to another of the image and turn green when the images in all the cameras have been static for a sufficient period of time. This is shown in the following screenshot:

With our noisy cameras, we will need support for the calibration pattern, such as a tripod or a panel, as shown in the following image:

Then, we can calibrate, as shown in the following screenshot:

This creates `tf` from the left-hand side camera to the right-hand side camera. However, although this is the most appropriate way to perform the camera pose calibration, we are going to use a simpler approach that is enough for a stereo pair. This is also required by `viso2`, as it needs the frame of the whole stereo pair as a single unit/sensor; internally, it uses the stereo calibration results of `cameracalibrator.py` to retrieve the baseline.

We have a launch file that uses `static_transform_publisher` for the camera link to the base link (robot base) and another from the camera link to the optical camera link because the optical one requires rotation; recall that the camera frame has the *z* axis pointing forward from the camera's optical lens, while the other frames (world, navigation, or odometry) have the *z* axis pointing up. This launch file is in `launch/frames/stereo_frames.launch`:

```
<launch>
  <arg name="camera" default="stereo" />

  <arg name="baseline/2" value="0.06"/>
  <arg name="optical_translation" value="0 -$(arg baseline/2) 0"/>

  <arg name="pi/2" value="1.5707963267948966"/>
  <arg name="optical_rotation" value="-$(arg pi/2) 0 -$(arg
  pi/2)"/>

  <node pkg="tf" type="static_transform_publisher" name="$(arg
  camera)_link"
  args="0 0 0.1 0 0 0 /base_link /$(arg camera) 100"/>
  <node pkg="tf" type="static_transform_publisher" name="$(arg
  camera)_optical_link"
  args="$(argoptical_translation) $(argoptical_rotation) /$(arg
  camera) /$(arg camera)_optical 100"/>
</launch>
```

This launch file is included in our stereo camera launch file and publishes these static frame transforms. Hence, we only have to run the following command to get the launch file to publish them:

```
$ roslaunch chapter5_tutorials camera_stereo.launchtf:=true
```

Then, you can check whether they are being published in `rqt_rviz` with the `tf` display, as we will see in the following running `viso2`; you can also use `rqt_tf_tree` for this (see *Chapter 3, Visualization and Debugging Tools*).

Running the viso2 online demo

At this point, we are ready to run the visual odometry algorithm: our stereo pair cameras are calibrated, their frame has the appropriate name for `viso2` (ends with `_optical`), and `tf` for the camera and optical frames has been published. However, before using our own stereo pair, we are going to test `viso2` with the bag files provided in `http://srv.uib.es/public/viso2_ros/sample_bagfiles/`; just run `bag/viso2_demo/download_amphoras_pool_bag_files.sh` to obtain all the bag files (this totals about 4 GB). Then, we have a launch file for both the monocular and stereo odometers in the `launch/visual_odometry` folder. In order to run the stereo demo, we have a launch file on top that plays the bag files and also allows you to inspect and visualize its contents. For instance, to calibrate the disparity image algorithm, run the following command:

```
$ roslaunch chapter5_tutorials viso2_demo.launch config_disparity:=true
view:=true
```

You will see that the left-hand side, right-hand side, disparity images, and the `rqt_reconfigure` interface configures the disparity algorithm. You need to perform this tuning because the bag files only have the RAW images. We have found good parameters that are in `config/viso2_demo/disparity.yaml`. In the following screenshot, you can see the results obtained using them, where you can clearly appreciate the depth of the rocks in the stereo images:

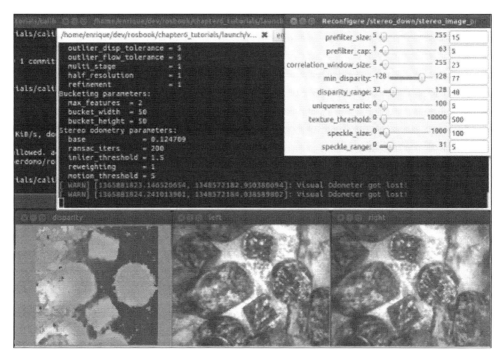

In order to run the stereo odometry and see the result in `rqt_rviz`, run the following command:

```
$ roslaunch chapter5_tutorials viso2_demo.launch odometry:=true
rviz:=true
```

Note that we have provided an adequate configuration for `rqt_rviz` in `config/viso2_demo/rviz.rviz`, which is automatically loaded by the launch file. The following sequence of images shows different instances of the texturized 3D point cloud and the `/odom` and `/stereo_optical` frames that show the camera pose estimate from the stereo odometer. The third image has a decay time of three seconds for the point cloud, so we can see how the points overlay over time. This way, with good images and odometry, we can even see a map drawn in `rqt_rviz`, but this is quite difficult and generally needs a SLAM algorithm (see *Chapter 8, Using Sensors and Actuators with ROS*). All of this is encapsulated in the following screenshots:

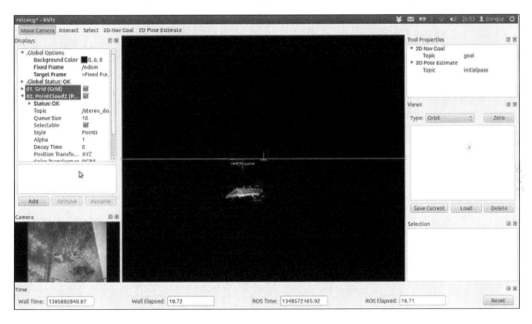

As new frames come, the algorithm is able to create a 3D reconstruction, as shown in the following screenshot, where we can see the heights of the rocks on the seabed:

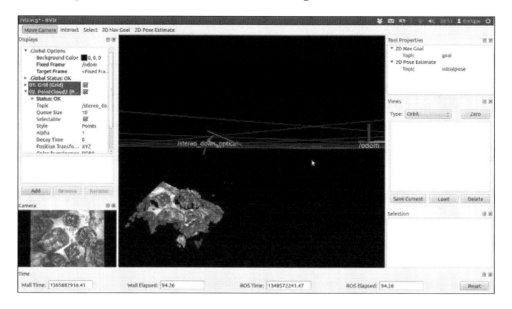

If we set a **Decay Time** of three seconds, the different point clouds from consecutive frames will be shown together, so we can see a map of the bottom of the sea. Remember that the map will contain some errors because of the drift of the visual odometry algorithm:

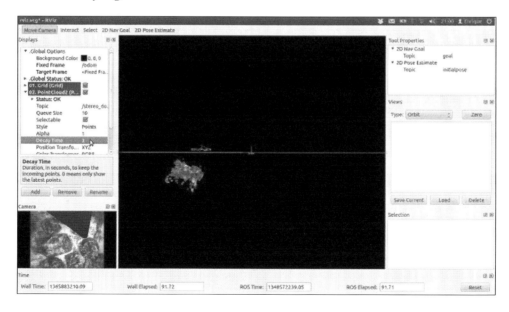

Performing visual odometry with viso2 with a stereo camera

Finally, we can do what `viso2_demo` does with our own stereo pair. We only have to run the following command to run the stereo odometry and see the results in `rqt_rviz` (note that the `tf` tree is published by default):

```
$ roslaunch chapter5_tutorials camera_stereo.launch odometry:=true
rviz:=true
```

The following image shows an example of the visual odometry system running for our low-cost stereo camera. If you move the camera, you should see the `/odom` frame moving. If the calibration is bad or the cameras are very noisy, the odometer may get lost, which is indicated by a warning message on the terminal. In that case, you should look for better cameras or recalibrate them to see whether better results can be obtained. You might also want to have to look for better parameters for the disparity algorithm.

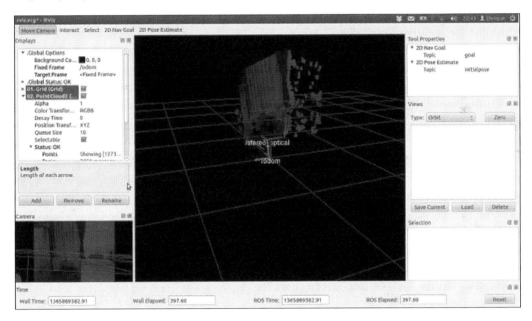

Performing visual odometry with an RGBD camera

Now we are going to see how to perform visual odometry using RGBD cameras using `fovis`.

Installing fovis

Since `fovis` is not provided as a Debian package, you must build it in your `catkin` workspace (use the same workspace as you used for `chapter5_tutorials`). Proceed with the following commands within any workspace:

```
$ cdsrc
$ git clone https://github.com/srv/libfovis.git
$ git clone https://github.com/srv/fovis.git
$ cd ..
$ catkin_make
```

This clones two repositories that allow us to have the `fovis` software integrated in ROS. Note that the original code is hosted on this Google Code Project at `http://fovis.github.io/`.

Once this has been built successfully, set up the environment for this workspace before using the software:

```
$ sourcedevel/setup.bash
```

Using fovis with the Kinect RGBD camera

At this point, we are going to run `fovis` for the Kinect RGBD camera. This means that we are going to have 3D information to compute the visual odometry, so better results are expected than when we use stereo vision or a monocular camera (as with `viso2`).

We simply have to launch the Kinect RGBD camera driver and `fovis`. For convenience, we provide a single `launch` file that runs both:

```
$ roslaunch chapter5_tutorials fovis_demo.launch
```

Move the camera around and you should be able to have a good odometry estimation of the trajectory followed by the camera. The next figure shows this on `rviz` in the initial state before moving the camera. You can see the RGBD point cloud and two arrows showing the odometry and the current position of the camera in the following screenshot:

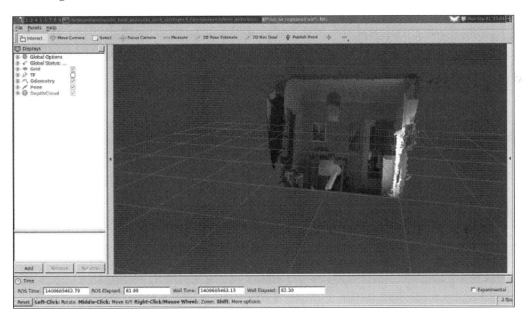

After moving the camera, you should see the arrows showing the camera pose (as shown in the following screenshot). Take into account that you have to move it quite slowly as the software needs time to compute the odometry, depending on the computer you are using:

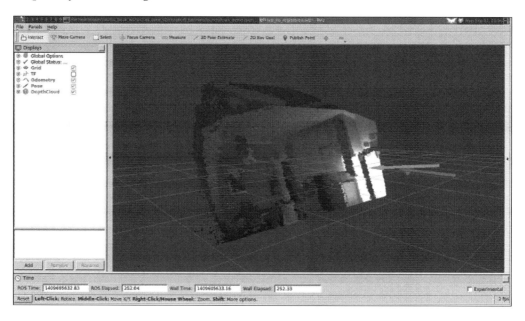

By default, the `fovis_demo.launch` file uses the `no_registered` depth information. This means that the depth image is not registered or transformed into the RGB camera frame. Although it is better to register it, this drops the frame rate dramatically from the raw throughput of 30 Hz provided by the Kinect sensor to something around 2.5 Hz depending on your computing resources.

You can use `throttle` on the RGB camera frames to use the registered version. This is automatically done by the `launch` file provided. You can select between the following modes: `no_registered` (default), `hw_registered`, and `sw_registered`. Note that, in principle, the Kinect sensor does not support the hardware registration mode (`hw_registered`), which is expected to be the fastest one. Therefore, you can try the software registration mode (`sw_registered`), for which we throttle the RGB camera messages to 2.5 Hz; you can change this in `fovis_sw_registered.launch`, as shown here:

```
$ roslaunch chapter5_tutorials fovis_demo.launch mode:=sw_registered
```

Computing the homography of two images

The homography matrix is a 3 x 3 matrix that provides transformation up to scale from a given image and a new one, which must be coplanar. In `src/homography.cpp`, there is an extensive example that takes the first image acquired by the camera and then computes the homography for every new frame in respect to the first image. In order to run the example, take something planar, such as a book cover, and run the following command:

```
$ roslaunch chapter5_tutorials homography.launch
```

This runs the camera driver that should grab frames from your camera (webcam), detect features (SURF by default), extract descriptors for each of them, and match them with the ones extracted from the first image using Flann-based matching with a cross-check filter. Once the program has the matches, the homography matrix H is computed. With H, we can warp the new frame to obtain the original one, as shown in the following screenshot (matches on the top, warped image using H, which is shown in plain text in the terminal):

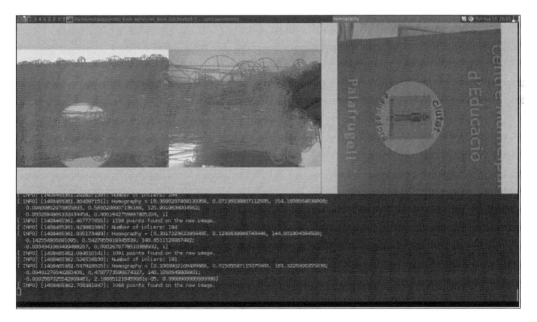

Summary

In this chapter, we have given you an overview of the Computer Vision tools provided by ROS. We started by showing how we can connect and run several types of cameras, particularly FireWire and USB ones. The basic functionality to change their parameters was presented, so now you can adjust certain parameters to obtain images of good quality. Additionally, we provided a complete USB camera driver example.

Then, we showed how you can calibrate the camera. The importance of calibration is the ability to correct the distortion of wide-angle cameras, particularly cheap ones. The calibration matrix also allows you to perform many Computer Vision tasks, such as visual odometry and perception.

We showed how you can work with stereo vision in ROS and how you can set up an easy solution with two inexpensive webcams. We also explained the image pipeline, several APIs that work with Computer Vision in ROS, such as `cv_bridge` and `image_transport`, and the integration of OpenCV within ROS packages.

Finally, we enumerated useful tasks and topics in Computer Vision that are supported by tools developed in ROS. In particular, we illustrated the example of visual odometry using the `viso2` and `fovis` libraries. We showed you an example of data recorded with a high-quality camera and also with the inexpensive stereo pair we proposed. Finally, feature detection, descriptor extraction, and matching was shown in order to illustrate how you can obtain homography between two images. All in all, after reading and running the code in this chapter, you will have seen the basics required to perform Computer Vision in ROS.

In the next chapter, you will learn how to work with point clouds using PCL, which allows you to work with RGBD cameras.

10
Point Clouds

Point clouds appeared in the robotics toolbox as a way to intuitively represent and manipulate the information provided by 3D sensors, such as time-of-flight cameras and laser scanners, in which the space is sampled in a finite set of points in a 3D frame of reference. The **Point Cloud Library** (**PCL**) provides a number of data types and data structures to easily represent not only the points of our sampled space, but also the different properties of the sampled space, such as color and normal vectors. PCL also provides a number of state-of-the-art algorithms to perform data processing on our data samples, such as filtering, model estimation, and surface reconstruction.

ROS provides a message-based interface through which PCL point clouds can be efficiently communicated, and a set of conversion functions from native PCL types to ROS messages, in much the same way as it is done with OpenCV images. Aside from the standard capabilities of the ROS API, there are a number of standard packages that can be used to interact with common 3D sensors, such as the widely used Microsoft Kinect or the Hokuyo laser, and visualize the data in different reference frames with the RViz visualizer.

This chapter will provide a background on the PCL, relevant data types, and ROS interface messages that will be used throughout the rest of the sections. Later, a number of techniques will be presented on how to perform data processing using the PCL library and how to communicate the incoming and outgoing data through ROS.

Understanding the Point Cloud Library

Before we dive into the code, it's important to understand the basic concepts of both the Point Cloud Library and the PCL interface for ROS. As mentioned earlier, the former provides a set of data structures and algorithms for 3D data processing, and the latter provides a set of messages and conversion functions between messages and PCL data structures. All these software packages and libraries, in combination with the capabilities of the distributed communication layer provided by ROS, open up possibilities for many new applications in the robotics field.

In general, PCL contains one very important data structure, which is `PointCloud`. This data structure is designed as a template class that takes the type of point to be used as a template parameter. As a result of this, the point cloud class is not much more than a container of points that includes all of the common information required by all point clouds regardless of their point type. The following are the most important public fields in a point cloud:

- `header`: This field is of the `pcl::PCLHeader` type and specifies the acquisition time of the point cloud.

- `points`: This field is of the `std::vector<PointT, ... >` type and is the container where all the points are stored. `PointT` in the vector definition corresponds to the class template parameter, that is, the point type.

- `width`: This field specifies the width of the point cloud when organized as an image; otherwise, it contains the number of points in the cloud.

- `height`: This field specifies the height of the point cloud when organized as an image; otherwise, it's always `1`.

- `is_dense`: This field specifies whether the cloud contains invalid values (infinite or NaN).

- `sensor_origin_`: This field is of the `Eigen::Vector4f` type, and it defines the sensor acquisition pose in terms of a translation from the origin.

- `sensor_orientation_`: This field is of the `Eigen::Quaternionf` type, and it defines the sensor acquisition pose as a rotation.

These fields are used by PCL algorithms to perform data processing and can be used by the user to create their own algorithms. Once the point cloud structure is understood, the next step is to understand the different point types a point cloud can contain, how PCL works, and the PCL interface for ROS.

Different point cloud types

As described earlier, `pcl::PointCloud` contains a field that serves as a container for the points; this field is of the `PointT` type, which is the template parameter of the `pcl::PointCloud` class and defines the type of point the cloud is meant to store. PCL defines many types of points, but a few of the most commonly used ones are the following:

- `pcl::PointXYZ`: This is the simplest type of point and probably one of the most used; it stores only 3D *XYZ* information.

- `pcl::PointXYZI`: This type of point is very similar to the previous one, but it also includes a field for the intensity of the point. Intensity can be useful when obtaining points based on a certain level of return from a sensor. There are two other standard identical point types to this one — the first one is `pcl::InterestPoint`, which has a field to store strength instead of intensity, and `pcl::PointWithRange`, which has a field to store the range instead of either intensity or strength.

- `pcl::PointXYZRGBA`: This type of point stores 3D information as well as color (RGB = red, green, blue) and transparency (A = alpha).

- `pcl::PointXYZRGB`: This type is similar to the previous point type, but it differs in that it lacks the transparency field.

- `pcl::Normal`: This is one of the most used types of points; it represents the surface normal at a given point and a measure of its curvature.

- `pcl::PointNormal`: This type is exactly the same as the previous one; it contains the surface normal and curvature information at a given point, but it also includes the 3D *XYZ* coordinates of the point. Variants of this point are `PointXYZRGBNormal` and `PointXYZINormal`, which, as the names suggest, include color (former) and intensity (latter).

Aside from these common types of points, there are many more standard PCL types, such as `PointWithViewpoint`, `MomentInvariants`, `Boundary`, `PrincipalCurvatures`, and `Histogram`. More importantly, the PCL algorithms are all converted to templates so that not only the available types can be used, but also semantically valid user-defined types can be used.

Algorithms in PCL

PCL uses a very specific design pattern throughout the entire library to define point cloud processing algorithms. In general, the problem with these types of algorithms is that they can be highly configurable, and in order to deliver their full potential, the library must provide a mechanism for the user to specify all of the parameters required as well as the commonly used defaults.

In order to solve this problem, PCL developers decided to make each algorithm a class belonging to a hierarchy of classes with specific commonalities. This approach allows PCL developers to reuse existing algorithms in the hierarchy by deriving from them and adding the required parameters for the new algorithm, and it also allows the user to easily provide the parameter values it requires through accessors, leaving the rest to their default value. The following snippet shows how using a PCL algorithm usually looks:

```
pcl::PointCloud<pcl::PointXYZ>::Ptr cloud(new
    pcl::PointCloud<pcl::PointXYZ>);
pcl::PointCloud<pcl::PointXYZ>::Ptr result(new
    pcl::PointCloud<pcl::PointXYZ>);

pcl::Algorithm<pcl::PointXYZ> algorithm;
  algorithm.setInputCloud(cloud);
  algorithm.setParameter(1.0);
  algorithm.setAnotherParameter(0.33);
  algorithm.process (*result);
```

This approach is only followed when required within the library, so there might be exceptions to the rule, such as the I/O functionality, which are not bound by the same requirements.

The PCL interface for ROS

The PCL interface for ROS provides the means required to communicate PCL data structures through the message-based communication system provided by ROS. To do so, there are several message types defined to hold point clouds as well as other data products from the PCL algorithms. In combination with these message types, a set of conversion functions are also provided to convert from native PCL data types to messages.

Some of the most useful message types are the following:

- `std_msgs::Header`: This is not really a message type, but it is usually part of every ROS message; it holds the information about when the message was sent as well a sequence number and the frame name. The PCL equivalent is `pcl::Header` type.

- `sensor_msgs::PointCloud2`: This is possibly the most important type; this message is used to transfer the `pcl::PointCloud` type. However, it is important to take into account that this message will be deprecated in future versions of PCL in favor of `pcl::PCLPointCloud2`.

- `pcl_msgs::PointIndices`: This type stores indices of points belonging to a point cloud; the PCL equivalent type is `pcl::PointIndices`.

- `pcl_msgs::PolygonMesh`: This holds the information required to describe meshes, that is, vertices and polygons; the PCL equivalent type is `pcl::PolygonMesh`.

- `pcl_msgs::Vertices`: This type holds a set of the vertices as indices in an array, for example, to describe a polygon. The PCL equivalent type is `pcl::Vertices`.

- `pcl_msgs::ModelCoefficients`: This stores the values of the different coefficients of a model, for example, the four coefficients required to describe a plane. The PCL equivalent type is `pcl::ModelCoefficients`.

The previous messages can be converted to and from PCL types with the conversion functions provided by the ROS PCL package. All of the functions have a similar signature, which means that once we know how to convert one type, we know how to convert them all. The following functions are provided in the `pcl_conversions` namespace:

```
void fromPCL(const <PCL Type> &, <ROS Message type> &);
void moveFromPCL(<PCL Type> &, <ROS Message type> &);
void toPCL(const <ROS Message type> &, <PCL Type> &);
void moveToPCL(<ROS Message type> &, <PCL Type> &);
```

Here, the PCL type must be replaced by one of the previously specified PCL types and the ROS message types by their message counterpart. `sensor_msgs::PointCloud2` has a specific set of functions to perform the conversions:

```
void toROSMsg(const pcl::PointCloud<T> &, sensor_msgs::PointCloud2
&);
void fromROSMsg(const sensor_msgs::PointCloud2 &,
pcl::PointCloud<T> &);
void moveFromROSMsg(sensor_msgs::PointCloud2 &, pcl::PointCloud<T>
&);
```

You might be wondering about what the difference between each function and its move version is. The answer is simple; the normal version performs a deep copy of the data, whereas the move versions perform a shallow copy and nullify the source data container. This is referred to as **move semantics**.

My first PCL program

In this section, you will learn how to integrate PCL and ROS. Knowledge and understanding of how ROS packages are laid out and how to compile are required although the steps will be repeated for simplicity. The example used in this first PCL program has no use whatsoever other than serving as a valid ROS node, which will successfully compile.

The first step is to create the ROS package for this entire chapter in your workspace. This package will depend on the `pcl_conversions`, `pcl_ros`, `pcl_msgs`, and `sensor_msgs` packages:

```
$ catkin_create_pkg chapter10_tutorials pcl_conversions pcl_ros pcl_msgs
sensor_msgs
```

The following step is to create the source directory in the package using the following commands:

```
$ rospack profile
$ roscd chapter10_tutorials
$ mkdir src
```

In this new source directory, you should create a file named `pcl_sample.cpp` with the following code, which creates a ROS node and publishes a point cloud with 100 elements. Again, what the code does should not really be of any concern to you as it is just for the purpose of having a valid node that uses PCL and compiles without problems:

```
#include <ros/ros.h>
#include <pcl/point_cloud.h>
#include <pcl_ros/point_cloud.h>
#include <pcl_conversions/pcl_conversions.h>
#include <sensor_msgs/PointCloud2.h>

main (int argc, char** argv)
{
```

```
ros::init (argc, argv, "pcl_sample");
ros::NodeHandle nh;
ros::Publisher pcl_pub =
nh.advertise<sensor_msgs::PointCloud2> ("pcl_output", 1);

sensor_msgs::PointCloud2 output;
pcl::PointCloud<pcl::PointXYZ>::Ptr cloud (new
pcl::PointCloud<pcl::PointXYZ>);

// Fill in the cloud data
cloud->width = 100;
cloud->height = 1;
cloud->points.resize (cloud->width * cloud->height);

//Convert the cloud to ROS message
pcl::toROSMsg (*cloud, output);

pcl_pub.publish(output);
ros::spinOnce();

return 0;
}
```

The next step is to add PCL libraries to `CMakeLists.txt` so that the ROS node executable can be properly linked against the system's PCL libraries:

```
find_package(PCL REQUIRED)

include_directories(include ${PCL_INCLUDE_DIRS})
link_directories(${PCL_LIBRARY_DIRS})
```

Finally, the lines to generate the executable and link against the appropriate libraries are added:

```
add_executable(pcl_sample src/pcl_sample.cpp)
target_link_libraries(pcl_sample ${catkin_LIBRARIES}
${PCL_LIBRARIES})
```

Once the final step has been reached, the package can be compiled by calling `catkin_make` as usual from the workspace `root` directory.

Creating point clouds

In this first example, the reader will learn how to create PCL point clouds composed solely of pseudorandom points. The PCL point clouds will then be published periodically through a topic named /pcl_output. This example provides practical knowledge on how to generate point clouds with custom data and how to convert them to the corresponding ROS message type in order to broadcast point clouds to subscribers. The source code for this first example can be found in the chapter10_tutorials/src folder, and it is named pcl_create.cpp:

```cpp
#include <ros/ros.h>
#include <pcl/point_cloud.h>
#include <pcl_conversions/pcl_conversions.h>
#include <sensor_msgs/PointCloud2.h>

main (int argc, char **argv)
{
    ros::init (argc, argv, "pcl_create");

    ros::NodeHandle nh;
    ros::Publisher pcl_pub =
    nh.advertise<sensor_msgs::PointCloud2> ("pcl_output", 1);
    pcl::PointCloud<pcl::PointXYZ> cloud;
    sensor_msgs::PointCloud2 output;

    // Fill in the cloud data
    cloud.width = 100;
    cloud.height = 1;
    cloud.points.resize(cloud.width * cloud.height);

    for (size_t i = 0; i < cloud.points.size (); ++i)
    {
        cloud.points[i].x = 1024 * rand () / (RAND_MAX + 1.0f);
        cloud.points[i].y = 1024 * rand () / (RAND_MAX + 1.0f);
        cloud.points[i].z = 1024 * rand () / (RAND_MAX + 1.0f);
    }

    //Convert the cloud to ROS message
    pcl::toROSMsg(cloud, output);
    output.header.frame_id = "odom";
```

```
    ros::Rate loop_rate(1);
    while (ros::ok())
    {
        pcl_pub.publish(output);
        ros::spinOnce();
        loop_rate.sleep();
    }

    return 0;
}
```

The first step in this, and every other snippet, is including the appropriate header files; in this case, we'll include a few PCL-specific headers as well as the standard ROS header and the one that contains the declarations for the `PointCloud2` message:

```
#include <ros/ros.h>
#include <pcl/point_cloud.h>
#include <pcl_conversions/pcl_conversions.h>
#include <sensor_msgs/PointCloud2.h>
```

After the node initialization, a `PointCloud2` ROS publisher is created and advertised; this publisher will later be used to publish the point clouds created through PCL. Once the publisher is created, two variables are defined. The first one, of the `PointCloud2` type, is the message type that will be used to store the information to be sent through the publisher. The second variable, of the `PointCloud<PointXYZ>` type, is the native PCL type that will be used to generate the point cloud in the first place:

```
ros::Publisher pcl_pub = nh.advertise<sensor_msgs::PointCloud2>
("pcl_output", 1);
pcl::PointCloud<pcl::PointXYZ> cloud;
sensor_msgs::PointCloud2 output;
```

The next step is to generate the point cloud with relevant data. In order to do so, we need to allocate the required space in the point cloud structure as well as set the appropriate field. In this case, the point cloud created will be of size `100`. Since this point cloud is not meant to represent an image, the height will only be of size `1`:

```
// Fill in the cloud data
cloud.width = 100;
cloud.height = 1;
cloud.points.resize(cloud.width * cloud.height);
```

With the space allocated and the appropriate fields set, the point cloud is filled with random points between 0 and 1024:

```
for (size_t i = 0; i < cloud.points.size (); ++i)
{
  cloud.points[i].x = 1024 * rand () / (RAND_MAX + 1.0f);
  cloud.points[i].y = 1024 * rand () / (RAND_MAX + 1.0f);
  cloud.points[i].z = 1024 * rand () / (RAND_MAX + 1.0f);
}
```

At this point, the cloud has been created and filled with data. Since this node is meant to be a data source, the next and last step in this snippet is to convert the PCL point cloud type into a ROS message type and publish it. In order to perform the conversion, the `toROSMsg` function will be used, performing a deep copy of the data from the PCL point cloud type to the `PointCloud2` message.

Finally, the `PointCloud2` message is published periodically at a rate of one hertz in order to have a constant source of information, albeit immutable:

```
//Convert the cloud to ROS message
pcl::toROSMsg(cloud, output);
output.header.frame_id = "odom";

ros::Rate loop_rate(1);
while (ros::ok())
{
  pcl_pub.publish(output);
  ros::spinOnce();
  loop_rate.sleep();
}
```

Perhaps the reader has also noticed that the `frame_id` field in the message header has been set to the `odom` value; this has been done in order to be able to visualize our `PointCloud2` message on the RViz visualizer.

In order to run this example, the first step is to open a terminal and run the `roscore` command:

```
$ roscore
```

In another terminal, the following command will run the example:

```
rosrun chapter10_tutorials pcl_create
```

To visualize the point cloud, the RViz visualizer must be run with the following command:

```
$ rosrun rviz rviz
```

Once `rviz` has been loaded, a `PointCloud2` object needs to be added by clicking on **Add** and adding the `pcl_output` topic. The reader must make sure to set `odom` as the fixed frame in the **Global Options** section. If everything has worked properly, a randomly spread point cloud should be shown in the 3D view, just as in the following screenshot:

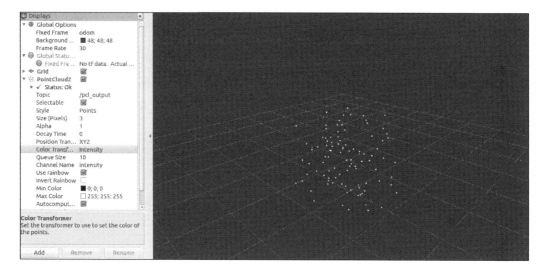

Loading and saving point clouds to the disk

PCL provides a standard file format to load and store point clouds to the disk as it is a common practice among researchers to share interesting datasets for other people to experiment with. This format is named PCD, and it has been designed to support PCL-specific extensions.

The format is very simple; it starts with a header containing information about the point type and the number of elements in the point cloud, followed by a list of points conforming to the specified type. The following lines are an example of a PCD file header:

```
# .PCD v.5 - Point Cloud Data file format
FIELDS x y z intensity distance sid
SIZE 4 4 4 4 4 4
```

```
TYPE F F F F F F
COUNT 1 1 1 1 1 1
WIDTH 460400
HEIGHT 1
POINTS 460400
DATA ascii
```

Reading PCD files can be done through the PCL API, which makes it a very straightforward process. The following example can be found in `chapter10_tutorials/src`, and it is named `pcl_read.cpp`. The following example shows how to load a PCD file and publish the resulting point cloud as an ROS message:

```cpp
#include <ros/ros.h>
#include <pcl/point_cloud.h>
#include <pcl_conversions/pcl_conversions.h>
#include <sensor_msgs/PointCloud2.h>
#include <pcl/io/pcd_io.h>

main(int argc, char **argv)
{
    ros::init (argc, argv, "pcl_read");

    ros::NodeHandle nh;
    ros::Publisher pcl_pub =
    nh.advertise<sensor_msgs::PointCloud2> ("pcl_output", 1);

    sensor_msgs::PointCloud2 output;
    pcl::PointCloud<pcl::PointXYZ> cloud;

    pcl::io::loadPCDFile ("test_pcd.pcd", cloud);

    pcl::toROSMsg(cloud, output);
    output.header.frame_id = "odom";

    ros::Rate loop_rate(1);
    while (ros::ok())
    {
        pcl_pub.publish(output);
        ros::spinOnce();
        loop_rate.sleep();
    }

    return 0;
}
```

As always, the first step is to include the required header files. In this particular case, the only new header file that has been added is `pcl/io/pcd_io.h`, which contains the required definitions to load and store point clouds to PCD and other file formats.

The main difference between the previous example and this new one is simply the mechanism used to obtain the point cloud. While in the first example, we manually filled the point cloud with random points, in this case, we just load them from the disk:

```
pcl::io::loadPCDFile ("test_pcd.pcd", cloud);
```

As we can see, the process of loading a PCD file has no complexity whatsoever. Further versions of the PCD file format also allow reading and writing of the current origin and orientation of the point cloud.

In order to run the previous example, we need to access the data directory in the package provided, which includes an example PCD file containing a point cloud that will be used further in this chapter:

```
$ roscd chapter10_tutorials/data
$ rosrun chapter10_tutorials pcl_read
```

As in the previous example, the point cloud can be easily visualized through the RViz visualizer:

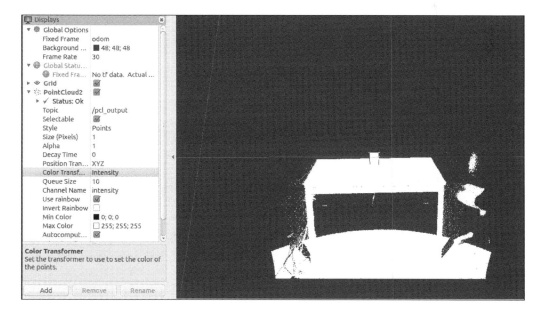

Obvious though it may sound, the second interesting operation when dealing with PCD files is creating them. In the following example, our goal is to subscribe to a `sensor_msgs/PointCloud2` topic and store the received point clouds into a file. The code can be found in `chapter10_tutorials`, and it is named `pcl_write.cpp`:

```
#include <ros/ros.h>
#include <pcl/point_cloud.h>
#include <pcl_conversions/pcl_conversions.h>
#include <sensor_msgs/PointCloud2.h>
#include <pcl/io/pcd_io.h>

void cloudCB(const sensor_msgs::PointCloud2 &input)
{
    pcl::PointCloud<pcl::PointXYZ> cloud;
    pcl::fromROSMsg(input, cloud);
    pcl::io::savePCDFileASCII ("write_pcd_test.pcd", cloud);
}

main (int argc, char **argv)
{
    ros::init (argc, argv, "pcl_write");

    ros::NodeHandle nh;
    ros::Subscriber bat_sub = nh.subscribe("pcl_output", 10,
    cloudCB);

    ros::spin();

    return 0;
}
```

The topic subscribed to is the same used in the two previous examples, namely `pcl_output`, so they can be linked together for testing:

```
ros::Subscriber bat_sub = nh.subscribe("pcl_output", 10, cloudCB);
```

When a message is received, the `callback` function is called. The first step in this `callback` function is to define a PCL cloud and convert `PointCloud2` that is received, using the `pcl_conversions` function `fromROSMsg`. Finally, the point cloud is saved to the disk in the ASCII format, but it could also be saved in the binary format, which will generate smaller PCD files:

```
void cloudCB(const sensor_msgs::PointCloud2 &input)
{
```

```
        pcl::PointCloud<pcl::PointXYZ> cloud;
        pcl::fromROSMsg(input, cloud);
        pcl::io::savePCDFileASCII ("write_pcd_test.pcd", cloud);
    }
```

In order to be able to run this example, it is necessary to have a publisher providing point clouds through the `pcl_output` topic. In this particular case, we will use the `pcl_read` example shown earlier, which fits this requirement. In three different terminals, we will run the `roscore`, `pcl_read`, and `pcl_write` node:

```
$ roscore
$ roscd chapter10_tutorials/data && rosrun chapter10_tutorials pcl_read
$ roscd chapter10_tutorials/data && rosrun chapter10_tutorials pcl_write
```

If everything worked properly, after the first (or second) message is produced, the `pcl_write` node should have created a file named `write_pcd_test.pcd` in the data directory of the `chapter10_tutorials` package.

Visualizing point clouds

PCL provides several ways of visualizing point clouds. The first and simplest is through the basic cloud viewer, which is capable of representing any sort of PCL point cloud in a 3D viewer, while at the same time providing a set of callbacks for user interaction. In the following example, we will create a small node that will subscribe to `sensor_msgs/PointCloud2` and the node will display `sensor_msgs/PointCloud2` using `cloud_viewer` (basic) from the library. The code for this example can be found in the `chapter10_tutorials/src` source directory, and it is named `pcl_visualize.cpp`:

```cpp
#include <iostream>
#include <ros/ros.h>
#include <pcl/visualization/cloud_viewer.h>
#include <sensor_msgs/PointCloud2.h>
#include <pcl_conversions/pcl_conversions.h>

class cloudHandler
{
public:
    cloudHandler()
    : viewer("Cloud Viewer")
    {
        pcl_sub = nh.subscribe("pcl_output", 10,
        &cloudHandler::cloudCB, this);
```

```
        viewer_timer = nh.createTimer(ros::Duration(0.1),
        &cloudHandler::timerCB, this);
    }

    void cloudCB(const sensor_msgs::PointCloud2 &input)
    {
        pcl::PointCloud<pcl::PointXYZ> cloud;
        pcl::fromROSMsg(input, cloud);

        viewer.showCloud(cloud.makeShared());
    }

    void timerCB(const ros::TimerEvent&)
    {
        if (viewer.wasStopped())
        {
            ros::shutdown();
        }
    }

protected:
    ros::NodeHandle nh;
    ros::Subscriber pcl_sub;
    pcl::visualization::CloudViewer viewer;
    ros::Timer viewer_timer;
};

main (int argc, char **argv)
{
    ros::init (argc, argv, "pcl_visualize");

    cloudHandler handler;

    ros::spin();

    return 0;
}
```

The code for this particular example introduces a different pattern; in this case, all of our functionality is encapsulated in a class, which provides a clean way of sharing variables with the `callback` functions, as opposed to using global variables.

The constructor implicitly initializes the node handle through the default constructor, which is automatically called for the missing objects in the initializer list. The cloud handle is explicitly initialized with a very simple string, which corresponds to the window name, after everything is correctly initialized. The subscriber to the `pcl_output` topic is set as well as a timer, which will trigger a callback every 100 milliseconds. This timer is used to periodically check whether the window has been closed and, if this is the case, shut down the node:

```
cloudHandler()
 : viewer("Cloud Viewer")
{
  pcl_sub = nh.subscribe("pcl_output", 10, &cloudHandler::cloudCB,
  this);
  viewer_timer = nh.createTimer(ros::Duration(0.1),
  &cloudHandler::timerCB, this);
}
```

The point cloud `callback` function is not very different from the previous examples except that, in this particular case, the PCL point cloud is passed directly to the viewer through the `showCloud` function, which automatically updates the display:

```
void cloudCB(const sensor_msgs::PointCloud2 &input)
{
  pcl::PointCloud<pcl::PointXYZ> cloud;
  pcl::fromROSMsg(input, cloud);

  viewer.showCloud(cloud.makeShared());
}
```

Since the viewer window usually comes with a close button as well as a keyboard shortcut to close the window, it is important to take into account this event and act upon it by, for example, shutting down the node. In this particular case, we are handling the current state of the window in a callback, which is called through a ROS timer every 100 milliseconds. If the viewer has been closed, our action is to simply shut down the node:

```
void timerCB(const ros::TimerEvent&)
{
  if (viewer.wasStopped())
  {
    ros::shutdown();
  }
}
```

To execute this example, and any other for that matter, the first step is to run the roscore command in a terminal:

```
$ roscore
```

In a second terminal, we will run the pcl_read example and a source of data, such as a reminder, using the following commands:

```
$ roscd chapter10_tutorials/data
$ rosrun chapter10_tutorials pcl_read
```

Finally, in a third terminal, we will run the following command:

```
$ rosrun chapter10_tutorials pcl_visualize
```

Running this code will cause a window to launch; this window will display the point cloud contained in the test PCD file provided with the examples. The following screenshot shows this:

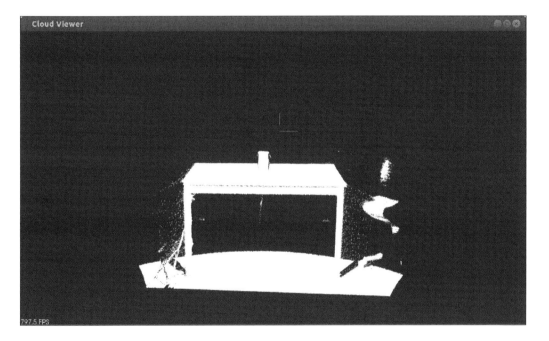

The current example uses the simplest possible viewer, namely the PCL `cloud_viewer`, but the library also provides a much more complex and complete visualization component named **PCLVisualizer**. This visualizer is capable of displaying point clouds, meshes, and surfaces, as well as including multiple viewports and color spaces. An example of how to use this particular visualizer is provided in the `chapter10_tutorials` source directory named `pcl_visualize2.cpp`.

In general, all the visualizers provided by PCL use the same underlying functionality and work in much the same way. The mouse can be used to move around the 3D view; in combination with the shift, it allows you to translate the image, and in combination with the control, it allows you to rotate the image. Finally, upon pressing *H*, the help text is printed in the current terminal, which should look like the following screenshot:

```
$ rosrun chapter6_tutorials pcl_visualize
| Help:
--------
        p, P   : switch to a point-based representation
        w, W   : switch to a wireframe-based representation (where available)
        s, S   : switch to a surface-based representation (where available)

        j, J   : take a .PNG snapshot of the current window view
        c, C   : display current camera/window parameters
        f, F   : fly to point mode

        e, E   : exit the interactor
        q, Q   : stop and call VTK's TerminateApp

        +/-    : increment/decrement overall point size
    +/- [+ ALT] : zoom in/out

        g, G   : display scale grid (on/off)
        u, U   : display lookup table (on/off)

    r, R [+ ALT] : reset camera [to viewpoint = {0, 0, 0} -> center_{x, y, z}]

    ALT + s, S   : turn stereo mode on/off
    ALT + f, F   : switch between maximized window mode and original size

        l, L            : list all available geometric and color handlers for the current actor map
    ALT + 0..9 [+ CTRL] : switch between different geometric handlers (where available)
        0..9 [+ CTRL]   : switch between different color handlers (where available)

    SHIFT + left click   : select a point

        x, X   : toggle rubber band selection mode for left mouse button
```

Filtering and downsampling

The two main issues that we may face when attempting to process point clouds are excessive noise and excessive density. The former causes our algorithms to misinterpret the data and produce incorrect or inaccurate results, whereas the latter makes our algorithms take a long time to complete their operation. In this section, we will provide insight into how to reduce the amount of noise or outliers of our point clouds and how to reduce the point density without losing valuable information.

The first part is to create a node that will take care of filtering outliers from the point clouds produced in the `pcl_output` topic and sending them back through the `pcl_filtered` topic. The example can be found in the source directory of the `chapter10_tutorials` package, and it is named `pcl_filter.cpp`:

```cpp
#include <ros/ros.h>
#include <pcl/point_cloud.h>
#include <pcl_conversions/pcl_conversions.h>
#include <sensor_msgs/PointCloud2.h>
#include <pcl/filters/statistical_outlier_removal.h>

class cloudHandler
{
public:
    cloudHandler()
    {
        pcl_sub = nh.subscribe("pcl_output", 10,
        &cloudHandler::cloudCB, this);
        pcl_pub =
        nh.advertise<sensor_msgs::PointCloud2>("pcl_filtered", 1);
    }

    void cloudCB(const sensor_msgs::PointCloud2& input)
    {
        pcl::PointCloud<pcl::PointXYZ> cloud;
        pcl::PointCloud<pcl::PointXYZ> cloud_filtered;
        sensor_msgs::PointCloud2 output;

        pcl::fromROSMsg(input, cloud);

        pcl::StatisticalOutlierRemoval<pcl::PointXYZ> statFilter;
        statFilter.setInputCloud(cloud.makeShared());
        statFilter.setMeanK(10);
```

```
        statFilter.setStddevMulThresh(0.2);
        statFilter.filter(cloud_filtered);

        pcl::toROSMsg(cloud_filtered, output);
        pcl_pub.publish(output);
    }

protected:
    ros::NodeHandle nh;
    ros::Subscriber pcl_sub;
    ros::Publisher pcl_pub;
};

main(int argc, char** argv)
{
    ros::init(argc, argv, "pcl_filter");

    cloudHandler handler;

    ros::spin();

    return 0;
}
```

Just as with the previous example, this one uses a class that contains a publisher as a member variable that is used in the `callback` function. The `callback` function defines two PCL point clouds, one for input messages and one for the filtered point cloud. As always, the input point cloud is converted using the standard conversion functions:

```
pcl::PointCloud<pcl::PointXYZ> cloud;
pcl::PointCloud<pcl::PointXYZ> cloud_filtered;
sensor_msgs::PointCloud2 output;

pcl::fromROSMsg(input, cloud);
```

Now, this is where things start getting interesting. In order to perform filtering, we will use the statistical outlier removal algorithm provided by PCL. This algorithm performs an analysis of the point cloud and removes those points that do not satisfy a specific statistical property, which, in this case, is the average distance in a neighborhood, removing all of those points that deviate too much from the average. The number of neighbors to use for the average computation can be set by the `setMeanK` function, and the multiplier on the standard deviation threshold can also be set through `setStddevMulThresh`.

The following piece of code handles the filtering and sets the `cloud_filtered` point cloud with our new *noiseless* cloud:

```
pcl::StatisticalOutlierRemoval<pcl::PointXYZ> statFilter;
statFilter.setInputCloud(cloud.makeShared());
statFilter.setMeanK(10);
statFilter.setStddevMulThresh(0.2);
statFilter.filter(cloud_filtered);
```

Finally, and as always, the filtered cloud is converted to `PointCloud2` and published so that our other algorithms can make use of this new point cloud to provide more accurate results:

```
pcl::toROSMsg (cloud_filtered, output);
pcl_pub.publish(output);
```

In the following screenshot, we can see the result of the previous code when it is applied on the point cloud provided in our test PCD file. The original point cloud can be seen on the left-hand side and the filtered one on the right-hand side. The results are not perfect, but we can observe how much of the noise has been removed, which means that we can now proceed with reducing the density of the filtered point cloud.

Reducing the density of a point cloud, or any other dataset for that matter, is called **downsampling**. There are several techniques that can be used to downsample a point cloud, but some of them are more rigorous or provide better results than others.

In general, the goal of downsampling a point cloud is to improve the performance of our algorithms; for that reason, we need our downsampling algorithms to keep the basic properties and structure of our point cloud so that the end result of our algorithms doesn't change too much.

In the following example, we are going to demonstrate how to perform downsampling on point clouds with **Voxel Grid Filter**. In this case, the input point clouds are going to be the filtered ones from the previous example so that we can chain both examples together to produce better results in further algorithms. The example can be found in the source directory of the `chapter10_tutorials` package, and it's named `pcl_downsampling.cpp`:

```cpp
#include <ros/ros.h>
#include <pcl/point_cloud.h>
#include <pcl_conversions/pcl_conversions.h>
#include <sensor_msgs/PointCloud2.h>
#include <pcl/filters/voxel_grid.h>

class cloudHandler
{
public:
    cloudHandler()
    {
        pcl_sub = nh.subscribe("pcl_filtered", 10,
        &cloudHandler::cloudCB, this);
        pcl_pub =
        nh.advertise<sensor_msgs::PointCloud2>("pcl_downsampled",
        1);
    }

    void cloudCB(const sensor_msgs::PointCloud2 &input)
    {
        pcl::PointCloud<pcl::PointXYZ> cloud;
        pcl::PointCloud<pcl::PointXYZ> cloud_downsampled;
        sensor_msgs::PointCloud2 output;

        pcl::fromROSMsg(input, cloud);
```

```
            pcl::VoxelGrid<pcl::PointXYZ> voxelSampler;
            voxelSampler.setInputCloud(cloud.makeShared());
            voxelSampler.setLeafSize(0.01f, 0.01f, 0.01f);
            voxelSampler.filter(cloud_downsampled);

            pcl::toROSMsg(cloud_downsampled, output);
            pcl_pub.publish(output);

        }
    protected:
        ros::NodeHandle nh;
        ros::Subscriber pcl_sub;
        ros::Publisher pcl_pub;
    };

    main(int argc, char **argv)
    {
        ros::init(argc, argv, "pcl_downsampling");

        cloudHandler handler;

        ros::spin();

        return 0;
    }
```

This example is exactly the same as the previous one, with the only differences being the topics subscribed and published, which, in this case, are `pcl_filtered` and `pcl_downsampled`, and the algorithms used to perform the filtering on the point cloud.

As said earlier, the algorithm used is Voxel Grid Filter, which partitions the point cloud into voxels, or more accurately a 3D grid, and replaces all of the points contained in each voxel with the centroid of that subcloud. The size of each voxel can be specified through `setLeafSize` and will determine the density of our point cloud:

```
pcl::VoxelGrid<pcl::PointXYZ> voxelSampler;
voxelSampler.setInputCloud(cloud.makeShared());
voxelSampler.setLeafSize(0.01f, 0.01f, 0.01f);
voxelSampler.filter(cloud_downsampled);
```

The following image shows the results of both the filtered and downsampled images when compared to the original one. You can appreciate how the structure has been kept, the density reduced, and much of the noise completely eliminated.

To execute both examples, as always we start running `roscore`:

```
$ roscore
```

In the second terminal, we will run the `pcl_read` example and a source of data:

```
$ roscd chapter10_tutorials/data
$ rosrun chapter10_tutorials pcl_read
```

In the third terminal, we will run the filtering example, which will produce the `pcl_filtered` image for the downsampling example:

```
$ rosrun chapter10_tutorials pcl_filter
```

Finally, in the fourth terminal, we will run the downsampling example:

```
$ rosrun chapter10_tutorials pcl_downsampling
```

As always, the results can be seen on `rviz`, but in this case, the `pcl_visualizer2` example provided in the package can also be used although you might need to tweak the subscribed topics.

Registration and matching

Registration and matching is a common technique used in several different fields that consists of finding common structures or features in two datasets and using them to stitch the datasets together. In the case of point cloud processing, this can be achieved as easily as finding where one point cloud ends and where the other one starts. These techniques are very useful when obtaining point clouds from moving sources at a high rate, and we have an estimate of the movement of the source. With this algorithm, we can stitch each of those point clouds together and reduce the uncertainty in our sensor pose estimation.

PCL provides an algorithm named **Iterative Closest Point (ICP)** to perform registration and matching. We will use this algorithm in the following example, which can be found in the source directory of the `chapter10_tutorials` package, and it's named `pcl_matching.cpp`:

```
#include <ros/ros.h>
#include <pcl/point_cloud.h>
#include <pcl/registration/icp.h>
#include <pcl_conversions/pcl_conversions.h>
#include <sensor_msgs/PointCloud2.h>

class cloudHandler
{
public:
    cloudHandler()
    {
        pcl_sub = nh.subscribe("pcl_downsampled", 10,
        &cloudHandler::cloudCB, this);
        pcl_pub =
        nh.advertise<sensor_msgs::PointCloud2>("pcl_matched", 1);
    }

    void cloudCB(const sensor_msgs::PointCloud2 &input)
    {
        pcl::PointCloud<pcl::PointXYZ> cloud_in;
        pcl::PointCloud<pcl::PointXYZ> cloud_out;
        pcl::PointCloud<pcl::PointXYZ> cloud_aligned;
        sensor_msgs::PointCloud2 output;

        pcl::fromROSMsg(input, cloud_in);
```

```
        cloud_out = cloud_in;

        for (size_t i = 0; i < cloud_in.points.size (); ++i)
        {
            cloud_out.points[i].x = cloud_in.points[i].x + 0.7f;
        }

        pcl::IterativeClosestPoint<pcl::PointXYZ, pcl::PointXYZ>
        icp;
        icp.setInputSource(cloud_in.makeShared());
        icp.setInputTarget(cloud_out.makeShared());

        icp.setMaxCorrespondenceDistance(5);
        icp.setMaximumIterations(100);
        icp.setTransformationEpsilon (1e-12);
        icp.setEuclideanFitnessEpsilon(0.1);

        icp.align(cloud_aligned);

        pcl::toROSMsg(cloud_aligned, output);
        pcl_pub.publish(output);
    }

protected:
    ros::NodeHandle nh;
    ros::Subscriber pcl_sub;
    ros::Publisher pcl_pub;
};

main(int argc, char **argv)
{
    ros::init(argc, argv, "pcl_matching");

    cloudHandler handler;

    ros::spin();

    return 0;
}
```

This example uses the `pcl_downsampled` topic as the input source of point clouds in order to improve the performance of the algorithm; the end result is published in the `pcl_matched` topic. The algorithm used for registration and matching takes three point clouds—the first one is the point cloud to transform, the second one is the fixed cloud to which the first one should be aligned, and the third one is the end result point cloud:

```
pcl::PointCloud<pcl::PointXYZ> cloud_in;
pcl::PointCloud<pcl::PointXYZ> cloud_out;
pcl::PointCloud<pcl::PointXYZ> cloud_aligned;
```

To simplify matters and since we don't have a continuous source of point clouds, we are going to use the same original point cloud as the fixed cloud but displaced on the *x* axis. The expected behavior of the algorithm would then be to align both point clouds together:

```
cloud_out = cloud_in;

for (size_t i = 0; i < cloud_in.points.size (); ++i)
{
   cloud_out.points[i].x = cloud_in.points[i].x + 0.7f;
}
```

The next step is to call the ICP algorithm to perform the registration and matching. This iterative algorithm uses **Singular Value Decomposition (SVD)** to calculate the transformations to be done on the input point cloud towards decreasing the gap to the fixed point cloud. The algorithm has three basic stopping conditions:

- The difference between the previous and current transformations is smaller than a certain threshold. This threshold can be set through the `setTransformationEpsilon` function.

- The number of iterations has reached the maximum set by the user. This maximum can be set through the `setMaximumIterations` function.

- Finally, the sum of the Euclidean squared errors between two consecutive steps in the loop is below a certain threshold. This specific threshold can be set through the `setEuclideanFitnessEpsilon` function.

Another interesting parameter that is used to improve the accuracy of the result is the correspondence distance, which can be set through the `setMaxCorrespondanceDistance` function. This parameter defines the minimum distance that two correspondent points need to have between them to be considered in the alignment process.

With all of these parameters, the fixed point cloud and the input point cloud, the algorithm is capable of performing the registration and matching and returning the end result point cloud after the iterative transformations:

```
pcl::IterativeClosestPoint<pcl::PointXYZ, pcl::PointXYZ> icp;
icp.setInputSource(cloud_in.makeShared());
icp.setInputTarget(cloud_out.makeShared());
icp.setMaxCorrespondenceDistance(5);
icp.setMaximumIterations(100);
icp.setTransformationEpsilon (1e-12);
icp.setEuclideanFitnessEpsilon(0.1);
icp.align(cloud_aligned);
```

Finally, the resulting point cloud is converted into PointCloud2 and published through the corresponding topic:

```
pcl::toROSMsg(cloud_aligned, output);
pcl_pub.publish(output);
```

In order to run this example, we need to follow the same instructions as the filtering and downsampling example, starting with roscore in one terminal:

```
$ roscore
```

In a second terminal, we will run the pcl_read example and a source of data:

```
$ roscd chapter10_tutorials/data
$ rosrun chapter10_tutorials pcl_read
```

In a third terminal, we will run the filtering example:

```
$ rosrun chapter10_tutorials pcl_filter
```

In a fourth terminal, we will run the downsampling example:

```
$ rosrun chapter10_tutorials pcl_downsampling
```

Finally, we will run the registration and matching node that requires the pcl_downsampled topic, which is produced by the chain of nodes run before:

```
$ rosrun chapter10_tutorials pcl_matching
```

The end result can be seen in the following image, which has been obtained from `rviz`. The blue one is the original point cloud obtained from the PCD file, and the white point cloud is the aligned one obtained from the ICP algorithm. It has to be noted that the original point cloud was translated in the x axis, so the results are consistent with the point cloud, completely overlapping the translated image, as shown in the following screenshot:

Partitioning point clouds

Often times, when processing our point clouds, we might need to perform operations that require accessing a local region of a point cloud or manipulating the neighborhood of specific points. Since point clouds store data in a one-dimensional data structure, these kinds of operations are inherently complex. In order to solve this issue, PCL provides two spatial data structures, named the **kd-tree** and the **octree**, which can provide an alternative and more structured representation of any point cloud.

As the name suggests, an octree is basically a tree structure in which each node has eight children, and which can be used to partition the 3D space. In contrast, the kd-tree is a binary tree in which nodes represent k-dimensional points. Both data structures are very interesting, but, in this particular example, we are going to learn how to use the octree to search and retrieve all the points surrounding a specific point. The example can be found in the source directory of the chapter10_ tutorials package, and it's named pcl_partitioning.cpp:

```
#include <ros/ros.h>
#include <pcl/point_cloud.h>
#include <pcl_conversions/pcl_conversions.h>
#include <sensor_msgs/PointCloud2.h>
#include <pcl/octree/octree.h>

class cloudHandler
{
public:
    cloudHandler()
    {
        pcl_sub = nh.subscribe("pcl_downsampled", 10,
        &cloudHandler::cloudCB, this);
        pcl_pub =
        nh.advertise<sensor_msgs::PointCloud2>("pcl_partitioned",
        1);
    }

    void cloudCB(const sensor_msgs::PointCloud2 &input)
    {
        pcl::PointCloud<pcl::PointXYZ> cloud;
        pcl::PointCloud<pcl::PointXYZ> cloud_partitioned;
        sensor_msgs::PointCloud2 output;

        pcl::fromROSMsg(input, cloud);

        float resolution = 128.0f;
        pcl::octree::OctreePointCloudSearch<pcl::PointXYZ> octree
        (resolution);

        octree.setInputCloud (cloud.makeShared());
        octree.addPointsFromInputCloud ();
```

```cpp
        pcl::PointXYZ center_point;
        center_point.x = 0 ;
        center_point.y = 0.4;
        center_point.z = -1.4;

        float radius = 0.5;
        std::vector<int> radiusIdx;
        std::vector<float> radiusSQDist;
        if (octree.radiusSearch (center_point, radius, radiusIdx,
        radiusSQDist) > 0)
        {
            for (size_t i = 0; i < radiusIdx.size (); ++i)
            {
                cloud_partitioned.points.push_back
                (cloud.points[radiusIdx[i]]);
            }
        }

        pcl::toROSMsg(cloud_partitioned, output);
        output.header.frame_id = "odom";
        pcl_pub.publish(output);
    }

protected:
    ros::NodeHandle nh;
    ros::Subscriber pcl_sub;
    ros::Publisher pcl_pub;
};

main(int argc, char **argv)
{
    ros::init(argc, argv, "pcl_partitioning");

    cloudHandler handler;

    ros::spin();

    return 0;
}
```

As usual, this example uses the `pcl_downsampled` topic as an input source of point clouds and publishes the resulting partitioned point cloud to the `pcl_partitioned` topic. The handler function starts by converting the input point cloud to a PCL point cloud. The next step is to create an octree-searching algorithm, which requires passing a resolution value that will determine the size of the voxels at the lowest level of the tree and, consequently, other properties such as the tree's depth. The algorithm also requires to be given the point cloud to explicitly load the points:

```
float resolution = 128.0f;
pcl::octree::OctreePointCloudSearch<pcl::PointXYZ>
    octree(resolution);

octree.setInputCloud (cloud.makeShared());
octree.addPointsFromInputCloud ();
```

The next step is to define the center point of the partition; in this case, it has been handpicked to be close to the top of the point cloud:

```
pcl::PointXYZ center_point;
center_point.x = 0;
center_point.y = 0.4;
center_point.z = -1.4;
```

We can now perform a search in a radius around that specific point using the `radiusSearch` function from the octree search algorithm. This particular function is used to output arguments that return the indices of the points that fall in that radius and the squared distance from those points to the center point provided. With those indices, we can then create a new point cloud containing only the points belonging to the partition:

```
float radius = 0.5;
std::vector<int> radiusIdx;
std::vector<float> radiusSQDist;
if (octree.radiusSearch (center_point, radius, radiusIdx,
radiusSQDist) > 0)
{
  for (size_t i = 0; i < radiusIdx.size (); ++i)
  {
    cloud_partitioned.points.push_back
    (cloud.points[radiusIdx[i]]);
  }
}
```

Finally, the point cloud is converted to the `PointCloud2` message type and published in the output topic:

```
pcl::toROSMsg( cloud_partitioned, output );
output.header.frame_id = "odom";
pcl_pub.publish( output );
```

In order to run this example, we need to run the usual chain of nodes, starting with `roscore`:

```
$ roscore
```

In the second terminal, we can run the `pcl_read` example and a source of data:

```
$ roscd chapter10_tutorials/data
$ rosrun chapter10_tutorials pcl_read
```

In the third terminal, we will run the filtering example:

```
$ rosrun chapter10_tutorials pcl_filter
```

In the fourth terminal, we will run the downsampling example:

```
$ rosrun chapter10_tutorials pcl_downsampling
```

Finally, we will run this example:

```
$ rosrun chapter10_tutorials pcl_partitioning
```

In the following image, we can see the end result of the partitioning process. Since we handpicked the point to be close to the top of the point cloud, we managed to extract part of the cup and the table. This example only shows a tiny fraction of the potential of the octree data structure, but it's a good starting point to further your understanding.

Segmentation

Segmentation is the process of partitioning a dataset into different blocks of data satisfying certain criteria. The segmentation process can be done in many different ways and with varied criteria; sometimes, it may involve extracting structured information from a point cloud based on a statistical property, and in other cases, it can simply require extracting points in a specific color range.

In many cases, our data might fit a specific mathematical model, such as a plane, line, or sphere, among others. When this is the case, it is possible to use a model estimation algorithm to calculate the parameters for the model that fits our data. With those parameters, it is then possible to extract the points belonging to that model and evaluate how well they fit it.

In this example, we are going to show how to perform model-based segmentation of a point cloud. We are going to constrain ourselves to a planar model, which is one of the most common mathematical models you can usually fit to a point cloud. For this example, we will also perform the model estimation using a widespread algorithm named **Random Sample Consensus (RANSAC)**, which is an iterative algorithm capable of performing accurate estimations even in the presence of outliers.

The example code can be found in the `chapter10_tutorials` package, and its named `pcl_planar_segmentation.cpp`:

```cpp
#include <ros/ros.h>
#include <pcl/point_cloud.h>
#include <pcl_conversions/pcl_conversions.h>
#include <pcl/ModelCoefficients.h>
#include <pcl/sample_consensus/method_types.h>
#include <pcl/sample_consensus/model_types.h>
#include <pcl/segmentation/sac_segmentation.h>
#include <pcl/filters/extract_indices.h>
#include <sensor_msgs/PointCloud2.h>

class cloudHandler
{
public:
    cloudHandler()
    {
        pcl_sub = nh.subscribe("pcl_downsampled", 10,
        &cloudHandler::cloudCB, this);
        pcl_pub =
        nh.advertise<sensor_msgs::PointCloud2>("pcl_segmented",
        1);
```

```
        ind_pub =
        nh.advertise<pcl_msgs::PointIndices>("point_indices", 1);
        coef_pub =
        nh.advertise<pcl_msgs::ModelCoefficients>("planar_coef",
        1);
}

void cloudCB(const sensor_msgs::PointCloud2 &input)
{
    pcl::PointCloud<pcl::PointXYZ> cloud;
    pcl::PointCloud<pcl::PointXYZ> cloud_segmented;

    pcl::fromROSMsg(input, cloud);

    pcl::ModelCoefficients coefficients;
    pcl::PointIndices::Ptr inliers(new pcl::PointIndices());

    pcl::SACSegmentation<pcl::PointXYZ> segmentation;
    segmentation.setModelType(pcl::SACMODEL_PLANE);
    segmentation.setMethodType(pcl::SAC_RANSAC);
    segmentation.setMaxIterations(1000);
    segmentation.setDistanceThreshold(0.01);
    segmentation.setInputCloud(cloud.makeShared());
    segmentation.segment(*inliers, coefficients);

    pcl_msgs::ModelCoefficients ros_coefficients;
    pcl_conversions::fromPCL(coefficients, ros_coefficients);
    ros_coefficients.header.stamp = input.header.stamp;
    coef_pub.publish(ros_coefficients);

    pcl_msgs::PointIndices ros_inliers;
    pcl_conversions::fromPCL(*inliers, ros_inliers);
    ros_inliers.header.stamp = input.header.stamp;
    ind_pub.publish(ros_inliers);

    pcl::ExtractIndices<pcl::PointXYZ> extract;
    extract.setInputCloud(cloud.makeShared());
    extract.setIndices(inliers);
    extract.setNegative(false);
    extract.filter(cloud_segmented);
```

```
        sensor_msgs::PointCloud2 output;
        pcl::toROSMsg(cloud_segmented, output);
        pcl_pub.publish(output);
    }

protected:
    ros::NodeHandle nh;
    ros::Subscriber pcl_sub;
    ros::Publisher pcl_pub, ind_pub, coef_pub;
};

main(int argc, char **argv)
{
    ros::init(argc, argv, "pcl_planar_segmentation");

    cloudHandler handler;

    ros::spin();

    return 0;
}
```

As the reader might have noticed, two new message types are being used in the advertised topics. As their names suggest, the `ModelCoefficients` messages store the coefficients of a mathematical model, and `PointIndices` stores the indices of the points of a point cloud. We will publish these as an alternative way of representing the extracted information, which could then be used in combination with the original point cloud (`pcl_downsampled`) to extract the correct point. As a hint, this can be done by setting the timestamp of the published objects to the same timestamp of the original point cloud message and using ROS message filters:

```
pcl_pub = nh.advertise<sensor_msgs::PointCloud2>("pcl_segmented",
1);
ind_pub = nh.advertise<pcl_msgs::PointIndices>("point_indices",
1);
coef_pub =
nh.advertise<pcl_msgs::ModelCoefficients>("planar_coef", 1);
```

As always, in the `callback` function, we perform the conversion from the `PointCloud2` message to the point cloud type. In this case, we also define two new objects that correspond to the native `ModelCoefficients` and `PointIndices` types, which will be used by the segmentation algorithm:

```
pcl::PointCloud<pcl::PointXYZ> cloud;
pcl::PointCloud<pcl::PointXYZ> cloud_segmented;

pcl::fromROSMsg(input, cloud);

pcl::ModelCoefficients coefficients;
pcl::PointIndices::Ptr inliers(new pcl::PointIndices());
```

The segmentation algorithm lets us define `ModelType` and `MethodType`, with the former being the mathematical model we are looking to fit and the latter being the algorithm to use. As we explained before, we are using RANSAC due to its robustness against outliers. The algorithm also lets us define the two stopping criteria: the maximum number of iterations (`setMaxIterations`) and the maximum distance to the model (`setDistanceThreshold`). With those parameters set, plus the input point cloud, the algorithm can then be performed, returning the inliers (points which fall in the model) and the coefficients of the model:

```
pcl::SACSegmentation<pcl::PointXYZ> segmentation;
segmentation.setModelType(pcl::SACMODEL_PLANE);
segmentation.setMethodType(pcl::SAC_RANSAC);
segmentation.setMaxIterations(1000);
segmentation.setDistanceThreshold(0.01);
segmentation.setInputCloud(cloud.makeShared());
segmentation.segment(*inliers, coefficients);
```

Our next step is to convert and publish the inliers and the model coefficients. As usual, conversions are performed with the standard functions, but you might notice that the namespace and signature of the conversion function is different from the one being used for point cloud conversions. To further improve this example, these messages also include the timestamp of the original point cloud in order to link them together. This also allows the use of the ROS message filters on other nodes to create callbacks containing objects that are linked together:

```
pcl_msgs::ModelCoefficients ros_coefficients;
pcl_conversions::fromPCL(coefficients, ros_coefficients);
ros_coefficients.header.stamp = input.header.stamp;
coef_pub.publish(ros_coefficients);
```

```
pcl_msgs::PointIndices ros_inliers;
pcl_conversions::fromPCL(*inliers, ros_inliers);
ros_inliers.header.stamp = input.header.stamp;
ind_pub.publish(ros_inliers);
```

In order to create the segmented point cloud, we extract the inliers from the point cloud. The easiest way to do this is with the `ExtractIndices` object, but it could be easily done by simply looping through the indices and pushing the corresponding points into a new point cloud:

```
pcl::ExtractIndices<pcl::PointXYZ> extract;
extract.setInputCloud(cloud.makeShared());
extract.setIndices(inliers);
extract.setNegative(false);
extract.filter(cloud_segmented);
```

Finally, we convert the segmented point cloud into a `PointCloud2` message type and we publish it:

```
sensor_msgs::PointCloud2 output;
pcl::toROSMsg (cloud_segmented, output);
pcl_pub.publish(output)
```

The result can be seen in the following image; the original point cloud is represented in white and the segmented inliers are represented in bluish. In this particular case, the floor was extracted as it's the biggest flat surface. This is quite convenient as it is probably one of the main elements we will usually want to extract from our point clouds.

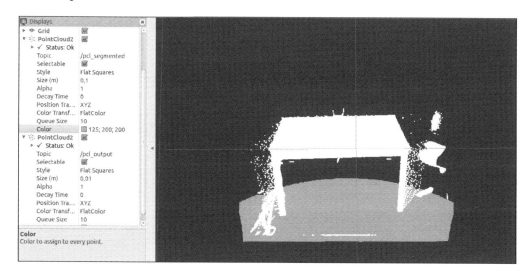

Summary

In this chapter, we have explored the different tools, algorithms, and interfaces that can be used to work with point clouds in ROS. The reader might have noticed that we have tried to link the examples together to provide more insight into how these kinds of nodes might be used in a reusable manner. In any case, given the computational price of point cloud processing, any kind of architectural design will be inextricably linked to the computational capabilities of the system at hand.

The data flow of our examples should start with all the data producers, which are `pcl_create` and `pcl_read`. It should continue to the data filters, which are `pcl_filter` and `pcl_downsampling`. After the filtering is performed, more complex information can be extracted through `pcl_planar_segmentation`, `pcl_partitioning` and `pcl_matching`. Finally, the data can be written to disk through `pcl_write` or visualized through `pcl_visualize`.

The main objective of this particular chapter was to provide clear and concise examples of how to integrate the basic capabilities of the **PCL** library with ROS, something which can be limited to messages and conversion functions. In order to accomplish this goal, we have taken the liberty of also explaining the basic techniques and common algorithms used to perform data processing on point clouds as we are aware of the growing importance of this kind of knowledge.

Index

Symbols

2D nav goal 212
3D model of robot
  creating, ROS used 137
3D visualization
  about 120
  data, visualizing with rqt_rviz 120-124
  frame transformations, visualizing 125-127
  relationship, between topics
     and frames 125
9DoF Razor IMU M0
  ADXL345 308
  BMP085 308
  HMC5883L 308
  L3G4200D 308
  reference link 307

A

actuators
  adding, Arduino used 291, 292
Adaptive Monte Carlo
     Localization (AMCL) 170
  about 223-225
  references 223-225
algorithms, Point Cloud Library (PCL) 396
Analog-to-Digital Converter (ADC) 355
Ångström 17
  URL, for installing 18
Arduino
  about 290
  robot motors, connecting to ROS 296-301
  used, for adding actuators 291
  used, for adding sensors 291

Arduino IDE
  reference link 291
ar_pose
  reference link 378
ARToolkit
  reference link 378
ArUco
  reference link 267
ATMega328 microcontroller 307
Augmented Reality (AR) 378

B

backtrace (bt) 88
bag file
  about 38, 42, 128
  data recording, with rosbag 129
  playing back 130
  rosbag 43
  rostopic 43
  rqt_bag 43
base controller
  creating 190-194
Bayer pattern 343
BeagleBone Black (BBB) 8
  environment, setting up 25
  reference link 19, 26
  ROS, example 25, 26
  ROS, installing 17, 18
  rosinstall, obtaining for 25
BeagleBone Black memory file system
  reference link 22
Berkeley Software Distribution (BSD) 3
blog
  URL 45

N

National Maritime Electronics Association
    (NMEA) **320**
navigation stack
  in ROS 170, 171
  launch file, creating 209-211
  rviz, setting up 211
  using, requisites 170
NMEA messages
  reference link 320
nodelets 39
nodes 37, 39
nodes diagnostics
  visualizing 111, 112

O

object recognition 378
Object Recognition Kitchen (ORK)
  reference link 378
objects
  adding, to planning scene 258, 259
  removing, from planning scene 260
obstacles
  avoiding 226-228
Occupancy Grid Map (OGM) 123, 196
Octomap Updater 261
octree 422
odometry
  creating 186-190
  creating, with Gazebo 181-186
  information, publishing 179-181
OMPL
  reference link 236
OpenCV
  reference link 344
  USB camera driver, making with 352-357
  using, in ROS 359, 360
OpenCV 3.0
  installing 359
Open Source Robotics
    Foundation (OSRF) 2
OSBOXES
  URL 11

P

package
  creating 202
package manifests 28
packages
  about 28-32
  catkin_create_pkg 31
  catkin_make 31
  CMakeLists.txt 31
  include/package_name/ 31
  msg/ 31
  package.xml 31
  rosdep 31
  rospack 31
  rqt_dep 32
  scripts/ 31
  src/ 31
  srv/ 31
parameters
  modifying, with rqt_reconfigure 225, 226
parameter server 37, 43
PC
  installing 4
PCLVisualizer 411
perception 378
pick and place task
  about 262, 263
  demo mode 278
  grasping 268-270
  perception 267, 268
  pickup action 272, 273
  place action 274-277
  planning scene 263, 264
  support surface 265, 266
  target object, grasping 264, 265
planning scene monitor
  about 236
  objects, adding to 258, 259
  objects, removing from 260
  reference link 236
Point Cloud Library (PCL)
  about 393, 394
  algorithms 396
  interface, for ROS 396, 397
  program 398, 399

44606443R00262